STRATEGIC
MARKET
MANAGEMENT

Strategic Market Management is supported by a free and fully interactive Companion website, available at www.wileyeurope.com/college/aaker and containing a wealth of additional teaching and learning material.

For the Lecturer:

- PowerPoint slides
- Solutions to test questions
- Sample syllabi
- Additional discussion questions

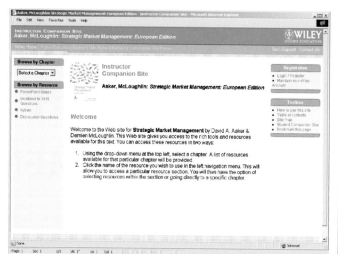

For Students:

- Additional case studies
- Self-test questions
- Further reading

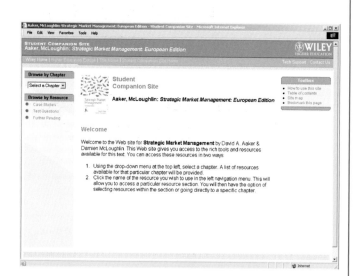

www.wileyeurope.com/college/aaker

STRATEGIC MARKET MANAGEMENT

EUROPEAN EDITION

David A. Aaker

Vice-Chairman, Prophet
Professor Emeritus, University of California,
at Berkeley

Damien McLoughlin

Senior Lecturer in Marketing,
Director, Marketing Development Programme,
University College Dublin Michael Smurfit
School of Business

John Wiley & Sons, Ltd

Copyright © 2007   John Wiley & Sons, Ltd
                    The Atrium, Southern Gate, Chichester,
                    West Sussex PO19 8SQ, England
                    Telephone (+44) 1243 779777

Email (for orders and customer service enquiries): cs-books@wiley.co.uk
Visit our Home Page on www.wiley.com

Authorised adaptation of the seventh edition by David A. Aaker, *Strategic Market Management* (ISBN 0-471-65903-7), published by John Wiley & Sons, Inc. Copyright © 2005 by John Wiley & Sons, Inc. All rights reserved.

Other Wiley Editorial Offices

John Wiley & Sons Inc., 111 River Street, Hoboken, NJ 07030, USA

Jossey-Bass, 989 Market Street, San Francisco, CA 94103-1741, USA

Wiley-VCH Verlag GmbH, Boschstr. 12, D-69469 Weinheim, Germany

John Wiley & Sons Australia Ltd, 42 McDougall Street, Milton, Queensland 4064, Australia

John Wiley & Sons (Asia) Pte Ltd, 2 Clementi Loop #02-01, Jin Xing Distripark, Singapore 129809

John Wiley & Sons Canada Ltd, 6045 Freemont Blvd, Mississauga, ONT, L5R 4J3

Wiley also publishes its books in a variety of electronic formats. Some content that appears in print may not be available in electronic books.

Anniversary logo design: Richard J. Pacifico

Library of Congress Cataloging-in-Publication Data
Aaker, David A.
Strategic market management / David A. Aaker, Damien McLoughlin. --
European ed.
     p. cm.
   Includes index.
   ISBN-13: 978-0-470-05986-9
     1. Marketing--Management. I. McLoughlin, Damien. II. Title.
HF5415.13.A23 2007
658.8'101--dc22   2006036925

A catalogue record for this book is available from the British Library

ISBN 13: 978-0-470-05986-9

Typeset by Thomson Digital, New Delhi, India
Printed and bound in Great Britain by Scotprint, Haddington, East Lothian

This book is printed on acid-free paper responsibly manufactured from sustainable forestry in which at least two trees are planted for each one used for paper production.

CONTENTS

Preface   ix

Acknowledgments   xiii

PART ONE   INTRODUCTION AND OVERVIEW   1

Chapter 1   *Business Strategy: The Concept and Trends in Its Management*   *3*
             What is a Business Strategy?   4
             Strategic Options   10
             Strategic Market Management: Characteristics and Trends   10
             Why Strategic Market Management?   14

Chapter 2   *Strategic Market Management: An Overview*   *17*
             External Analysis   18
             Internal Analysis   23
             Creating a Vision for the Business   26
             Strategy Identification and Selection   28
             Selecting Among Strategic Alternatives   31
             The Process   33

PART TWO   STRATEGIC ANALYSIS   35

Chapter 3   *External and Customer Analysis*   *37*
             External Analysis   37
             The Scope of Customer Analysis   41
             Segmentation   42
             Customer Motivations   46
             Unmet Needs   50

Chapter 4   *Competitor Analysis*   *56*
             Identifying Competitors – Customer-Based Approaches   57
             Identifying Competitors – Strategic Groups   59
             Potential Competitors   62
             Competitor Analysis – Understanding Competitors   63
             Competitor Strengths and Weaknesses   67
             Obtaining Information on Competitors   73

Chapter 5   *Market Analysis*   *76*
             Dimensions of a Market Analysis   77
             Actual and Potential Market Size   80
             Market and Submarket Growth   81

	Market and Submarket Profitability Analysis	83
	Cost Structure	86
	Distribution Systems	87
	Market Trends	87
	Key Success Factors	89
	Risks in High-Growth Markets	89
Chapter 6	**Environmental Analysis and Strategic Uncertainty**	**95**
	Dimensions of Environmental Analysis	96
	Dealing with Strategic Uncertainty	103
	Impact Analysis – Assessing the Impact of Strategic Uncertainties	103
	Scenario Analysis	106
Chapter 7	**Internal Analysis**	**111**
	Financial Performance – Sales and Profitability	112
	Performance Measurement – Beyond Profitability	115
	Determinants of Strategic Options	119
	From Analysis to Strategy	121
	Business Portfolio Analysis	123
	The BCG Growth-share Matrix	124
	Case Challenges for Part Two	**130**
	The Soft Drinks Market	136
	Tesco	134

PART THREE   ALTERNATIVE BUSINESS STRATEGIES   139

Chapter 8	**Creating Advantage – Synergy and Vision Versus Opportunism**	**141**
	The Sustainable Competitive Advantage	141
	The Role of Synergy	147
	Strategic Vision Versus Strategic Opportunism	149
	A Dynamic Vision	156
Chapter 9	**Strategic Options: Quality and Brand Equity**	**162**
	Business Strategy Challenges	163
	Strategic Options	165
	The Quality Option	167
	The Brand Equity Option	172
Chapter 10	**Strategic Options: Value, Focus, Innovation and Customer Relationships**	**184**
	The Value Option	184
	Focus	192
	Innovation	195
	The Customer Relationship Option	199

Chapter 11	***Global Strategies***	***206***
	Motivations Underlying Global Strategies	207
	Indicators that Strategies should be Global	209
	What Country to Enter?	210
	Standardisation Versus Customisation	211
	Global Brand Management	215
	Strategic Alliances	218
Chapter 12	***Strategic Positioning***	***225***
	The Role of the Strategic Position	226
	Strategic Position Options	233
	Developing and Selecting a Strategic Position	242
	Case Challenges for Part Three	***247***
	Neau	247
	Innocent	250

PART FOUR   GROWTH STRATEGIES   255

Chapter 13	***Growth Strategies: Penetration, Product–Market Expansion, Vertical Integration, and the Big Idea***	***257***
	Growth in Existing Product Markets	259
	Product Development for the Existing Market	264
	Market Development Using Existing Products	267
	Vertical Integration Strategies	269
	The Big Idea	273
Chapter 14	***Diversification***	***277***
	Related Diversification	278
	The Mirage of Synergy	283
	Unrelated Diversification	285
	Entry Strategies	290
Chapter 15	***Strategies in Declining and Hostile Markets***	***296***
	Creating Growth in Declining Industries	297
	Be the Profitable Survivor	299
	Milk or Harvest	300
	Divestment or Liquidation	302
	Selecting the Right Strategy for the Declining Environment	303
	Hostile Markets	306
	Case Challenges for Part Four	***312***
	Dove	312
	Green & Black's	315

PART FIVE   IMPLEMENTATION ISSUES   319

Chapter 16	*Organisational Issues*	*321*
	A Conceptual Framework	322
	Structure	323
	Systems	325
	People	327
	Culture	329
	Obtaining Strategic Congruence	331
	Organising for Innovation	336
	A Recap of Strategic Market Management	339
	Case Challenges for Part V	*342*
	Vodafone	342
	Index	*345*

PREFACE

This European edition of *Strategic Market Management* has been prepared with the objective of taking David Aaker's outstanding and well-established textbook and making it more accessible for a European audience. The core value of the original text, that the development, evaluation and implementation of business strategies are essential to successful management, is retained, as is the view that the key to achieving this is a management system that will help managers

- monitor and understand a dynamic environment
- generate visionary and creative strategic options that will be responsive to changes facing a business
- develop strategies based on sustainable competitive advantages
- provide vision to their businesses

Within this, I wanted to retain the culture of the original text, to maintain its accessibility and continue its emphasis on practical action. This edition also keeps the compactness that has made it so popular with graduate and executive students and managers, while retaining comprehensive coverage of major and emerging themes in strategy. Building on a strong base, the European edition focuses changes in four main areas:

- Hundreds of new European relevant examples and vignettes.
- Seven new cases, including cases on Tesco, Innocent, Dove, Neau, The soft drinks market, Cadbury/Green & Blacks and Vodafone.
- Completely new coverage of Brand Equity and CRM.
- Revised coverage of topics such as creating new market space, environmental scanning, consumer ethnography, webnography and feature fatigue.

A WORD TO INSTRUCTORS

For instructors, a fully revised Web-based package of supplementary materials including Power Point slides, a test bank, case studies and a comprehensive instructors manual are available at **www.wileyeurope.com/college/aaker.**

FIVE THRUSTS

Strategic Market Management has five thrusts. The first is external analysis, a structure and methodology for analysing the external environment. Strategic planning that represents an automatic extension of what was done last year and that is dominated by financial objectives and spreadsheets will be inadequate and may even inhibit or prevent strategy change and innovation. Rather, strategy development should look outside the business to sense changes, trends, threats, and opportunities and then create strategies that are responsive. This book describes and illustrates a structured approach to external analysis that business managers will find helpful in generating strategic options. This approach is supported by a summary flow diagram, a set of agendas to help start the process, and a set of planning forms.

The second thrust is toward sustainable competitive advantages (SCAs). Having SCAs is crucial to long-term success. Without them a business will eventually be treading water – if it survives at all. Sustainable competitive advantages need to be based on organisational assets and competencies. Thus, this book presents methods and concepts that will help readers to select relevant assets and competencies and our understanding of the strengths, weaknesses, and strategic problems of the organisation. Thus, this book presents methods and concepts that will help readers to conduct an internal analysis to select relevant assets and competencies.

The third thrust is to create customer-oriented business strategies, each with a value proposition that is relevant, meaningful, and sustainable. A business strategy, whose primary focus is inside of the firm, rather than on its customers, will eventually be vulnerable and lose its relevance. A customer orientation implies not only that customers are understood in some depth but that competitors are monitored, that markets are tracked and that the firm may have to invest in anticipation of emerging submarkets.

The fourth thrust involves the investment decision. The need is to select investment or disinvestment levels for existing product-market business areas and to chart growth directions. Among the alternative growth directions are market penetration, product expansion, market expansion, diversification, and vertical integration. By using a variety of concepts and methods, such as strategic uncertainties, portfolio models and scenario analysis, this book will help managers identify and evaluate numerous strategic investment alternatives. The fifth thrust is implementation. It is important to understand how an organisation's structure, systems, people, and culture contribute to strategic success. In addition, how can an organisation create dynamic strategies that are responsive to changing conditions? How can alliances be used to gain strategic advantage? What are the implementation issues when markets are hostile or declining or when competition is global in scope?

OBJECTIVES OF THE BOOK

This book has a number of objectives that influence its approach and style. The book attempts to:

- Introduce a long-term perspective that may help a business avoid weaknesses or problems caused by the dominance of short-term goals or operational problems. The focus on assets and competencies and away from short-term financials provides one approach.

- Provide methods and structures to create entrepreneurial thrusts. In many organisations the key problem is how to support both efficiency and an entrepreneurial spirit.

- Emphasise a global perspective: Increasingly, effective strategies must consider – and be responsive to – international competitors and markets.

- Present a proactive approach to strategic market management in which, rather than merely detecting and reacting to change, a business anticipates or even creates it. In this approach, the strategy development process is driven by a dynamic analysis of the market and the environment. The inclusion of the term *market* into the phrase 'strategic market management' emphasises the external orientation and the proactive approach.

- Encourage online strategy development, which involves gathering information, analysing the strategic context, precipitating strategic decisions, and developing strategic implementation plans outside the annual planning cycle.

- Draw on multiple disciplines. During the past decade many disciplines have made relevant and important contributions to strategic market management. An effort has been made to draw on and integrate developments in marketing, economics, organisational behaviour, finance, accounting, management science and the field of strategy itself.

- Incorporate several important empirical research streams that have helped strategic market management become more professional and scientific.

- Introduce concepts, models, and methods that are or have promise of being useful to the strategy development process. Among the concepts covered are business strategies, value proposition, and strategic groups; exit, entry, and mobility barriers; industry structure; segmentation; unmet needs; positioning; strategic problems; strategic uncertainties; strengths; weaknesses; strategic assets and competencies; brand equity; flexibility; sustainable competitive advantage; synergy; relevance challenges, business strategy options; strategic alliances; key success factors; corporate culture; organisational structure; the virtual corporation; strategic types; strategic vision; strategic opportunism; strategic intent and global strategies. The models and methods covered include researching lead customers, scenario analysis, impact analysis, total quality control, reengineering, the competitor strength grid, technological forecasting, the experience curve, value chain analysis, portfolio models, customer-based competitor identification, and shareholder value analysis.

AN OVERVIEW

This book is divided into five parts. The first part, Chapters 1 and 2, defines a business strategy and provides an overview of the book. The second part, Chapters 3 to 7, covers strategic analysis that includes external analysis (the analysis of the customer, competitors, market, and environment) and internal analysis (which includes performance analysis, the analysis of strategically important organisational characteristics, and portfolio analysis). The third part, Chapters 8 to 12, focuses on the development of successful strategies. It discusses the role of synergy, the tension between vision and opportunism, strategic options (such as quality, value, innovation, brand equity, customer relationships, focus, and being global), and strategic positioning. The fourth part, Chapters 13 to 15, covers growth strategies, including competing in mature and hostile markets. The fifth part, Chapter 16, contains material on how organisational components interact with strategy. Seven case challenges are positioned at the end of Parts II, III, IV, and V.

THE AUDIENCE

This book is suitable for any management or business school course that focuses on the management of strategies. It is especially appropriate for:

- marketing strategy courses, such as strategic market management, strategic market planning, strategic marketing, or marketing strategy
- policy or entrepreneurship courses, such as strategic management, strategic planning, business policy, entrepreneurship, or policy administration
- executive or short programmes with a similar focus will also benefit from the breadth of coverage and the accessible style

The book is also designed to be used by managers who need to develop strategies – especially those who have recently moved into a general management position or who run a small business and want to improve their strategy development and planning processes. Another intended audience consists of those general managers, top executives, and planning specialists who would like an overview of recent issues and methods in strategic market management.

Damien McLoughlin

ACKNOWLEDGMENTS

I would like to thank Scott Dacko of Warwick Business School and John Roberts of LBS and other reviewers for their excellent comments. They played a strong role in shaping the final manuscript.

Yvonne Mcnamara and Yansong Hu played a large and important role in preparing the manuscript and the case studies contained in this edition. I am grateful to them both. The Dean of UCD Smurfit School, Professor Tom Begley, and the head of the Marketing Group, Professor Tony Meenaghan both provided strong support. I had a number of very useful and formative discussions about the book with Professor Frank Bradley and Dr Andrew Keating. I offer thanks also to my other Marketing Group colleagues and Antoinette, Derek and Nicola, my colleagues on the Marketing Development Programme.

I have been lucky to work with a great team at John Wiley & Sons. This project began with Steve Hardman, a good friend over many years. But the book was completed with the support of an outstanding team led by Sarah Booth and including Anneli Anderson, Mark Styles and Emma Cooper.

I thank also my wonderful children Dearbhla and Bebhinn who did their best to be quiet while I was working. When that didn't work they tried to entertain me, which was almost as useful. Finally, I offer most thanks to my wife Brenda for her love, support and friendship.

This book is dedicated to Alan Sattell, a good friend, an inspiration and a role model for me in the past and today.

Damien McLoughlin

Dr Damien McLoughlin is a senior lecturer in marketing and Director of the Marketing Development Programme at the UCD Michael Smurfit School of Business. His teaching is highly regarded and he has been recognised with a number of teaching awards and distinctions. His research, teaching and consulting interests are in areas of strategic marketing, market making and B2B marketing. His work has been published in leading international journals such as the *Journal of Business Research*, *Industrial Marketing Management* and the *European Journal of Marketing*. He is a member of the editorial board of a number of leading marketing journals including *Industrial Marketing Management*. He was a visiting Professor in Marketing at the S.C. Johnson Graduate School of Management, Cornell University in 2004. In 2007 he will be a visiting Professor in Marketing at the Indian School of Business, Hyderabad. Professionally he has worked with leading international firms such as Alltech, Microsoft and Hewlett-Packard.

PART
ONE

INTRODUCTION AND
OVERVIEW

CHAPTER ONE

Business Strategy: The Concept and Trends in Its Management

To accomplish great things, we must not only act, but also dream, not only plan but also believe.
— *Anatole France, Nobel Laureate in Literature 1921*

Even if you are on the right track, you'll get run over if you just sit there.
— *Will Rodgers*

Where absolute superiority is not attainable, you must produce a relative one at the decisive point by making skilful use of what you have.
— *Karl von Clausewitz*, On War, *1832*

*F*ounded in 1947 Golden Wonder was the first company to sell crisps in packets. It was also first to make and sell flavoured crisps and by 1964 it operated the largest crisp factory in the world. Its best known brands have included the iconic Golden Wonder, Wotsits, Golden Lights and Wheat Crunchies. In addition they supplied large retailers with own-label crisps. In 2006 they went into receivership and were subsequently sold to a competitor. Much of the blame for the demise of Golden Wonder was directed towards the relentless competition of Walker's crisps, owned by PepsiCo since 1989. Walkers had a similar long history in the British market and enjoyed much of the same nostalgic halo but it also has a long history of consistent investment in its brands, product innovation and responding to market trends. It started an advertising campaign with Gary Lineker, an English football legend and a man famous for being pleasant, in the early 1990s. More than 10 years later Lineker was still the brand spokesman and Walkers had a library of outstanding commercials featuring the footballer to their credit. Golden Wonder's response was to launch an advertising campaign with the slogan 'Employ celebrities to sell crisps ... we'd rather use newsagents.'

3

In 2002 Walkers launched its Sensations range of crisps designed to take advantage of the trend towards adult crisps and to counterweight the decline in the crisps market. Golden Wonder's response was to mock the trend and employ the slogan 'where a crisp is a crisp' to indicate its unwillingness to change. As part of a corporate restructuring in 2002, Golden Wonder sold a prized asset, Wotsits, to Walkers. In the mid-2000s the issues of salt and fat content of food and obesity began to affect consumer attitudes and behaviours towards the snack foods business. Walkers' response was radical. It did not simply launch a new product: it changed the way it manufactured all of its crisps to reduce the amount of saturated fat in its products by 70% and the level of salt to 8% of the recommended daily allowance. This change was supported by an advertising campaign featuring Mr Lineker. Golden Wonder's response to this emerging trend was to launch a subbrand, Golden Lights. Finally, Walkers refused to supply crisps on an own label basis, preferring to keep the focus on developing its own products and brands. Where did the blame for the demise of Golden Wonder truly lie?[1]

The story of Walkers and Golden Wonder is the story of many markets and industries today. Clearly, they were and are dependent upon their ability to analyse their competitive context, make sound strategic choices and support those choices with needed strategic initiatives. The fact is that nearly every organisation is affected by strategic decisions or, sometimes, nondecisions.

This book is concerned with helping managers identify, select, and implement strategies. The intent is to provide decision makers with concepts, methods, and procedures by which they can improve the quality of their strategic decision making. This and the following chapter have several functions. First, they identify the approach toward strategy and its management that is taken in this book. Second, they introduce and position most of the concepts and methods that are covered in the book. Third, they position and structure the other parts and chapters. Fourth, they provide a general overview and summary. Thus the reader can productively reread these two chapters as a way to review.

This chapter begins by defining the concept of a business strategy. It then describes strategic options and the building blocks of a business strategy, provides a historical perspective to strategy and, finally, presents some characteristics, trends, and rationales of strategic market management.

WHAT IS A BUSINESS STRATEGY?

Before discussing the process of developing sound business strategies, it is fair to address two questions. What is a business? What is a business strategy? Having groups of managers provide answers to these questions can be particularly interesting and useful. You quickly learn from such an exercise that the issues are complex and there is no consensus answer.

A Business Is …

A business is generally an organisational unit that has a distinct business strategy and a manager with sales and profit responsibility. An organisation will thus have many business units that relate to each other horizontally and vertically. For example, Nestlé needs to set strategic directions for the many product markets in which it competes, and each product market will typically have its own business strategy. Thus, there may be a business strategy for the Nestlé Waters product group but within that line there may also be separate business strategies for products such as the premium water brand San Pellegrino, for segments such as national supermarket chains and for geographies such as the UK or Italy. Organisationally and strategically, there are tradeoffs in deciding how many businesses should be operated. It can be compelling to have many businesses because then each can develop a strategy that is optimal for its market.

Thus, a strategy for each country or each region or each major segment may have some benefits. Having too many business units, on the other hand, can result in inefficiency through programmes that lack scale economies and fail to leverage the strategic skills of the best managers. These considerations create pressure to combine businesses into larger entities.

Business units can be aggregated to create a critical mass, to coordinate strategies and leverage similarities in markets and strategies. Businesses that are too small to justify a strategy will need to be aggregated so that the management structure, even if small, can be supportable. Larger business units afford staff and programmes that enhance changes of success. Of course, two business units can share some elements of operations, such as a sales force or a facility, to gain economies without merging. Another benefit of larger business units is to achieve synergy with closer strategic interaction among the subunits. For example, Unilever aggregates brands such as Dove, Lux and Ponds into a personal care category to share learning about consumers, to optimise the application of product innovations and to provide shelf space guidance of retailers. Diageo, owner of leading brands such as Guinness and J&B Scotch, organises countries into regions, and others merge regions into global business units. In fact, the choice between country, regional, or global aggregation is a crucial decision facing many firms. A final incentive toward aggregation is leveraging the knowledge of similar markets and strategies. Thus, in Eastern Europe, Coca-Cola might consider aggregating its Coke and Diet Coke business units but not Fanta and Sprite. Hewlett Packard might aggregate its LaserJet and InkJet printers in some countries, as they face very similar market contexts and will have overlapping strategies.

A Business Strategy Is ...

Four dimensions define a business strategy: the product-market investment strategy, the customer value proposition, assets and competencies, and functional strategies and programmes. The first specifies where to compete, and the remaining three indicate how to compete to win (see Figure 1.1).

The Product-Market Investment Strategy – Where to Compete

The scope of the business and the dynamics within that scope represent a very basic strategy dimension. Which sectors are receiving investments in resources

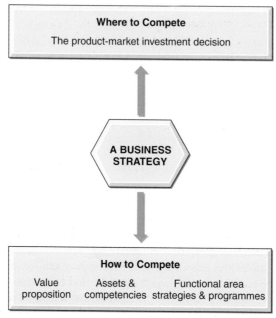

Figure 1.1   A business strategy

and management attention? The scope of a business is defined by the products it offers and chooses not to offer, by the markets it does and does not seek to serve, by the competitors it chooses to compete with or to avoid and by its level of vertical integration. Sometimes the most important business scope decision is what products or segments to avoid because such a decision (if followed with discipline) can conserve resources needed to compete successfully elsewhere. Such judgements can sometimes involve painful decisions to divest or liquidate a business.

Many organisations have demonstrated the advantages of having a well-defined business scope. IKEA sells well designed, functional furniture for the home. *OK!* magazine in the UK features exclusive stories and pictures of leading celebrities. Gucci offers luxury goods. Heinz provides a broad spectrum of packaged consumer goods. Trailfinders offers individual, tailor made holidays for long haul travellers. Occasionally, business scope can be too well defined. For example, the Spanish owned, UK published Hello! magazine has suffered from its over-reliance on stories about European royalty, a business definition which was central to its early success.

More important than the scope itself are its dynamics. What product markets will be entered or exited in coming years? Which will be dialled up or down? Financial resources, generated either internally or externally, plus nonfinancial resources such as plant, equipment, and people, all need to be allocated based on these decisions.

Which business sectors will receive investment resources because of their increased importance in the future? Even for a small organisation, the allocation decision is key to strategy. The investment pattern will determine the future direction of the firm. Although there are obvious variations and refinements, the broad conceptual choices are as follows:

- invest to grow (or enter the product market)
- invest only to maintain the existing position
- milk the business by minimising investment
- recover as many of the assets as possible by liquidating or divesting the business

In 2004 one of the world's most famous retailers, Marks & Spencer (M&S), was in crisis. Its share price was at £3.45 and the company was the subject of a hostile takeover bid. By mid-2006 the CEO Stuart Rose, appointed to fend off the takeover and rebuild the business, was cautiously optimistic that a successful Christmas 2005 trading period had provided a solid foundation for the future. Mr Rose had set out with the ambition that M&S would 'trade its socks off'. The key to the turnaround was improved product ranges. Marks & Spencer continued to sell thousands of traditional V-neck men's sweaters in 15 colours but also had success with new ranges, in clothing and food, such as mini-fish and chips and chocolate puddings. Rose also steered the retailer to respond more quickly to consumer demand in-store, devoted more shelf space to cheaper items, invested in a strong TV advertising campaign and initiated a well received programme of store renovations. Finally, a direct contribution to bottom line achievement was made through re-negotiating supplier terms. By the middle of 2006 the share price was north of £5.75 and the 63 000 staff of Marks and Spencer were set to share in a bonus pool of around £70 000 000.[2]

The Customer Value Proposition

A customer value proposition is the perceived functional, emotional, social, or self-expressive benefit that is provided by the organisation's offering. One or more value propositions need to be relevant and meaningful to the customer and reflected in the positioning of the product or service. To support a successful strategy, the propositions should be sustainable over time and differentiate the offering from its competitors.

The customer value proposition can involve elements such as providing:

- good value (Aldi)
- excellence on an important product or service attribute (Noilly Prat vermouth)
- the best overall quality (Organix, organic baby food)

- product line breadth (Gillette razor and blades)
- innovative offerings (Body Shop)
- a shared passion for an activity or a product (Innocent drinks)
- global prestige (Louis Vuitton)

While many of Italy's traditional Italian clothing and footwear firms are suffering from the low cost competition of Chinese manufacturers, one firm stands out in its defiance, Tod's, Italy's largest luxury shoe manufacturer. Led by its charismatic CEO, Diego della Valle, the core idea behind Tod's, inspired originally by the elegance of people such as Gianni Agnelli and John F. Kennedy, is to bring the casual freedom of weekend dress into everyday life through high quality and innovative footwear. The commitment to this proposition is relentless and supported by heavy investment in the Tod's brand. The result is a brand that sells more than 2 million pairs of shoes each year at an average price of €250. At a corporate level the revenues of Tod's S.p.A grew from €319 million in 2001 to €503 million in 2005, with profits climbing from €60 million to more than €90 million in the same period. For Tod's the Chinese are a market for luxury brands not an insurmountable competitive threat.[3]

Assets and Competencies

The strategic assets or competencies that underlie the strategy provide the sustainable competitive advantage (SCA). A *strategic competency* is what a business unit does exceptionally well, such as manufacturing or promotion, which has strategic importance to the business. It is usually based on knowledge or a process. A *strategic asset* is a resource, such as a brand name or installed customer base, which is strong relative to that of competitors. Strategy formulation must consider the cost and feasibility of generating or maintaining assets or competencies that will provide the basis for a sustainable competitive advantage.

Assets and competencies can involve a wide spectrum, from buildings and locations to research-and-development expertise or a metaphorical symbol, such as the Mercedes star. Though a strong asset or competency is often difficult to build, it can result in an advantage that is significant and enduring. An important asset and SCA source can be the synergies obtained from operating a business that spans product markets. Synergy occurs, for example, when two businesses can reduce costs or increase sales by sharing a sales force, a logistics system or brand management expertise. L'Oréal's acquisition of The Body Shop in 2006 was designed to generate synergy through using its marketing and research-and-development competency in the luxury cosmetics market to drive growth in The Body Shop brand franchise. It was also hoped that the ethical dimensions of The Body Shop brand and business model might have benefits for L'Oréal, although these benefits could not be as readily anticipated. Businesses may also be able to offer retailers and/or customers a combination of coordinated products (such as sports shoes and clothing) thereby creating a value that would not exist if the two businesses were distinct.

Organisational synergy-based SCAs tend to be sustainable because they are defined with respect to an organisation, its product-market scope and its business strategy, which are not easily duplicated. Synergies and the concept of a sustainable competitive advantage are both discussed in more depth in Chapter 8.

The ability of an organisation's assets and competencies to support a strategy will in part depend on their power relative to those of competitors. To what extent are the assets and competencies strong and in place? To what extent are they ownable because of a symbol trademark or long-standing investment in a capability? To what extent are they based on synergy within a unique organisation that others cannot duplicate?

Functional Strategies and Programmes

A target value proposition or a set of assets and competencies should mandate some strategy imperatives, in the form of a supportive set of functional strategies or programmes. These strategies and programmes, in turn, will be implemented with a host of short-term tactics. Some of the functional strategies or programmes that could drive the business strategy include the following:

- manufacturing strategy
- distribution strategy
- brand-building strategy
- communication strategy
- information technology strategy
- global strategy
- segmentation strategy
- quality programme
- customer relationship programme

The need for functional strategies and programmes can be determined by asking a few questions. What must happen for the firm to be able to deliver on the value proposition? Are the assets and competencies needed in place? Do they need to be created, strengthened, or supported? How?

The Airbus A380 super-jumbo is the largest passenger aircraft in the world. Its value proposition lies in its ability to carry a greater number of passengers between international hubs, such as London–Hong Kong and Frankfurt–Singapore, where landing slots are increasingly hard to come by. In order to deliver on this value proposition Airbus needed each of its functional areas, such as sales, manufacturing and quality to be closely coordinated. Initial sales were promising but manufacturing problems with the installation of onboard entertainment and other electrical systems imposed bottlenecks in delivery to customers. The outcomes of this problem were key customers placing orders for the A380's leading competitor the Boeing 787 'Dreamliner'. Also the surge in sales that follow the entry of an aircraft into service will be delayed. The total cost to the airline was estimated at €500 million per year between 2007 and 2010.[4]

STRATEGIC OPTIONS

A business strategy will involve a host of elements organised by these four dimensions (the product-market investment strategy, the customer value proposition, assets and competencies and functional strategies and programmes). The complexity and apparent number of alternative strategies can become overwhelming. Usually, however, a business strategy will be based on a limited number of strategic options. A strategic option is a particular value proposition for a specific product market with supporting assets and competencies and functional strategies and programmes. Conceptualising and labelling strategic options help crystallise and describe alternative business strategies. It also provides a way to describe the selected business strategy to employees, partners, investors, and customers.

A strategy can involve more than one strategic option; in fact, most successful strategies do. Philips, for example, has a customer-focus strategy organised around the principles of making products that make sense and are simple to use. To fulfil this strategy Philips must continuously invest in technology leadership while at the same time supporting its design function with fresh ideas from a variety of sources such as the human sciences and technology. So, strategic options can be viewed as the building blocks of a business strategy. Analogously, a business strategy can be perceived as a set of integrated strategic options. Several of the most common and important strategic options – such as quality, customer intimacy, value, innovation, focus, being global and developing brand equity – are explored in some detail in Chapters 9, 10, and 11. Chapter 9 also discusses strategic options driven by a product attribute, product design, product line breadth, and corporate social responsibility. These discussions provide an overview of strategic options that are widely used, are often successful, and for which a body of knowledge exists. The list of possible options discussed is not complete but those that are described can provide insights into others.

STRATEGIC MARKET MANAGEMENT: CHARACTERISTICS AND TRENDS

Strategic market management is motivated by the assumption that the planning cycle is inadequate to deal with the rapid rate of change that can occur in a firm's external environment. To cope with strategic surprises and fast-developing threats and opportunities, strategic decisions need to be precipitated and made outside the planning cycle. Recognition of the demands of a rapidly changing environment has stimulated the development or increased use of methods, systems, and options that are responsive. In particular, it suggests a need for continuous, real-time information systems rather than, or in addition to, periodic analysis. More sensitive environmental scanning, the identification and continuous monitoring of information-need areas, efforts to develop strategic flexibility, and the enhancement of the entrepreneurial thrust of the organisation may be helpful. An information-need area is an area of uncertainty that will affect strategy, such as an emerging consumer-interest area. Strategic flexibility involves strategic options that allow quick and appropriate responses to sudden changes in the environment. Strategic market management is proactive and future oriented. Rather than simply accepting the environment as given, with the strategic role confined to adaptation and reaction, strategy may be proactive, affecting environmental change. Thus, governmental policies, customer needs, and technological developments can be influenced – and perhaps even controlled – with creative, active strategies.

Gary Hamel and C. K. Prahalad argue that managers should have a clear and shared understanding of how their industry may be different in ten years and a strategy for competing in that world.[5] They challenge managers to evaluate the extent to which:

- management has a distinctive and farsighted view, rather than a conventional and reactive view, about the future
- senior management focuses on regenerating core strategies rather than on reengineering core processes
- competitors view the company as a rule maker rather than a rule follower
- the company's strength is in innovation and growth rather than in operational efficiency
- the company is mostly out in front rather than catching up

In strategic market management, a periodic planning process is normally supplemented by techniques that allow the organisation to be strategically responsive outside the planning process.

The inclusion of the term *market* in the phrase 'strategic market management' emphasises that strategy development needs to be driven by the market and its environment rather than by an internal orientation. It also points out that the process should be proactive rather than reactive and that the task should be to try to influence the environment as well as respond to it.

Several distinct characteristics and trends have emerged in the strategy field, some of which have already been mentioned. A review of these thrusts or trends will provide additional insight into strategic market management and into the perspective and orientation of the balance of the book.

External Market Orientation

As already noted, organisations need to be oriented externally – toward customers, competitors, the market, and the market's environment. In sharp contrast to projection-based, internally oriented, long-range planning systems, the goal is to develop market-driven strategies that are sensitive to the customer.

Proactive Strategies

A proactive strategy attempts to influence events in the environment rather than simply reacting to environmental forces as they occur. A proactive strategy is important for at least two reasons. First, one way to be sure of detecting and quickly reacting to major environmental changes is to participate in their creation. Second, because environmental changes can be significant it may be important to be able to influence them. For example, it may be beneficial for an insurance firm to be involved in tort reform strategy.

Importance of the Information System

An external orientation puts demands on the supporting information system. The determination of what information is needed, how it can be obtained efficiently and effectively and how it should best be analysed, processed, and stored can be key to an effective strategy development process.

Knowledge Management

Knowledge management is becoming critical because the knowledge is increasingly the key issue for companies, whether it be knowledge of technology, marketing, processes or other ingredient of success. Knowledge resides in the minds of individuals, so the challenge is to capture that knowledge in a form that can be retained and nurtured over time and can be shared by a wide group of people.

Online Analysis and Decision Making

Organisations are moving away from relying only on the annual planning cycle and toward a more continuous, online system of information gathering, analysis, and strategic decision making. The design of such a system is demanding and requires new methods and concepts. The system must be structured enough to provide assistance in an inherently complex decision context, sensitive enough to detect the need to precipitate a strategic choice and flexible enough to be applied in a variety of situations.

Entrepreneurial Thrust

The importance of developing and maintaining an entrepreneurial thrust is increasingly being recognised. There is a need for the development of organisational forms and strategic-market management support systems that allow the firm to be responsive to opportunities. The entrepreneurial skill is particularly important to large, diversified firms and to firms involved in extremely fast-moving industries, such as high-tech firms or industries that produce 'hit' products such as video games, music or cinema. The strategy in such contexts must include providing an environment in which entrepreneurs can flourish.

Implementation

Implementation of strategy is critical. There needs to be a concern about whether the strategy fits the organisation – its structure, systems, people, and culture – or whether the organisation can be adapted to the strategy. The strategy needs to be linked to the functional area policies and the operating plan. Chapter 16 is devoted to implementation issues.

Globalisation

Increasingly, the global dimension is affecting strategy. Globalisation of markets are affecting just about every business today, from Zara to Volvo. The global element represents both direct and indirect opportunities and threats. The financial difficulty of a major country or a worldwide shortage of some raw material may have a dramatic impact on an organisation's strategy. Chapter 11 focuses on global strategies.

Longer Time Horizon

A longer time horizon is needed for most businesses in order to create and implement strategic initiatives needed to develop assets and competences. This requires the ability to balance discipline and patience with the need for real-time analysis and the pressures for short-term results. It also requires methods and measures that reflect a long-term perspective.

Empirical Research

Historically, the field of strategy has been dominated by conceptual contributions based on personal experience and insights, as the writings of Alfred Sloan, the architect of General Motors, and Peter Drucker, the author of the classic book, *The Practice of Management,* illustrate.[6] More recently, an empirical research tradition has begun. The qualitative case-study approach provides useful hypotheses and insights. In addition, a host of quantitative research streams compare and study the performance and characteristics of samples of business units over time. These research streams can now be found in most of the basic disciplines and in the field of strategy itself. They are an important indication that the field is finally reaching a maturity in which theories can be and are being subjected to scientific testing.

WHY STRATEGIC MARKET MANAGEMENT?

Strategic market management is often frustrating because the environment is so difficult to understand and predict. The communication and choices required within the organisation can create strain and internal resistance. The most valuable organisational resource, management time, is absorbed. The alternative of simply waiting for and reacting to exceptional opportunities often seems efficient and adequate. Despite these costs and problems, strategic market management has the potential to:

- *Precipitate the consideration of strategic choices.* What is happening externally that is creating opportunities and threats to which a timely and appropriate reaction should be generated? What strategic issues face the firm? What strategic options should be considered? The alternative to strategic market management is usually to drift strategically, becoming absorbed in day-to-day problems. Nothing is more tragic than an organisation that fails because a strategic decision was not addressed until it was too late.

- *Force a long-range view.* The pressures to manage with a short-term focus are strong and frequently lead to strategic errors.

- *Make visible the resource allocation decision.* Allowing allocation of resources to be dictated by the accounting system, political strengths, or inertia (the same as last year) is too easy. One result of this approach is that the small but promising business with 'no problems' or the unborn business may suffer from a lack of resources, whereas the larger business areas with 'problems' may absorb an excessive amount.

- *Aid strategic analysis and decision making.* Concepts, models, and methodologies are available to help a business collect and analyse information and address difficult strategic decisions.

- *Provide a strategic management and control system.* The focus on assets and competencies and the development of objectives and programmes associated with strategic thrusts provide the basis for managing a business strategically.

- *Provide both horizontal and vertical communication and coordination systems.* Strategic market management provides a way to communicate problems and proposed strategies within an organisation; in particular, its vocabulary adds precision.

- *Help a business cope with change.* If a particular environment is extremely stable and the sales patterns are satisfactory, there may be little need for meaningful strategic change – either in direction or intensity.
  In that case, strategic market management is much less crucial. However, most organisations now exist in rapidly changing and increasingly unpredictable environments and therefore need approaches for coping strategically.

KEY LEARNINGS

- A business strategy includes the determination of the product-market scope and its dynamics (as reflected in the intensity of the business investment), the customer value proposition, assets and competencies and functional strategies and programmes.
- Available strategy options include quality, value, focus, innovation, global, product attribute, product design, product line breadth, corporate social responsibility, brand familiarity, and customer intimacy. A business strategy involves the selection and integration of a set of strategic options.
- Strategic market management has evolved from and encompasses budgeting, long-range planning, and strategy planning.
- Strategic market management is externally oriented, proactive, timely, entrepreneurial and globally supported by information systems and knowledge management programmes.

FOR DISCUSSION

1. What is a business strategy? Do you agree with the definition proposed in this chapter? Illustrate your answer with examples.

2. Consider one of the firms in the list below. Read the description in the text, then go to the firm's website and use it to gain an understanding of the business strategy. Look at elements such as the products and services offered, the history of the firm, and its values. What is the business strategy? What product markets does the firm serve? What value propositions does it use? How are the value propositions delivered? What are the firm's assets and competencies? What strategic options has it pursued?

   a. IKEA

   b. Aldi

   c. Diesel

   d. A firm of your choice

NOTES

1. WWW.GoldenWonder.Com; http://walkers.corpex.com/cr15p5/index.htm.
2. Mark Tran 'M&S sales rise sharply', *Guardian Unlimited*, Tuesday 11 July 2006. http://business.guardian.co.uk/story/0,,1817742,00.html. Mark Tran, "M&S shines in retail gloom", *Guardian Unlimited*, Tuesday 11 April 2006. http://business.guardian.co.uk/story/0,,1751455,00.html

3. Putting the boot in. *The Economist*, 18 May 2006. How we shop now. *Time Magazine* supplement, Spring 2006.

4. Testing times, *The Economist*, 30 May 2006. Stuck on the runaway. *The Economist*, 15 June 2006.

5. Gary Hamel and C. K. Prahalad, Competing for the future, *Harvard Business Review*, July–August 1994, pp. 122–8.

6. Alfred P. Sloan, Jr. (1963) *My Years with General Motors*, Doubleday, New York and Peter F. Drucker (1954) *The Practice of Management*, Harper & Row, New York.

CHAPTER TWO

Strategic Market Management: An Overview

Chance favours the prepared mind.
—*Louis Pasteur*

Far better an approximate answer to the right question, which is often vague, than an exact answer to the wrong question, which can always be made precise.
—*John Tukey*, statistician

If you don't know where you're going, you might end up somewhere else.
—*Casey Stengel*

Strategic market management is a system designed to help management both precipitate and make strategic decisions, as well as create strategic visions. A strategic decision involves the creation, change, or retention of a strategy. In contrast to a tactical decision, a strategic decision is usually costly in terms of the resources and time required to reverse or change it. The cost of altering a wrong decision may be so high as to threaten the very existence of an organisation. Normally, a strategic decision has a time frame greater than one year; sometimes decades are involved. A strategic vision is a vision of a future strategy or sets of strategies. The realisation of an optimal strategy for a firm may involve a delay because the firm is not ready or the emerging conditions are not yet in place. A vision will provide direction and purpose for interim strategies and strategic activities. An important role of the system is to precipitate as well as make strategic decisions. The identification of the need for a strategic response is frequently a critical step. Many strategic blunders occur because a strategic decision process was never activated, not because an incorrect decision was made. Furthermore, the role of strategic market management is not limited to selecting from among decision alternatives, but it includes the identification of alternatives as well. Much of the analysis is therefore concerned with identifying alternatives. Figure 2.1 shows an overview of the external analysis and internal analysis that

17

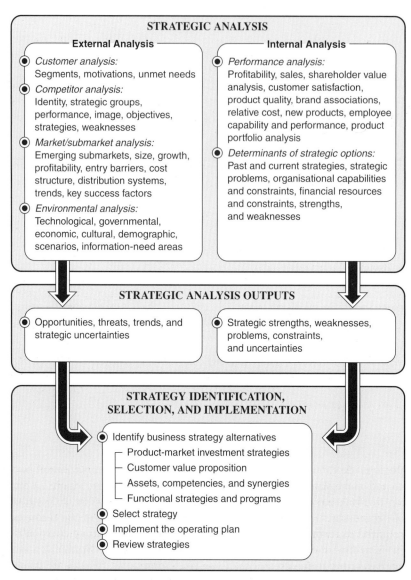

Figure 2.1   Overview of strategic market management

provide the input to strategy development and the set of strategic decisions that is the ultimate output. It provides a structure for strategic market management and for this book. A brief overview of its three principal elements and an introduction to the key concepts will be provided in this chapter.

EXTERNAL ANALYSIS

External analysis involves an examination of the relevant elements external to an organisation. The analysis should be purposeful, focusing on the identification of opportunities, threats, trends, strategic uncertainties, and strategic choices. There is a danger in being excessively descriptive. There is literally no limit to the scope of a descriptive study so the result can be a considerable expenditure of resources with little impact on strategy. One output of external analysis is an identification and understanding of opportunities and threats, both present and potential, facing the organisation. An opportunity is a trend or event that could lead to a significant upward change in sales and profit patterns – given the appropriate strategic response. A threat is a trend or event that will result, in the absence of a strategic response, in a significant downward departure from current sales and profit patterns. For example, the recent trend for women to wear their hair longer and with less styling presents a strategic challenge to the owners of hairstyling brands. Another output is the identification of strategic uncertainties regarding a business or its environment that have the potential to affect strategy. If the uncertainty is important and urgent, an in-depth analysis leading to a strategy decision may be needed; otherwise, an information-gathering effort is usually appropriate. The frame of reference for an external analysis is typically a defined business but it is useful to conduct the analysis at several levels. External analyses of submarkets provide insight sometimes critical to developing strategy. Thus, an external analysis of the market for hairstyling products might contain analysis of the male submarket, which is growing and has important differences. It is also possible to conduct external analyses for groups of businesses, such as divisions, that have characteristics in common, such as segments served, competition, and environmental trends. External analysis, discussed at the outset of Chapter 3, is divided into four sections or components: customer analysis, competitor analysis, market analysis, and environmental analysis.

Customer Analysis

Customer analysis, the first step of external analysis and a focus of Chapter 3, involves identifying the organisation's customer segments and each segment's motivations and unmet needs. Segment identification defines alternative product markets and thus structures the strategic investment decision (what investment levels to assign to each market). The analysis of customer motivations provides information needed to decide which customer value proposition to pursue. An unmet need (a need not currently being met by existing products) can be strategically important because it may represent a way to dislodge entrenched competitors. For example, consider the adult soft-drinks market. Amongst the segments in this market are fruit juices, mineral water and cola. Consumers in each segment have different motivations. The fruit juice drinker might be concerned with taste, the mineral water drinker with health and the cola consumer with avoiding alcohol. An example of an unmet need might be for a branded, adult, soft drink primarily intended for consumption in pubs.

Competitor Analysis

Competitor analysis, covered in Chapter 4, starts with the identification of competitors, current and potential. Some competitors compete more intensely than others.

Polo mints compete most intensely with other mints (for example Tic Tac). However, they also compete with chewing gum and other forms of confectionery. Although intense competitors should be examined most closely, all competitors are usually relevant to strategy development. Especially when there are many competitors, it is helpful to combine those with similar characteristics (for example, size and resources), strengths (for example, brand name, distribution), and strategies (for example, high quality) into strategic groups. The luxury hotel industry might be divided into hotels that offer business-oriented amenities and hotels that are ultra-plush and prestigious. These two groups might be further divided into those that are members of chains with central reservation systems and those that are autonomous.

To develop a strategy, it is important to understand the competitor's:

- *Performance.* What do this competitor's sales, sales growth, and profitability indicate about its health?
- *Image and personality.* How is the competitor positioned and perceived?
- *Objectives.* Is this competitor committed to the business? Does this competitor aim for high growth?
- *Current and past strategy.* What are the implications for future strategic moves?
- *Culture.* What is most important to the organisation – cost control, entrepreneurship or the customer?
- *Cost structure.* Does the competitor have a cost advantage?
- *Strengths and weaknesses.* Is the brand name, distribution, or research-and-development a strength or a weakness?

Of special interest are the competitor's strengths and weaknesses. Strategy development often focuses on exploiting a competitor's weakness or neutralising or bypassing a competitor's strength.

Market/Submarket Analysis

Market analysis, the subject of Chapter 5, has two primary objectives. The first is to determine the attractiveness of the market and submarkets. On average, will competitors earn attractive profits or will they lose money? If the market is so difficult that everyone is losing money then it is not a place in which to invest. The second objective is to understand the dynamics of the market so that threats and opportunities can be detected and strategies adapted. The analysis should include an examination of the market size, growth, profitability, cost structure, channels, trends and key success factors.

Emerging Submarkets

The evolution of submarkets is a key market dynamic. Even a strong business can become irrelevant if it is not attached to the emerging submarkets. The men's toiletries market has grown quickly in recent times with growth in areas such as fragrance, shaving preparation and deodorant products. The expectation amongst owners of toiletry brands for men, such as Nivea, L'Oréal and Brylcream, is that future high-growth prospects lie in the skincare submarket. Given this, major brand owners are focusing product development and promotional efforts in this area.

Size

A basic characteristic of a market (or a submarket) is its size. In addition to current sales, the analysis should consider the market's potential, that is, the additional sales that could be obtained if new users were attracted, new uses were found, or existing buyers were enticed to use the product or service more frequently.

Growth Prospects

The analysis needs to assess the growth trend and product life-cycle stage for the industry and its submarkets. An investment in a declining industry is not always unwise, but it would be if the strategist held the erroneous impression that it was a growth situation. Conversely, it is important to recognise growth contexts even though they will not always be attractive investments for a given firm.

Market Profitability

The profitability of the market depends on five factors – the number and vigour of existing competitors, the threat of new competitors, the threat of substitute products, the profit impact of powerful suppliers, and the power of customers to force price concessions. For example, cold and flu treatments have historically been sold through pharmacies but supermarket sales are rapidly increasing. The power of supermarket retail buyers to put downward pressure on prices and thus the profitability of the market as a whole should be a cause for concern for brand owners. Important structural components are the barriers to entry that must be overcome by potential competitors entering the industry. A barrier to entry for the luxury hotel business in Rome is the availability of desirable sites.

Cost Structures

One issue is what value-added stage represents the most important cost component. In the parcel delivery system, there is local pickup and delivery versus sorting and combining versus between-city transportation versus customer service. Achieving a cost advantage in an important value-added stage can be crucial. Another cost issue is whether the industry is appropriate for a low-cost strategy based on the experience curve model, discussed in Chapter 10.

Distribution Channels

An understanding of the alternative distribution channels and trends can be of strategic value. As more homes have access to broadband the emergence of Internet

Protocol Television (IPTV) is likely to revolutionise the distribution of television programming. IPTV allows consumer to access programmes when they want rather than according to channels schedules. There are many strategic implications of this but primary is the change it makes in the relationship between the channel and the viewer from a 'push' to 'pull'. There are two major challenges for TV companies in this new distribution environment, the first is to learn how consumers will behave in this space and the types of services will they want. With its public service remit the BBC announced the launch of BBCiPlayer in 2006, which would allow viewers to catch up on TV programmes they had missed (and presumably offer an opportunity to the BBC to learn about the new technology). The second challenge is how to maintain advertising revenues. Television technology, such as PVR, already allows consumers to avoid advertising. TV companies need to find a way to keep consumers watching commercials to maintain their own revenues. In the US, ABC has made some of its most popular shows, such as *Lost* and *Desperate Housewives,* available for download free but with embedded advertising as they experiment with ways to maintain their revenues in the new distribution environment.

Market Trends

Trends within the market can affect current or future strategies and assessments of market profitability. For example, a trend in the battery market is consumers growing need for long life batteries to operate high-drain products such as digital cameras and gaming devices. To meet this need Energiser Rechargeable has launched a 15-minute charge product, which lasts up to four times longer in digital cameras and can be re-charged in 15 minutes in a car adapter. Trends in the confectionery industry include the demand for 'healthy' snacks. Cadbury have responded to this with the Cadbury Under 99 Calorie Range, which allows people to have a chocolate treat while control-ling their calorie intake.

Key Success Factors

A key success factor is any competitive asset or competence that is needed to win in the marketplace, whether it is a sustainable competitive advantage (SCA) (ac-tually representing a sustainable point of advantage) or merely a point of parity with the company's competitors. In the luxury hotel business, key success factors might be characteristics that contribute to image, such as ambience or quality of service.

In the e-commerce arena, three key success factors are emerging that impact the emerging ability to track individual buying habits and motivations, to tailor the prod-uct offering and its presentation to specific customers, and to interact with customers. The firms that gain position in the short run and become contenders for winning in the long run will address those key success factors.

Environmental Analysis

Important forces outside an organisation's immediate markets and competitors will shape its operation and thrust. Environmental analysis, the subject of Chapter 6, is the process of identifying and understanding emerging opportunities and threats created by these forces. It is important to limit environmental analysis to what is manageable and relevant because it can easily become bogged down by excessive scope and volume. It is helpful to divide environmental analysis into five components: technological, governmental, cultural, economic, and demographic. A technological development can change an industry dramatically and create difficult decisions for those who are committed to profitable, old technologies. For example, the microprocessor, the Internet, and wireless communication have changed a host of industries. Information technology has created a significant advantage for those hotels able to develop and exploit systems that allow them to service customers more efficiently and with a personalised touch. The governmental environment can be especially important to multinational corporations that operate in politically sensitive countries. A food company may be interested in new EU regulations on food labelling restricting the use of terminology such as 'low fat' or 'high fibre'. Strategic judgements in many contexts are affected by the cultural environment. For example, the key success factor for many clothing industries is the capability to keep in tune with current fashion, and understanding the reasons behind the public's interest in nutrition and health is important to strategists in the confectionery industry.

Knowledge of the economic environment facing a country or an industry helps in projecting that industry's sales over time and in identifying special risks or threats. The hotel industry, for example, can see a link between the overall health of the economy and its primary customer segments. When the economy is down, travel, especially business travel, also turns down. Demographic trends are important to many firms. Age patterns are crucial to those whose customers are in certain age groups, such as infants, students, baby boomers, or retirees. The DIY industry has seen strong growth over the past ten years, benefiting from the large number of middle aged men who have DIY skills. A strategic issue for those in the DIY sector is how to maintain growth as this cohort matures and their ability to DIY declines. Geographic patterns can affect the investment decisions of service firms such as hotels.

A strategic uncertainty stimulated by any external analysis component can generate an information-need area, a strategically important area for which there is likely to be a continuing need for information. Special studies and ongoing information gathering might be justified. A strategic uncertainty can also be used to create two or three future scenarios, relatively comprehensive views of the future environment. One scenario might be optimistic, another pessimistic, and a third in between. For example, a pessimistic scenario for the DIY business in ten years might depict a low level of consumer demand and a high level of intense competition. Each scenario should have strategic implications.

INTERNAL ANALYSIS

Internal analysis, presented in Chapter 7 and summarised in Figure 2.1, aims to provide a detailed understanding of strategically important aspects of the organisation.

In particular, it covers performance analysis and an examination of the key determinants of strategy such as strengths, weaknesses, and strategic problems. Internal analysis, like external analysis, usually has a business unit as a frame of reference but can also be productive at the level of aggregations of businesses, such as divisions or firms.

Performance Analysis

Profitability and sales provide an evaluation of past strategies and an indication of the current market viability of a product line. Return on assets (ROA), the most commonly used measure of profitability, needs to be compared to the cost of capital in order to determine if the business is adding value for the shareholder. Return on assets can be distorted by the limitations of accounting measures – in particular, it ignores intangible assets, such as brand equity. Sales are another performance measure that can reflect changes in the customer base that have long-term implications. Shareholder value analysis is based on generating a discounted present value of the cash flow associated with a strategy. It is theoretically sound and appropriately forward-looking (as opposed to current financials that measure the results of past strategies). However, it focuses attention on financial measures rather than on other indicators of strategic performance. Developing the needed estimates is difficult and subject to a variety of biases. Other, nonfinancial performance measures often provide better measures of long-term business health:

- *Customer satisfaction/brand loyalty.* How are we doing relative to our competitors at attracting customers and building loyalty?
- *Product/service quality.* Is our product delivering value to the customer and is it performing as intended?
- *Brand/firm associations.* What do our customers associate with our business in terms of perceived quality, innovativeness, product class expertise, customer orientation, and so on?
- *Relative cost.* Are we at a cost disadvantage with respect to materials, assembly, product design, or wages?
- *New product activity.* Do we have a stream of new products or product improvements that have made an impact?
- *Manager/employee capability and performance.* Have we created the type, quantity, and depth of personnel needed to support projected strategies?

Product Portfolio Analysis

This analysis considers the performance/strength of each business area, together with the attractiveness of the business area in which it competes. One goal is to generate a business mix with an appropriate balance between new and mature products. An organisation that lacks a flow of new products faces stagnation or decline. A balance must also exist between products that generate cash and those that use cash.

Determinants of Strategic Options

Internal analysis should also review characteristics of the business that will influence strategic options. Five areas are noted in Figure 2.1: past and current strategy, strategic problems, organisational capabilities and constraints, financial resources and constraints, and strengths and weaknesses.

Strategy Review

The past and current strategy provides an important reference point and should be understood. Has the strategy been one of milking, maintenance, or growth? What has been the value proposition? What are its target segments? What are the assets and competencies that would be the basis for a sustainable competitive advantage?

Strategic Problems

A strategic problem is one that, if uncorrected, could have damaging strategic implications. An airline faces a strategic problem if it needs to finance new equipment. An instrument firm may have a quality problem. A weakness is more a characteristic, such as a bad location, that the organisation may have to endure. In general, problems are corrected, and weaknesses are neutralised by a strategy or overcome by strengths.

Organisational Capabilities and Constraints

Internal analysis includes an examination of the internal organisation, its structure, systems, people, and culture. The internal organisation can be important strategically when it is a source of:

- A *strength.* The culture in some firms can be so strong and positive as to provide the basis for a sustainable competitive advantage.
- A *weakness.* A firm may lack the marketing personnel to compete in a business in which a key success factor is marketing.
- A *constraint.* A proposed strategy must fit the internal organisation. A realistic appraisal of an organisation may preclude some strategies.

Financial Resources and Constraints

An analysis of the financial resources available for investment, either from planned cash flow or from debt financing, helps determine how much net investment should be considered. One result could be a financial constraint, such as having only €20 million per year available for investment during the next few years.

Strengths and Weaknesses

Future strategies are often developed by building on strengths and neutralising weaknesses. Strengths and weaknesses are based on assets, such as a brand name, or competencies, such as advertising or manufacturing.

SENOKOT: A CASE STUDY[1]

Senokot has been the market leader in the treatment of constipation in the UK for many years. However in 2004 there was a feeling that the brand sales had stagnated but could benefit if the market for constipation remedies could be expanded. Research revealed that those who suffered from constipation could be divided into three groups: 'treaters' who used remedies, 'diet modifiers' who changed their diets to deal with symptoms and 'combos' who preferred to modify their diets but used a remedy if the symptoms persisted. The problem with the latter two groups was that they did not consider constipation to be serious and felt it was not worth taking a remedy for. However, constipation can be a serious condition with potentially unpleasant symptoms and side effects. Senokot needed to engage the 'combos' more actively with remedies in general and Senokot in particular. At the same time it needed to get the 'diet modifiers' to more actively consider their condition and the use of remedies. The brands solution was to reframe the condition as an issue of inner health. To achieve this Senokot developed an advertising concept using the handbag as a metaphor for the stomach, with TV advertisement showing meals being tipped into the bag over a period of days. The intended effect was to highlight to consumers what constipation actually means for the body and to encourage them to reconsider how they treated their symptoms. The result was a sales uplift in major multiples of 31.4% and in chemists of 21.7%. Overall Senokot increased its share of the market from 30.5% to 34.1%.

The success of the campaign was aided by Senokot's competitors who had not approached the issue in such stark fashion and by the existing strength of Senokot's distribution and brand name.

CREATING A VISION FOR THE BUSINESS

A business vision can play several roles for many decades. First, it can guide strategy, suggesting strategic paths for the business. Second, it can help perpetuate the core of the business and ensure that its core competencies are preserved. Third and perhaps most important, it can inspire those in the organisation by providing a purpose that is worthwhile and ennobling and that goes beyond maximising shareholder wealth. James Collins and Jerry Porras, in an insightful study of visionary companies, suggested that a business vision should include the following three components, as shown in Figure 2.2: core values, a core purpose, and one or more BHAGs, or 'Big, Hairy, Audacious Goals'.[2]

Core values, up to three to five in number, are the timeless, passionately held guiding principles of an organisation. At Nestlé, the core values are creating value for all stakeholders, over the long term, through strong customer focus, effective employee management and a commitment to compliance with legislative requirements. For Nokia the core values are customer satisfaction, respect, achievement and renewal. Mobile phone operator O2 identifies its core values as being bold, open, trusted and clear. Core values come from within the organisation; they

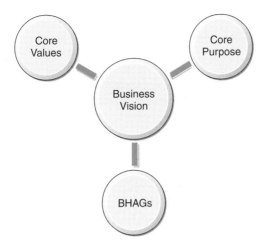

Figure 2.2 The business vision

represent what the organisation is at its very essence, as opposed to what it might like to be.

The core purpose, which should last for at least a hundred years, is the organisation's reason for being, which goes beyond current products and services. Tesco identifies the purpose of its business as being to create value for customers to earn their long-term loyalty. For Ikea the core purpose is to offer a wide range of well designed, functional home furnishing products at prices so low that as many people as possible will be able to afford them. Nokia's core purpose is connecting people. One approach to finding a core purpose is to ask five whys. Start with a description of the business and ask 'why is that important?' five times; after a few whys you get to the very essence of the business.

Big, hairy, audacious goals provide a clear and compelling aspiration and challenge. They can take several forms, such as focusing on a:

- *Sales goal.* Throughout its history, the Irish commercial bank, Anglo-Irish Bank has set extremely specific and ambitious sales goals to drive its growth.
- *Common enemy.* Virgin Atlantic has been focused on and been energised by the goal of competing with a common enemy, British Airways.
- *Role model.* Ryanair originally modelled itself on the low-cost model of Southwest Airlines.
- *Internal transformation.* Since the mid-1990s BP has been working to transform itself into a twenty-first century energy company.

One challenge is to distinguish between BHAGs that are simply bravado or wishful thinking and those that are genuinely effective. James Collins identified 11 companies (which he termed 'good to great' companies) which achieved a return three times that of the stock market over 15 years.[3] One conclusion he reached is that in comparison to reference companies, the good-to-great firms had BHAGs which satisfied three criteria:

- *The BHAG leveraged something in which the organisation excelled.* For Abbott Laboratories, it was creating hospital nutritional products and diagnostic devices, rather than being a pharmaceutical company.
- *The BHAG resulted in economic value by moving the needle with respect to key economic metrics.* For Abbott Laboratories, the key metric was profit-per-employee (as opposed to profit per loan or profit per precut line).
- *The BHAG was something the organisation was deeply passionate about.* It went beyond short-term financials into something that made employees feel worthwhile and provided a customer value proposition which mattered.

STRATEGY IDENTIFICATION AND SELECTION

The purpose of external analysis and internal analysis is twofold: to help generate strategic alternatives and to provide criteria for selecting from among them. Figure 2.3 highlights the four dimensions of a business strategy. The first is selecting

---

IDENTIFICATION OF STRATEGIC ALTERNATIVES
- Product-market investment strategies
  - Product-market scope
  - Growth directions
  - Investment strategies
- Customer value proposition
- Bases of competitive advantage – assets, competencies, synergies
- Functional area strategies

CRITERIA FOR STRATEGY SELECTION
- Consider scenarios suggested by strategic uncertainties and environmental opportunities/threats
- Generate an attractive ROI
- Pursue a sustainable competitive advantage
  - Exploit organisational strengths or competitor weaknesses
  - Neutralise organisational weaknesses or competitor strengths
- Be consistent with organisational vision/objectives
  - Achieve a long-term return on investment
  - Be compatible with vision/objectives
- Be feasible
  - Resources are available
  - Be compatible with the internal organisation
- Consider the relationship to other strategies within the firm
  - Foster product portfolio balance
  - Consider flexibility
  - Exploit synergy

Figure 2.3   Selecting strategic alternatives

the product markets in which the firm will operate and deciding how much investment should be allocated to each; the second is determining the customer value proposition; the third is identifying the assets and competencies leading to sustainable competitive advantages; and the fourth is to develop functional area strategies.

GENERIC CUSTOMER NEED

In his classic article, 'Marketing myopia', Theodore Levitt suggested that firms that myopically define their business in product terms can stagnate even though the basic customer need that they are serving is enjoying healthy growth.[4] Because of a myopic product focus, others gain the benefits of growth. Thus, if firms regard themselves as being in the transportation rather than the railroad business, the energy instead of the petroleum business, or the communication rather than the telephone business, they are more likely to exploit opportunities. The concept is simple. Define the business in terms of the basic customer need rather than the product. Xerox changed its focus from copiers when it became the 'document' company. Visa has defined itself as being in the business of enabling a customer to exchange value – to exchange any asset including cash on deposit, the cash value of life insurance, the equity in a home – for virtually anything anywhere in the world. As the business is redefined, both the set of competitors and the range of opportunities are often radically expanded. After redefining its business, Visa estimated that it had reached only 5% of its potential given the new definition. Defining a business in terms of generic need can be extremely useful for fostering creativity, in generating strategic options, and avoiding an internally oriented product/production focus.

Product-Market Investment Strategies

Product Definition

As a practical matter, many strategic decisions involve products – which product lines to continue, which to add, and which to delete. Green & Blacks market organic, fair-trade confectionery products; they are not simply in the confectionery business. Nike got back on track when it decided it was in the sports and fitness business rather than the business of making casual sportswear.

Market Definition

Businesses need to select markets in which they will have a competitive advantage. Northern Rock bank defines its business as specialised lending for residential mortgages, secured commercial lending and personal finance. HSBC seeks to be the world's leading financial service provider and operates in four major markets: personal financial services, commercial banking, corporate and investment banking and private banking. Such statements of focus can drive the operations of a firm.

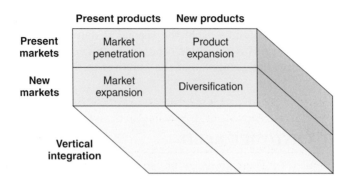

Figure 2.4   Product-market growth directions

Vertical Integration

A strategic option not covered by product-market scope is vertical integration. Some publishing companies have integrated backward into paper and wood products. Inditex, the Spanish owner of high-street fashion retailers Zara, and Massimo Dutti is involved in textile design, manufacturing and distribution. They have used the flexibility of vertical integration to respond quickly to marketplace demand and to build sales. The question is, at what vertical levels should the business operate? The trade-offs between increased control and potential return from vertical integration on the one hand, and increased risk and loss of flexibility caused by the associated investment on the other, are discussed in detail in Chapter 13.

Growth Directions

It is crucial in strategy development to have a focus that is dynamic rather than static. The concept of a product-market matrix shown in Figure 2.4 is helpful for identifying options and encouraging a dynamic perspective. In the product-market matrix, five growth options are shown. The first is to penetrate the existing product market. A firm may attempt to attract customers from competitors or increase usage by existing customers. A second option involves product expansion while remaining in the current market. Thus, a firm offering cleaning services to public service facilities might expand into supervision of other functions, such as grounds and building maintenance. A third option is to apply the same products in new markets. The cleaning firm could expand its cleaning services into other industries. These first three growth options are explored in more detail in Chapter 12. The fourth growth option, to diversify into new product markets, is discussed in detail in Chapter 13. Figure 2.4 also adds another dimension to the product-market matrix representing a fifth growth option: vertical integration.

Investment Strategies

For each product market, four investment options are possible. The firm could invest to enter or grow, invest to hold the existing position, milk the business by avoiding any investment, or exit. The exit option might arise if prospects become extremely unattractive or if the business area becomes incompatible with the overall thrust of the firm.

Strategic Options

Even given a specification of a product-market investment plan, a business strategy will still involve choices. An organisation cannot be good at all things or create an infinite number of assets and competencies. Value propositions and programmes that are too broad and ambitious will lack credibility with customers and may end up demoralising employees. There are an unlimited number of such choices that involve specifying the value proposition, functional area strategies, and assets and competencies that will be the bases for a sustainable competitive advantage. These choices can be conceptualised in the form of one or more strategic options, as introduced in the last chapter and elaborated in Chapters 9, 10, and 11.

These options include, but are not limited to: quality, value, focus, innovation, globalisation, product attributes, product design, product-line breadth, corporate social responsibility, brand equity, and customer relationships. Of course, each of these options has many variants, depending on the industry and firm context.

The strategic options will specify the following:

- *Value propositions* – what the offering provides to the buyer and user of the product or service. The value proposition is not limited to functional benefits but can include social, emotional, and self-expressive benefits.
- *Assets and competencies* – the bases for a sustainable competitive advantage. Assets and competencies usually require time, resources, and talent to create, and they are sustainable because they are often hard to replicate. Approaches to identifying candidate assets and competencies are presented in Chapter 4.
- *Functional strategies and programmes* – to support the value proposition and the development and enhancement of the assets and competencies. These strategies and programmes can involve such functional areas as manufacturing, distribution, information technology, quality, customer relationships, brand building, and communications.

Strategic positioning, the subject of Chapter 12, specifies how the business is to be perceived relative to its competitors and market by its customers and employees/partners. As such, it often represents the essence of a business strategy.

SELECTING AMONG STRATEGIC ALTERNATIVES

Figure 2.3 provides a list of some of the criteria useful for selecting alternatives, grouped into five general areas.

- *Consider scenarios.* A future scenario can be stimulated by strategic uncertainties or environmental opportunities or threats. Thus, the strategic uncertainty 'will a breakthrough in storage batteries make a general-use electric car feasible?' could lead to both 'yes' and 'no' scenarios. The threat of severe pollution controls could also generate scenarios relevant to the strategies of car and energy firms. It is useful and prudent to evaluate strategic options in the context of any major scenarios identified.

- *Generate an attractive ROI.* Creating a value proposition that is appealing to customers may not be worthwhile if the investment or operating cost is excessive.

- *Pursue a sustainable competitive advantage.* A useful operational criterion is whether a sustainable competitive advantage exists as part of the strategy. Unless the business unit has or can develop a real competitive advantage that is sustainable over time in the face of competitor reaction, an attractive long-term return will be unlikely. To achieve a sustainable competitive advantage, a strategy should exploit organisational assets and competencies and neutralise weaknesses.

- *Be consistent with organisational vision and objectives.* A primary purpose of an organisation's vision – what a future strategy should be – and objectives is to help make strategic decisions. Thus, it is appropriate to look toward them for guidance. They can be changed, of course, if circumstances warrant. An explicit decision to change a strategy is very different from ignoring it in the face of a tempting alternative.

- *Be feasible.* A practical criterion is that the strategy be feasible. It should be within the resources of the organisation. It also should be internally consistent with other organisational characteristics, such as structure, systems, people, and culture. These organisational considerations will be covered in Chapter 16.

- *Consider the relationship to other firm strategies.* A strategy can relate to other business units by:

  - *Balancing the sources and uses of cash flow.* Some business units should generate cash and others should provide attractive places to invest that cash. Chapter 7 and 15 elaborate.
  - *Enhancing flexibility.* Flexibility is generally reduced when heavy commitments are made in the form of fixed investment, long-term contracts, and vertical integration.
  - *Exploiting synergy.* A firm that does not exploit potential synergy may be missing an opportunity.

Implementation

The implementation stage involves converting strategic alternatives into an operating plan. If a new product market is to be entered then a systematic programme is required to develop or acquire products as an entry vehicle. If a strong research-and-development group is to be assembled, a programme to hire people, organise them and obtain facilities will be needed. The operating plan may span more than one year. It might be useful to provide a detailed plan for the upcoming year that contains specific short-term objectives.

Strategy Review

One of the key questions in a strategic market management system is to determine when a strategy requires review and change. It is usually necessary to monitor a limited number of key measures of strategy performance and the environment. Thus, sales, market share, margins, profit, and ROA may be regularly reported and analysed. Externally, the process is more difficult, requiring an effective information-scanning system. The heart of such a system will be an identified set of strategic uncertainties or issues that need to be continuously considered.

THE PROCESS

Figure 2.1 implies a logical, sequential process. After external and internal analyses are completed, the strategic options are then detailed and the optimal ones selected. Finally, the operating plan and strategy review programme are implemented. Later, perhaps in the next annual planning cycle, the process is repeated and the plan updated. Although Figure 2.1 provides a useful structure, the process should be more iterative and circular than sequential. The identification and selection of strategies should occur during external and internal analysis. Furthermore, the process of evaluating strategies often suggests the need for additional external analysis, making it necessary to cycle through the process several times. As suggested earlier, strategies and indicators of the need to change them should be continually monitored to avoid being tied to an annual planning cycle. The process supporting the development of business strategies is covered in Chapter 16.

KEY LEARNINGS

- External analysis includes analyses of customers, competitors, markets and the environment. The role of these analyses is to identify existing or emerging opportunities, threats, trends, strategic uncertainties, and strategic options.
- Internal analysis includes a performance appraisal and an examination of organisational strengths, weaknesses, problems, constraints, and strategic options.
- Business vision should specify the core values (timeless guiding principles), core purpose (reason for being), and BHAGs (big, hairy, audacious goals).
- A business strategy specification includes the product-market scope and the selection of a set of strategic options that include the value proposition, assets and competencies, and strategies for functional areas.
- Strategy selection should consider scenarios, ROI prospects, SCAs, the organisation vision, strategy feasibility, and other firm strategies.

FOR DISCUSSION

1. Consider the Gallo strategic decision. Evaluate or describe how you would go about evaluating that decision with respect to the criteria in Figure 2.3. Create a hypothetical BHAG for Gallo and evaluate it with respect to the three criteria for good BHAGs.

2. What is the difference between key success factors and sustainable competitive advantages? Illustrate your understanding by discussing several constructs such as the cola market or the luxury car market.

3. Which quote from the beginning of either Chapter 1 or Chapter 2 do you find the most insightful? Why?

NOTES

1. Senokot – The Transformation of a Constipation Remedy to an Inner-Health Product, IPA Effectiveness Awards, Institute of Practitioners in Advertising, London, 2005. © 2006 Copyright and database rights owned by WARC.

2. For a discussion of the business vision see James C. Collins and Jerry I. Porras (1996) Building your company's vision. *Harvard Business Review*, September-October, pp. 65–77. The authors also include a fourth element: a 'vivid description' of the envisioned future. For a description of the study of visionary companies see the authors' excellent book: James C. Collins and Jerry I. Porras (1994) *Built to Last: Successful Habits of Visionary Companies*, HarperBusiness, New York.

3. Jim Collins (2003) Good to Great, Harper Business, New York, p. 95.

4. Theodore Levitt (1960) Marketing myopia. Harvard Business Review, July–August, p. 45–56.

PART
TWO

STRATEGIC ANALYSIS

CHAPTER THREE

External and Customer Analysis

To be prepared is half the victory.
—*Miguel Cervantes*

The purpose of an enterprise is to create and keep a customer.
—*Theodore Levitt*

You can't just ask customers what they want and then try to give that to them. By the time you get it built, they'll want something new.
—*Steve Jobs*

Strategy development or review logically starts with external analysis, an analysis of the factors external to a business that can affect strategy. The first four chapters of Part Two present concepts and methods useful in conducting an external analysis. The final chapter of Part Two turns to internal analysis: the analysis of the firm's strengths, weaknesses, problems, constraints, and options.

EXTERNAL ANALYSIS

A successful external analysis needs to be directed and purposeful. There is always the danger that it will become an endless process resulting in an excessively descriptive report. In any business there is no end to the material that appears potentially relevant. Without discipline and direction, volumes of useless descriptive material can easily be generated.

Affecting Strategic Decisions

The external analysis process should not be an end in itself. Rather, it should be motivated throughout by a desire to affect strategy, to generate or evaluate strategic options. As Figure 3.1 shows, it can impact strategy directly by suggesting strategic decision alternatives or influencing a choice among them. More specifically, it should contribute to the investment decision and the development of a strategic option that includes the value proposition, assets and competencies, and functional strategies and programmes.

The investment decision – where to compete – involves questions like:

- Should existing business areas be liquidated, milked, maintained, or a target for investment?
- What growth directions should receive investment?
- Should there be market penetration, product expansion, or market expansion?
- Should new business areas be entered?

The selection of strategic options – that is, how to compete – suggests questions like the following:

- What are the value propositions?
- What are the key success factors?
- What assets and competencies should be created, enhanced or maintained?
- What strategies and programmes should be implemented in functional areas?
- What should be the positioning strategy, segmentation strategy, distribution strategy, brand-building strategy, manufacturing strategy and so on?

Additional Analysis Objectives

Figure 3.1 also suggests that an external analysis can contribute to strategy indirectly by identifying:

- significant trends and future events
- threats and opportunities
- strategic uncertainties that could affect strategy outcomes

A significant trend or event, such as concern about saturated fat or the emergence of a new competitor, can dramatically affect the evaluation of strategy options. A new

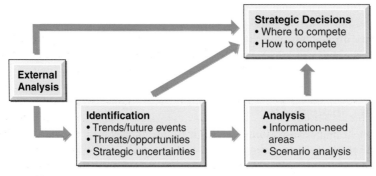

Figure 3.1   The role of external analysis

technology can represent both a threat to an established firm and an opportunity to a prospective competitor.

Strategic Uncertainties

Strategic uncertainty is a particularly useful concept in conducting an external analysis. If you could know the answer to one question prior to making a strategic commitment, what would that question be? If Alfa Romeo were to consider whether to add a petrol-electric hybrid to its line, important strategy uncertainties might include the following:

- What will the sales profile of hybrids be in upcoming years? How many will be sold in what categories?
- What will be the hybrid strategies of Alfa Romeo's direct competitors?
- What new technologies might emerge that will affect the demand for hybrids?

Strategic uncertainties focus on specific unknown elements that will affect the outcome of strategic decisions. 'Should Alfa Romeo extend its line to hybrids?' is a strategic decision, whereas 'what is the future demand for hybrids?' is a strategic uncertainty. Most strategic decisions will be driven by a set of these uncertainties. Below are some examples of strategic uncertainties and the strategic decisions to which they might relate. A strategic uncertainty can often lead to additional sources of strategic uncertainty. One common strategic uncertainty, as portrayed in the figure on the top of p. 45, is what the future demand for a product (such as ultrasound diagnostic equipment) will be. Asking 'on what does that depend?' will usually generate additional strategic uncertainties. One uncertainty might address technological improvements, whereas another might consider the technological development and cost/benefit levels achieved by competitive technologies. Still another might look into the financial capacity of the telecommunications industry to continue capital improvements. Each of these strategic uncertainties can, in turn, generate still another level of strategic uncertainties.

Analysis

There are three ways of handling uncertainty, as suggested by Figure 3.1. First, a strategic decision can be precipitated because the logic for a decision is compelling and/or because a delay would be costly or risky. Second, it may be worthwhile to attempt to reduce the uncertainty by information acquisition and analysis of an information-need area. The effort could range from a high-priority task force to a low-key monitoring effort. The level of resources expended will depend on the potential impact on strategy and its immediacy. Third, the uncertainty could be modelled by a scenario analysis. A scenario is an alternative view of the future environment that is usually prompted by an alternative possible answer to a strategic uncertainty or by a prospective future event or trend. Is the current popularity of male grooming a fad associated with the popularity of metrosexuality and which will recede as male-ness reasserts itself? Such a question could be the basis for a positive and a negative scenario. Each could be associated with very different environmental profiles and strategy recommendations. In Chapter 6, information-need areas and scenario analy-sis will be covered in more detail. A host of concepts and methods are introduced in this and the following three chapters. It would, of course, be unusual to employ all of them in any given context, and the strategist should resist any compulsion to do so. Rather, those that are most relevant to the situation at hand should be selected. Furthermore, some areas of analysis will be more fruitful than others and will merit more effort.

External Analysis as a Creative Exercise

In part, external analysis is an exercise in creative thinking. In fact, there is often too little effort devoted to developing new strategic options and too much effort di-rected to solving operational problems of the day. The essence of creative thinking is considering different perspectives, and that is exactly what an external analysis does. The strategist is challenged to look at strategy from the perspectives of customer, competitor, market, and environment as well as from an internal perspective. Within each there are several subdimensions. In Figure 2.1 more than two dozen are identi-fied. The hope is that by examining strategy from different viewpoints, options will be generated that would otherwise be missed.

The Level of Analysis – Defining the Market

An external analysis of what? To conduct an external analysis, the market or submar-ket boundaries need to be specified. The scope of external analysis can involve an industry such as:

- sporting goods
- ski clothing and equipment
- skis and snowboards
- downhill skis
- high-performance skis

The level of analysis will depend on the organisational unit and strategic deci-sions involved. A sporting goods company, such as Adidas, will be making resource decisions across a number of sports and thus needs to be concerned with the whole industry. A ski equipment manufacturer, such as Salomon, may only be concerned with elements of sporting goods relating to skis, boots and clothing. The maker of high-performance skis might be interested in only a subsegment of the ski industry. One approach to defining the market is to specify the business scope. The scope can be identified in terms of the product market and in terms of the competitors. Relevant, of course, are the future product market and competitors as well as the present.

There is always a tradeoff to be made. A narrow scope specification will inhibit a business from identifying trends and opportunities that could lead to some attractive options and directions. Thus, a maker of downhill skis may want to include snowboards and cross-country skis because they represent business options or because they will impact the ski equipment business. On the other hand, depth of analysis might be sacrificed when the scope is excessively broad. A more focused analysis may generate more insight. The analysis usually needs to be conducted at several levels. The downhill ski and snowboard industry might be the major focus of the analysis. However, an analysis of sporting goods might suggest and shed light on some substitute product pressures and market trends. Also, an analysis may be needed at the segment level (for example, high-performance skis) because entry, investment, and strategy decisions are often made at that level. Furthermore, the key success factors could differ for different product markets within a market or industry. One approach is a layered analysis, with the primary level receiving the greatest depth of analysis. Another approach could be multiple analyses, perhaps consecutively conducted. The first analysis might stimulate an opportunity that would justify a second analysis.

When Should an External Analysis Be Conducted?

There is often a tendency to relegate the external analysis to an annual exercise. Each year, of course, it may not require the same depth as the initial effort. It may be more productive to focus on a part of the analysis in the years immediately following a major effort.

The annual planning cycle can provide a healthy stimulus to review and change strategies. However, a substantial risk exists in maintaining external analysis as an annual event. The need for strategic review and change is often continuous. Information sensing and analysis therefore also need to be continuous. The framework and concepts of external analysis can still play a key role in providing structure even when the analysis is continuous and addresses only a portion of the whole.

External analysis deliberately commences with customer and competitor analyses because they can help define the relevant industry or industries. An industry can be defined in terms of the needs of a specific group of customers – buyers of ice cream in France, for instance. Such an industry definition then forms the basis for the identification of competitors and the balance of external analysis. An industry such as the ice cream industry can also be defined in terms of all its competitors. Customers have such a direct relationship to a firm's operation, so they are usually a rich source of relevant operational opportunities, threats, and uncertainties.

THE SCOPE OF CUSTOMER ANALYSIS

In most strategic market-planning contexts, the first logical step is to analyse the customers. Customer analysis can be usefully partitioned into an understanding of how the market segments, an analysis of customer motivations, and an exploration of unmet needs. Figure 3.2 presents a basic set of questions for each area of inquiry.

SEGMENTATION
- Who are the biggest customers? The most profitable? The most attractive potential customers? Do the customers fall into any logical groups based on needs, motivations, or characteristics?
- How could the market be segmented into groups that would require a unique business strategy?

CUSTOMER MOTIVATIONS
- What elements of the product/service do customers value most?
- What are the customers' objectives? What are they really buying?
- How do segments differ in their motivation priorities?
- What changes are occurring in customer motivation? In customer priorities?

UNMET NEEDS
- Why are some customers dissatisfied? Why are some changing brands or suppliers?
- What are the severity and incidence of consumer problems?
- What are unmet needs that customers can identify? Are there some of which consumers are unaware?
- Do these unmet needs represent leverage points for competitors?

Figure 3.2   Customer analysis

SEGMENTATION

Segmentation is often the key to developing a sustainable competitive advantage. In a strategic context, *segmentation* means the identification of customer groups that respond differently from other groups to competitive offerings. A segmentation strategy couples the identified segments with a programme to deliver an offering to those segments. Thus, the development of a successful segmentation strategy requires the conceptualisation, development, and evaluation of a targeted competitive offering. A segmentation strategy should be judged on three dimensions. First, can a competitive offering be developed and implemented that will be appealing to the target segment? Second, can the appeal of the offering and the subsequent relationship with the target segment be maintained over time despite competitive responses? Third, is the resulting business from the target segment worthwhile, given the investment required to develop and market an offering tailored to it? The concept behind a successful segmentation strategy is that within a reduced market space it is possible to create a dominant position that competitors will be unwilling or unable to attack successfully.

How Should Segments Be Defined?

The task of identifying segments is difficult, in part, because in any given context there are literally hundreds of ways to divide up the market. Typically, the analysis will consider five, ten, or more segmentation variables. To avoid missing a useful way of defining segments, it is important to consider a wide range of variables. These variables need to be evaluated on the basis of their ability to identify segments for which different strategies are (or should be) pursued.

CUSTOMER CHARACTERISTICS

- Geographic
- Type of organisation

- Size of firm
- Lifestyle

- Sex
- Age
- Occupation

- Small regional communities as markets for discount stores
- Computer needs of restaurants versus manufacturing firms versus banks versus retailers
- Large hospital versus medium versus small
- Jaguar buyers tend to be more adventurous, less conservative than buyers of Mercedes-Benz and BMW
- Mothers of young children
- Cereals for children versus adults
- The paper copier needs of lawyers versus bankers versus dentists

PRODUCT-RELATED APPROACHES

- User type
- Usage
- Benefits sought

- Price sensitivity

- Competitor
- Application
- Brand loyalty

- Appliance buyer—home builder, remodeler, home owner
- Concert—season ticket holders, occasional patrons, nonusers
- Dessert eaters—those who are calorie-conscious versus those who are more concerned with convenience
- Price-sensitive Skoda buyer versus the luxury Mercedes-Benz buyer
- Users of competing products
- Professional users of chain saws versus home owners
- Those committed to Heinz ketchup versus price buyers

Figure 3.3 Examples of approaches to defining segments

The most useful segment-defining variables for an offering are rarely obvious. Among the variables frequently used are those shown in Figure 3.3. The first set of variables describes segments in terms of general characteristics unrelated to the product involved. Thus, a bakery might be concerned with geographically defined segments related to communities or even neighbourhoods. A consulting company may specialise in the hotel industry. A financial services firm in Germany may target the over-60 market as this segment is projected to double to 28 million by 2050.

Demographics are particularly powerful for defining segments, in part because a person's life stage affects his or her activities, interests and brand loyalties. Another reason is that demographic trends are predictable. The European population of over 65s is expected to grow to over 136 million in 2020, with more than 36 million over the age of 80. A British firm, Comfort Plus Products, has recognised this trend and established itself as a source of mobility products designed for the elderly. Adjustable beds, rise and decline chairs and scooters are just some of the Comfort Plus products that appeal to this long-ignored demographic segment.

Another attempt to employ demographics was made by Volvo with their concept car the YCC (your concept car) designed by an all-female team for the independent, professional, woman driver.[1] This is a growing segment in Europe and more than half of all car buyers in the US. The car has all of the things you expect from Volvo in terms of performance and reliability but it also has features that are intended to be attractive to women. Amongst these features are extra storage space for personal items such as mobile phones, coins and keys. The car also has gull-wing doors (upward opening) to emphasises storage and ease of access. While only a concept car at this stage it is expected that many of the popular features will be employed in future models and the launch of the concept car is intended to signal to women drivers that Volvo takes its needs seriously.

The second category of segment variables includes those that are related to the product. One of the most frequently employed is usage. A bakery may follow a very different strategy in serving restaurants that rely heavily on bakery products than in serving those that use fewer such products. A manufacturer of light bulbs may design a special line for a large customer such as B&Q but sell through distributors using another brand name. Four other useful segment variables are benefits, price sensitivity, loyalty, and applications.

Benefits

If there is a most useful segmentation variable, it would be benefits sought from a product because the selection of benefits can determine a total business strategy. In the baby food market twin (and apparently conflicting) benefits of convenience and healthy products have driven growth. German company Hipp has used these benefits to segment the baby food market and offer a range of organic ready made meals that provide parents with both benefits.

Price Sensitivity

The benefit dimension representing the tradeoff between low price and high quality is both useful and pervasive; hence it is appropriate to consider it separately. In many product classes there is a well-defined breakdown between those customers concerned first about price and others who are willing to pay extra for higher quality and features. Food retailers operate along a well-defined hierarchy from discounters such as Aldi and Lidl, through Asda, Sainsbury, to Marks and Spencer food halls and on to prestige food emporia. Hotels similarly operate from the Inn concept (such as Jury's Inn) through branded chains like Accor to the great prestige hotels such as George V in Paris and Claridges of London. In each case the segment dictates the strategy.

Loyalty

Brand loyalty, an important consideration in allocating resources, can be structured using a loyalty matrix as shown in Figure 3.4.[2] Each cell represents a very different strategic priority and can justify a very different programme. Generally it is too easy to take the loyal customer for granted. However, a perspective of total profits over the life of a customer makes the value of an increase in loyalty more vivid. A study by Bain shows that a 5% increase in loyalty can nearly double the lifetime profits generated by customers in several industries, including banking, insurance, publishing and credit cards.[3] The key is often to reward the loyal customer by living up to expectations consistently, providing an ongoing relationship and offering extras that surprise and delight. The loyalty matrix suggests that the brand fencesitters, including those of competitors, should also have high priority. Using the matrix involves estimating the

	Low Loyalty	Moderate Loyalty	Loyal
Customer	Medium	High	Highest
Noncustomer	Low to Medium	High	Zero

Figure 3.4   The loyalty matrix: priorities about here

size of each of the six cells, identifying the customers in each group, and designing programmes that will influence their brand choice and loyalty level.

Applications

Some products and services, particularly industrial products, can best be segmented by use or application. A laptop computer may be needed by some for use while travelling, whereas others may need a computer at the office that can be conveniently stored when not in use. One segment may use a computer for word processing and another may be more interested in data processing. Some might use a four-wheel drive for light industrial hauling and others may be buying primarily for recreation. The sportswear industry segments into the serious athletes (small in number but influential), the weekend warriors and the casual wearers using sportswear for street wear. Recognising that the casual wearer segment is a large majority of users, Puma and the fashion designer Alexander McQueen have joined forces to produce a sport-fashion collection to appeal to this market.

Multiple Segments versus a Focus Strategy

Two distinct segmentation strategies are possible. The first focuses on a single segment, which can be much smaller than the market as a whole. Anglo-Irish Bank has built great success through a focus strategy of providing banking, treasury and wealth management services to business clients. Customers deal directly with a dedicated relationship manager and a product specialist. With a very strong commitment to customer service Anglo Irish have been able to use their focus to drive high growth for more than 10 years.

An alternative to a focusing strategy is to involve multiple segments. In many industries aggressive firms are moving toward multiple-segment strategies. L'Oréal competes in four segments with multiple brands. These are consumer (L'Oréal Paris and Garnier), professional (Redken and Mizani), luxury (Lancôme and Cacharel) and active (La Roche Posay and Skinceuticals). Campbell Soup has introduced different flavour soups for different areas in Europe. For example, in countries like Ireland and the UK they offer Oxtail-flavoured soup. They have also developed different flavours specific to countries such as Sweden.

Developing multiple strategies is costly and often must be justified by an enhanced aggregate impact. There can be important synergies between segment offerings. For example, in the Alpine ski industry, the image developed by high-performance skis is important to sales at the recreational-ski end of the business. Thus, a manufacturer that is weak at the high end will have difficulty at the low end. Conversely, a successful high-end firm will want to exploit that success by having entries in the other segments. A key success factor in the general aviation industry is a broad product line, ranging from fixedgear, single-engine piston aircraft to turboprop planes, because customers tend to trade up and will switch to a different firm if the product line has major gaps.

CUSTOMER MOTIVATIONS

After identifying customer segments, the next step is to consider their motivations: What lies behind their purchase decisions? And how does that differ by segment? It is helpful to list the segments and the motivation priorities of each, as shown in Figure 3.5 for air travellers. Internet retailers have learned that there are distinct shopper segments, and each has a very different set of driving motivations.[4]

- *newbie shoppers* – need a simple interface, as well as a lot of hand-holding and reassurance
- *reluctant shoppers* – need information, reassurance, and access to live customer support
- *frugal shoppers* – need to be convinced that the price is good and they don't have to search elsewhere
- *strategic shoppers* – need access to the opinions of peers or experts, and choices in configuring the products they buy
- *enthusiastic shoppers* – need community tools to share their experiences, as well as engaging tools to view the merchandise and personalised recommendations
- *convenience shoppers* – (the largest group) want efficient navigation, a lot of information from customers and experts, and superior customer service

Some motivations will help to define strategy. A car from Audi, for example, might be designed and positioned with respect to power and prestige. Before making a strategic commitment to such a positioning it is crucial to know where power fits in the motivation set. Other motivations may not define a strategy or differentiate a business but represent a dimension for which adequate performance must be obtained or the battle will be lost. If the prime motivation for buyers of juice drinks is health, a viable firm must be able to deliver at least acceptable health benefits.

Segment	Motivation
Business	Reliable service, convenient schedules, easy-to-use airports, frequent-flyer programs, and comfortable service
Vacationers	Price, feasible schedules

Figure 3.5   Customer motivation grid: air travellers

Figure 3.6 Customer motivation analysis

Determining Motivations

As Figure 3.6 suggests, consumer motivation analysis starts with the task of identifying motivations for a given segment. Although a group of managers can identify motivations, a more valid list is usually obtained by getting customers to discuss the product or service in a systematic way. Why is it being used? What is the objective? What is associated with a good or bad use experience? For a motivation such as car safety, respondents might be asked why safety is important. Such probes might result in the identification of more basic motives, such as the desire to feel calm and secure rather than anxious.

Customers can be accessed with group or individual interviews. Griffin and Hauser of the MIT Quality Function Deployment (QFD) programme compared the two approaches in a study of food-carrying devices.[5] They found that individual interviews were more cost effective and that the group processes did not generate enough extra information to warrant the added expense. They also explored the number of interviews needed to gain a complete list of motivations and concluded that 20 to 30 will cover 90% to 95% of the motivations. The number of motivations can be in the hundreds so the next task is to cluster them into groups and subgroups. Affinity charts developed by a managerial team are commonly used. Each team member is given a set of motives on cards. One member puts a motive on the table or pins it to a wall, and the others add similar cards to the pile, discussing the decision to do so. The process continues until there is a consensus that the piles represent reasonable groupings. Each pile is then structured into a hierarchy with the more general and strategic motives at the top and the more specific and tactical at the bottom.

BUYER HOT BUTTONS

Motivations can be categorised as important or unimportant, yet the dynamics of the market may be better captured by identifying current buyer hot buttons. Hot buttons are motivations whose salience and impact on markets are significant and growing. What are buyers talking about? What are stimulating changes in buying decisions and use patterns? In consumer retail food products, for example, hot buttors include:

- Freshness and naturalness. Supermarkets like Dunnes Stores and Sainsburys have responded with salad bars, packaged precut vegetables and efforts to upgrade the quality and selection of their fresh produce.

- Healthy eating. Low fat is a prime driver but concern about sodium, sugar, and processed foods is also growing and affecting product offerings in most food categories.
- Ethnic eating. A growing interest in ethnic flavours and cooking such as Asian, Eastern European and African cuisines, has led to an explosion of new offerings. Brands usually start in ethnic neighbourhoods, move into natural food and gourmet stores and finally reach the mainstream markets.
- Gourmet eating. The success of Forman and Field, a fine food mail order company, and similar retailers reflects the growth of gourmet cooking and has led to the introduction of a broader array of interesting cooking aids and devices.
- Meal solutions. The desire for meal solutions has led to groups of products being bundled together as a meal and to a host of carryout prepared foods offered by both supermarkets and restaurants.
- Low-carbohydrate foods. The influence of low-carbohydrate diets has created a demand for reduced carbohydrate food variants in both supermarkets and restaurants.

An alternative is to use customers or groups of customers to sort the motives into piles. The customers are then asked to select one card from each pile that best represents their motives. When a set of customers or groups go through the exercise, the judgements can be combined using cluster analysis statistical programs. Although managers gain buy-in and learning by going through the process themselves, Griffin and Hauser report that in the 20 applications at one firm, the managers considered customer-based approaches better representations than their own. Another task of customer motivation analysis is to determine the relative importance of the motivations. Again, the management team can address this issue. Alternatively, customers can be asked to assess the importance of the motivations directly or perhaps through trade-off questions. If an engineer had to sacrifice response time or accuracy in an oscilloscope, which would it be? Or, how would an airline passenger trade off convenient departure time with price? The trade-off question asks customers to make difficult judgments about attributes. Another approach is to see which judgements are associated with actual purchase decisions. Such an approach revealed that mothers often selected snack food based on what 'the child likes' and what was 'juicy' instead of qualities they had said were important (nourishing and easy to eat).

A fourth task is to identify the motivations that will play a role in defining the strategy of the business. The selection of motivations central to strategy will depend not only on customer motivations, but on other factors as well, such as competitors' strategies that emerge in the competitor analysis. Another factor is how feasible and practical the resulting strategy is for the business. Internal analysis will be involved in making that determination, as will an analysis of the strategy's implementation.

Qualitative Research

Qualitative research is a powerful tool in understanding customer motivation. It can involve focus-group sessions, in-depth interviews, customer case studies, or on-site customer visits. The concept is to search for the real motivations that do not emerge from structured lists. For instance, buyers of active lifestyle brands, like Quiksilver, might really be expressing their rebellious or adventurous attitude. The perception that a product is too expensive might really reflect a financing gap. Getting inside the customer can provide strategic insights that do not emerge any other way.

Modelling the customer experience from beginning to end, then analysing each step, can result in detailed insights that can generate real change. Clarks, the UK footwear manufacturer and retailer, employed such an approach in its walking boots product line where comfort is a prime buying motivation. Through observation they noted that buyers often feel the tongue of the boot to test for comfort. This insight was used in the future design of Clarks walking boots.[6] Similarly, when Ford was developing the Ford Focus one of the target segments was older people. In order to model the experience of an older person in a car Ford designers wore Michelin man suits to understand the challenges faced by older people in accessing their cars.[7]

Although a representative cross section of customers is usually sought, special attention to some is often merited. Very loyal customers are often best able to articulate the bonds that the firm is capable of establishing. Lost customers (those who have defected) are often particularly good at graphically communicating problems with the product or service. New customers or customers who have recently increased their usage may suggest new applications. Those using multiple vendors may have a good perspective of the firm relative to the competition.

Changing Customer Priorities

It is particularly critical to gain insight into changes in customers' priorities.[8] In the high-tech area, customer priorities often evolve from needing help in selecting and installing the right equipment to wanting performance to looking for low cost. In the coffee business, customer tastes and habits have evolved from buying coffee at grocery stores to drinking coffee at gourmet cafés to buying their own whole-bean gourmet coffees. Assuming that customer priorities are not changing can be risky. It is essential to ask whether a significant and growing segment has developed priorities that are different from the basic business model.

The Customer as Active Partner

Customers are increasingly becoming active partners in the buying process, rather than passive targets of product development and advertising. The trend is illustrated by the Lego Mindstorm product, which was software developed to allow consumers to create their own robots. This software quickly became popular both with children and adults and sharing of ideas via websites became the norm. One user became so involved with the product that he re-wrote the software and made it available to other users. Lego took advantage of this trend and made the original code available to its user community and allowed them to improve on it and circulate it for use.[9] This example particularly illustrates the power-enhancing access to information and fellow customers provided by the Internet. To harness this change, managers should:[10]

- *Encourage active dialogue.* Contact with customers must now be considered a dialogue of equals. Blogs provide a way for customers to create dialogue on a particular topic.
- *Mobilise customer communities.* The Internet facilitates stronger and more widespread online customer communities. The challenge is to organise and create the context for the communities so that they become an extension of the brand experience and a source of customer input into the product and its use.
- *Manage customer diversity.* Particularly in technology products there will be a wide range of sophistication among customers and the challenge will be to deal with multiple levels. The more sophisticated groups will be the most active partners.
- *Cocreating personalised experiences.* An online florist might let customers design the type and arrangement of flowers and vases, rather than merely providing a menu of choices. Cocreating experiences go beyond customisation in tailoring the offering to the needs of individuals.

UNMET NEEDS

An unmet need is a customer need that is not being met by the existing product offerings. For example, ski areas have a need for snowmaking equipment that can access steep, advanced trails. A major extension of the temporary-services industry has been created by firms responding to an unmet need for temporary lawyers, high-tech specialists and doctors. NetJets Europe was set up to sell one-sixteenth interests (and greater) in corporate jets to customers who needed the flexibility of a private jet but were unwilling or unable to buy their own aircraft.

Unmet needs are strategically important because they represent opportunities for firms to increase their market share, break into a market, or create and own new markets. They can also represent threats to established firms in that they can be a lever that enables competitors to disrupt an established position. The Swiss company Ricola, manufacturer of herb drops and candy, has entered a number of international markets, including the UK, by offering consumers a sugar-free candy. Its path has been smoothed because of a lack of competitors in this market and consumers increasing desire to reduce their sugar intake. Sometimes customers may not be aware of their unmet needs because they are so accustomed to the implicit limitations of existing equipment. The farmer of the 1890s would have longed for a horse that worked harder and ate less but would not have mentioned a tractor in his or her wish list. Unmet needs that are not obvious may be more difficult to identify but they can also represent a greater opportunity for an aggressive business because there will be little pressure on established firms to be responsive. The key is to stretch the technology or apply new technologies in order to expose unmet needs.

Using Customers to Identify Unmet Needs

Customers are a prime source of unmet needs. The trick is to access them – to get customers to detect and communicate unmet needs. The first step is to conduct market research using individual or group interviews. The research usually starts with a discussion of an actual product-use experience. What problems have emerged? What is frustrating about it? How does it compare with other product experiences? With expectations? Are there problems with the total-use system in which the product is embedded? How can the product be improved? Launched in the late 1980s, Magnum was the first adult premium ice-cream brand in Europe and enjoyed the growth and price premium of the first mover. However, as the 1990s wore on and the premium adult market became more crowded, sales began to sag and qualitative research indicated that consumers viewed it as 'predictable' and 'nothing special'. Using qualitative research it was also revealed that for women the product (chocolate and ice cream) and the brand had to combine to give permission to 'sin' as she wished. The result was the Magnum 7 sins range, seven unique magnum products available for a limited period. Each products unique recipe providing an opportunity for the customer to "sin" in an original way. The introduction revitalised the brand with a 20% sales increase in 2003 and no cannibalisation of the core brand.[11]

Ethnography has recently become very popular as a way to provide more in-depth insights into customer needs and to drive the accuracy of new product development. The US firm Sirius Satellite Radio wanted to use product innovation to close the gap with its large competitor XM Satellite Radio Holdings. To do this it used a team of ethnographers to shadow 45 consumers and study how they were listening to music, watching TV and reading magazines. They concluded that a portable satellite radio device that was easy to use and was the killer application desired. The result was the launch in late 2005 of the Sirius S50, a cigarette-packet sized device that could store 50 hours of music and chat. It had easy-to-use features and once slipped into a docking station would automatically download content from Sirius channels based on listening patterns. The S50 was one of the hottest consumer electronic items in the last quarter of 2005 and helped Sirius sign up more subscribers than XM since its launch.[12]

Webnography[13] has joined customer surveys and the monitoring of customer complaints as an important perspective on what consumers experience with brands. Most brands today have chat rooms, newsgroups or blogs associated with them. The invisibility of researchers in these environments and the real-time nature of the insight make them valuable sources of insight. For example, Apple agreed to replace defective screens on its iPod nano after receiving complaints from customers that it cracked too easily and after discovering websites dedicated to complaints about the device.

A structured approach, termed *problem research*, develops a list of potential problems with the product.[14]

The problems are then prioritised by asking a group of 100 to 200 respondents to rate each problem as to whether

- the problem is important
- the problem occurs frequently, and
- a solution exists

A problem score is obtained by combining these ratings. A dog-food problem research study found that buyers felt dog food smelled bad, cost too much and was not available in different sizes for different dogs. Subsequently, products responsive to these criticisms emerged. Another study led an airline to modify its cabins to provide more legroom.

Technological developments are likely to change the way marketers approach the problem of identifying customers needs. Erik Brynjolfsson of MIT Sloan School has suggested that consumers' increasing ability to access the Internet while they are on the move and RFID tags will mean that they can constantly monitor the availability of goods they seek. He sees the questions changing from producers asking consumers if they will buy products from them at this price to consumers saying what they want and the price they are willing to pay.[15]

USER-DEVELOPED PRODUCTS

BMW developed a customer innovation lab called BMW ConnectedDrive where users could register on a website that allowed them to create new ideas for services. The BMW ConnectedDrive pilot project allowed users to contact BMW directly and submit ideas for evaluation. A team of experts would then evaluate the proposals and select the best option from the customer submissions.

In the early 1970s, store owners and sales personnel in southern California began to notice that youngsters were fixing up their bicycles to look like motorcycles complete with imitation tailpipes and chopper-type handlebars. Sporting crash helmets and Honda motorcycle T-shirts, the youngsters raced fancy 20-inchers on dirt tracks. Obviously onto a good thing, the manufacturers came out with a whole new line of motorcross models. California users refined this concept into the mountain bike. Manufacturers were guided by the California customers to develop new refinements including the 21-speed gearshift that doesn't require removing one's hands from the bars. Mountain bike firms are enjoying booming growth and are still watching their West Coast customers.

Eric von Hippel, a researcher at MIT who studies customers as sources of service innovations, suggests that lead users provide a particularly fertile ground for discovering unmet needs and new product concepts. Lead users are users who:[16]

- Face needs that will be general in the marketplace but face them months or years before the bulk of the marketplace. A person who is very much into health foods and nutrition would be a lead user with respect to health foods, if we assume that there is a trend toward health foods.

- They are positioned to benefit significantly by obtaining a solution to those needs. Lead users of office automation would be firms that today would benefit significantly from technological advancement.

The Ideal Experience

The conceptualisation of an ideal experience can also help to identify unmet needs. A major publisher of directories polled its customers, asking each to describe its ideal experience with the firm. The publisher found that its very large customers (the top 4 % that were generating 45 % of its business) wanted a single contact point to resolve problems, customised products, consultation on using the service and help in tracking results. In contrast, smaller customers wanted a simple ordering process and to be left alone. These responses provided insights into improving service while cutting costs.[17]

Use Creative Thinking

Thinking out of the box (or just throwing away the box) is a key challenge in discovering new offerings that are responsive to unmet needs. Thinking differently can generate a new offering that creates or changes a category, making the existing competitors less relevant as the new offering becomes the frame of reference and the standard. What could be better? For example, in 2001 a man tried to repair an old cricket bat that was infested with woodworm, shaving and shaping the rear of the bat to eliminate the pests. His son took the more curvaceous bat to the crease and scored 142 not out. The Wooodworm cricket bat and brand franchise was born. Bob Sillet and his son Joe had the option to sell the idea to a number of bat manufacturers but instead they kept ownership of the brand and subcontracted the manufacturing. The winning value proposition of the Woodworm bat was that it actually improved the performance of the cricketer in a way that no other bat innovation did. Woodworm have used the success of their original product to move into a range of other cricket equipment and more recently into golf wear.

Creative thinking is a route to big ideas that lead to significant growth opportunities. It can be the difference between repairing your son's cricket bat and creating a multimillion-Euro brand franchise. The creative thinking process is based on three principles that, with discipline, any organisational unit can follow. First, separate ideation from evaluation. Rather than killing ideas prematurely by burying them in negatives, give seemingly bad ideas enough breathing room to perhaps lead you to good ones. Second, approach the problem from different mental and physical perspectives – walking in the hills of County Mayo, a camping site in the South of France or the top of a roller coaster ride in Euro Disney – whatever. Finally, have a mechanism to take the most promising ideas and improve them until they turn into potential winners worth trying. Some further creative thinking guidelines are presented in Chapter 13.

KEY LEARNINGS

- External analysis should influence strategy by identifying opportunities, threats, trends, and strategic uncertainties. The ultimate goal is to improve strategic choices – decisions as to where and how to compete.

- Customer motivation analysis can provide insights into what assets and competencies are needed to compete as well as indicate possible sustainable competitive advantages.
- Unmet needs that represent opportunities (or threats) can be identified by projecting technologies, by accessing lead users, and by systematic creative thinking.

FOR DISCUSSION

1. Why do a strategic analysis? What are the objectives? What, in your view, are the three keys to making a strategic analysis helpful and important? Is there a downside to conducting a full-blown strategic analysis?
2. Consider the buyer 'hot buttons' described in the insert. What are the implications for frozen food firms such as Findus or Birds Eye? What new business areas might be considered, given each hot button? Answer the same questions for a grocery store chain such as El Corte Ingles, Dunnes Stores or Sainsbury's.
3. What is a customer buying at Harrods? At Zara? At H&M?
4. Pick a company or brand/business on which to focus. What are the major segments? What are the customer motivations by segments? What are the unmet needs?

NOTES

1. "Girl Power softens Volvo's edges" BBC.Co.UK, 3 March 2004, http://news.bbc. co.uk/1/hi/business/3528757.stm. Accessed on 1 December 2006.
2. International Data Group (1993) How to Target: A Profit-Based Segmentation of the PC Industry, November.
3. Patricia Sellers (1993) Keeping the buyers you already have. *Fortune*, Autumn/ Winter, pp. 56–58.
4. Melinda Cuthbert (2000) All buyers not alike. *Business 2.0*, 26 December.
5. Abbie Griffin and John R. Hauser (1993) The voice of the customer. *Marketing Science*, Winter, pp. 1–27.
6. Keith Goffin and Rick Mitchell (2006) The customer holds the key to great products. *Financial Times*, 23 March.
7. Ibid.
8. For a fuller discussion of customer priorities see Adrian J. Slywotzky (1996) *Value Migration*, Harvard Business School Press, Boston.
9. G. Traynor (2006) Open source thinking: From passive consumers to active creators. Market Research Society Annual Conference, 2006. Market Research Society, London.

10. C. K. Prahalad and Venkatram Ramaswamy (2000) Co-opting customer competence.*Harvard Business Review*, January-February, pp. 79–87.

11. Dawn Coulter (2004) Magnum 7 Sins: Europe. IPA Effectiveness Awards, Institute of Practitioners in Advertising, London, 2004.

12. Spencer E. Ante and Cliff Edwards (2006) The science of desire. *Business Week Online*, 5 June.

13. Anjai Puri, The Web of Insights: The Art and Practice of Webnography. Market Research Society Conference, 2006. Market Research Society, London.

14. E. E. Norris (1975) Seek out the consumer's problem. *Advertising Age*, 17 March, pp. 43–44.

15. Happy e-birthdays. *The Economist*, 21 July 2005.

16. Eric von Hippel (1986) Lead users: a source of novel product concepts. *Management Science*, July, p. 802.

17. George S. Day (2003) Creating a superior customer-relating capability, *Sloan Management Review*, Spring, p. 81.

CHAPTER FOUR

Competitor Analysis

Induce your competitors not to invest in those products, markets and services where you expect to invest the most ... that is the fundamental rule of strategy.
—*Bruce Henderson, founder of BCG*

There is nothing more exhilarating than to be shot at without result.
—*Winston Churchill*

The best and fastest way to learn a sport is to watch and imitate a champion.
—*Jean-Claude Killy, skier*

*T*here are numerous well-documented reasons why the Japanese automobile firms were able to penetrate the US market successfully, especially during the 1970s. One important reason, however, is that they were much better than US firms at doing competitor analysis.[1] David Halberstam, in his account of the automobile industry, graphically described the Japanese efforts at competitor analysis in the 1960s. 'They came in groups ... They measured, they photographed, they sketched, and they taperecorded everything they could. Their questions were precise. They were surprised how open the Americans were.'[2] The Japanese similarly studied European manufacturers, especially their design approaches. In contrast, according to Halberstam, the Americans were late in even recognising the competitive threat from Japan and never did well at analysing Japanese firms or understanding the new strategic imperatives created by the revised competitive environment.

As the BRIC economies (Brazil, Russia, India and China) continue to develop as economic powerhouses, are similar mistakes being made by Western managers again? How realistic is the assumption that India's threat lies mainly in its low cost base when 112 000 engineers graduated there in 2004? How seriously should companies take the ambition of the Chinese government to increase from 14 to 50 the number of Chinese firms in the 500 by 2010? Who will lose out and why?

Competitor analysis is the second phase of external analysis. Again, the goal should be insights that will influence the product-market investment decision or the

WHO ARE THE COMPETITORS?
- Against whom do we usually compete? Who are our most intense competitors? Less intense but still serious competitors? Makers of substitute products?
- Can these competitors be grouped into strategic groups on the basis of their assets, competencies and/or strategies?
- Who are the potential competitive entrants? What are their barriers to entry? Is there anything that can be done to discourage them?

EVALUATING THE COMPETITORS
- What are their objectives and strategies? Their level of commitment? Their exit barriers?
- What is their cost structure? Do they have a cost advantage or disadvantage?
- What is their image and positioning strategy?
- Which are the most successful/unsuccessful competitors over time? Why?
- What are the strengths and weaknesses of each competitor or strategic group?
- What leverage points (our strategic weaknesses or customer problems or unmet needs) could competitors exploit to enter the market or become more serious competitors?
- Evaluate the competitors with respect to their assets and competencies. Generate a competitor strength grid.

Figure 4.1   Questions to structure competitor analysis

effort to obtain or maintain an SCA. The analysis should focus on the identification of threats, opportunities, or strategic uncertainties created by emerging or potential competitor moves, weaknesses, or strengths.

Competitor analysis starts with identifying current and potential competitors. There are two very different ways of identifying current competitors. The first examines the perspective of the customer who must make choices among competitors. This approach groups competitors according to the degree they compete for a buyer's choice. The second approach attempts to place competitors in strategic groups on the basis of their competitive strategy. After competitors are identified, the focus shifts to attempting to understand them and their strategies. Of particular interest is an analysis of the strengths and weaknesses of each competitor or strategic group of competitors. Figure 4.1 summarises a set of questions that can provide a structure for competitor analysis.

IDENTIFYING COMPETITORS – CUSTOMER-BASED APPROACHES

In most instances, primary competitors are quite visible and easily identified. Thus, Heineken competes with Carlsberg, Stella Artois, Guinness and other beers. The BBC competes with ITV, Channel 4 and Sky. And Kellogg's competes with Nestlé cereals. However, the businesses that compete most directly will often use the same business model and the same assumptions about customers. Winning within this common competitive framework requires doing similar things better and focusing on price. The result can be an erosion of profitability.

In many markets the basic business model is eroding because customer priorities are changing and indirect competitors are strategically relevant. Colas are no longer as dominant in beverages. Television viewers have options outside network programming. Banks are no longer the only transaction game in town. Because some of the new competitors are small or appear to be very different, they may not appear on the radar screen. Expanding the radar screen's sensitivity can allow these key industry dynamics to surface:[3]

- As mobile phones become more feature-laden with MP3 players, cameras and videos, handset manufacturers such as Nokia have had to expand their understanding of competitors to include consumer electronics firms such as Sony and Apple.

- While major television stations struggle to compete against each other, digital TV packages like Sky Digital and NTL have flourished, increasing the variety of channels that consumers have access to. In addition, the average person in the UK spends about 28 hours per week watching television but around 20 hours per week online, a figure likely to increase both as broadband penetration increases and as consumers engage in more intensive social activity such as blogging and using social network sites.

- While Coca Cola focused on Cola wars consumers became concerned about how soft drinks were affecting their health and also had their head turned by other liquid consumables such as tea, coffee, juices and bottled water. Pepsi saw this trend and reacted. Coca Cola reacted later and is playing catch-up.

- While Nescafe, Maxwell House and others compete for supermarket business and shelf space using low pricing strategies and advertising campaigns, firms like Starbucks, Insomnia and Costa are changing the way that coffee drinkers enjoy the product.

The competitive analysis in nearly all cases will benefit from extending the perspective beyond the obvious direct competitors. By explicitly considering indirect competitors, the strategic horizon is expanded and the analysis more realistically mirrors what the customer sees. In the real world, the customer is never restricted to a firm's direct competitors but instead is always poised to consider other options. The energy drink market includes direct competitors such as Lucozade, Club Energise, Red Bull, Powerade and V. But there are also a host of indirect competitors with similar products: bottled water brands like Evian, soft drinks brands like Tango, 7-UP and Sprite and juice brands like Tropicana. Understanding the positioning and new product strategies of these indirect competitors will be strategically important to businesses in the energy drink category.

Both direct and indirect competitors can be further categorised in terms of how relevant they are, as determined by similar positioning. Thus, Lucozade and Club Energise are relevant to each other as they are all sports energy drinks positioned specifically to appeal to athletes rather than the regular day-to-day consumer. Red Bull and V are relevant to each other as they are positioned to be daytime energy drinks offering a 'pick-me-up' at any time of the day for those who are tired and in need of an extra energy boost.

A key issue with respect to strategic analysis in general, and competitor analysis in particular, is the level at which the analysis is conducted. Is it at the level of a business unit, the firm, or some other aggregation of businesses? Because an analysis will be needed at all levels at which strategies are developed, multiple analyses might ultimately be necessary. For example when Walkers introduced its Sensations range, the 'posh crisp' for an everyday treat, they would have benefitted from a competitor analysis of premium and kettle chips, in which case other crisp brands might be considered indirect competitors.

Customer Choices

One approach to identifying competitor sets is to look at competitors from the perspective of customers – what choices are customers making? A Keymile buyer could be asked what brand would have been purchased had Keymile not made the required item. A buyer for a hospital meal service could be asked what would be substituted for chicken fillets if they increased in price. A sample of wine buyers could be asked what other wines they considered and perhaps what other varieties of grape or regions they favoured.

Product-Use Associations

Another approach that provides insights is the association of products with specific use contexts or applications.[4] Perhaps 20 or 30 product users could be asked to identify a list of use situations or applications. For each use context they would then name all the products that are appropriate. Then for each product they would identify appropriate use contexts so that the list of use contexts would be more complete. Another group of respondents would then be asked to make judgements about how appropriate each product is for each use context. Then products would be clustered based on the similarity of their appropriate use contexts. Thus, if Cadbury's Time-Out was regarded as appropriate for snack occasions, it would compete primarily with products similarly perceived. The same approach will work with an industrial product that might be used in several distinct applications.

Both the customer-choice and product-use approaches suggest a conceptual basis for identifying competitors that can be employed by managers even when marketing research is not available. The concept of alternatives from which customers choose and the concept of appropriateness to a use context can be powerful tools in helping to understand the competitive environment.

IDENTIFYING COMPETITORS – STRATEGIC GROUPS

The concept of a strategic group provides a very different approach toward understanding the competitive structure of an industry. A strategic group is a group of firms that:

- over time pursues similar competitive strategies (for example, the use of the same distribution channel, the same type of communication strategies or the same price/quality position)
- have similar characteristics (such as size, aggressiveness)
- have similar assets and competencies (such as brand associations, logistics capability, global presence, or research and development)

For example, three strategic groups could be identified in the European airline business. One strategic group consists of the flag carriers. These are large and medium sized airlines with established brands, some of them strong. Historically they dominated the airline travel market in Europe and competed using services, destinations and their participation in alliances such as Oneworld and the Star Alliance. The large players within this group are British Airways, Air France-KLM and Lufthansa. The second tier of airlines includes British Midland, Aer Lingus, Alitalia and Iberia. All are historically strong but suffering from their lack of scale and the impact of low cost carriers.

A second strategic group is of the low-cost carriers such as Ryanair, easyJet, Air Berlin and about 30 others. They fly point-to-point, offer rock bottom fares and fly to second-tier airports to take advantage of cheaper airport charges. These airlines sell tickets mainly via the Internet and have significant market share in the European airline market. There has been some consolidation in the market, with easyJet buying Go and Ryanair acquiring Buzz, but new airlines appear to be entering (and exiting) the market on an ongoing basis. In strategy terms these are very aggressive competitors and price wars on routes are the norm, as is aggressive and comparative advertising.

The third group consists of charter airlines such as Air 2000, MyTravel Airways or Thomsonfly. These airlines typically fly holidaymakers to destinations around Europe and the rest of the world. Some have developed low-cost scheduled route strategies to compete more directly with the low cost carriers who threaten them most.

Each strategic group has mobility barriers that inhibit or prevent businesses from moving from one strategic group to another. For example, each of the flag carriers has been protected by barriers such as access to airport slots, brand equity, alliance membership and ability to feed into international flight hubs. Perhaps the biggest barrier to flag carriers becoming low-cost carriers is the cultural change required. Being low cost is not just a strategy decision but requires a completely different business model and culture of implementation.

It is possible to bypass or overcome the barriers, of course. The low cost carriers have overcome these barriers most obviously by offering radically lower prices to consumers to encourage them to accept lower convenience on multiple dimensions. Additionally, the low-cost carriers carry people who have never flown before. Prior to the emergence of this sector people travelled less and stayed longer. The short break and casual travel market has exploded as a result of low fares and new segments of travellers now exist. The barriers are real, however, and a firm competing across strategic groups is usually at a disadvantage.

A member of a strategic group can have exit as well as entry barriers. For example, assets such as aircraft investment or a specialised labour force can represent a meaningful exit barrier, as can the need to protect a brand's reputation. The mobility barrier concept is crucial because one way to develop a sustainable competitive advantage is to pursue a strategy that is protected from competition by assets and competencies that represent barriers to competitors. Consider the PC and server market. Dell and a few others have marketed computers direct to consumers – first by catalogues and telephone, and then by the Internet. They developed a host of assets and competencies to support their direct channels, including an impressive product support system. Competitors such as Hewlett Packard – which have used indirect channels involving retailers and systems firms – have found it very difficult to shift strategies. Not only is the development of assets and competencies costly and difficult, their links with their existing channels create significant barriers.

Using the Strategic Group Concept

The conceptualisation of strategic groups can make the process of competitor analysis more manageable. Numerous industries contain many more competitors than can be analysed individually. Often it is simply not feasible to consider 30 competitors, to say nothing of hundreds. Reducing this set to a small number of strategic groups makes the analysis compact, feasible, and more usable. For example, in the wine industry, competitor analysis by a firm like Piat'dor might examine three strategic groups: jug wines (under €12), premium wines (€12 to €20), and super-premium wines (over €25). Little strategic content and insight will be lost in most cases because firms in a strategic group will be affected by and react to industry developments in similar ways. Thus, in projecting future strategies of competitors, the concept of strategic groups can be helpful. Strategic groupings can refine the strategic investment decision. Instead of determining in which industries to invest, the decision can focus on what strategic group warrants investment. Thus, it will be necessary to determine the current profitability and future potential profitability of each strategic group. One strategic objective is to invest in attractive strategic groups in which assets and competencies can be employed to create strategic advantage. Ultimately, the selection of a strategy and its supporting assets and competencies will often mean selecting or creating a strategic group. Thus, a knowledge of the strategic group structure can be extremely useful.

Projecting Strategic Groups

The concept of strategic groups can also be helpful in projecting competitive strategies into the future. A classic McKinsey study of the effects of deregulation on five deregulated industries (summarised in Figure 4.2) forecasts with remarkable accuracy that successful firms will move toward one of three strategic groups.[5] The evolution of the first group involves three phases. During the first phase, the medium and small firms attempt – usually unsuccessfully – to gain enough market share by merging to compete with the large firms. In the second phase, strong firms make acquisitions to fill in product lines or market gaps. During this phase, which occurs about three to five years following deregulation, the major firms try to develop broad product lines and distribution coverage. In the third phase, interindustry mergers occur. Strong firms merge with others outside their industry. The second strategic group consists of low-cost producers entering the industry after deregulation by providing simple product lines with minimal service to the price-sensitive segment. The third group includes those pursuing a focus strategy, with a specialised service targeted toward a specific customer group.

Group	Industry	Examples
1. National distribution company with full line of differentiated products and emphasis on attractive service/price trade-offs	Brokerage Airlines Trucking Railroads Business terminals	Merrill Lynch Delta Consolidated Freightways Burlington Northern Lucent Technologies
2. Low-cost producer—often a new entrant following deregulation	Brokerage Airlines Trucking Railroads Business terminals	Charles Schwab Southwest Airlines Overnite Transportation Oki
3. Specialty firm with strong customer loyalty and specialised service targeted toward an attractive customer group	Brokerage Airlines Trucking Railroads Business terminals	Goldman Sachs Air Wisconsin Ryder Systems Santa Fe Northern Telecom

Figure 4.2   Strategic groups emerging from deregulation

POTENTIAL COMPETITORS

In addition to current competitors, it is important to consider potential market entrants, such as firms that might engage in:

- *Market expansion.* Perhaps the most obvious source of potential competitors is firms operating in other geographic regions or in other countries. A biscuit company may want to keep a close eye on a competing firm in a nearby country, for example.
- *Product expansion.* The leading French firm Danone, originally a plate glass manufacturer, expanded into the food industry and then withdrew from the plate glass manufacturing industry when they realised that growth had dropped. Danone continued to expand their product portfolio to include dairy products, bottled water and ready-made meals.
- *Backward integration.* Customers are another potential source of competition. For example, Kingspan, an Irish company active in the manufacture and supply of building materials, has acquired dozens of manufacturers of components over the years including a manufacturer of insulation materials.
- *Forward integration.* Suppliers attracted by margins are also potential competitors. The German giant, Oracle, for example purchased a couple of major software retailers. Suppliers, believing they have the critical ingredients to succeed in a market, may be attracted by the margins and control that come with integrating forward.
- *The export of assets or competencies.* A current small competitor with critical strategic weaknesses can turn into a major entrant if it is purchased by a firm

that can reduce or eliminate those weaknesses. Predicting such moves can be difficult but sometimes an analysis of competitor strengths and weaknesses will suggest some possible synergistic mergers. A competitor in an above-average growth industry that does not have the financial or managerial resources for the long haul might be a particularly attractive candidate for merger.

- *Retaliatory or defensive strategies.* Firms that are threatened by a potential or actual move into their market might retaliate. Thus, British Midlands set up BMI Baby, a low fares airline, as a defence against the encroachment of other low fare airlines, particularly Rynair and easyJet, on its market position and market share.

COMPETITOR ANALYSIS – UNDERSTANDING COMPETITORS

Understanding competitors and their activities can provide several benefits. First, an understanding of the current strategy strengths and weaknesses of a competitor can suggest opportunities and threats that will merit a response. Second, insights into future competitor strategies may allow the prediction of emerging threats and opportunities. Third, a decision about strategic alternatives might easily hinge on the ability to forecast the likely reaction of key competitors. Finally, competitor analysis may result in the identification of some strategic uncertainties that will be worth monitoring closely over time. A strategic uncertainty might be, for example, 'Will Competitor A decide to move into the Eastern European market?' As Figure 4.3 indicates,

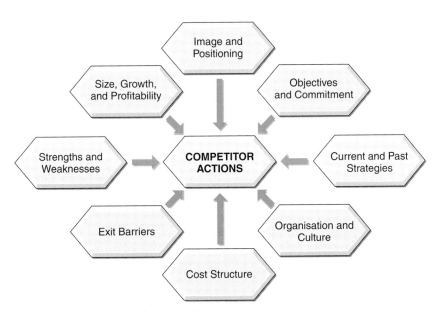

Figure 4.3   Understanding the competitors

competitor actions are influenced by eight elements. The first of these reflects financial performance, as measured by size, growth and profitability.

Size, Growth, and Profitability

The level and growth of sales and market share provide indicators of the vitality of a business strategy. The maintenance of a strong market position or the achievement of rapid growth usually reflects a strong competitor (or strategic group) and a successful strategy. In contrast, a deteriorating market position can signal financial or organisational strains that might affect the interest and ability of the business to pursue certain strategies. To provide a crude sales estimate for businesses that are buried in a large company, take the number of employees and multiply it by the average sales per employee in the industry. For many businesses this method is very feasible and remarkably accurate. After size and growth comes profitability. A profitable business will generally have access to capital for investment unless it has been designated by the parent to be milked. A business that has lost money over an extended time period or has experienced a recent sharp decrease in profitability may find it difficult to gain access to capital either externally or internally.

Image and Positioning Strategy

A cornerstone of a business strategy can be an association, such as being the strongest truck, the most durable car, the smallest consumer electronics equipment or the most effective cleaner. More often, it is useful to move beyond class-related product attributes to intangibles that span product class, such as quality, innovation, sensitivity to the environment or brand personality. Chapter 12, on strategic positioning, elaborates. In order to develop positioning alternatives it is helpful to determine the image and brand personality of the major competitors. Weaknesses of competitors on relevant attributes or personality traits can represent an opportunity to differentiate and develop advantage. Strengths of competitors on important dimensions may represent challenges to exceed them or to outflank them. In any case it is important to know the competitive profiles.

Competitor image and positioning information can be deduced in part by studying a firm's products, advertising, website, and actions, but often customer research is helpful to ensure that an accurate current portrayal is obtained. The conventional approach is to start with qualitative customer research to find out what a business and its brands mean to customers. What are the associations? If the business were a person, what kind of person would it be? What visual imagery, books, animals, trees, or activities are associated with the business? What is its essence?

Competitor Objectives and Commitment

A knowledge of competitor objectives provides the potential to predict whether or not a competitor's present performance is satisfactory or strategic changes are likely. The financial objectives of the business unit can indicate the competitor's willingness to invest in that business even if the payout is relatively long term. In particular, what are the competitor's objectives with respect to market share, sales growth and profitability? Nonfinancial objectives are also helpful. Does the competitor want to be a technological leader? Or to develop a service organisation? Or to expand distribution? Such objectives provide a good indication of the competitor's possible future strategy.

The objectives of the competitor's parent company (if one exists) are also relevant. What are the current performance levels and financial objectives of the parent? If the business unit is not performing as well as the parent, pressure might be exerted to improve or the investment might be withdrawn. Of critical importance is the role attached to the business unit. Is it central to the parent's long-term plans or is it peripheral? Is it seen as a growth area, or is it expected to supply cash to fund other areas? Does the business create synergy with other operations? Does the parent have an emotional attachment to the business unit for any reason? Deep pockets can sometimes be accompanied by short arms; just because resources exist does not mean they are available.

Current and Past Strategies of Competitors

The competitor's current and past strategies should be reviewed. In particular, past strategies that have failed should be noted, because such experiences can inhibit the competitor from trying similar strategies again. Also, a knowledge of a competitor's pattern of new product or new market moves can help anticipate its future growth directions.

Is the strategy based on product-line breadth, product quality, service, distribution type, or brand identification? If a low-cost strategy is employed, is it based on economies of scale, the experience curve, manufacturing facilities and equipment, or access to raw material? What is its cost structure? If a focus strategy is evident, describe the business scope.

Competitor Organisation and Culture

Knowledge about the background and experience of the competitor's top management can provide insight into future actions. Are the managers drawn from marketing, engineering, or manufacturing? Are they largely from another industry or company? Premier Foods, owner of brands such as Branston, Ambrosia and Crosse & Blackwell, has employed a number of marketers previously employed by Heinz.[6] This information provides some sense of how the brands mentioned and the others owned by Premier might be managed in the future.

An organisation's culture, supported by its structure, systems, and people, often has a pervasive influence on strategy. A cost-oriented, highly structured organisation that relies on tight controls to achieve objectives and motivate employees may have difficulty innovating or shifting into an aggressive, marketing-oriented strategy. A loose, flat organisation that emphasises innovation and risk taking may similarly have difficulty pursuing a disciplined product-refinement and cost-reduction programme. In general, as Chapter 16 will make clearer, organisational elements such as culture, structure, systems, and people limit the range of strategies that should be considered.

Cost Structure

Knowledge of a competitor's cost structure, especially when the competitor is relying on a low-cost strategy, can provide an indication of its likely future pricing strategy and its staying power. The goal should be to obtain a feel for both direct costs and fixed costs, which will determine breakeven levels. The following information can usually be obtained and can provide insights into cost structures:

- the number of employees and a rough breakdown of direct labour (variable labour cost) and overhead (which will be part of fixed cost)
- the relative costs of raw materials and purchased components
- the investment in inventory, plant, and equipment (also fixed cost)
- sales levels and number of plants (on which the allocation of fixed costs is based)

Exit Barriers

Exit barriers can be crucial to a firm's ability to withdraw from a business area and thus are indicators of commitment. They include:[7]

- specialised assets – plant, equipment, or other assets that are costly to transform to another application and therefore have little salvage value
- fixed costs, such as labour agreements, leases, and a need to maintain parts for existing equipment
- relationships to other business units in the firm resulting from the firm's image or from shared facilities, distribution channels, or sales force
- government and social barriers – for example, governments may regulate whether a railroad can exit from a passenger service responsibility, or firms may feel a sense of loyalty to workers, thereby inhibiting strategic moves
- managerial pride or an emotional attachment to a business or its employees that affects economic decisions

Assessing Strengths and Weaknesses

Knowledge of a competitor's strengths and weaknesses provides insight that is key to a firm's ability to pursue various strategies. It also offers important input into the process of identifying and selecting strategic alternatives. One approach is to attempt to exploit a competitor's weakness in an area where the firm has an existing or developing strength. The desired pattern is to develop a strategy that will pit 'our' strength against a competitor's weakness. Conversely, a knowledge of 'their' strength is important so it can be bypassed or neutralised.

One firm that developed a strategy to neutralise a competitor's strength was a small software firm that lacked a retail distribution capability or the resources to engage in retail advertising. It targeted value-added software systems firms, which sell total software and sometimes hardware systems to organisations such as investment firms or hospitals.

These value-added systems firms could understand and exploit the power of the product, integrate it into their systems, and use it in quantity. The competitor's superior access to a distribution channel or resources to support an advertising effort was thus neutralised.

The assessment of a competitor's strengths and weaknesses starts with an identification of relevant assets and competencies for the industry and then evaluates the competitor on the basis of those assets and competencies. We now turn to these topics.

COMPETITOR STRENGTHS AND WEAKNESSES

What are the Relevant Assets and Competencies?

Competitor strengths and weaknesses are based on the existence or absence of assets or competencies. Thus, an asset such as a well-known name or a prime location could represent a strength, as could a competency such as the ability to develop a strong promotional programme. Conversely, the absence of an asset or competency can represent a weakness. To analyse competitor strengths and weaknesses, it is thus necessary to identify the assets and competencies that are relevant to the industry. As Figure 4.4 summarises, five sets of questions can be helpful.

1. What businesses have been successful over time? What assets or competencies have contributed to their success? What businesses have had chronically low perfor-mance? Why? What assets or competencies do they lack?

By definition, assets and competencies that provide SCAs should affect perfor-mance over time. Thus, businesses that differ with respect to performance over time should also differ with respect to their assets and competencies. Analysis of the causes of the performance usually suggests sets of relevant competencies and assets. Typi-cally, the superior performers have developed and maintained key assets and com-petencies that have been the basis for their performance. Conversely, weakness in several assets and competencies relevant to the industry and its strategy should vis-ibly contribute to the inferior performance of the weak competitors over time. For example, in the auto industry, one of the top performers, BMW, has superior driving technology, quality and research and development consistent strong performance and credibility as a premium auto manufacturer based on decades of innovation that all reflect the BMW idea.

2. What are the key customer motivations? What is really important to the customer?
Customer motivations usually drive buying decisions and thus can dictate what assets or competencies potentially create meaningful advantages. In the mobile phone

---

1. Why are successful businesses successful? Why are unsuccessful businesses unsuccessful?
2. What are the key customer motivations?
3. What are the large cost components?
4. What are the industry mobility barriers?
5. Which components of the value chain can create competitive advantage?

Figure 4.4 Identifying relevant assets and competencies

industry, Carphone Warehouse's promise of 'we won't be beaten on price' has been an important asset in their growth. An analysis of customer motivations can also identify assets and competencies that a business will need to deliver unless a strategy can be devised that will make them unimportant. If the prime buying criterion for shampoo is smell, a brand will have to develop the skills to deliver that attribute. A business that lacks competence in an area important to the customer segment can experience problems even if it has other substantial SCAs.

3. *What are the large value-added parts of the product or service? What are the large cost components?*

An analysis of the cost structure of an industry can reveal which value added stage represents the largest percentage of total cost. Obtaining a cost advantage in a key value-added stage can represent a significant SCA whether that advantage is used to support a low price or another strategy. Cost advantages in lower value-added stages have less leverage. In the metal can business, transportation costs are relatively high; thus a competitor that can locate plants near customers or on a customer's premises will have a significant cost advantage.

4. *Consider the components of the value chain. Do any provide the potential to generate competitive advantage?*

One tool to identify significant value-added components is the value chain, a conceptual model developed by Michael Porter.[8] A business's value chain (see Figure 4.5) consists of two types of value-creating activities and should be considered in assessing a competitor. The components of the value chain are defined as follows:

Primary Value Activities

- *inbound logistics* – material handling and warehousing
- *operations* – transforming inputs into the final product
- *outbound logistics* – order processing and distribution

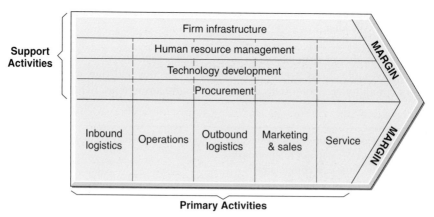

Figure 4.5   The value chain

- *marketing and sales* – communication, pricing, and channel management
- *service* – installation, repair, and parts

Secondary Value Activities

- *procurement* – procedures and information systems
- *technology development* – improving the product and processes/systems
- *human resource management* – hiring, training, and compensation
- *firm infrastructure* – general management, finance, accounting, government relations, and quality management

The linear flow suggested by the value chain may not always be the most useful representation of a competitor, especially in the Internet space. Another perspective is to simply address the question – what are the significant added-value components for a competitor, components that yield either customer benefits or reduced cost.[9] For eBid, for example, these components might be found in free selling, more selling options than competitors, a good customer service and auction services.

A Checklist of Strengths and Weaknesses

Figure 4.6 provides an overview checklist of the areas in which a competitor can have strengths and weaknesses. The first category is innovation. In the Biotech sector firms are judged not just by the products they have in the market but also on those which they have in their research-and-development pipelines. For example, Shire Pharmaceuticals is a specialist pharmaceutical firm that focuses on conditions of the central nervous system, gastrointestinal conditions and renal problems. While it currently has a number of very successful products, particularly in the treatment of ADHD, it is the firm's deep research-and-development pipeline, planned product launches and its history of growth that makes it admired.

The second area of competitor strengths and weaknesses is manufacturing. Perhaps the greatest strength of Toyota is the Toyota Production System (TPS) which is organised to reduce waste of all kinds and to constantly improve quality. One of the key potential strength areas in manufacturing involves sources of sustainable cost advantages. Is there anything about the nature of the plant or equipment, the raw material access, the level of vertical integration, or the type of workforce that would support a sustainable cost advantage? Excess capacity can increase fixed costs, but it can also be a source of strength if the market is volatile or growing.

The third area is finance, the ability to generate or acquire funds in the short as well as the long run. Companies with deep pockets (financial resources) have a decisive advantage because they can pursue strategies not available to smaller firms. Compare giant pharmaceutical companies like Roche with smaller companies like EiRx Therapeutics, for example, or Heineken and Carlsberg with some of the smaller regional breweries. Operations provide one major source of funds. What is the nature

INNOVATION
- Technical product or service superiority
- New product capability
- R&D
- Technologies
- Patents

MANUFACTURING
- Cost structure
- Flexible production operations
- Equipment
- Access to raw materials
- Vertical integration
- Workforce attitude and motivation
- Capacity

FINANCE—ACCESS TO CAPITAL
- From operations
- From net short-term assets
- Ability to use debt and equity financing
- Parent's willingness to finance

MANAGEMENT
- Quality of top and middle management
- Knowledge of business
- Culture
- Strategic goals and plans
- Entrepreneurial thrust
- Planning/operation system
- Loyalty—turnover
- Quality of strategic decision making

MARKETING
- Product quality reputation
- Product characteristics/differentiation
- Brand name recognition
- Breadth of the product line—systems capability
- Customer orientation
- Segmentation/focus
- Distribution
- Retailer relationship
- Advertising/promotion skills
- Sales force
- Customer service/product support

CUSTOMER BASE
- Size and loyalty
- Market share
- Growth of segments served

Figure 4.6   Analysis of strengths and weaknesses

of cash flow that is being generated and will be generated given the known uses for funds? Cash or other liquid assets provide other sources, as does a parent firm. The key is the ability of the business to justify the use of debt or equity and the will to access this source.

Management is the fourth area. Controlling and motivating a set of highly disparate business operations are strengths for L'Oréal, Danone, Nestlé and other firms that have successfully diversified. The quality, depth, and loyalty (as measured by turnover) of top and middle management provide an important asset for others. Another aspect to analyse is the culture. The values and norms that permeate an organisation can energise some strategies and inhibit others. In particular, some organisations, such as Virgin, possess both an entrepreneurial culture that allows them to initiate new directions and the organisational skill to nurture them. The ability to set strategic goals and plans can represent significant competencies. To what extent does the business have a vision and the will and competence to pursue it?

The fifth area is marketing. Often the most important marketing strength, particularly in the high-tech field, involves the product line: its quality reputation, breadth, and the features that differentiate it from other products. Brand image and distribution have been key assets for businesses such as Puma, Mercedes-Benz and UBS. The ability to develop a true customer orientation can be an important strength. Another strength can be based on the ability and willingness to advertise effectively. The success of Diesel is due in part to its ability to generate superior advertising. Other elements of the marketing mix, such as the sales force and service operation, can also be sources of sustainable competitive advantage. Part of Dyson's original success in the vacuum cleaner market was its ability to enroll the support of retail sales people and the quality of their customer service operation. Still another possible strength, particularly in the high-tech field, is a competitor's ability to stay close to its customers. The final area of interest is the customer base. How substantial is the customer base and how loyal is it? How are the competitor's offerings evaluated by its customers? What are the costs that customers will have to absorb if they switch to another supplier? Extremely loyal and happy customers are going to be difficult to dislodge. What are the size and growth potentials of the segments served?

The Competitive Strength Grid

With the relevant assets and competencies identified, the next step is to scale your own firm and the major competitors or strategic groups of competitors on those assets and competencies. The result is termed a competitive strength grid and serves to summarise the position of the competitors with respect to assets and competencies.

A sustainable competitive advantage is almost always based on having a position superior to that of the target competitors in one or more asset or competence area that is relevant both to the industry and to the strategy employed. Thus, information about each competitor's position with respect to relevant assets and competencies is central to strategy development and evaluation. If a superior position does not exist with respect to assets and competencies important to the strategy, it probably will have to be created or the strategy may have to be modified or abandoned. Sometimes there simply is no point of difference with respect to the firms regarded as competitors. A competency that all competitors have will not be the basis for an SCA. For example, car safety is important among car buyers and drivers but if car brands are perceived to be equal with respect to strength of car frame and airbag features it cannot be the basis for an SCA. Of course, if some car manufacturers can convince passengers that they are superior with respect to wheels and skidding safety, then an SCA could indeed emerge.

The Luxury Car Market

A competitor strength grid is illustrated in Figure 4.7 for the European car market. The relevant assets and competencies are listed on the left, grouped as to whether they are considered keys to success or are of secondary importance. The principal competitors are shown as column headings across the top. Each cell is coded as to whether the brand is strong, above average, average, below average, or weak in that asset or competence category. The resulting figure provides a summary of the profile of the strengths and weaknesses of ten brands. Two can be compared, such as Ford and Lexus or BMW and Audi. BMW and Lexus have enviable positions.

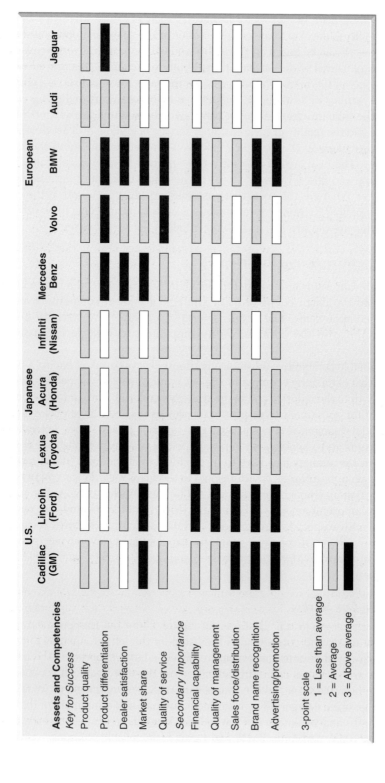

Figure 4.7   Illustrative example of a competitive strength grid for the European car market

Analysing Submarkets

It is often desirable to conduct an analysis for submarkets or strategic groups and perhaps for different products. A firm may not compete with all other firms in the industry but only with those engaged in similar strategies and markets. For example, a competitive strength grid may look very different for the safety submarket, with Volvo having more strength. Similarly, the handling submarket may also involve a competitive grid that will look different, with BMW having more strength.

The Analysis Process

The process of developing a competitive strength grid can be extremely informative and useful. One approach is to have several managers create their own grids independently. The differences can usually illuminate different assumptions and information bases. A reconciliation stage can disseminate relevant information and identify and structure strategic uncertainties. For example, different opinions about the quality reputation of a competitor may stimulate a strategic uncertainty that justifies marketing research. Another approach is to develop the grid in a group setting, perhaps supported by preliminary staff work. When possible, objective information based on laboratory tests or customer perception studies should be used. The need for such information becomes clear when disagreements arise about where competitors should be scaled on the various dimensions.

OBTAINING INFORMATION ON COMPETITORS

A competitor's website is usually a rich source of information and the first place to look. The strategic vision (along with a statement about values and culture) is often posted and the portfolio of businesses is usually laid out. The way that the latter is organised can provide clues as to business priorities and strategies. Visitors to the Dyson website will be in no doubt but that product technology leadership is its goal. Similarly the website of fashion company Diesel emphasises its uniqueness and design qualities, a useful indication of its direction. The website also can provide information about such business assets as plants, global access, and brand symbols. Research on the competitor's site can be supplemented with search-engines, access to articles and financial reports about the business. General-information sites (such as thebiz. co.uk, countryweb.co.uk, kompass.ie), and websites for trade shows, trade magazines, channel members (such as retailers) and financial analysts can also provide useful information.

Detailed information on competitors is generally available from a variety of sources. Competitors usually communicate extensively with their suppliers, customers, and distributors; security analysts and stockholders and government legislators and regulators. Contact with any of these can provide information. Monitoring of trade magazines, trade shows, advertising, speeches, annual reports, and the like can be informative. Technical meetings and journals can provide information about technical developments and activities. Thousands of databases accessible by computer now make available detailed information on most companies.

Detailed information about a competitor's standing with its customers can be obtained through market research. For example, regular telephone surveys could provide information about the successes and vulnerabilities of competitors' strategies. Respondents could be asked questions such as the following. Which store is closest to your home? Which do you shop at most often? Are you satisfied? Which has the lowest prices? Best specials? Best customer service? Cleanest stores? Best quality meat? Best-quality produce? And so on. Those chains that were well positioned on value, on service or on product quality could be identified and tracking would show whether they were gaining or losing position. The loyalty of their customer base (and thus their vulnerability) could be indicated in part by satisfaction scores and the willingness of customers to patronise stores even when they were not the most convenient or the least expensive.

KEY LEARNINGS

- Competitors can be identified by customer choice (the set from which customers select) or by clustering them into strategic groups, (firms that pursue similar strategies and have similar assets, competencies, and other characteristics). In either case, competitors will vary in terms of how intensely they compete.

- Competitors should be analysed along several dimensions, including their size, growth and profitability, image, objectives, business strategies, organisational culture, cost structure, exit barriers and strengths and weaknesses.

- Potential strengths and weaknesses can be identified by considering the characteristics of successful and unsuccessful businesses, key customer motivation and value-added components.

- The competitive strength grid, which arrays competitors or strategic groups on each of the relevant assets and competencies, provides a compact summary of key strategic information.

FOR DISCUSSION

1. Consider the television industry. Identify the BBC's competitors and organise them in terms of their intensity of competition. Also organise them in terms of strategic groups. Are there differences in the two methods of organisation?

2. Evaluate Figure 4.7. What surprises are there in the figure? What are the implications for Toyota? For Audi?

3. Pick a company or brand/business on which to focus. What business is it in? Who are its direct and indirect competitors? Which in each category are the most relevant competitors?

4. Consider the car industry. Identify competitors to BMW and organise them in terms of their intensity of competition. Also organise them into strategic groups. What are the KSFs for the strategic groups? Do you think that will change in the next five years?

NOTES

1. David Halberstam (1986) *The Reckoning*, William Morrow, New York, p. 310.
2. Ibid.
3. For a fuller discussion of expanding the radar screen see Adrian J. Slywotzky (1996) *Value Migration*, Harvard Business School Press, Boston.
4. George S. Day, Allan D. Shocker and Rajendra K. Srivastava (1979) Customer-oriented approaches to identifying product markets. *Journal of Marketing*, 43, pp. 8–19.
5. Donald C. Waite (1982) Deregulation and the banking industry. *Bankers Magazine*, 163, January–February, pp. 76–85.
6. Claire Murphy (2006) The trouble with Heinz. *Marketing*, 14 June, pp. 26–8.
7. Michael E. Porter (1980) *Competitive Strategy*, The Free Press, New York, pp. 20–1. The concept of exit barriers will be discussed again in Chapter 13.
8. Michael E. Porter (1985) *Competitive Advantage*, New York: The Free Press, Chapter 2.
9. Shawn D. Cartwight and Richard W. Oliver (2000) Untangling the value web. *Journal of Business*, January–February, pp. 22–7.

CHAPTER FIVE

Market Analysis

As the economy, led by the automobile industry, rose to a new high level in the twenties, a complex of new elements came into existence to transform the market: instalment selling, the used-car trade-in, the closed body, and the annual model. (I would add improved roads if I were to take into account the environment of the automobile.)
— *Alfred P. Sloan, Jr., General Motors*

Before you build a better mousetrap, it helps to know if there are any mice out there.
— *Mortimer B. Zuckerman*

The most effective way to cope with change is to help create it.
— *I. W. Lynett*

*M*arket analysis builds on customer and competitor analyses to make some strategic judgements about a market (and submarket) and its dynamics. One of the primary objectives of a market analysis is to determine the attractiveness of a market (or submarket) to current and potential participants. Market attractiveness, the market's profit potential as measured by the long-term return on investment achieved by its participants, will provide important input into the product-market investment decision. The frame of reference is all participants. Of course, participating in an attractive market will not guarantee success for all competitors. Whether a market is appropriate for a particular firm is a related but very different question, depending not only on the market attractiveness but also on how the firm's strengths and weaknesses match up against those of its competitors. A second objective of market analysis is to understand the dynamics of the market. The need is to identify emerging submarkets, key success factors, trends, threats, opportunities, and strategic uncertainties that can guide information gathering and analysis. A key success factor is an asset or competency that is needed to play the game. If a firm has a strategic weakness in a key success factor that isn't neutralised by a well-conceived strategy, its ability to compete will be limited. The market trends can include those identified in customer or competitor analysis, but the perspective here is broader and others will usually emerge as well.

DIMENSIONS OF A MARKET ANALYSIS

The nature and content of an analysis of a market and its relevant product markets will depend on context but will often include the following dimensions:

- emerging submarkets
- actual and potential market and submarket size
- market and submarket growth
- market and submarket profitability
- distribution systems
- trends and developments
- key success factors

Figure 5.1 provides a set of questions structured around these dimensions that can serve to stimulate a discussion identifying opportunities, threats, and strategic uncertainties. Each dimension will be addressed in turn, starting with assessment

---

SUBMARKETS

Are forces such as augmented products, the emerging of niches, a trend toward systems, new applications, repositioned product classes, customer trends, or new technologies creating worthwhile submarkets? How should they be defined?

SIZE AND GROWTH

What are the important and potentially important submarkets? What are their size and growth characteristics? What submarkets are declining or will soon decline? How fast? What are the driving forces behind sales trends?

PROFITABILITY

For each major submarket consider the following: Is this a business area in which the average firm will make money? How intense is the competition among existing firms? Evaluate the threats from potential entrants and substitute products. What is the bargaining power of suppliers and customers? How attractive/profitable are the market and its submarkets both now and in the future?

COST STRUCTURE

What are the major cost and value-added components for various types of competitors?

DISTRIBUTION SYSTEMS

What are the alternative channels of distribution? How are they changing?

MARKET TRENDS

What are the trends in the market?

KEY SUCCESS FACTORS

What are the key success factors, assets, and competencies needed to compete successfully? How will these change in the future? How can the assets and competencies of competitors be neutralised by strategies?

Figure 5.1   Questions to help structure a market analysis

of market size. The chapter concludes with a discussion of the risks of growth markets.

Emerging Submarkets

The management of a firm in any dynamic market requires addressing the challenge and opportunity of relevance, as described in the boxed insert (p. 79). In essence, the challenge is to detect and understand emerging submarkets, identify those that are attractive to the firm given its assets and competencies, and then adjust offerings and brand portfolios in order to increase their relevance to the chosen submarkets. The opportunity is to influence these emerging submarkets so that competitors become less relevant. A review of some of the many forces and events behind the rise or fall of submarkets will be helpful in the difficult task of detecting and understanding them.

First, the product or service can be augmented or expanded to include a new dimension.The move by personal care brands into the male grooming market has led to the emergence of submarkets, such as male hair removal, and brands to serve them, such as Veet for men which is an extension of an established brand for women.

Second, the market can be broken into niches. The energy drink market is fragmented into a variety of submarkets, including the sports drink market for athletes needing rehydration (for example Club Energise Sport and Lucozade Sport), the energy drink market for customers needing an energy boost (for example Club Energy and Lucozade Energy) and the recovery drink market, which allows athletes recover more quickly after training using protein based drinks (for example, Club Energise Sport Recovery 20). Third, the application scope can be expanded from components to systems or turnkey solutions; in essence there is an aggregation into submarkets, the inverse of breaking the category up into submarkets. In the late 1990s, Siebel took the lead in creating Internet-based customer relationship management (CRM) solutions by pulling together a host of application areas, including customer loyalty programmes, customer acquisition, call centres, customer service, customer contact and sales force automation.

Fourth, the emergence of a new and distinct application can define relevant brand options. The emergence in recent years of laptops as truly mobile (as opposed to portable and luggable) devices has led to the development of the design driven laptop. The Sony Vaio FJ range, for example, offers laptop options from a selection of core colours (sky blue for inventive thinkers and optimists; jade green for earth lovers and forward thinkers) and also limited edition colour options (such as wild violet).

Fifth, a product class can be repositioned. For example, the dental care market has changed its emphasis from health to beauty. The key players in the market have moved their attention and investment towards dental floss, tooth whitener and powered toothbrushes and similar products with a primarily cosmetic emphasis. The repositioning of the product class has provided growth in what is an otherwise mature market.

Sixth, a customer trend can be a driver of a submarket. The dual trends toward wellness and food quality have supported the emergence of smoothie bars where customers can buy healthy fruit shakes and even add shots of natural health supplements like wheatgerm. Emerging from this market is the submarket of readymade smoothies, such as Innocent smoothies, available for easy purchase in supermarkets and shops.

Seventh, a new technology – such as disposable razors, laptop computers, a new fabric, or hybrid cars – can drive the perception of a submarket. Through its creation of the iPod, Apple made other producers of portable music devices like Sony and Panasonic irrelevant for a segment of customers who wanted a way to store music without having to rely on CD's and minidiscs. The introduction of the iPod drove customers perceptions in the music market away from Walkmans, CDs and minidiscs forcing other companies to innovate and introduce MP3 players.

Finally, a whole market can simply be invented. First Direct was launched by the Midland Bank in 1989 and for several years it was the UK's first and only person-to-person telephone banking service, which was open 24 hours a day, 365 days a year. eBay created an online auction category that has spawned many imitators, who have had difficulty matching both the operational performance and the critical mass of users established by eBay around the world.

RELEVANCE

All too frequently, despite retaining high levels of awareness, attitude and even loyalty, a brand loses market share because it is not perceived to be relevant to emerging submarkets. If a group of customers want hybrid cars, it simply does not matter how good they think your firm's four-wheel drive is. They might love it and recommend it to others, but if they are interested in an hybrid because of their changing needs and desires, then your brand is irrelevant to them. This may be true even if your firm also makes hybrids under the same brand. The hybrid submarket is different than four wheel drives and has a different set of relevant brands.

Relevance for a brand occurs when two conditions are met. First, there must be a perceived need or desire by customers for a submarket defined by some combination of an attribute set, an application, a user group, or other distinguishing characteristic. Second, the brand needs to be among the set considered to be relevant for that submarket by the prospective customers.

Winning among brands within a submarket, however, is not enough. There are two additional relevance challenges. One is to make sure that the submarket associated with the brand is relevant. The problem may not be that the customer picks the wrong brand, but rather that the wrong submarket (and brand set) is picked. The second challenge is to make sure that the brand is considered by customers to be an option with respect to a submarket. This implies that a brand needs to be positioned against the submarket in addition to whatever other positioning strategies may be pursued. It must also be visible and be perceived to meet minimal performance levels.

Nearly every marketplace is undergoing change-often dramatic, rapid change – that creates relevance issues. Examples appear in nearly every industry, from computers, consulting, airlines, power generators, and financial services to snack food, beverages, pet food, and toys. Hardware, paint and flooring stores struggle with the reality of B&Q, electronics stores struggle against the reality of Curry's and computers and communications stores struggle against the reality of Harvey Norman's. Marks & Spencer's and Debenhams face the challenge of a variety of other retailers including H&M and Zara who are advancing in the apparel industry. Supermarket chains like Iceland and Asda face threats to their value propositions as discount stores like Aldi and Lidl continue to grow. Relevance is also an issue for brands attempting to open up new business arenas such as Armani's new range of hotels and Nivea's venture into the men's skincare market.

The key to managing such change is twofold. First, a business must detect and understand emerging submarkets, projecting how they are evolving. Second, it must maintain relevance in the face of these emerging submarkets. Businesses that perform these tasks successfully have organisational skills at detecting change, the organisational vitality to respond, and a well-conceived brand strategy.

There is also the option of creating or influencing the emergence of submarkets that will serve to make competitors less relevant. Apple did it with their iPod, Tesco did it with their online store and home delivery service, Magners/Bulmer's did it twice with the introduction of the original pint bottle and Bulmer's Light, Guinness did it with their canned Guinness draught which used a widget to improve product quality. Creating and owning subcategories can only occur when the right firm, armed with the right idea and offering, is ready to act at the right time. But when it happens, it can be a strategic home run.[1]

ACTUAL AND POTENTIAL MARKET SIZE

A basic starting point for the analysis of a market or submarket is the total sales level. If it is reasonable to believe that a successful strategy can be developed to gain a 15% share, it is important to know the total market size. Among the sources that can be helpful are published financial analyses of the firm, customers, government data and trade magazines and associations. The ultimate source is often a survey of product users in which the usage levels are projected to the population.

Potential Market – The User Gap

In addition to the size of the current, relevant market, it is often useful to consider the potential market. A new use, new user group, or more frequent usage could dramatically change the size and prospects for the market. There is unrealised potential for the cereal market in Europe;[2] Europeans buy only about 25% as much cereal as their US counterparts. If technology allowed cereals to be used more conveniently away from home by providing shelf-stable milk products, usage could be further expanded. There is also unrealised potential for the childcare market in Europe as the traditional family structure disappears. Of course, the key is not only to recognise the potential, but also to have the vision and programme in place to exploit it. A host of strategists have dismissed investment opportunities in industries because they lacked the insight to see the available potential and take advantage of it.

Ghost Potential

Sometimes an area becomes so topical and the need so apparent that potential growth seems assured. As a Lewis Carroll character observed, 'What I tell you three times is true.' However, this potential can have a ghostlike quality caused by factors inhibiting or preventing its realisation. Many dot-com firms such as Boo.com and Pets.com were the beneficiaries of considerable hype, but failed because the growth of their application never materialised. For example, the demand for computers exists in many underdeveloped countries but a lack of funds inhibits buying and government regulations make productive, efficient operations difficult if not impossible.

Small Can Be Beautiful

Some firms have investment criteria that prohibit them from investing in small markets. Unilever, Diageo and Nestle for example, have historically looked to new products that would generate large sales levels within a few years. Yet in an era of micromarketing, much of the action is in smaller niche segments. If a firm avoids them, it can lock itself out of much of the vitality and profitability of a business area. Furthermore, most substantial business areas were small at the outset, sometimes for many years. Avoiding the small market can thus mean that a firm must later overcome the first-mover advantage of others.

MARKET AND SUBMARKET GROWTH

After the size of the market and its important submarkets have been estimated, the focus turns to growth rate. What will be the size of the market's submarkets in the future? If all else remains constant, growth means more sales and profits even without increasing market share. It can also mean less price pressure when demand increases faster than supply and firms are not engaged in experience curve pricing, anticipating future lower costs. Conversely, declining sales can mean reduced sales and often increased price pressure as firms struggle to hold their shares of a diminishing pie.

It may seem that the strategy of choice would thus be to identify and avoid or disinvest in declining situations and to identify and invest in growth contexts. Of course, the reality is not that simple. In particular, declining product markets can represent a real opportunity for a firm, in part because competitors may be exiting and disinvesting, instead of entering and investing for growth. The firm may attempt to become a profitable survivor by encouraging others to exit and by becoming dominant in the most viable segments. The pursuit of this strategy is considered in detail in Chapter 15.

The other half of the conventional wisdom, that growth contexts are always attractive, can also fail to hold true. Growth situations can involve substantial risks. Because of the importance of correctly assessing growth contexts, a discussion of these risks is presented at the end of this chapter.

Identifying Driving Forces

In many contexts, the most important strategic uncertainty involves the prediction of market sales. A key strategic decision, often an investment decision, can hinge on not only being correct but also understanding the driving forces behind market dynamics. One begins to address most key strategic uncertainties by asking on what the answer depends. In the case of projecting sales of a major market, the need is to determine which forces will drive those sales. For example, the sales of a new consumer electronics device may be driven by machine costs, the evolution of an industry standard, or the emergence of alternative technologies. Each of these three drivers will provide the basis for key second-level uncertainties. In the cigarette market, the impact of anti-smoking movements (such as ASH in the UK), government tax policies, the medical link between smoking and serious illnesses like cancer and heart disease and the development of products like Nicorette to help customers quit smoking might be driving forces. One second-level strategic uncertainty might then focus on the likely strength of the anti-smoking movements.

Forecasting Growth

Historical data can provide a useful perspective and help to separate hope from reality, but they need to be used with care. Apparent trends in data such as those shown in Figure 5.2 can be caused by random fluctuations or by short-term economic conditions, and the urge to extrapolate should be resisted. Furthermore, the strategic interest is not on projections of history but rather on the prediction of turning points, times when the rate and perhaps direction of growth change. Sometimes leading indicators of market sales may help in forecasting and predicting turning points. Examples of leading indicators include:

- *Demographic data.* The number of births is a leading indicator of the demand for education, and the number of people reaching age 65 is a leading indicator of the demand for retirement facilities.
- *Sales of related equipment.* Personal computer and printer sales provide a leading indicator of the demand for supplies and service needs.

Market sales forecasts, especially of new markets, can be based on the experience of analogous industries. The trick is to identify a prior market with similar characteristics. Sales of high-definition televisions might be expected to have a pattern similar to sales of colour televisions, for example. Sales of a new type of snack might look to the history of other previously introduced snack categories or other consumer products such as cereal bars or breakfast bars. The most value will be obtained if several analogous product classes can be examined and the differences in the product class experiences related to their characteristics. Methods now exist to provide re-

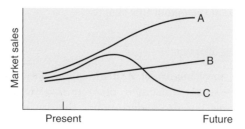

Figure 5.2 Sales patterns

markably accurate forecasts of sales patterns for durable products such as appliances and cameras. They are based, in part, on decomposing sales into first purchases and replacement sales.

Detecting Maturity and Decline

One particularly important set of turning points in market sales occurs when the growth phase of the product-life cycle changes to a flat maturity phase and when the maturity phase changes into a decline phase. These transitions are important indicators of the health and nature of the market. Often they are accompanied by changes in key success factors. Historical sales and profit patterns of a market can help to identify the onset of maturity or decline, but the following often are more sensitive indicators:

- *Price pressure caused by overcapacity and the lack of product differentiation.*When growth slows or even reverses, capacity developed under a more optimistic scenario becomes excessive. Furthermore, the product evolution process often results in most competitors matching product improvements. Thus, it becomes more difficult to maintain meaningful differentiation.

- *Buyer sophistication and knowledge.* Buyers tend to become more familiar and knowledgeable as a product matures and thus they become less willing to pay a premium price to obtain the security of an established name. Airline travellers have gained more confidence and knowledge over the years in their ability to select which airline offers the cheapest price; the Internet, websites and travel agents like SAYIT that search for the cheapest flights for customers have resulted in a reduction in the value of brand names like KLM and Lufthansa as search cues.

- *Substitute products or technologies.* The sales of personal video recorders (PVRs) provide an indicator of the decline of VCRs.

- *Saturation.* When the number of potential first-time buyers declines, market sales should mature or decline.

- *No growth sources.* The market is fully penetrated and there are no visible sources of growth from new uses or users.

- *Customer disinterest.* The interest of customers in applications, new product announcements, and so on falls off.

MARKET AND SUBMARKET PROFITABILITY ANALYSIS

Economists have long studied why some industries or markets are profitable and others are not. Harvard economist and business strategy guru Michael Porter applied his theories and findings to the business strategy problem of evaluating the investment value of an industry or market.[3] The problem is to estimate how profitable the average firm will be. It is hoped, of course, that a firm will develop a strategy that will bring above-average profits. If the average profit level is low, however, the task of succeeding

Figure 5.3   Porter's five-factor model of market profitability

financially will be much more difficult than if the average profitability were high. Porter's approach can be applied to any industry, but it also can be applied to a market or submarket within an industry. The basic idea is that the attractiveness of an industry or market as measured by the long-term return on investment of the average firm depends largely on five factors that influence profitability, shown in Figure 5.3:

- the intensity of competition among existing competitors
- the existence of potential competitors who will enter if profits are high
- substitute products that will attract customers if prices become high
- the bargaining power of customers
- the bargaining power of suppliers

Each factor plays a role in explaining why some industries are historically more profitable than others. An understanding of this structure can also suggest which key success factors are necessary to cope with the competitive forces.

Existing Competitors

The intensity of competition from existing competitors will depend on several factors, including:

- the number of competitors, their size, and their commitment
- whether their product offerings and strategies are similar

- the existence of high fixed costs
- the size of exit barriers

The first question to ask is 'how many competitors are already in the market or making plans to enter soon?' The more competitors that exist, the more competition intensifies. Are they large firms with staying power and commitment or small and vulnerable ones? The second consideration is the amount of differentiation. Are the competitors similar, or are some (or all) insulated by points of uniqueness valued by customers? The third factor is the level of fixed costs. A high fixed-cost industry like telecommunications or airlines experiences debilitating price pressures when over-capacity gets large. Finally, one should assess the presence of exit barriers such as specialised assets, long-term contract commitments to customers and distributors, and relationships to other parts of a firm.

One major factor in the shakeout of both e-commerce and content Internet firms was the excessive number of competitors. Because the barriers to entry were low and the offered products so similar, margins were insufficient (and often nonexistent), especially given the significant investment in infrastructure and brand building that was needed. Given the hysterical market growth and the low barriers to entry, the results should have been anticipated; at one time there were a host of pet-supply and pharmacy e-commerce offerings competing for a still-embryonic market.

Potential Competitors

Chapter 4 discusses identifying potential competitors that might have an interest in entering an industry or market. Whether potential competitors, identified or not, actually do enter depends in large part on the size and nature of barriers to entry. Thus, an analysis of barriers to entry is important in projecting likely competitive intensity and profitability levels in the future.

Various barriers to entry include required capital investment (the infrastructure involved in developing a mobile phone network like Vodafone or the network needed for a digital TV service like NTL or SKY), economies of scale (the success of super-markets like French retailer Carrefour and German retailer Otto is contributed to by scale economies), distribution channels (Volkswagen and Nescafe have access to customers that is not easily duplicated) and product differentiation (Evian and Apple have highly differentiated products that protect them from new entrants).

Substitute Products

Substitute products compete with less intensity than do the primary competitors. They are still relevant, however. They can influence the profitability of the market and can be a major threat or problem. Therefore, soft drinks, fruit juices, energy drinks and even alcoholic beverage products exert pressure on the bottled water market. Mobile phones are substitutes for a house landline in many cases and online music stores create a threat for high street music stores. Substitutes that show a steady im-provement in relative price/performance and for which the customer's cost of switch-ing is minimal are of particular interest.

Customer Power

When customers have relatively more power than sellers, they can force prices down or demand more services, thereby affecting profitability. A customer's power will be greater when its purchase size is a large proportion of the seller's business, when alternative suppliers are available, and when the customer can integrate backward and make all or part of the product. Thus, tyre manufacturers face powerful customers in the car firms. The customers of metal can manufacturers are large packaged-goods manufacturers who have over time demanded price and service concessions and who have engaged in backward integration. Cereal firms face a supermarket industry that has become strong and assertive in part because of its developing strengths in information technology. Soft-drink firms sell to fast-food and other restaurant chains that have strong bargaining power.

Supplier Power

When the supplier industry is concentrated and sells to a variety of customers in diverse markets, it will have relative power that can be used to influence prices. Power will also be enhanced when the costs to customers of switching suppliers are high. Thus, the highly concentrated oil industry is often powerful enough to influence profits in customer industries that find it expensive to convert from oil. However, the potential for regeneration whereby industries can create their own energy supplies, perhaps by recycling waste, may have changed the balance of power in some contexts.

COST STRUCTURE

An understanding of the cost structure of a market can provide insights into present and future key success factors. The first step is to conduct an analysis of the value chain presented in Figure 5.4 to determine where value is added to the product (or service). As suggested in Figure 5.4, the proportion of value added attributed to one value chain stage can become so important that a key success factor is associated with that stage. It may be possible to develop control over a resource or technology, as did the OPEC oil cartel. More likely, competitors will aim to be the lowest-cost competitor in a high value-added stage of the value chain. Advantages in lower value added stages will simply have less leverage. Thus, in the metal can business, transportation costs are relatively high and a competitor that can locate plants near customers will have a significant cost advantage. It may not be possible to gain an advantage at high value-added stages. For example, a raw material, such as flour for bakery firms, may represent a high value added, but because the raw material is widely available at commodity prices, it will not be a key success factor. Nevertheless, it is often useful to look first at the highest value-added stages, especially if changes are occurring. For example, the cement market was very regional when it was restricted to rail or truck transportation. With the development of specialised ships, however, waterborne transportation costs dropped dramatically. Key success factors changed from local ground transportation to production scale and access to the specialised ships.

Production State	**Markets that Have Key Success Factors Associated with the Production Stage**
• Raw material procurement	• Gold mining, wine making
• Raw material processing	• Steel, paper
• Production fabricating	• Integrated circuits, tyres
• Assembly	• Apparel, instrumentation
• Physical distribution	• Bottled water, metal cans
• Marketing	• Branded cosmetics, spirits
• Service backup	• Software, cars
• Technology development	• Razors, medical systems

Figure 5.4   Value added and key success factors

DISTRIBUTION SYSTEMS

An analysis of distribution systems should include three types of questions:

- What are the alternative distribution channels?
- What are the trends? What channels are growing in importance? What new channels have emerged or are likely to emerge?
- Who has the power in the channel and how is that likely to shift?

Sometimes the creation of a new channel of distribution can lead to a sustainable competitive advantage. A dramatic example is the success that Tesco's online operation experienced and it heralded the development of a new channel of distribution that lead to an SCA for the company. The group has also had remarkable success with its online offering. Tesco.com is now the largest Internet grocery home shopping service in the world. At the beginning of 2001, the operation overtook Amazon.co.uk to become the UK's biggest e-tailer, and revenues grew by a further 32 % in 2005/6 to just under £1 billion. Customers value the time savings of not having to go to the store, walk around, queue, pay and unload again when they get home. Thus, it is useful to consider not only existing channels but also potential ones.

An analysis of likely or emerging changes within distribution channels can be important in understanding a market and its key success factors. The increased sale of alcohol in supermarkets and local shops have made it much more important for alcoholic beverage producers to focus on packaging and advertising. The emergence of e-commerce, the growth of mini supermarkets in petrol stations, the success of category dominating stores like Harvey Norman's and Woodies and the growth of online retailers illustrate trends that have strategic importance to firms affected by these channels.

MARKET TRENDS

Often one of the most useful elements of external analysis comes from addressing the question 'what are the market trends?' The question has two important attributes:

it focuses on change and it tends to identify what is important. Strategically useful insights almost always result. A discussion of market trends can serve as a useful summary of customer, competitor, and market analyses. It is thus helpful to identify trends near the end of market analysis.

Since the Irish government introduced a ban on smoking in pubs and restaurants a trend towards entertaining at home rather than the pub has accelerated. This presents opportunities for the off-licence sector. Related to this is the growth of wine as a category in the alcohol markets and its purchase for consumption at home. Ireland has become one of the fastest growing markets for wine consumption in recent years. Wine consumption has quadrupled since 1990, with wine drinkers totalling 728 000 in 1990 and 1 441 900 in 2003. It should also be pointed out that while the wine market has been growing so has the smoothie market. In 2006 the Irish smoothie market was estimated to be worth €4 million and had grown by 214% since 2002 with no signs of slowing down.

Trends versus Fads

It is crucial to distinguish between trends that will drive growth and reward those who develop differentiated strategies and fads that will only last long enough to attract investment (which is subsequently underemployed or lost forever). Kellogg's Special K was positioned as a diet food; however, with the emergence of several diet fads customers no longer felt that Special K was relevant in the world of fad diets so Kellogg's developed the two-week challenge campaign, which catered to the fad dieters in the industry. The mistaken belief that certain e-commerce markets, such as those for cosmetics and pet supplies, were solid trends caused strategists to undertake initial share-building strategies that eventually led to the ventures' demise. One firm, the Zandl Group, suggests that three questions can help detect a real trend, as opposed to a fad.[4]

- *What is driving it?* A trend will have a solid foundation with legs. Trends are more likely to be driven by demographics (rather than pop culture), values (rather than fashion), lifestyle (rather than a trendy crowd) or technology (rather than media).

- *How accessible is it in the mainstream?* Will it be constrained to a niche market for the foreseeable future? Will it require a major change in ingrained habits? Is the required investment in time or resources a barrier (perhaps because the product is priced too high or is too hard to use)?

- *Is it broadly based?* Does it find expression across categories or industries? Eastern influences, for example, are apparent in healthcare, food, fitness and design – a sign of a trend.

Faith Popcorn observes that fads are about products while trends are about what drives consumers to buy products. She also suggests that trends (which are big and broad, lasting an average of ten years) cannot be created or changed, only observed.[5] Still another perspective on fads comes from Peter Drucker, who opined that a change is something that people do whereas a fad is something people talk about. The implication is that a trend demands substance and action supported by data, rather than simply an idea that captures the imagination. Drucker also suggests that the leaders of today need to move beyond innovation to be change agents – the real payoff comes not from simply detecting and reacting to trends, even when they arereal, but from creating and driving them.[6]

KEY SUCCESS FACTORS

An important output of market analysis is the identification of key success factors (KSFs) for strategic groups in the market. These are assets and competencies that provide the basis for competing successfully. There are two types. Strategic necessities do not necessarily provide an advantage, because others have them, but their absence will create a substantial weakness. The second type, strategic strengths, are those at which a firm excels, the assets or competencies that are superior to those of competitors and provide a base of advantage. The set of assets and competencies developed in competitor analysis provides a base set from which key success factors can be identified. The points to consider are which are the most critical assets and competencies now and, more important, which will be most critical in the future. It is important not only to identify KSFs, but also to project them into the future and, in particular, to identify emerging KSFs. Many firms have faltered when KSFs changed and the competencies and assets on which they were relying became less relevant.

For example, for industrial firms, technology and innovation tend to be most important during the introduction and growth phases, whereas the roles of systems capability, marketing, and service backup become more dominant as the market matures. In consumer products, marketing and distribution skills are crucial during the introduction and growth phases, but operations and manufacturing become more crucial as the product settles into the maturity and decline phases.

RISKS IN HIGH-GROWTH MARKETS

The conventional wisdom that the strategist should seek out growth areas often overlooks a substantial set of associated risks. As shown in Figure 5.5, there are the risks that:

- the number and commitment of competitors may be greater than the market can support
- a competitor may enter with a superior product or low-cost advantage
- key success factors might change and the organisation may be unable to adapt
- technology might change
- the market growth may fail to meet expectations
- price instability may result from overcapacity or from retailers' practice of pricing hot products low to attract customers
- resources might be inadequate to maintain a high growth rate
- adequate distribution may not be available

Figure 5.5   Risks of high-growth markets

Competitive Overcrowding

Perhaps the most serious risk is that too many competitors will be attracted by a growth situation and enter with unrealistic market share expectations. The reality may be that sales volume is insufficient to support all competitors. Overcrowding has been observed in virtually all hyped markets, from railroads to airplanes, radio stations and equipment, televisions sets and personal computers. Overcrowding was never more vividly apparent (in retrospect, at least) than in the dot-com frenzy. At one point there were at least 150 online brokerages, 1000 travel-related sites and 30 health and beauty sites that were competing for attention. Dot-com business-to-business (B2B) exchanges were created for the buying and selling of goods and services, information exchanges, logistics services, sourcing industry data and forecasts and a host of other services. The number of B2B companies grew from under 250 to over 1500 during the year 2000, then fell to under 250 again in 2003. At the peak, there were estimated to be more than 140 such exchanges in the industrial supplies industry alone.[7]

The following conditions are found in markets in which a surplus of competitors is likely to be attracted and a subsequent shakeout is highly probable. These factors were all present in the B2B dot-com experience:

- The market and its growth rate have high visibility. As a result, strategists in related firms are encouraged to consider the market seriously and may even fear the consequences of turning their backs on an obvious growth direction.
- Very high forecast and actual growth in the early stages are seen as evidence confirming high market growth as a proven phenomenon.
- Threats to the growth rate are not considered or are discounted, and little exists to dampen the enthusiasm surrounding the market. The enthusiasm may be contagious when venture capitalists and stock analysts become advocates.

- Few initial barriers exist to prevent firms from entering the market. There may be barriers to eventual success (such as limited retail space), however, that may not be evident at the outset.

- Some potential entrants have low visibility, and their intentions are unknown or uncertain. As a result, the quantity and commitment of the competitors are likely to be underestimated.

Superior Competitive Entry

The ultimate risk is that a position will be established in a healthy growth market and a competitor will enter late with a product that is demonstrably superior or that has an inherent cost advantage. In the 1960's the only international sports brand was Adidas. In 1962, Nike was developed by an American athlete hoping to steal some market share from Adidas. The heart of Nike's success lay in the revolutionary Nike Air cushioning system that was developed by NASA. Adidas' main area of strength resided in their dominance of the football market, but in 2004 lost its lead in football boots to Nike.

Changing Key Success Factors

A firm may successfully establish a strong position during the early stages of market development, only to lose ground later when key success factors change. One forecast is that the surviving personal computer makers will be those able to achieve low-cost production through vertical integration or exploitation of the experience curve, those able to obtain efficient, low-cost distribution, and those able to provide software for their customers – capabilities not necessarily critical during the early stages of market evolution. Many product markets have experienced a shift over time from a focus on product technology to a focus on process technology. A firm that might be capable of achieving product-technology-based advantages may not have the resources, competencies, and orientation/culture needed to develop the process technology-based advantages that the evolving market demands.

Changing Technology

Developing first-generation technology can involve a commitment to a product line and production facilities that may become obsolete and to a technology that may not survive. A safe strategy is to wait until it is clear which technology will dominate and then attempt to improve it with a compatible entry. When the principal competitors have committed themselves, the most promising avenues for the development of a sustainable competitive advantage become more visible. In contrast, the early entrant has to navigate with a great deal of uncertainty.

Disappointing Market Growth

Many shakeouts and price wars occur when market growth falls below expectations. Sometimes the market was an illusion to begin with. Business-to-business exchanges did not provide value to firms that already had systems built with relationships that were, on balance, superior to the B2B exchanges. There was an absence of a compelling value proposition to overcome marketplace inertia. In other cases, the demand may be healthy, but the market is still hostile because competitors have built capacity to match overoptimistic expectations. Or the demand might simply take longer to materialise because the technology is not ready, or because customers are slow to change. For example, Iceland entered the Irish market in the 1990s as part of its overall growth strategy. In the midst of an economy enjoying explosive economic growth sales might have been expected to thrive but in 2005 Iceland left the Irish market on the back of disappointing sales.

Forecasting demand is difficult, especially when the market is new, dynamic and glamourised. In 2002 the future of the mobile phone industry was uncertain. The market was relatively new and there was a tremendous amount of technological optimism surrounding it. In addition to this there were doubts over the availability of new handsets, the capabilities of networks and a difficulty in forecasting the demand for new services this period was the eve of the introduction of digital audio and visual handsets which posed a problem for providers in forecasting demand, deciding tariffs, design and security.

Price Instability

When the creation of excess capacity results in price pressures, industry profitability may be short lived, especially in an industry, such as airlines or steel, in which fixed costs are high and economies of scale are crucial. However, it is also possible that some will use a hot product as a loss leader just to attract customer flow. Compact discs, a hot growth area in the American market in the late 1980s, fuelled the over-expansion of retailers from 5500 in 1987 to over 7000 in 1992.[8] The retailers were very profitable when they sold CDs for about $15. However, when Best Buy, a home-electronics chain, decided to sell CDs for under $10 to attract customers to their off-mall locations, and when Circuit City followed suit, the result was a dramatic erosion in margins and volume and the ultimate bankruptcy of a substantial number of the major CD retailers. A hot growth area had spawned a disaster, not by a self-inflicted price cut but by price instability from a firm that chose to treat the retailing of CDs as nothing more than a permanent loss leader.

Resource Constraints

The substantial financing requirements associated with a rapidly growing business are a major constraint for small firms. Royal Crown's Diet-Rite cola lost its leadership position to Coca-Cola's Tab and Diet Pepsi in the mid 1960s when it could not match the advertising and distribution clout of its larger rivals. Furthermore, financing requirements frequently are increased by higher than expected product development and market entry costs and by price erosion caused by aggressive or desperate competitors. The organisational pressures and problems created by growth can be even more difficult to predict and deal with than financial strains. Many firms have failed to survive the rapid-growth phase because they were unable to obtain and train people to handle the expanded business or to adjust their systems and structures.

Distribution Constraints

Most distribution channels can support only a small number of brands. For example, few retailers are willing to provide shelf space for more than four or five brands of a houseware appliance. As a consequence, some competitors, even those with attractive products and marketing programmes, will not gain adequate distribution and their marketing programmes will become less effective. Distribution limitations fuelled the shakeout that began in the software business in the mid-1980s. More than 120 firms were making financial spreadsheet programmes, whereas the market and distribution channels could not support more than a handful.

A corollary of the scarcity and selectivity of distributors as market growth begins to slow is a marked increase in distributor power. Their willingness to use this power to extract price and promotion concessions from manufacturers or to drop suppliers is often heightened by their own problems in maintaining margins in the face of extreme competition for their customers. Many of the same factors that drew in an overabundance of manufacturers also contribute to overcrowding in subsequent stages of a distribution channel. The eventual shakeout at this level can have equally serious repercussions for suppliers.

KEY LEARNINGS

- The emergence of submarkets can signal a relevance problem.
- Market analysis should assess the attractiveness of a market, as well as its structure and dynamics.
- A usage gap can cause the market size to be understated.
- Market growth can be forecast by looking at driving forces, leading indicators and analogous industries.
- Market profitability will depend on five factors – existing competitors, supplier power, customer power, substitute products and potential entrants.
- Cost structure can be analysed by looking at the value added at each production stage.
- Distribution channels and trends will often affect who wins.
- Market trends will affect both the profitability of strategies and key success factors.
- Key success factors are the skills and competencies needed to compete in a market.
- Growth-market challenges involve the threat of competitors, market changes and firm limitations.

FOR DISCUSSION

1. What are the emerging submarkets in the adult snack food industry? What are the alternative responses available to confectionery companies like Cadbury and Walker's, assuming that it wants to stay relevant to customers interested in healthier eating habits?

2. Identify markets in which actual sales and growth was less than expected. Why was that the case? What would you say was the most important reason that the bottom fell out of the dot-com boom? Why did all the B2B sites emerge, and why did they collapse so suddenly?

3. Why were some brands (like Lucozade) able to fight off competitors in high-growth markets and other (like Palm) were not?

4. Pick a company or brand/business on which to focus. What are the emerging submarkets? What are the trends? What are the strategic implications of the submarkets and trends for the major players?

NOTES

1. For more details about the relevance concept see David A. Aaker (2004) The brand relevance challenge. *Strategy and Business*, Spring; also David A. Aaker (2004) *Brand Portfolio Strategy*, The Free Press, New York, Chapter 3.

2. Greg Stanger, Clark Newby, Todd Andrews *et al.* (1991) *The Ready to Eat Cereal Market*, unpublished paper.

3. This section draws on Michael E. Porter (1985) *Competitive Advantage*, TheFree Press, New York, Chapter 1.

4. Irma Zandl (2000) How to separate trends from fads. *Brandweek*, 23 October, pp. 30–5.

5. Faith Popcorn and Lys Marigold (1997) *Clicking*, HarperCollins, Oxford, pp. 11–12.

6. James Daly (2000) Sage advice – interview with Peter Drucker. *Business 2.0*, 22 August, pp. 134–44.

7. George S. Day, Adam J. Fein, Gregg Ruppersberger (2003) Shakeouts in digital markets: lessons for GB2B exchanges. *California Management Review*, Winter, p. 131–3.

8. Tim Carvell (1997) These prices really are insane. *Fortune*, 4 August, pp. 109–14.

CHAPTER SIX

Environmental Analysis and Strategic Uncertainty

We are watching the dinosaurs die, but we don't know what will take their place.
—*Lester Thurow, MIT economist*

There is something in the wind.
—*William Shakespeare, The Comedy of Errors*

A poorly observed fact is more treacherous than a faulty train of reasoning.
—*Paul Valéry, French philosopher*

*I*n this chapter the focus changes from the market to the environment surrounding the market. The interest is in environmental trends and events that have the potential to affect strategy, either directly or indirectly. Environmental analysis should identify such trends and events and estimate their likelihood and impact. Although environmental analysis is one step removed from the market or industry, it is only one step. When conducting environmental analysis, it is very easy to become bogged down in an extensive, broad survey of trends. However, it is necessary to restrict the analysis to those areas relevant enough to have a significant impact on strategy.

Environmental analysis can be divided usefully, as shown in Figure 6.1, into five areas: technological, governmental, economic, cultural and demographic. Each area is discussed and illustrated. Then, methods of forecasting trends and events are presented.

After describing environmental analysis, the last of the four dimensions of external analysis, the chapter will turn to the task of dealing with strategic uncertainty, a key output of external analysis. Impact analysis and scenario analysis are tools that help to evolve that uncertainty into strategy. Impact analysis – the assessment of the relative importance of strategic uncertainties – is addressed first. Scenario analysis – ways of creating and using future scenarios to help generate and evaluate strategies – follows.

TECHNOLOGY
- To what extent are existing technologies maturing?
- What technological developments or trends are affecting or could affect the industry?

GOVERNMENT
- What changes in regulation are possible? What will their impact be?
- What tax or other incentives are being developed that might affect strategy?
- What are the political risks of operating in a governmental jurisdiction?

ECONOMICS
- What are the economic prospects and inflation outlets for the countries in which the firm operates? How will they affect strategy?

CULTURE
- What are the current or emerging trends in lifestyles, fashions, and other components of culture? Why? What are their implications?

DEMOGRAPHICS
- What demographic trends will affect the market size of the industry or its submarkets? What demographic trends represent opportunities or threats?

GENERAL EXTERNAL ANALYSIS QUESTIONS
- What are the significant trends and future events?
- What threats and opportunities do you see?
- What are the key areas of uncertainty as to trends or events that have the potential to impact strategy? Evaluate these strategic uncertainties in terms of their impact.

SCENARIOS
- What strategic uncertainties are worth being the basis of a scenario analysis?

Figure 6.1   Environmental analysis

DIMENSIONS OF ENVIRONMENTAL ANALYSIS

Technology

One dimension of environmental analysis is technological trends or technological events occurring outside the market or industry that have the potential to impact strategies. They can represent opportunities and threats to those in a position to capitalise. The rise of biofuels such as biodiesel and ethanol offer new product opportunities for energy firms but also present uncertainty regarding how the technology will evolve in the future and which of several alternatives will come to the fore. In the radio industry, podcasting is revolutionising how consumers are using radio. With a wider range of shows to choose from and consumers deciding when they will listen, radio stations are being forced to re-examine their business models both in terms of content production and advertising revenue generation.

Disruptive and Sustaining Technologies

Clayton Christensen, a Harvard Business School professor, developed a theory about disruptive versus sustaining innovations that explains the dynamics of many industries.[1] Sustaining innovations are those that help incumbent companies sell better products for more money to their best customers. Both simple, incremental improvements and breakthrough leaps in technology can be sustaining as long as the focus is on improving margins for the best existing customers. Successful organisations develop structures, staff, incentives and skills designed to generate and implement a continuous flow of sustaining innovations – the pursuit of which is considered a reliable route to profitable growth and the absence of which risks loss of position. Incumbent organisations are not always the first to market with a sustaining innovation, but they usually win because of their resources and motivation.

Disruptive innovations, in contrast, appeal to customers who are unattractive to incumbents, usually because they are not in the high-volume, high-margin 'sweet spot' of the market. Instead, these innovations take one of two routes into the marketplace.[2] First, they look toward potential customers who are not currently buying the product because it is too complex or expensive. Examples of this would include how monitor makers attracted new users in the entertainment market by offering LCD monitors with the same image quality as plasma screens but at a much cheaper price. Tesco developed its 'Finest' range to cater for customers who wanted gourmet food products but at a cheaper price.

A second route for disruptive technologies is to enter the market at the low end, focusing on customers who are 'overserved'. As sustainable innovation drives performance upward there will be a segment that simply does not need the extra capabilities and would be satisfied with (indeed, would prefer) a simpler, cheaper product with satisfactory performance. Wikipedia's entry into the encyclopaedia market met a requirement for Internet access to a simple to use and reasonably reliable reference site that was free. It entered a mature market for encyclopaedias in 2001 with a number of strong incumbents operating on a fee based membership basis. In 2005 Wikipedia calculated it had 2.5 billion page views per month.

Disruptive innovations are often the basis for attractive growth, but incumbent firms – especially successful ones – rarely participate. When an organisation is doing well, there is pressure to enhance short-term growth and margins, which can best be achieved through sustaining innovations. When the business turns downward (perhaps because of a competitor's disruptive technology) there are no resources available to support an initiative to catch up to the disruptive innovation.

To participate in disruptive innovations, a firm needs to recognise that its existing organisation is likely to be a liability. Thus, a separate organisation may be required, or at least a group within the current organisation that has very different people, processes and culture. Further, it is important to explore disruptive innovations before performance turns bad, resources are less available and others have achieved a first-mover advantage. Finally, top management should participate in the decision to develop a disruptive innovation; without a high-level commitment, the pursuit may become an endless exercise in observation and fact-finding.

Impact of New Technologies

Certainly it can be important, even critical, to manage the transition to a new technology. The appearance of a new technology, however, even a successful one, does not necessarily mean that businesses based on the prior technology will suddenly become unhealthy. A group of researchers at Purdue studied 15 companies in five industries in which a dramatic new technology had emerged:[3]

- diesel-electric trains versus steam trains
- transistors versus vacuum tubes
- ballpoint pens versus fountain pens
- nuclear power versus boilers for fossil-fuel plants
- electric razors versus safety razors

Two interesting conclusions emerged that should give pause to anyone attempting to predict the impact of a dramatic new technology. First, the sales of the old technology continued for a substantial period, in part because the firms involved continued to improve it. Safety-razor sales have actually increased 800% since the advent of the electric razor. Thus, a new technology may not signal the end of the growth phase of an existing technology. In all cases, firms involved with the old technology had a substantial amount of time to react to the new technology. Second, it is relatively difficult to predict the outcome of a new technology. The new technologies studied tended to be expensive and crude at first. Furthermore, they started by invading submarkets. Transistors, for example, were first used in hearing aids and pocket radios. In addition, new technologies tended to create new markets instead of simply encroaching on existing ones. Throwaway ballpoint pens and many of the transistor applications opened up completely new market areas.

Government

The addition or removal of legislative or regulatory constraints can pose major strategic threats and opportunities. For example, the ban of some ingredients in food products or cosmetics has dramatically affected the strategies of numerous firms. The impact of governmental efforts to reduce piracy in industries such as software (more than one-fourth of all software used is copied), CDs, DVDs and movie videos is of crucial import to those affected. The Restriction on Hazardous Substances regulation (RoHS) involving the importation and manufacturing of electronic goods into Europe could affect up to 300 companies in Ireland alone. European Union financial directives and regulations such as the Financial Services and Markets Act 2000 (FSMA) are having enormous implications for firms involved. Regulations concerning data protection, privacy, such as the EU Data Protection Act 1998 and e-commerce also pose major strategic questions and threats for firms.

In an increasingly global economy with interdependencies in markets and in the sourcing of products and services, possible political hot spots need to be understood and tracked. In a classic study of environmental trends and events that were forecast in *Fortune* magazine during the 1930s and 1940s, predictions were found to be remarkably good in many areas such as synthetic vitamins, genetic breakthroughs, the decline of railroads, and the advent of TVs, house-trailers, and superhighways. However, forecasting was extremely poor when international events were involved.[4] Thus, a mid-1930s article did not consider the possibility of US involvement in a European war. A 1945 article incorrectly forecast a huge growth in trade with the Soviet Union, not anticipating the advent of the Cold War. A Middle East scenario failed to forecast the emergence of Israel. International political developments, which can be critical to multinational firms, are still extremely difficult to forecast. A prudent strategy is one that is both diversified and flexible, so that a political surprise will not be devastating.

Environment

Organisations are increasingly making assessments of strategy and markets on the basis of the environmental cost and impact of their involvement. The environment, in particular carbon emissions, is of concern to business for three reasons. Firstly, consumers may be less willing to buy a brand that is harmful to the environment. Secondly, the rising cost of fuels and the emergence of alternatives means that fuel-intensive organisations must keep abreast of developments and trends in the environmental arena. Finally, as the environment moves up the political agenda the willingness of government to intervene and impose sanctions and taxes on those damaging the environment will increase. The European Union's Emissions Trading Scheme (ETS) imposes emission caps on certain industries with particularly high emissions and provides an opportunity for companies to trade their carbon and meet their emission targets, although this process has not been without criticism. Organisations such as the Neutral Carbon Company have worked with clients like British Sky Broadcasting, DHL and Barclays to go beyond regulatory limits and achieve carbon neutral status. The band Coldplay have ensured that some of their albums 'A Rush of Blood to the Head' and 'X&Y' are carbon neutral. This involved them measuring the carbon dioxide emissions from these projects and countering them by planting a Coldplay forest and supporting carbon reducing projects in lesser developed nations.[5]

Economics

The evaluation of some strategies will be affected by judgements made about the economy, particularly about inflation and general economic health as measured by unemployment and economic growth. Heavy investment in a capital-intensive industry might need to be timed to coincide with a strong economy to avoid a damaging period of losses. Usually it is necessary to look beyond the general economy to the health of individual industries. Over the past decade the housing markets of many of the world's economies have seen meteoric house price growth despite the weakness of some of those economies. A forecast of the relative valuations of currencies can be relevant for industries with multinational competitors. Thus, an analysis of the balance of payments and other factors affecting currency valuations might be needed.

IBM AND THE INTERNET

In 1993, an IBM engineer wrote a research paper entitled 'Get Connected', which outlined six principles of Internet-based communication. This led to a total refocus of IBM toward the Internet years before Microsoft and others got the message. It has to be one of the most influential environmental analyses of our time. The principles were that e-mail would become pervasive; e-mail directory assistance would be needed; e-mail would allow vertical communication within an organisation; e-mail addresses would be on all communication; companies would create websites with information repositories and e-commerce would explode. These insights seem obvious in retrospect, but they were visionary at the time. In 1994, the then-new CEO, Lou Gerstner, bought into the idea. He 'got it' – during the first e-commerce demonstration Gerstner was reported to ask 'where is the Buy button?' A flurry of initiatives followed, turning IBM from a sick firm on the brink of collapse to a leader of the new economy. Among the more visible strategic moves were the purchase of Lotus Notes, the creation of NetCommerce (an outgrowth of the IBM support for the 1996 Olympics), a general e-business positioning and the renaming of the server line to 'e-servers'.[6]

Culture

Cultural trends can present both threats and opportunities for a wide variety of firms, as the following examples illustrate. A dress designer conducted a study that projected women's lifestyles. It predicted that a more varied lifestyle would prevail, that more time would be spent outside the home, and that those who worked would be more career oriented. These predictions had several implications relevant to the dress designer's product line and pricing strategies. For example, a growing number and variety of activities would lead to a broader range of styles and larger wardrobes, with perhaps somewhat less spent on each garment. Furthermore, consumers' increased financial and social independence would probably reduce the number of follow-the-leader fashions and the perception that certain outfits were required for certain occasions.

There is a trend toward tribing, the affinity toward a social unit that is centred around an interest or activity and is not bound by conventional social links.[7] These can range from festivals like La DolceVita, an Italian festival in London, designed to entertain and create an Italian experience for all who like to indulge in Italian food and wine and learn about Italian property, to the Bulldog Bash biker event held in England annually by bikers wishing to celebrate hard rock music, custom motorcycles and similar lifestyle activities. The Internet has also generated a host of communities and chat groups ranging from parenting forums, to golf forums and the now ubiquitous Myspace and Bebo social networking sites. Tribing has significance for brand-building and communication programmes, both positively and negatively.

Faith Popcorn has uncovered and studied cultural trends that, in her judgement, will shape the future. Her efforts provide a provocative view of the future environment of many organisations. Consider, for example, the following trends:[8]

- *Cocooning.* Consumers are retreating into safe, cosy 'homelike' environments to shield themselves from the harsh realities of the outside world. This trend supports online and catalogue shopping, home security systems, gardening and smart homes.

- *Fantasy adventure.* Consumers crave low-risk excitement and stimulation to escape from stress and boredom. Responsive firms offer theme restaurants, exotic cosmetics, adventure travel, fantasy clothes that suggest roleplaying, fantasy-based entertainment, and fantasy cars.

- *Pleasure revenge.* Consumers are rebelling against rules to cut loose and savour forbidden fruits (for example, indulgent ice creams, cigars, Martinis, tanning salons and furs).

- *Small indulgences.* Busy, stressed-out people are rewarding themselves with affordable luxuries that will provide quick gratification: Haagen-Dazs ice cream, Cuisine de France, technically advanced Nokia mobile phones, readymade Marks and Spencer meals. For the luxury market, the range of possibilities might include Louis Vuitton bags, a Mercedes S550 or a luxury expensive Bulthaup kitchen.

- *Down-aging.* Consumers seek symbols of youth, renewal, and rejuvenation to counterbalance the intensity of their adult lives. The over-55 crowd going to school and participating in active sports (including ironman competitions and outdoor adventures) reflect this trend but it really extends to a wide age group that favours products, apparel, activities and entertainment that capture the nostalgia of youth.

- *Being alive.* Consumers focus on the quality of life and the importance of wellness, taking charge of their personal health rather than delegating it to the health care industry. Examples of this include the use of herbal tea ranges such as Twinings green tea, homeopathic solutions to medical problems, organic and free range products available in supermarkets and restaurants, smoothie bars offering healthy shots of products like wheatgerm in smoothies, gyms and water-coolers in work places and health stores.

- *99 lives.* Consumers are forced to assume multiple roles to cope with their increasingly busy lives. Retailers serving multiple needs, ever-faster ways to get prepared food, a service that manages your second home and prepares it for visits, noise neutralisers, e-commerce and yoga are all responsive to this trend.

INFORMATION TECHNOLOGY

In nearly every industry it is useful to ask what potential impact new information technology based on new databases will have on strategies. How will it create SCAs and key success factors? For example, Zara sets itself apart from competitors through its supply-chain management system, which links stores to design shops and company-owned factories in real time. This allows them to use technology to respond rapidly to changing customer tastes. Deploying this system provides them with an SCA given the difficulty competitors have with imitating their system. Jumbo supermarkets, a leading Dutch supermarket retailer, was the first to go live with the latest version of Lawson Retail Operations which enables them to get automated forecasting and ordering for each store individually and allows Jumbo to maintain less inventory. Sky's partnership with Digital Rum enabled Sky subscribers to purchase goods and services through Sky's Net Portal, a mechanism were customers can access and use the Internet and e-business services through interactive TV. In supermarket retailing, 'smart cards' – cards that customers present during checkout to pay for purchases – provide a record of all purchases that allow:

- stores to build loyalty by rewarding cumulative purchase volume
- promotions to target individual customers based on their brand preferences and household characteristics
- the use of cents-off coupons without the customer or store having to handle pieces of paper; the purchase of a promoted product can be discounted automatically
- the store to identify buyers of slow-moving items and predict the impact on the store's choice of dropping an item
- decisions as to shelf-space allocation, special displays, and store layout to be refined based on detailed information about customer shopping

Demographics

Demographic trends can be a powerful underlying force in a market and it can be predictable. Among the influential demographic variables are age, income, education, and geographic location.

The older demographic group is of particular interest because it is growing rapidly and is blessed with not only resources but the time to use them. The over-65 population in Europe will grow from 115 million in 2005 to 136 million in 2020. The over-80 group will grow from 25 million to over 36 million in the same time period and its members will be much more likely to live independently. Women tend to outlive men, so their portion of the population increases sharply with age; within the 80-year-old group there are only 30 men per 100 women. Between 1975 and 1995 the EU's population grew by over 6%, but from 1995 to 2025 this growth is expected to fall to 3.7%. To profit from this trend marketers must move away from the image of the over-50s as being a slippers and blanket-over-the-knee market. In France, Danone has targeted the senior market with its Actimel brand and its promise to boost immune systems. In the cosmetics market L'Oréal and Revlon have both developed products targeted at older women and used mature stars such as Catherine Deneuve, Diane Keaton, Jane Fonda and Susan Sarandon to endorse and promote them.

Ethnic populations in Europe, however, are rising rapidly and some analysts believe that immigration could be the magic bullet that will solve Europe's labour problem. For example, the UK population is set to rise by about 5 million people over

25 years to 2032 with immigrants accounting for two-thirds of this growth. This has implications for a range of organisations such as supermarket owners, who may need to adjust their product lines to stock more ethnic products. Dunnes Stores, Ireland's leading retailer, has recently begun to offer a wide range of Polish brands, in response to a large and relatively recent influx of Polish emigrants, and to advertise in Polish to support its new product range.

The nuclear family, which was once traditional in European homes, has declined rapidly due to various technological and social developments and changes (for example, contraception, abortion, the Internet, TV, women's emancipation, education and changes in cultural values). This has lead to an increase in the prevalence of one-parent families and 55 % of females in the EU employed outside of the home. One implication in this demographic evolution is an increased demand for DIY services, home help, domestic cleaners, meal preparation and child minding.

DEALING WITH STRATEGIC UNCERTAINTY

Strategic uncertainty, which that has strategic implications, is a key construct in external analysis. A typical external analysis will emerge with dozens of strategic uncertainties. To be manageable, they need to be grouped into logical clusters or themes. It is then useful to assess the importance of each cluster in order to set priorities with respect to information gathering and analysis. Impact analysis, described in the next section, is designed to accomplish that assessment. Sometimes the strategic uncertainty is represented by an inherently unpredictable future trend or event. Information gathering and additional analysis will not be able to reduce the uncertainty. In that case, scenario analysis can be employed. Scenario analysis basically accepts the uncertainty as given and uses it to drive a description of two or more future scenarios. Strategies are then developed for each. One outcome could be a decision to create organisational and strategic flexibility so that as the business context changes the strategy will adapt. Scenario analysis will be detailed in the final section of this chapter.

IMPACT ANALYSIS – ASSESSING THE IMPACT OF STRATEGIC UNCERTAINTIES

An important objective of external analysis is to rank the strategic uncertainties and decide how they are to be managed over time. Which uncertainties merit intensive investment in information gathering and in-depth analysis, and which merit only a low-key monitoring effort? The problem is that dozens of strategic uncertainties and many second-level strategic uncertainties are often generated. These strategic uncertainties can lead to an endless process of information gathering and analysis that can absorb resources indefinitely. A publishing company may be concerned about digital TV, lifestyle patterns, educational trends, geographic population shifts and printing technology. Any one of these issues involves a host of subfields and could easily spur limitless research. For example, digital TV might involve a variety of pay-per-view-TV concepts, suppliers, technologies, and viewer reactions. Unless distinct priorities are established, external analysis can become descriptive, ill focused and inefficient. The extent to which a strategic uncertainty should be monitored and analysed depends on its impact and immediacy.

- The impact of a strategic uncertainty is related to:
  - the extent to which it involves trends or events that will impact existing or potential businesses
  - the importance of the involved businesses
  - the number of involved businesses
- The immediacy of a strategic uncertainty is related to:
  - The probability that the involved trends or events will occur
  - The time frame of the trends or events
  - The reaction time likely to be available, compared with the time required to develop and implement appropriate strategy

THE NEED FOR A WIDER LENS

Wharton professors George Day and Paul Shoemaker have drawn attention to the value of examining the periphery of the business environment as part of the strategy development process. Their observations are that businesses are being regularly buffeted by unanticipated events, that these occurrences are being flagged in advance but the signals are not seen or interpreted in the correct way. In order to anticipate and deal with such shocks, managers must seek and interpret weak signals, small issues that have a vague resonance but in a particular set of circumstances could translate into a strategic problem for the firm. Information may be provided by staff, customers or competitors. Internally, signals can be identified by asking hard questions about the future of the business, the types of changes that might be particularly damaging for it and also by keeping a close eye on emerging technologies within the industry and adjacent sectors. However, while some suggest that paranoia is a positive state for a manager, overexamination of the environment can be a waste of time and resources for a business if it distracts attention from core activities.[9]

Impact of a Strategic Uncertainty

Each strategic uncertainty involves potential trends or events that could have an impact on present, proposed, and even potential businesses. For example, a strategic uncertainty for a beer firm could be based on the future prospects of the microbrewery market. If the beer firm has both a proposed microbrewery entry and an imported beer positioned in the same area, trends in the microbrewery beer market could have a high impact on the firm. The trend toward natural foods may present opportunities for a sparkling water product line for the same firm and be the basis of a strategic uncertainty.

The impact of a strategic uncertainty will depend on the importance of the impacted business to a firm. Some businesses are more important than others. The importance of established businesses may be indicated by their associated sales, profits, or costs. However, such measures might need to be supplemented for proposed or growth businesses for which present sales, profits, or costs may not reflect the true value to a firm. Finally, because an information-need area may affect several businesses, the number of involved businesses can also be relevant to a strategic uncertainty's impact.

Immediacy of Strategic Uncertainties

Events or trends associated with strategic uncertainties may have a high impact but such a low probability of occurrence that it is not worth actively expending resources to gather or analyse information. Similarly, if occurrence is far in the future relative to the strategic-decision horizon, then it may be of little concern. Thus, the harnessing of tide energy may be so unlikely or may occur so far in the future that it is of no concern to a utility. Finally, there is the reaction time available to a firm, compared with the reaction time likely to be needed. After a trend or event crystallises, a firm needs to develop a reaction strategy. If the available reaction time is inadequate, it becomes important to anticipate emerging trends and events better so that future reaction strategies can be initiated sooner.

Managing Strategic Uncertainties

Figure 6.2 suggests a categorisation of strategic uncertainties for a given business. If both the immediacy and impact are low, then a low level of monitoring may suffice. If

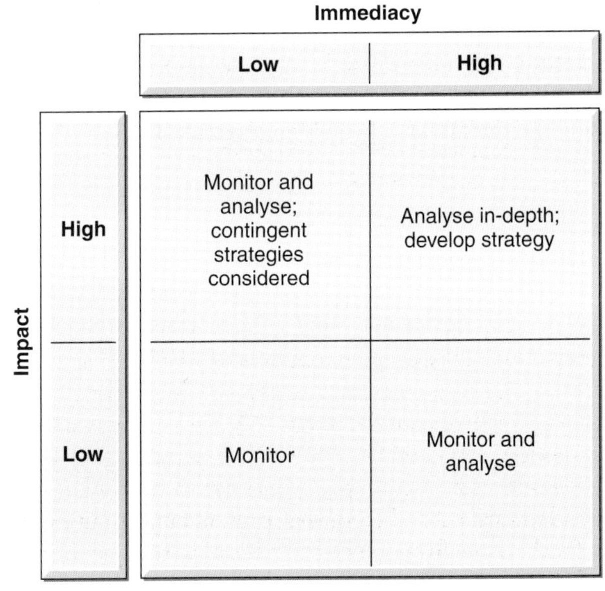

Figure 6.2   Strategic uncertainty categories

the impact is thought to be low but the immediacy is high, the area may merit monitoring and analysis. If the immediacy is low and the impact high, then the area may require monitoring and analysis in more depth, and contingent strategies may be considered but not necessarily developed and implemented. When both the immediacy and potential impact of the underlying trends and events are high, then an in-depth analysis will be appropriate, as will be the development of reaction plans or strategies. An active task force may provide initiative.

SCENARIO ANALYSIS

Scenario analysis can help deal with uncertainly. It provides an alternative to investing in information to reduce uncertainty, which is often an expensive and futile process. By creating a small number of marketplace or market context scenarios and assessing their likelihood and impact, scenario analysis can be a powerful way to deal with complex environments. There are two types of scenario analyses. In the first type, strategy-developing scenarios, the objective is to provide insights into future competitive contexts, then use these insights to evaluate existing business strategies and stimulate the creation of new ones. Such analyses can help create contingency plans to guard against disasters – an airline adjusting to a terror incident, for example, or a pharmaceutical company reacting to a product safety problem. They can also suggest investment strategies that enable the organisation to capitalise on future opportunities caused by customer trends or technological breakthroughs. In the second type of analyses, decision-driven scenarios, a strategy is proposed and tested against several scenarios that are developed.[10] The goal is to challenge the strategies, thereby helping to make the go/no-go decision and suggesting ways to make the strategy more robust in withstanding competitive forces. If the decision is to enter a market with a technology strategy, alternative scenarios could be built around variables such as marketplace acceptance of the technology, competitor response and the stimulation of customer applications. In either case, a scenario analysis will involve three general steps: the creation of scenarios, relating those scenarios to existing or potential strategies, and assessing the probability of the scenarios (see Figure 6.3).

Identify Scenarios

Strategic uncertainties can drive scenario development. The impact analysis will identify the strategic uncertainty with the highest priority for a firm. A manufacturer of a medical imagery device may want to know whether a technological advance

Figure 6.3   Scenario analysis

will allow its machine to be made at a substantially lower cost. A farm equipment manufacturer or ski resort operator may believe that the weather – whether a drought will continue, for example – is the most important area of uncertainty. A server firm may want to know whether a single software standard will emerge or multiple standards will coexist. The chosen uncertainty could then stimulate two or more scenarios. A competitor scenario analysis can be driven by the uncertainly surrounding a competitor's strategy. For example, could the competitor aggressively extend its brand? Or might it divest a product line or make a major acquisition? Perhaps the competitor could change its value proposition, or become more aggressive in its pricing.[11] When a set of scenarios is based largely on a single strategic uncertainty, the scenarios themselves can usually be enriched by related events and circumstances. Thus, an inflation-stimulated recession scenario would be expected to generate a host of conditions for the appliance industry, such as price increases and retail failures. Similarly, a competitor scenario can be comprehensive, specifying such strategy dimensions as product-market investment, acquisition or joint ventures, pricing, positioning, product, and promotions.

It is sometimes useful to generate scenarios based on probable outcomes: optimistic, pessimistic, and most likely. The consideration of a pessimistic scenario is often useful in testing existing assumptions and plans. The aura of optimism that often surrounds a strategic plan may include implicit assumptions that competitors will not respond aggressively, the market will not fade or collapse, or technological problems will not surface. Scenario analysis provides a nonthreatening way to consider the possibility of clouds or even rain on the picnic. Often, of course, several variables are relevant to the future period of interest. The combination can define a relatively large number of scenarios. For example, a large greeting-card firm might consider three variables important: the success of small boutique card companies, the life of a certain card type and the nature of future distribution channels. The combination can result in many possible scenarios. Experience has shown that two or three scenarios are the ideal number with which to work; any more and the process becomes unwieldy and any value is largely lost. Thus, it is important to reduce the number of scenarios by identifying a small set that ideally includes those that are plausible/credible and those that represent departures from the present that are substantial enough to affect strategy development.

Relate Scenarios to Strategies

After scenarios have been identified, the next step is to relate them to strategy – both existing strategies and new options. If an existing strategy is in place, it can be tested with respect to each scenario. Which scenario will be the best one? How bad will the strategy be if the wrong scenario emerges? What will its prospects be with respect to customer acceptance, competitor reactions, and sales and profits? Could it be modified to enhance its prospects? Even if the scenario analysis is not motivated by a desire to generate new strategy options, it is always useful to consider what strategies would be optimal for each scenario. A scenario by its nature will provide a perspective that is different from the status quo. Any strategy that is optimal for a given scenario

THE FUTURE OF THE INTERNET

Technology Magazine Red Herring interviewed Internet leaders for their opinions on how the net might be shaping our lives in 2016. The consensus was that the connection between people and in the Internet would be more organic. The devices that we take for granted today will disappear as they become integrated into our environment, into clothing and even spectacles. Human interaction with the Internet will be speech based but not necessarily in English, which will no longer be the dominant Internet language. Bandwidth of 100 mbs per second will be the norm and the global online population will triple to 3 billion people and connecting to the Internet will no longer be a conscious act. The commercial implications of this are immense. John Hagel III sees opportunities for customer relationship businesses that can bundle services and offer branded advice to consumers faced with overwhelming demand. Household devices such as heating and security will be controlled via the Internet. Consumers will also take control of the design of their own products. For example, car makers might make their parts catalogue available with consumers designing their own vehicles and even selling their designs back to the manufacturers.[12]

should become a viable option. Even if it is not considered superior or even feasible, some elements of it might be captured.

Estimate Scenario Probabilities

To evaluate alternative strategies it is useful to determine the scenario probabilities. The task is actually one of environmental forecasting, except that the total scenario may be a rich combination of several variables. Experts could be asked to assess probabilities directly. A deeper understanding will often emerge, however, if causal factors underlying each scenario can be determined. For example, the construction equipment industry might develop scenarios based on three alternative levels of construction activity. These levels would have several contributing causes. One would be the interest rate. Another could be the availability of funds to the homebuilding sector, which in turn would depend on the emerging structure of financial institutions and markets. A third cause might be the level of government spending on roads, energy, and other areas.

KEY LEARNINGS

- Environmental analysis of changes in technology, demographics, culture, the economy, and governmental actions should detect and analyse current and potential trends and events that will create opportunities or threats to an organisation.

- Impact analysis involves assessing systematically the impact and immediacy of the trends and events that underlie each strategy uncertainty.

• Scenario analysis, a vehicle to explore different assumptions about the future, involves the creation of two to three plausible scenarios, the development of strategies appropriate to each, the assessment of scenario probabilities, and the evaluation of the resulting strategies across the scenarios.

FOR DISCUSSION

1. What did the fax machine replace, if anything? What will replace (or has replaced) the fax machine? When will the fax machine disappear?

2. Develop a scenario based on the proposition that hybrid cars will continue to improve and take 30% of the automotive market in a few years. Analyse it from the point of view of an energy company like Shell or a car company like Mercedes. What are the top three or four dimensions to consider?

3. A recent important technology development is Wi-Fi, the wireless Internet access concept. Supported by Intel's Centrino chip (which frees computers from hard-wired connections), the development has raised expectations throughout the computer industry.

   a. Will this change the use of computers? How many people will actually use computers connected to the Internet in coffee shops and airports? Think of some other similarly hyped phenomena, from railroads to airplanes to television to VCRs. What happened in those cases?

   b. What are the action alternatives for organisations such as Pret A Manger and Starbucks?

4. Pick a company or brand/business on which to focus. What are the major trends that come out of an environmental analysis? What are the major areas of uncertainty? How would a major company in the industry handle those best?

5. Focusing on the airline industry, develop a list of strategic uncertainties and possible strategic actions.

NOTES

1. Clayton M. Christensen, Mark W. Johnson and Darrell K. Rigby (2002) Foundations for growth. *MIT Sloan Management Review*, Spring, pp. 22–31.

2. Clayton M. Christensen, Mark W. Johnson, and Darrell K. Rigby (2002) Foundations for growth. *MIT Sloan Management Review*, Spring, pp. 22–31.

3. Arnold Cooper, Edward Demuzilo, Kenneth Hatten *et al.* (1976) Strategic responses to technological threats. *Academy of Management Proceedings*, pp. 54–60.

4. Richard N. Farmer (1973) Looking back at looking forward. *Business Horizons*, February, pp. 21–8.

5. The Carbon Neutral Company website http://www.carbonneutral.com/.

6. IBM *Red Herring*, November, 1999, pp. 120–8.

7. Sam Hill (2003) *60 Trends in 60 Minutes*, John Wiley & Sons, New Yori, p. 96.

8. Faith Popcorn and Lys Marigold (1997) *Clicking*, HarperCollins, Oxford, pp. 11–12.

9. George S. Day and Paul J.H. Schoemaker (2006) *Peripheral Vision*, Harvard Business School Press, Cambridge MA.

10. Hugh Courtney (2003) Decision-driven scenarios for assessing four levels of uncertainty. *Strategy & Leadership*, 31(1), pp. 14–16.

11. Liam Fahey (2003) Competitor scenarios. *Strategy and Leadership*, 31(1), pp. 32–44.

12. The future of the Internet. *Red Herring*, 10 April 2006.

CHAPTER SEVEN

Internal Analysis

We have met the enemy and he is us.
—*Pogo*

Self-conceit may lead to self-destruction.
—*Aesop,* The Frog and the Ox

The fish is last to know if it swims in water.
—*Chinese proverb*

*I*n addition to external threats and opportunities, strategy development must be based on the objectives, strengths, and capabilities of a business. For example, Airness, a youthful French apparel company, has become the biggest selling French sportswear company thanks to the strength it has developed in creating vibrant designs, the emotional strength they have created around their powerful red and black panther logo and the positioning of the brand as a counter example of the racial and economic struggles encountered by most young black immigrants in France. Using these strengths, Airness widened its product mix to include mobile phones. In the sports market its objectives are to expand further into the sports field to basketball and rugby and to develop its football business in other European countries.[1]

Understanding a business in depth is the goal of internal analysis. A business internal analysis is similar to a competitor analysis, but it has a greater focus on performance assessment and is much richer and deeper. It is more detailed because of its importance to strategy and because much more information is available. The analysis is based on specific, current information on sales, profits, costs, organisational structure, management style, and other factors.

Just as strategy can be developed at the level of a business, a group of businesses, or the firm, internal analysis can also be conducted at each of these levels. Of course, analyses at different levels will differ from each other in emphasis and content but their structure and thrust will be the same. The common goal is to identify organisational strengths, weaknesses, constraints and, ultimately, to develop responsive strategies, either exploiting strengths or correcting or compensating for weaknesses.

Internal analysis begins by examining the financial performance of a business, its profitability and sales. Indications of unsatisfactory or deteriorating performance might stimulate strategy change. In contrast, the conclusion that current or future performance is acceptable can suggest the old adage 'if it ain't broke, don't fix it.' Of course, something that is not broken may still need some maintenance, refurbishing, or vitalisation. Performance analysis is especially relevant to the strategic decision of how much to invest in or disinvest from a business.

The first section of this chapter considers financial performance, as measured by sales, return on assets, and the shareholder value concept. The next section covers other performance dimensions linked to future profitability, such as customer satisfaction, product quality, brand associations, relative cost, new products, and employee capability.

Another perspective on internal analysis considers those business characteristics that limit or drive strategy choice. The third section of this chapter examines five issues: past and current strategy, strategic problems, organisational capabilities and constraints, financial resources and constraints, and organisational strengths and weaknesses. The final section discusses business portfolio analysis, which evaluates each business by assessing its performance and the attractiveness of the market in which it competes.

FINANCIAL PERFORMANCE – SALES AND PROFITABILITY

Internal analysis often starts with an analysis of current financials, measures of sales and profitability. Changes in either can signal a change in the market viability of a product line and the ability to produce competitively. Furthermore, they provide an indicator of the success of past strategies and thus can often help in evaluating whether strategic changes are needed. In addition, sales and profitability at least appear to be specific and easily measured. As a result, it is not surprising that they are so widely used as performance evaluation tools.

Sales and Market Share

A sensitive measure of how customers regard a product or service can be sales or market share. After all, if the relative value to a customer changes, sales and share should be affected, although there may be an occasional delay caused by market and customer inertia.

Sales levels can be strategically important. Increased sales can mean that the customer base has grown. An enlarged customer base, if we assume that new customers will develop loyalty, will mean future sales and profits. Increased share can provide the potential to gain SCAs in the form of economies of scale and experience curve effects. Conversely, decreased sales can mean decreases in customer bases and a loss of scale economies.

A problem with using sales as a measure is that they can be affected by short-term actions, such as promotions by a brand and its competitors. Thus, it is necessary to separate changes in sales that are caused by tactical actions from those that represent fundamental changes in the value delivered to the customer, and it is important to couple an analysis of sales or share with an analysis of customer satisfaction, which will be discussed shortly.

Profitability

The ultimate measure of a firm's ability to prosper and survive is its profitability. Although both growth and profitability are desirable, establishing a priority between the two can help guide strategic decision making. A host of measures and ratios reflect profitability, including margins, costs, and profits. Building on the assets employed leads to the return on assets (ROA) measure, which can be decomposed with a formula developed by General Motors and DuPont in the 1920s.

$$ROA = Profits/Sales \times Sales/Assets$$

Thus, return on assets can be considered as having two causal factors. The first is the profit margin, which depends on the selling price and cost structure. The second is the asset turnover, which depends on inventory control and asset utilisation. The determination of both the numerator and denominator of the ROA terms is not as straightforward as might be assumed. Substantial issues surround each, such as the distortions caused by depreciation and the fact that book assets do not reflect intangible assets, such as brand equity, or the market value of tangible assets.

Measuring Performance: Shareholder Value Analysis

Shareholder value, an enormously influential concept during the past two decades, provides an answer to this question. Each business should earn an ROA (based on a flow of profits emanating from an investment), that meets or exceeds the costs of capital, which is the weighted average of the cost of equity and cost of debt. Thus, if the cost of equity is 16% and the cost of debt is 8, the cost of capital would be 12% if the amount of debt was equal to the amount of equity; if there were only one-fourth as much debt as equity, then the cost of capital would be 14%. If the return is greater, the cost of capital shareholder value will increase and if it is less shareholder value will decrease.

Some of the routes to increasing shareholder value are as follows:

- Earn more profit by reducing costs or increasing revenue without using more capital.
- Invest in high-return products (this, of course, is what strategy is all about).
- Reduce the cost of capital by increasing the debt to equity ratio or by buying back stock to reduce the cost of equity.
- Use less capital. Under shareholder value analysis, the assets employed are no longer a free good, so there is an incentive to reduce it. If improved just-in-time operations can reduce the inventory, it directly affects shareholder value.

The concept of shareholder value is theoretically valid.[2] If a profit stream can be estimated accurately from a strategic move, the analysis will be sound. The problem is that short-term profits (known to affect stock return and thus shareholder wealth) are easier to estimate and manipulate than long-term profits. Investors who assume that short-term profits predict longer-term profits pay undue attention to the former, as does the top management of a company with numerical targets to meet. The discipline to invest in a strategy that will sacrifice short-term financial performance for long-term prospects is not easy to come by, especially if some of the future prospects are in the form of options. For example, the investment by Italian jewellery company Bulgari into a joint venture with Marriott International Inc. to create Bulgari Hotels and Resorts gave it the option to expand its brand name into a different sector. When Diageo bought the Chalone Wine Group it bought the option to enhance its business in the alcoholic beverage area specifically in the North American wine business. The impact of reducing investment also has risks. When, for example, Coca-Cola sold off its bottlers to reduce investment and improve shareholder value, its control of the quality of its product may have been reduced. In general, investment reduction often means outsourcing, with its balancing act between flexibility and loss of control over operations. A broadband company that outsources its installations loses a chance to interact with its customers. One danger of shareholder value analysis is that it reduces the priority given to other stakeholders such as employees, suppliers, and customers, each of whom represents assets that can form the basis for long-term success. The radical downsizing of some firms has resulted in going beyond trimming fat to reducing future prospects. For example, by the end of 2006 in an effort to provide shareholders with more value, Nokia aimed to reduce its overall expenditure on research and development to 9%–10% of net sales. Strategically this may turn out to be a dangerous move as the product offerings in the mobile phone industry are increasing in complexity and customer demands are growing more sophisticated. An effort to reduce costs can too easily cut into customer service and thus customer loyalty.

In fact, shareholder value management has met with very mixed results. However, one study of the experience of 125 firms found similarities among those that had applied shareholder value concepts successfully.[3] These companies:

- gave priority to shareholder value over other goals, particularly growth goals
- provided intensive training throughout the organisation regarding shareholder value and made it a practical tool for business managers at all levels – the philosophy was not restricted to the executive suite
- were disciplined in identifying the drivers of shareholder value – for example, for a call centre, drivers could be the length of time to answer calls and the quality of responses
- reduced overhead by adapting the current accounting system and integrating shareholder value analysis with strategic planning

These firms found a variety of benefits. First, the concept led to value-creating divestments that otherwise would not have occurred. Second, firms were able to transfer corporate planning and decision making to decentralised business units because all units tended to use the same logic, metrics and mindset. Third, the business investment horizon tended to be longer, with projects with multi-year time frames being approved. Fourth, the new recognition that capital had a cost tended to generate better strategic decisions.

PERFORMANCE MEASUREMENT – BEYOND PROFITABILITY

One of the difficulties in strategic market management is developing performance indicators that convincingly represent long-term prospects. The temptation is to focus on short-term profitability measures and to reduce investment in new products and brand images that have long-term payoffs. The concept of net present value represents a long-term profit stream but it is not always operational. It often provides neither a criterion for decision making nor a useful performance measure. It is somewhat analogous to preferring €6 million to €4 million. The real question involves determining which strategic alternative will generate €6 million and which will generate €4 million.

It is necessary to develop performance measures that will reflect long-term viability and health. The focus should be on the assets and competencies that underlie the current and future strategies and their SCAs. What are the key assets and competencies for a business during the planning horizon? What strategic dimensions are most crucial: to become more competitive with respect to product offerings, to develop new products, or to become more productive? These types of questions can help identify performance areas that a business should examine. Answers will vary depending on the situation, but, as suggested by Figure 7.1, they will often include customer satisfaction/brand loyalty, product/service quality, brand/firm associations, relative cost, new product activity and manager/employee capability and performance.

Customer Satisfaction/Brand Loyalty

Perhaps the most important asset of many firms is the loyalty of the customer base. Measures of sales and market share are useful but potentially inaccurate indicators of how customers really feel about a firm. Such measures can reflect market inertia

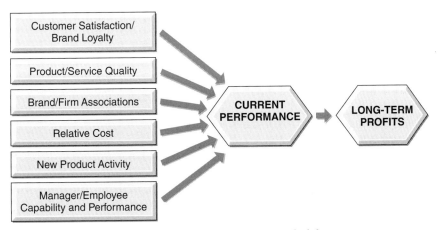

Figure 7.1 Performance measures reflecting long-term profitability

and are noisy, in part, because of competitor actions and market fluctuations. Measures of customer satisfaction and brand loyalty are much more sensitive and provide diagnostic value as well.

Guidelines for Measuring Satisfaction and Loyalty

First, problems and causes of dissatisfaction that may motivate customers to change brands or firms should be identified. Second, often the most sensitive and insightful information comes from those who have decided to leave a brand or firm. Thus, exit interviews for customers who have abandoned a brand can be productive. Third, there is a big difference between a brand or firm being liked and the absence of dissatisfaction. The size and intensity of the customer group that truly likes a brand or firm should be known. Fourth, measures should be tracked over time and compared with those of competitors. Relative comparisons and changes are most important.

Product and Service Quality

A product (or service) and its components should be critically and objectively compared both with the competition and with customer expectations and needs. How good a value is it? Can it really deliver superior performance? How does it compare with competitor offerings? How will it compare with competitor offerings in the future given competitive innovations? One common failing of firms is to avoid tough comparisons with a realistic assessment of competitors' current and potential offerings. Product and service quality are usually based on several critical dimensions that can be identified and measured over time. For example, an automobile manufacturer can measure defects, ability to perform to specifications, durability, repairability, and features. A bank might be concerned with waiting time, accuracy of transactions, and the quality of the customer experience. A computer manufacturer can examine relative performance specifications and product reliability as reflected by repair data. A business that requires better marketing of a good product line is very different from one that has basic product deficiencies.

Brand/Firm Associations

An often-overlooked asset of a brand or firm is what customers think of it. What are its associations? What is its perceived quality? Perceived quality, sometimes very different from actual quality, can be based on experience with past products or services and on quality cues, such as retailer types, pricing strategies, packaging, advertising, and typical customers. Is a brand or firm regarded as expert in a product or technology area (such as designing and making sailboats)? Innovative? Expensive? For the country club set? Is it associated with a country, a user type, or an application area (such as racing)? Such associations can be key strategic assets for a brand or firm. Associations can be monitored by regularly asking customers in focus groups to describe their use experiences and to tell what a brand or firm means to them. The identification of changes in important associations will likely emerge from such efforts. Structured surveys using a representative sample of customers can provide even more precise tracking information.

Figure 7.2   Relative cost versus relative performance – strategic implications

Relative Cost

A careful cost analysis of a product (or service) and its components, which can be critical when a strategy is dependent on achieving a cost advantage or cost parity, involves tearing down competitors' products and analysing their systems in detail. The Japanese consultant Ohmae suggested that such an analysis, when coupled with performance analysis, can lead to one of the four situations shown in Figure 7.2.[4] If a component such as a car's braking system or a bank's teller operation is both more expensive than and inferior to that of the competition, a strategic problem requiring change may exist. An analysis could show, however, that the component is such a small item both in terms of cost and customer impact that it should be ignored. If the component is competitively superior, however, a cost-reduction programmeme may not be the only appropriate strategy. A value analysis, in which the component's value to the customer is quantified, may suggest that the point of superiority could support a price increase or promotion campaign. If, on the other hand, a component is less expensive than that of the competition, but inferior, a value analysis might suggest that it be de-emphasised. Thus, for a car with a cost advantage but handling disadvantage, a company might de-emphasise its driving performance and position it as an economy car. An alternative is to upgrade this component. Conversely, if a component is both less expensive and superior, a value analysis may suggest that the component be emphasised, perhaps playing a key role in positioning and promotion strategies.

Sources of Cost Advantage

The many routes to cost advantage will be discussed in Chapter 10. They include economies of scale, the experience curve, product design innovations, and the use of a no-frills product offering. Each provides a different perspective to the concept of competing on the basis of a cost advantage.

Average Costing

In average costing, some elements of fixed or semi-variable costs are not carefully allocated but instead are averaged over total production. Thus, a plant may contain new machines and older machines that differ in the amount of support required for their operation. If support expenses are averaged over all output, the new machines will appear less profitable than they are and some inappropriate decisions could be precipitated.

Average costing can provide an opening for competitors to enter an otherwise secure market. For example, the J. B. Kunz Company, a maker of passbooks for banks, created a situation in which large-order customers were subsidising small-order customers because of average costing.[5] The cost system inflated the costs of processing very large orders and thus provided an opportunity for competitors to underbid Kunz on the very profitable large orders. A product line that is subsidising other lines is vulnerable, representing an opportunity to competitors and thus a potential threat to a business.

New Product Activity

Does the research and development operation generate a stream of new product concepts? Is the process from product concept to new product introduction well managed? Is there a track record of successful new products that have affected the product performance pro-file and market position? One measure of new product innovation is the numbers of patents awarded. In the UK in 2004, 1835 patents were granted. European companies like Schlumberger, a leading oilfield services provider, Ericsson and Nokia were among the top 10 companies awarded patents in the UK in 2004. All also have a good track record of getting their innovations into the marketplace. Time-to-market is another measure of successful innovations.[6]

Manager/Employee Capability and Performance

Also key to a firm's long-term prospects are the people who must implement strategies. Are the human resources in place to support current and future strategies? Do those who are added to the organisation match its needs in terms of types and quality or are there gaps that are not being filled? In contrast, a host of firms that enjoyed explosive growth could not develop the systems, people, and structure to cope with expansion and subsequently failed. An organisation should be evaluated not only on how well it obtains human resources but also on how well it nurtures them. A healthy organisation will consist of individuals who are motivated, challenged, fulfilled, and growing in their professions.

Each of these dimensions can be observed and measured by employee surveys and group discussions. Certainly the attitude of production workers was a key factor in the quality and cost advantage that Japanese automobile firms enjoyed throughout the past three decades. In service industries such as banking and fast foods, the ability to sustain positive employee performance and attitude is usually a key success factor.

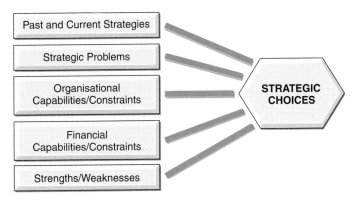

Figure 7.3   Determinants of strategic options and choices

DETERMINANTS OF STRATEGIC OPTIONS

Another approach to internal analysis is to consider the determinants of strategic options. What characteristics of a business make some options unfeasible without a major organisational change? What characteristic will be pivotal in choosing among strategic options? Again, the answers to these questions will depend on the situation, but as noted in Figure 7.3, five areas warrant close scrutiny.

Past and Current Strategies

To understand the bases of past performance and attempt to sort out new options it is important to be able to make an accurate profile of past and current strategies. Sometimes a strategy has evolved into something very different from what was assumed. For example, a firm positioned itself as an innovator and spent heavily on research and development to repeat its early breakthrough innovation. However, an honest analysis of its operations over the previous two decades indicated that its success was based on manufacturing strengths and scale economies. Other companies had introduced almost all the meaningful innovations in the industry during that period. A recognition that the R&D effort had been successful in improving product features, reliability, and cost, but not in developing any technological breakthroughs, was helpful in structuring strategic options.

BENCHMARKING

Comparing the performance of a business component with others is called benchmarking. The goal is to generate specific ideas for improvement, and also to define standards at which to aim. One target may be competitors: what cost and performance levels are they achieving, and how? Knowing your deficits with respect to the competition is the first step to developing programmes to eliminate them. Another target is best practice companies. Thus many companies compare themselves against Disney in terms of delivering consistent service, or Dell as the standard for e-commerce operations and customer support. Looking outside one's own industry is often a way to break away from the status quo and thereby create a real advantage.

Strategic Problems

Another relevant and helpful construct is the strategic problem – that is, a problem with strategic implications. For example, when the Mercedes A-Class was introduced to the market Mercedes failed to spot a problem with the cars high centre of gravity. A reporter from a Swedish motor journal rolled over while test driving it, leading customers across Europe to cancel their orders. This required Mercedes to make strategic moves to recall cars and fit (for free) ESP systems and different tyres to rectify the problem. A strategic problem differs from a weakness or liability, which is the absence of an asset (such as good location) or competence (for example, new-product introduction skills). A business copes over time with a weakness or liability by adjusting strategies. Strategic problems, in contrast, need to be addressed aggressively and corrected even if the fix is difficult and expensive.

Organisational Capabilities/Constraints

The internal organisation of a company – its structure, systems, people, and culture – can be an important source of both strengths and weaknesses. One of BMW's strengths is that during a car development process all project team members are relocated to one area to ensure proximity to facilitate car development and efficient communication.

Internal organisation can affect the cost and even the feasibility of some strategies. There must be a fit between a strategy and the elements of an organisation. If the strategy does not fit well, making it work might be expensive or even impossible. For example, an established centralised organisation with a background oriented to one industry may have difficulty implementing a diversification strategy requiring a decentralised organisation and an entrepreneurial thrust. Internal organisation is considered in more detail in Chapter 16, which discusses strategy implementation and the concept of fit.

Financial Resources and Constraints

Ultimately, judgements need to be made about whether or not to invest in a business or withdraw cash from it. A similar decision needs to be made about the aggregate of businesses. Should a firm increase its net investment or decrease it by holding liquid assets or returning cash to shareholders or debt holders? A basic consideration is the firm's ability to supply investment resources. A financial analysis to determine probable, actual, and potential sources and uses of funds can help provide an estimate of this ability. A cash flow analysis projects the cash that will be available from operations and depreciation and other assets. In particular, a growth strategy, even if it simply involves greater penetration of the existing product market, usually requires working capital and other assets, which may exceed the funds available from operations. The appendix to this chapter provides a discussion of how to conduct a cash flow analysis.

In addition, funds may be obtained either by debt or equity financing. To determine the desirability and feasibility of either option, an analysis of the balance sheet may be needed. In particular, the current debt structure and a firm's ability to support it will be relevant. The appendix also reviews some financial ratios that are helpful in this regard. A division or subsidiary may need to consider how much support and involvement it can expect from a parent organisation, particularly in regard to its investment proposals. The scenario of multiple businesses all planning investments that, in the aggregate, are far beyond a firm's willingness and ability to support, is all too common. A realistic appraisal of a firm's resources can make strategy development more effective.

Organisational Strengths and Weaknesses

A key step in internal analysis is to identify the strengths and weaknesses of an organisation that are based on its assets and competencies. In fact, much internal analysis is motivated by the need to detect strengths and weaknesses. There are, of course, many possible sources of strengths and weaknesses. In Chapter 4, methods to identify such sources are presented; in Chapter 8, we discuss how assets and competencies become the bases of sustainable competitive advantages.

FROM ANALYSIS TO STRATEGY

In internal analysis, organisational strengths and weaknesses need to be not only identified but also related to competitors and the market. Strategic market management, as noted in Chapter 1, has four interrelated elements. The first is to determine areas in which to invest or disinvest. Investment could go to growth areas, such as new product markets or programmemes designed to create new strength areas, or to existing ones. The second is the value proposition offered to customers. The third is the development of assets and competencies to provide the bases of competitive advantage. The fourth is the specification and implementation of functional area strategies and programmes such as product policy, manufacturing strategy, distribution choices, and so on.

In making strategic decisions, inputs from a variety of assessments are relevant, as the last several chapters have already made clear. However, the core of any strategic decision should be based on three types of assessments. The first concerns organisational strengths and weaknesses. The second evaluates competitor strengths, weaknesses, and strategies, because an organisation's strength is of less value if it is neutralised by a competitor's strength or strategy. The third assesses the competitive context, the customers and their needs, the market, and the market environment. These assessments focus on determining how attractive the selected market will be, given the strategy selected.

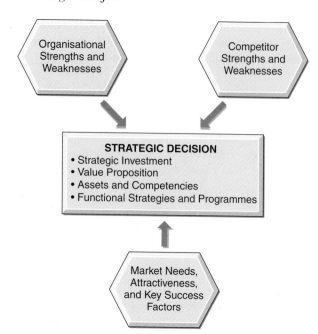

Figure 7.4   Structuring strategic decisions

The goal is to develop a strategy that exploits business strengths and competitor weaknesses and neutralises business weaknesses and competitor strengths. The ideal is to compete in a healthy, growing industry with a strategy based on strengths that are unlikely to be acquired or neutralised by competitors. Figure 7.4 summarises how these three assessments combine to influence strategy.

Vodafone's decision to sell its Japanese business in 2006 illustrates these strategic principles.[7] Vodafone had originally entered the Japanese market through the acquisition of J-phone, Japans third place player in 2001. The logic of the acquisition was twofold: to take advantage of Vodafone's global economies of scale to grow in the Japanese market and to use the advanced business model of the Japanese market to drive it's activities in other markets. The latter worked well but in the former problems arose. Firstly, plans to switch the Japanese market to the 3G technology used in Europe did not work, consumers were unenthusiastic about the handsets on offer and so Vodafone had to develop a Japan specific range of phones, undermining the economies of scale aspect of their business model. In competitive terms Vodafone faced two strong incumbents in NTTDoCoMo and KDDI and the Japanese government created three new mobile phone licences and introduced new legislation to allow consumers keep their numbers when they switched providers, a move likely to encourage switching behaviour. Finally, the market for phone services is changing rapidly. Vodafone had built its strategy on being a global mobile only provider. In 2001 this looked like a winning strategy but by 2006 it seemed as if the market was questionable as key success factor had switched to being able to provide customers with converged services of mobile, fixed line, broadband and TV. Faced with such a decision environment the move to sell the Japanese business offered an opportunity for Vodafone to re-evaluate its overall position and to find a more competitive way to deploy it's assets and competencies.

BUSINESS PORTFOLIO ANALYSIS

Business portfolio analysis provides a structured way to evaluate business units on two key dimensions: the attractiveness of the market involved and the strength of the firm's position in that market. The result is a graphical portrayal of the various business units on these key dimensions. The analysis and representation naturally lead to a resource allocation decision. Which businesses merit investment and which should be spun off? These are very basic strategic investment issues. The resource allocation question is usually very difficult organisationally. In a decentralised organisation, it is natural for the managers of cash-generating businesses to control the available cash that funds investment opportunities and for each business to be required or encouraged to fund its own growth. As a result, however, a fast-growing business with enormous potential but low profit or even losses will often be starved of needed cash. The irony is that businesses involving mature products may have inferior investment alternatives, but because cash flow is plentiful, their investments will still be funded. The net effect is that available cash is channelled to areas of low potential and withheld from the most attractive areas. A business portfolio analysis helps force the issue of which businesses should receive the available cash.

The Market Attractiveness–Business Position Matrix

Figure 7.5 shows the market attractiveness–business position matrix into which each business unit is to be positioned. The concept is credited to strategy efforts of General Electric planners and the consulting firm McKinsey & Company. Consider first market attractiveness, the horizontal axis. The basic question is: how attractive is the market for a competitor in terms of the cash flow that it will generate? Scaling a market should start with the Porter five-factor model of industry attractiveness (Chapter 5). However, the other elements of the market analysis as well as the analyses of customers, competitors, and the environment of the business should also contribute. A set of nine factors is set forth in the figure as a point of departure. The actual factors will depend on what is relevant for the context. Consider next the business-position assessment, as shown on the vertical axis. The business position should be based on the internal analysis of the business and, in particular, on an evaluation of its assets and competencies relative to those of its competitors. Eleven dimensions are suggested in the figure, but an appropriate set will need to be generated for each particular context.

Applying the Matrix

The market attractiveness–business position matrix is a formal, structured way to match a firm's strengths with market opportunities. One implication is that when

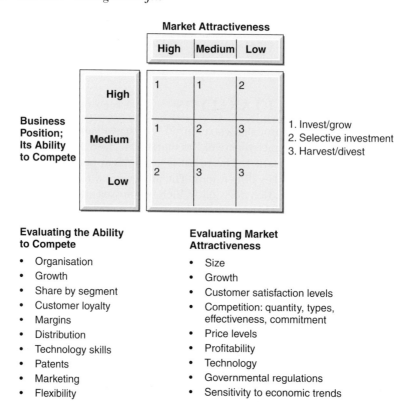

Figure 7.5   The market attractiveness–business position matrix

both firm position and market attractiveness are positive, as in the boxes marked 1 in Figure 7.5, a firm should probably invest and attempt to grow. When the assessment is more negative, as in the boxes marked 3, however, the recommendation would be either harvest or divest. For the three boxes marked 2, a selective decision to invest would be made only when there was a specific reason to believe the investment would be profitable. A useful exercise is to attempt to predict whether either your position or the attractiveness of the market will change if it is assumed the current strategy is followed. A predicted movement to another cell can signal the need to consider a change in strategy.

THE BCG GROWTH-SHARE MATRIX

Portfolio analysis started in the mid-1960s with the BCG growth-share matrix which was pioneered and used extensively by the BCG consulting group. The concept was to position each business within a firm on the two-dimensional matrix shown in Figure 7.6. The market-share dimension (actually the ratio of share to that of the largest competitor) was regarded as pivotal because it reflected cost advantages resulting from scale economies and manufacturing experience. The growth dimension was considered the best single indicator of market strength.

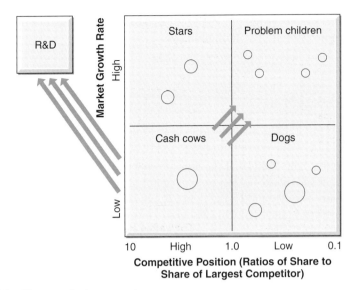

Figure 7.6   The growth-share matrix

The BCG growth-share matrix is associated with a colourful cast of characters representing strategy recommendations. The stars (the high-share, high-growth quadrant) are important to the current businesses and should receive resources if needed. Cash cows (the high-share, low-growth quadrant) should be the source of substantial amounts of cash that can be channelled to other business areas. Dogs (low-growth, low-share quadrant) are potential cash traps because they perpetually absorb cash. Problem children (low-share, high-growth quadrant) are assumed to have heavy cash needs before they can convert into stars and eventually cash cows. The BCG growth-share model was very influential in its day. It made visible the issue of allocation across business units, that some businesses should generate cash that supports others. It also introduced the experience curve into strategy and showed that, under some conditions, market share could lead to experience-curve-based advantage. The experience curve is discussed in more detail in Chapter 10.

In structuring strategies, the following are among the logical alternatives:

- *Invest to hold.* Attempt to stop erosion in position by investing enough to compensate for environmental and competitive forces.
- *Invest to penetrate.* Aggressively attempt to move the position up, even at the sacrifice of earnings.
- *Invest to rebuild.* Attempt to regain a previously held position that was lost by a milking strategy that, for whatever reason, is no longer appropriate.
- *Selective investment.* Attempt to strengthen position in some segments and let position weaken in other segments.

- *Low investment.* Attempt to harvest the business, drawing cash out and cutting investment to a minimum.
- *Divestiture.* Sell or liquidate the business.

KEY LEARNINGS

- Sales and profitability analysis provide an evaluation of past strategies and an indication of the current market viability of a product line.
- Shareholder value holds that the flow of profits emanating from an investment should exceed the cost of capital (which is the weighted average of the cost of equity and cost of debt). Routes to achieving shareholder value – such as downsizing, reducing assets employed, and outsourcing – can be risky when they undercut assets and competences.
- Performance assessment should go beyond financials to include such dimensions as customer satisfaction/brand loyalty, product/service quality, brand/firm associations, relative cost, new product activity, and manager/employee capability and performance.
- Five business characteristics limit or drive strategic choice: past and current strategy, strategic problems, organisational capabilities and constraints, financial resources and constraints, and strengths and weaknesses.
- Business portfolio analysis provides a structured way to evaluate businesses on two key dimensions: the attractiveness of the market involved, and the strength of the firm's position in that market. The analysis and representation lead naturally to a resource allocation decision.

FOR DISCUSSION

1. Explain shareholder value analysis. Why might it help firms? Why might it result in bad decisions?

2. Explain the market attractiveness–business position matrix. What role should it have in strategy development? Choose an industry (such as confectionary, hotels or alcoholic beverages) and attempt to identify brands that are high or low on each dimension.

3. Look at the quotations that begin Chapters 3 through 7. Which one do you find the most insightful? Why? Under what circumstances would its implications not hold?

4. In implementing a market attractiveness-business position matrix, what metrics are likely to be applied in any industry context? Pick an industry and determine if specialised metrics would be needed.

NOTES

1. Rachel Tiplady (2006) The ascent of Airness Apparel. *Business Week* online, 2 May 2006. http://www.businessweek.com/globalbiz/content/may2006/gb20060501_745574.htm?chan=search

2. For an excellent review of the risks of shareholder value see Allan A. Kennedy (2000) *The End of Shareholder Value*, Cambridge, MA: Perseus Publishing. For a marketing perspective on the same issue see Peter V. Doyle (2000) *Value Based Marketing*, John Wiley & Sons, Chichester.

3. Philippe Haspeslagh, Tomo Noda and Fares Boulos (2001) It's not just about the numbers. *Harvard Business Review*, July–August, pp. 65–73.

4. Kenichi Ohmae (1982) *The Mind of the Strategist*, Penguin Books, New York, p. 26.

5. J. B. Kunz (1977) *Company A, Case 9-577-115*, Intercollegiate Case Clearing House, Boston.

6. IBM, *Red Herring*, November, 1999, pp. 120–8.

7. Not-so-big is beautiful. *The Economist*, 9 May 2006. Calling for a rethink, *The Economist*, 26 January 2006.

APPENDIX: PROJECTING CASH FLOW – SOURCES AND USES OF FUNDS

A projection of cash flow during the strategy horizon is essential to determine what base of cash resources is available and what cash needs will be required. At the outset, a reasonable baseline assumption might be that current strategies and trends will extend into the near future. It can be helpful also to project the flow of funds given both optimistic and pessimistic scenarios. The impact of changes in strategies and the introduction of new strategies can then be determined. Figure 7.7 shows a simplified balance sheet and the major categories of sources and uses of funds. It will provide a context in which to discuss the principal elements of a cash flow analysis. As the sources and uses of funds are presented, some useful balance-sheet ratios will be introduced. They provide measures of the financial health of a firm in terms of its assets and debt structure. As such, they are helpful in making judgements concerning the desirability and feasibility of raising money through debt or equity financing.

The first item under the sources and uses of funds in Figure 7.7 is changes in net working capital. Working capital is defined as current assets less current liabilities (generally liabilities under one year). The current ratio is one way of measuring the adequacy of working capital:

$$current\ ratio = current\ assets/current\ liabilities$$

The most desirable ratio will depend, of course, on the nature of a business. In particular, firms with large amounts of assets in inventories may require a higher ratio. Another ratio that deletes inventories is called the quick or acid-test ratio: As sales grow, of course, working capital will have to grow also so that it will continue to be adequate for supporting operations.

Balance Sheet, December 31 (Millions)

Current Assets		6.0	Current Liabilities		3.0
• Cash, receivables, investments	3.5		• Accounts payable	2.0	
			• Other	1.0	
• Inventory	2.5				
			Long-term Liabilities		2.0
Fixed Assets		6.0			
• Property, plant, and equipment	10.0		**Equity**		7.0
			• Capital stock	4.0	
• Less accumulated depreciations	4.0		• Retained earnings and other	3.0	
Total Assets		12.0	**Total Liabilities and Equity**		12.0

Projected Sources and Uses of Funds

Sources of Funds		Uses of Funds	
• Decrease in net working capital	0.0	• Increase in net working capital	1.0
• Sale of fixed assets	0.0	• Purchase of fixed assets	2.5
• Issue long-term liabilities	2.0	• Retire long-term liabilities	0.0
• Sell capital stock	0.0	• Buy back capital stock	0.0
• Operations: net income	1.0	• Operations: net losses	0.0
• Depreciation	0.5	• Dividends	0.0
Total Sources of Funds	3.5	**Total Uses of Funds**	3.5

Figure 7.7   Balance sheet and sources and uses of funds statement

The second item concerning the sources and uses of funds in Figure 7.7 is the sale or purchase of fixed assets. The acquisition of fixed assets might be divided into those necessary for maintaining current operation levels and those needed for more discretionary expenditures to generate growth. Again, the analysis of the sources and uses of funds should reflect the implications of any proposed growth strategy.

The third category is the issue or retirement of long-term debt. In determining the appropriate debt level, useful ratios are:

$$\text{quick ratio} = \text{current assets less inventory/current liabilities}$$
$$\text{total debt-to-equity ratio} = \text{total liabilities/equity}$$
$$\text{debt-to-equity ratio} = \text{long-term liabilities/equity}$$

Of course, the higher these ratios are, the larger the interest burden in a downturn and the lower the ability to obtain new debt in an emergency. The optimal level will depend on the ability of the earnings to carry added interest expense, the policy of a firm toward debt and its associated risk, the return expected on future investment, and the debt-to-equity ratio of competing firms. The use of funds obtained from debt financing will be relevant for determining how much debt to undertake. If the funds are to be used to buy a firm, the structure of the resulting combined balance sheet and funds flow must be considered. The fourth category shown in Figure 7.7 is changes in capital stock. To what extent is it feasible and desirable to raise capital through the sale of stock? Conversely, it may be beneficial to use funds to buy stock if the stock is undervalued compared with alternative investments.

Finally, there are the sources of funds from operations, which provide the base from which investment planning will begin. Depreciation expense is added to, and dividends to be paid are subtracted from, net income. Depreciation is an expense item that does not involve cash outflow. Thus, depreciation is actually a source of funds. Obviously, the net income from operations will interact with other sources. For example, increasing debt will increase interest expense, which will reduce the funds available for future operations. And the ability to raise stock may depend on dividend policy. Furthermore, investment or disinvestment in assets will affect depreciation in future years.

In evaluating the balance sheet, considerable judgment and reservation may be appropriate. There may be bad debts among the reported receivables, the depreciation may not reflect plant deterioration, and assets and liabilities may have market values that differ substantially from their reported book value. Inflation effects contribute to the interpretation difficulties. Thus, it might be appropriate to interpret or adjust the ratios and cash-flow projection accordingly.

CASE CHALLENGES FOR PART II

CASE STUDY I: A MATURE INDUSTRY WITH DYNAMIC NICHES: THE IRISH SOFT DRINKS INDUSTRY

The total Irish soft drinks market consists of several subcategories including carbonates, bottled water, energy and sports drinks and fruit juices. After seeing an average growth of approximately 7 % per year between 1994 and 2002, the market has remained relatively stagnant over the past few years. Although the industry is facing new and challenging obstacles as health becomes a consumer concern, companies are continuing to perform relatively well.

The chilled juice, the bottled water market and sports and functional drinks are the fastest growing segments of the soft drinks market and are experiencing strong growth, poor carbonated drinks category sales in recent years have contributed to stagnation in the overall soft drinks market. Carbonated drinks grew at a rate of 7 % in the four years to the end of 2001 but began to decline after that with the emergence of a more health conscious Irish nation as customers became concerned with obesity and health issues in general. The Irish carbonated soft drinks market is dominated by several strong competitors with colas and diet carbonates dominating the sector. Coca-Cola is the number one selling grocery brand in Ireland targeting teens and young adults. In 2005, Coca-Cola held 32 % of the Irish grocery carbonates market and was valued at €114 million. Diet Coke is the number one diet carbonate drink in Ireland and accounts for nearly half of all diet carbonated soft drinks sold. The brand grew by over 40 % between 2000 and 2005 and held 12 % of the carbonates market in 2005. In general it has outperformed competitors in the Irish soft drinks market and is growing faster than the carbonates market as a whole. In 2005 their marketing emphasis shifted from a female-only targeting strategy to a unisex strategy to recognise that 50 % of their consumers are male. In response to changing consumer attitudes on health Diet Coke's campaigns focus heavily on the 'sugar-free' message in order to curb a decrease in carbonate sales. This is also a strategy that is currently being pursued by Pepsi in promoting their Pepsi Max product. Pepsi Max is expected to grow in light of consumer health concerns by emphasising their 'Don't worry – there's no sugar' selling proposition. Pepsi's regular cola drink is a strong performer in the Irish carbonated drinks market with 12 % growth in 2004. Lemon and lime is the second most popular flavour of carbonates in the Irish soft drinks market behind colas and held 25 % of the category in 2005. 7up is Ireland's favourite lemon and lime drink and second biggest selling soft drink with several product lines launched in 2005 including 7up Ice and Diet 7up which was rebranded as 7up Free. Sprite, the number one lemon and lime brand worldwide, grew by 9 % in Ireland in 2005 behind 7up. Their diet product, Sprite Zero, is one of the most successful beverage innovations and is the fastest growing diet brand, growing 30 % annually. Launched in 2004, the brand has become extremely popular and has driven huge growth in the diet lemon-and-lime beverages category. Fanta Orange is the fastest growing brand in orange flavoured beverages and increased its volume share by 2 % in 2005 by being one of the most innovative brands by introducing of the new flavours.

Their main competitors in the orange flavour sector are Finches Orange and C&C Ireland's Club Orange brand.

As Irish consumers have become more health-conscious and time poor, fruit juice has become a popular refreshment alternative to carbonates, providing both refreshment and nutrition throughout the day, not just for breakfast. Fruit juices, particularly smoothies, have become very popular in Ireland with 53% of Irish people in 2004 drinking fruit juice daily and an increase in the number of juice and smoothie bars due to the consumer focus on health and obesity issues. The fruit-juice industry in Ireland has many competitors and is such an attractive, lucrative market that larger soft drink companies like PepsiCo and Coca-Cola are attempting to enter it to counter slow growth in the traditional carbonated soft drinks market. However, the Irish juice market already has several established competitors. Tropicana was Ireland's number one selling chilled juice brand with the chilled juice category worth €51 million in 2005, growing at 9% annually in comparison to the ambient juice category which grew at just 0.3%; the diluteables juice category which grew at 0.6%; and the carbonates category which declined by 3.8%. Tropicana was the first company in the juice market in Ireland to use 'Not From Concentrate' juice, which has become a driver of growth in the category. This sector has boosted chilled juice growth and accounts for nearly half of chilled fruit juice category sales. Sqeez was the number one selling ambient fruit juice brand in Ireland in 2005, with 40% share of value, worth €27 million, outselling all other competitors. Fruice is a premium juice produced by Coca-Cola Bottlers Ireland and in 2005 was the fastest growing juice brand on the Irish market with a share growth of 24%. Ocean Spray is one of the most popular and fastest growing juice drinks available in Ireland with 58% share of the cranberry juice market in 2005. Capri-Sun is the number one single serve, ready to drink juice drink in Ireland, with 23% value share in 2005. MiWadi is the biggest selling cordial in Ireland with 37.4% share of the cordial market in 2004, competing against other diluteables like Ribena. It experienced strong growth in the 'No added sugar' range, reflecting consumer health concerns.

In Ireland people are concerned about their health and strive to get fit. This 'get fit' obsession has ensured that energy drinks and sports drinks have become a huge area of growth in recent years, with Ireland's energy drinks sector experiencing the highest level of consumption per capita in the world, after Japan. While the initial growth experienced at the beginning of the millennium has slowed slightly, the energy and sports drinks sector continues to increase, promoting investment from drinks giants.

Emerging from the original energy drinks market are three sub-sectors in the Irish market. The energy drinks market, sports drinks market and the recovery drinks market. The energy drinks market in Ireland consists of several dominant brands. The Lucozade Energy brand is currently the number one in the Irish market and number two within the carbonates market. However, Lucozade Energy's position in the Irish market has come under threat from competitors due to the attractiveness and growth opportunity that it represents. Red Bull is a carbonated energy drink and functional beverage that was launched in Europe in 1987 and is now one of the top functional energy drinks in Ireland. In this market there are also a number of smaller competitors vying for market share; C&C (Ireland) Ltd introduced

Club Energise to their product line in 2005 to compete with Lucozade Energy. BPM Energy, launched in 2003, is also a key player in the energy drinks category in Ireland. The sports drink market in Ireland is also dominated by a few brands; it is the fastest growing category of the soft drinks market and has experienced extraordinary success over recent years. Lucozade introduced Lucozade Sport positioned as a sports drink containing glucose in the early 1990s which is now Ireland's number one sports drinks. In 2003, C&C entered the sports drink category with their Club Energise Sport product which has performed exceptionally well in the market. In its first year it outperformed the market and its international competitors to move to the number two position in the sports drink category, stealing market share from Lucozade Energy Sport, its key international competitor. Inside a year it had 18.6% of the €37 million sports drink market which was valued at €6.9 million and took 14% of Lucozade's market share in a year. Powerade has become very successful in the sports drink category gaining a market share of 16.6% in its first year on the market. C&C also developed a new product called Club Energise Sport Recovery 20, the first protein based sports drink in Ireland, therefore creating a new sector in the sports drinks market.

There have been a number of social and economic factors that have continued to drive growth in the bottled water market. In Ireland bottled water was classified as a luxury product in the past but in recent years shifting consumer attitudes and demands for a healthy soft-drink option has created an acceptance of buying water and resulted in steady growth in the market. There is still the potential for massive growth in the water market in Ireland as spending on bottled water is set to continue to increase. In 2002 Irish people consumed 83 million litres of bottled water and this is set to increase to 125 million litres by 2007, which will make bottled water the category expected to increase most in the soft drinks market. Ballygowan is positioned as a premium brand with a share of approximately 50% of total market volume, making it the brand leader in the mineral water market across all channels. Volvic is the number two bottled water brand within the still-water market in Ireland. Deep RiverRock is Ireland's fastest growing water brand. San Pellegrino was launched into the Irish market in 2001, as the only naturally carbonated water in the market. Evian is the number one natural mineral water in the world. Lucozade has positioned their Lucozade Sport Hydro Active product in a niche in the bottled water category which continues to grow.

FOR DISCUSSION

1. Conduct a thorough analysis of this industry's customers, competitors, market, and environment from the perspective of Coca-Cola. What are the key strategic questions? What additional information would you like to obtain? How would you obtain it? What are the threats and opportunities? In particular, address the following issues:

a. How is the market segmented? What are the key customer motivations and unmet needs? What are the similarities and differences among the segments? How might companies link customer motivations to value propositions?

b. Identify the competitors. Who are the most direct competitors? The indirect competitors? Substitute products? What are the strategic groups?

c. What are the market trends? The growth submarkets? The key success factors?

d. What are the environmental trends that will affect the industry? Generate two or three viable future scenarios.

2. How would you go about evaluating emerging submarkets? What criteria would you use to enter each?

3. What innovation would support a new entry? How should entries be branded? Can brands such as Red Bull, V and Club Energise and others be leveraged?

4. Is there potential for any of the products or brands in this market to expand into other areas, drinks and food products with trends like diet and reduced sugar consumption dominating the market?

5. At what stage is the soft drinks market relative to the product-life cycle? What strategies can be used to extend the life cycle? Do you see any dramatic changes on the horizon?

6. Develop a positioning map and note if there are any obvious customer needs that are currently not being met.

CASE STUDY II: COMPETING AGAINST INDUSTRY GIANTS

Competing Against Tesco

Tesco is the largest supermarket retailer in the UK and the fourth largest retailer in the world behind Wal-Mart, Carrefour and Home Depot. Since 1999 it has been the UK's most profitable retailer.[1] At the beginning of 2006 it had 30.6% of the market share up 29% from the previous year, with gross turnover for the year ending 2006 up 13% to £41.8 billion and pre-tax profits of £2.2 billion. In 2006 it had 2334 stores (including 1780 in Britain), 360000 employees worldwide and is the world's biggest online grocery retailer. It is estimated that over £1 in every £8 of UK retail sales is spent in Tesco.[2]

Tesco was established in London by Jack Cohen, a veteran from the First World War who, upon returning from military service, opened a stall in East London in 1919. Gradually his business began to grow to include markets all over London. He also began wholesale trade and the first line of Cohen brand goods placed on the market was tea. Five years later the first Tesco brand appeared. This was the name that the company would later take on – it contains the initials of the owner of the firm, Mr. T. E. Stockwell, who supplied the firm with tea, and the first two letters of Jack Cohen's surname.

In 1929 Cohen opened the first Tesco store in North London. In 1934 he purchased land to construct a modern head office and warehouse that employed then new ways of materials inventory control, a first for the country. During the Second World War, Jack Cohen once again demonstrated vision when he launched food rationing (before the government did) to make sure everyone received an equal food supply.

In 1947 Tesco was floated on the London Stock Exchange, the first Tesco self-service store opened in 1948, in 1956 the first supermarket opened in Essex, the first superstore opened in 1968 in West Sussex. They began selling petrol in 1974 and in 1995 introduced the loyalty Clubcard which helped push their market share and is the UK's most popular loyalty reward scheme with ten million accounts. Tesco began its quest for international expansion in 1994 when they took over Scottish supermarket chain William Low and then proceeded to expand into Central Europe, Ireland and East Asia. In its international expansion it has used both acquisition, such as the purchase of the Quinnsworth and Crazy Prices stores in Ireland in 1997, and joint ventures with local retailers, for example, in Thailand with Tesco Lotus.

Tesco began specialising in food, later moving into areas like clothing, consumer electronics, financial services, internet services, customer telecoms and fuel services. They expanded the company's services in the 1990s and 2000s by using a joint venture strategy. For example, in 1994 Tesco began operating an Internet service, Tesco.com, and in 2001 it became involved with a US Internet grocery retailing company called GroceryWorks. Today it has the world's biggest online market, offering not only just Tesco grocery products but also a wide range of services from telecom services, financial services to extra services offered in partnership with other companies like flights, holidays, electricity, gas, music and DVD rental. In 2003 it launched a UK telecoms division by partnering with existing telecoms.

For example Tesco Mobile was launched as a joint venture with O2. In 2004 they launched a broadband service as a joint partnership with NTL. By April 2006 Tesco announced that it had signed up one and a half million customers for a telecom account which included mobile, fixed line and broadband accounts. Tesco also entered into a joint venture with Royal Bank of Scotland to provide customers with a financial service package called Tesco Personal Finance. There are 11 financial products including credit cards, insurance, loans and mortgages and in 2006 they managed over 5 million customer account.

The founder, Jack Cohen, was determined to drive people to patronise his stores by using particular strategies. He signed Tesco up to Green Shield Stamps in 1963, which was a sales promotion technique used in the UK in the 1960s and 1970s. However customers began to realise that although they were accumulating stamps, grocery prices were being increased in supermarkets to cover the cost of the scheme. So Tesco abandoned this approach for a simpler value-for-money approach using the money invested in Green Shield stamps to implement cost reductions.

Initially Jack Cohen's successful approach was to use the selling proposition 'pile it high and sell it cheap' but by the middle of the 1970s this approach had caused Tesco cost problems and the company was beginning to overstretch itself. Middle-class customers were also beginning to have a poor perception of Tesco stores as a result of this which, in the late 1970s, Tesco faced a crisis over the negative image that was associated with the brand – so much so that consultants advised that they rebrand their store name. It did not accept this as an option and the managing director at the time, Ian MacLaurin, instead fought to change the company strategy and revitalise the brand. Over the past two or three decades, using a range of innovative schemes, Tesco managed to develop its brand name and grow to become the UK's leading supermarket chain in 2006.

The key to Tesco's success and growth over the past three decades lies in its change of strategy and image. Firstly, it needed to appeal to all segments of the market, lower, middle and upper, with an 'inclusive offer' strategy, which is based on a plain vision of selling high quality goods at a reasonable price to cater for all segments of the population. Tesco managed to achieve this by offering four differing levels of its own-brand products. The 'Finest' range of premium products was introduced in 1998 and in 2006 this comprised of approximately 2 300 product lines. This was followed by the 'Tesco Organic' range which was introduced in 1986 and in 2006 extended to 1 400 product lines. Following this was the 'Tesco Healthy Living' range which in 2006 had 500 product lines. Finally the 'Value' range designed to appeal to the price conscious customer in 2006 encompassed 2 200 product lines.[3] By developing a wide range of own brands they succeeded in changing customers perceptions toward own brand products which allows Tesco to achieve higher profits margins than it does for other branded products. Secondly, the company mantra has shifted from maximising shareholder value to maximising customer value. While the underlying objective is naturally to make higher profits this is specifically done while focusing on customer service. They believe that they need to continuously improve the standard of services provided and respond to customers' needs. Their offers reflect trends of a new lifestyle, stressing health and the environment both in relation to customer, employees and business partners. Thirdly, Tesco developed a diversification strategy based on four main areas: innovating and expanding in the core UK grocery market and into areas like convenience stores. Innovating and expanding into non-food businesses like consumer electronics, clothing, health, beauty, CDs, DVDs and has even developed their non-food Finest and Value ranges. Innovating and expanding into retail services like personal Finance, Telecoms and utilities by entering into joint ventures with major players in these industry sectors. Finally expanding internationally which accounted for 20 % of sales or £7 billion in 2005 with plans for further expansion into the US market in 2006.[4]

Tesco has faced controversy in the UK and has been targeted by people who believe that supermarkets have a negative affect on suppliers, smaller competitors and local farmers.[5] Recently supermarkets, particularly the big four in the UK – Tesco, ASDA, Sainsbury's and Morrison's – have been scrutinised because of a belief that they have become too powerful despite lower than ever before prices for consumers. They have faced three inquiries over seven years.[6] In 2000/2001 a regulatory inquiry into the big four's market domination in the UK found no evidence of anti-competitive behaviour leaving retailers to expand as they wanted. In 2006 there were two fresh inquires initiated. In March 2006 there was an investigation into the big four's dominance of the UK's grocery retail market which is estimated to be worth £95 billion annually.[7] The second inquiry in 2006 looks set to span two years and pay particular attention to the planning regime of supermarkets and the accusations that supermarkets buy up plots of land and leave them idle to create barriers to entry and prevent competitors entering the market.[8] But what does the future hold for Tesco? For years retail companies have battled it out over price and value propositions. However, recently competition has moved from price to the environment, with all the chains trying to prove their green credentials and caring image. The new consumer trend of being more concerned about the environment is having a significant impact on Tesco's strategies. For example, in May 2006 Tesco unveiled a 10-point plan aimed at changing the image of the giant into one of a good neighbour and improve its green credentials in light of mounting customer concern over the giant supermarket group's power. The new 'community plan' outlines initiatives to sponsor youth football and offer more local produce and biodegradable carrier bags. Tesco continues to make regular acquisitions to drive its international expansion and plans to enter the US market on the West Coast in 2007. But how will Tesco measure up in direct competition with US giants like Wal-Mart and Home Depot?

For Discussion

Supermarkets in the UK must expect a more competitive Tesco in the future and these supermarkets need to understand Tesco and how it competes. What strategies that led to Tesco's success could be used in the future? What future direction is Tesco likely to pursue? Are there plans to expand their business into new industries and product lines? Consider two competitors in the UK market, ASDA and Sainsbury's, who need to design a strategy that will help them increase their industry market share and compete with Tesco.

ASDA

Asda became a subsidiary of Wal-Mart in 1999 and is the UK's second largest retailer.[9] It was founded in 1965 by a group of Yorkshire farmers to provide an outlet for their farm produce. As other supermarkets moved upmarket in the 1970s and 1980s Asda remained relatively focussed on low prices. In the late 1980s Asda tried to expand its product offering to help it compete, most significant was including a clothing line. This started slowly. In the early 1990s Asda was on the brink of collapse until the introduction of aggressive marketing practices saw sales increase and by 1995 it had become the UK's number three supermarket group. Instead of expanding internationally Asda stayed in the UK and focused on building its range. In 1999 Asda was acquired by Wal-Mart and in 2000 an Asda hypermarket in Bristol was refurbished to become the first Wal-Mart store in the UK, with two more launched in 2001. In 2006 Asda had a market share of 16.6%, there were 21 Asda/Wal-Mart Supercentres, 234 Asda Living Stores, 10 Georges and 24 depots (distribution centres) and it employed 150 000 employees. In May 2006 Asda announced plans to expand into the estate agency sector.

Sainsbury's

Sainsbury's was once the market leader in the UK but it is now ranked third largest retailer having been overtaken by Tesco in 1995 and Asda in 2003.[10] Sainsbury's was established as a partnership by John James Sainsbury and his wife in 1869 in London, initially selling basic products like eggs and bacon. In 1922 it was incorporated as a private company and in 1973 it floated on the stock exchange. In the 1980s the company began to expand overseas when it acquired the US chain, Shaw's.

However, in the early 1990s Sainsbury's expansion threatened to take away Sainsbury's competitive edge in its core markets and the company experienced some difficulties. This, combined with Tesco's aggressive strategy, saw Sainsbury's lose its number-one spot. The company's fortunes improved after the launch of a recovery programme in 2004.

At the beginning of 2006 it held 16.3% of the market up 1% from the previous year. It had 752 outlets, profits were up 12% to £267 million, it was attracting 1.5 million new customers a week, like-for-like sales were ahead 3.7%, it was gaining ground on Asda and was expected to oust them as the UK's number-two grocer. Sainsbury's had historically adopted an approach of retaining a middle-upper class image with such a wide lead on quality that it did not need to position itself to customers on price as it was not interested in attracting lower income customers. However after it lost its number-one position to Tesco in 1995 it had to reconsider its strategy to be more customer focused and, in effect, re-position closer to Tesco. In May 2006 Sainsbury's announced expansion plans costing £1.3 billion over two years. It planned to increase its store opening rate fivefold within two to five years and to buy more land to develop supermarkets. In late 2006, Sainsbury's portfolio of sites offered it the potential to expand by 1% a year. Its aim was increase this pace to 4–5%.

FOR DISCUSSION

1. What are the strengths and weaknesses of Tesco from ASDA's and Sainsbury's perspective?
2. What strategies should each company adopt to compete with Tesco and what strategies should they avoid?
3. Does Tesco have any areas of weakness or strategies that ASDA and Sainsbury's could exploit?
4. Are there any market segments that Tesco is not currently serving that ASDA and Sainsbury's could exploit?

NOTES

1. "Tesco" http://en.wikipedia.org/wiki/Tesco
2. ibid
3. "Tesco" Company Profile, WARC, http://www.warc.com/ © 2006 Copyright and database rights owned by WARC
4. "Tesco" http://en.wikipedia.org/wiki/Tesco
5. "Tesco" http://en.wikipedia.org/wiki/Tesco
6. Fiona Walsh "Supermarkets face third inquiry in seven years", *The Guardian*, 10 May 2006.
7. Fiona Walsh "Supermarkets promise to end confusion in online pricing", *The Guardian*, 17 March 2006.
8. Fiona Walsh "Land Locked" Guardian Unlimited, 9 May 2006. http://business.guardian.co.uk/comment/story/0,,1771155,00.html
9. www.Asda.co.uk ; "Asda" http://en.wikipedia.org/wiki/Asda
10. www.sainsburys.co.uk/ J. Sainsbury http://en.wikipedia.org/wiki/Sainsbury

ALTERNATIVE BUSINESS STRATEGIES

CHAPTER EIGHT

Creating Advantage – Synergy and Vision Versus Opportunism

Vision is the art of seeing things invisible.
—*Jonathan Swift*

All men can see the tactics whereby I conquer, but what none can see is the strategy out of which great victory is evolved.
—*Sun-Tzu, Chinese military strategist*

The possibilities are numerous once we decide to act and not react.
—*George Bernard Shaw*

Our attention now shifts from strategic analysis to the development of a business strategy. Which strategic alternatives should be considered? Which one is optimal? These questions will be the focus of Chapters 8 through 12. One goal will be to provide a wide scope of available strategic alternatives in order to increase the likelihood that the best choices will be considered. Even a poor decision among superior alternatives is preferable to a good decision among inferior alternatives.

This chapter discusses the concept and creation of a sustainable competitive advantage (SCA), the key to a successful strategy. It then turns to the challenge of creating and leveraging synergy as one basis for an SCA. Finally, two very different routes to developing winning strategies are presented: strategic vision and strategic opportunism. Chapters 9, 10, and 11 discuss a variety of strategic options, including quality, brand equity focus, value, innovation, customer relationships and being global. Chapter 12 then introduces strategic position – the face of the business strategy, both internally and externally. In the next section of the book, Chapters 13, 14, and 15 discuss growth strategies. The final section covers organisational issues.

THE SUSTAINABLE COMPETITIVE ADVANTAGE

As defined earlier in this book, a sustainable competitive advantage is an element (or combination of elements) of the business strategy that provides a meaningful

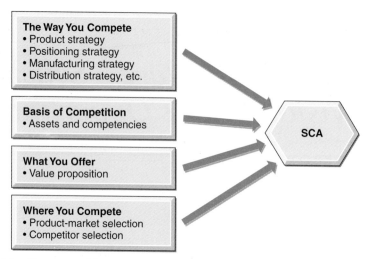

Figure 8.1   The sustainable competitive advantage

advantage over both existing and future competitors (see Figure 8.1). Carrefour has a cost advantage due to its scale economies, market power, logistical efficiencies, value proposition for the customer and international location assets. UBS has a strong position as one of the world's largest financial services company and its strength lies in a powerfully constructed global brand. The Spanish retailer Mango has built a global fashion franchise by using concept driven design and high quality products in a focused segment of young, urban women.

An SCA needs to be both meaningful and sustainable. It should be substantial enough to make a difference; a marginal superiority in quality, especially when 'good' quality is good enough for most customers, will not generate an SCA. Meanwhile, sustainability (in the absence of an effective patent) means that any advantage needs to be supported and enhanced over time. There needs to be a moving target for competitors. For example, Smirnoff has maintained its leading position in the alcoholic beverages market over a long period with a succession of innovations like Smirnoff Ice, the Smirnoff Twist range and Smirnoff Black Ice. This approach to product introduction makes it more difficult for competitors to copy Smirnoff's advantage.

An SCA will in part depend on the functional strategies and programmes, how you compete. H&M's value proposition, Easyjets's point-to-point system and Ikea's cheap and simple delivery of designer furniture all have SCAs based in part on their functional strategies and programmes. In these cases and others, however, an effective SCA will also involve other aspects of the business strategy – assets and competencies, the value proposition, and the selection of the product market.

The Basis of Competition: Assets and Competencies

The assets and competencies of an organisation represent the most sustainable element of a business strategy because these are usually difficult to copy or counter. There is no point in pursuing a quality strategy, for example, without the design and manufacturing competencies needed to deliver quality products. Anyone can try to distribute cereal or detergent through supermarkets but few have the competencies in logistics, shelf-space management and promotions or relationships with chain executives that make product distribution efficient and effective. Similarly, a department store's premium-service positioning strategy will not succeed unless the right people and culture are in place and are supported. Who you are, in other words, is as important as what you do.

As discussed in Chapter 4, several questions can help to identify relevant assets and competencies. What are the key motivations of the major market segments? What are the large value-added components? What are the mobility barriers? What elements of the value chain can generate an advantage? What assets and competencies are possessed by successful businesses and lacking in unsuccessful businesses?

What You Offer – The Value Proposition

An effective SCA should be visible to customers and provide or enhance a value position. The key is to link an SCA with the positioning of a business. A product's reliability may not be apparent to customers but if it can be made visible through advertising or product design it can support a reliability positioning strategy. For example, Volkswagen positions their cars based on reliability and this is supported by advertising that communicates the SCA provided by its product design and performance.

A reputation for delivering a value proposition can be a more important asset than the substance that underlies that reputation. A business with such a reputation can falter for a time and the market will either never become aware of the weakness or will forgive the firm. Conversely, competitors often have a much easier time in matching the quality or performance of a market offering than in convincing customers that it indeed has done so. Enduring impressions like these are why a visible value proposition that is meaningful to customers is strategically valuable.

A solid value proposition can fail if a key ingredient is missing or if consumer needs change. For example, many confectionery firms are suffering stagnant or fallings sales as consumer concerns about obesity and fat and sugar content of food grow. Consumers still desire treats but they want ones that are less threatening to their health. Many companies in the food and beverage sector such as Coca-Cola, Cadbury and Kellogg's are responding with revised marketing or new product offerings.

Where You Compete: The Product Market Served

An important determinant for an SCA is the choice of the target product market. A well-defined strategy supported by assets and competencies can fail because it does not work in the marketplace. One way to create marketplace value is to be relevant to customers. It is no good offering customers the best stout or bitter on the market when they really want to purchase and consume light beers or lagers. The scope of the business also involves the identity of competitors. Sometimes an asset or competency will form an SCA only given the right set of competitors. Thus, it is vital to assess whether a competitor or strategic group is weak, adequate, or strong with respect to assets and competencies. The goal is to engage in a strategy that will match up with competitors' weak points in relevant areas.

Sustainable Competitive Advantages Versus Key Success Factors

What is the difference between key success factors (KSFs), introduced in Chapters 2 and 5, and SCAs? A KSF is an asset or competence needed to compete. An SCA is an asset or competence that is the basis for a continuing advantage. For example, a car manufacturer needs to have adequate distribution given its business model and objectives, so distribution is a KSF. Lexus has turned its dealer network into an SCA, however, because it is capable of delivering a superior customer experience. A KSF for value-priced economy cars is the ability to control costs in order to create profit margins. Hyundai's ability in this regard is markedly superior to its competitors, and thus it becomes an SCA.

To be a winner at poker requires skill, nerve, and money. It also requires a player to ante – to put up a certain amount of money just to see the cards and engage in betting. A KSF can be an ante in terms of the marketplace. Generating a superior quality car may have been an SCA for Porsche or Mercedes and a point of differentiation in the mid-1990s. But as Audi and BMW improve their own quality the quality dimension starts to be an attribute all luxury cars are assumed to have, and thus a KSF but not a basis for an SCA. Instead of winning the competitive hand, a KSF merely buys an organisation a seat at the table.

In the branding arena, Keller talks about points of parity (POPs) and points of differentiation (PODs), which provide additional insight into this distinction.[1] PODs are strong, favourable, and unique brand associations based on some attribute or benefit associations. Ikea, for example, provides home furnishings at accessible prices with unique designs which customers handle and assemble themselves. A POP, in contrast, is an association that is not necessarily unique to the brand. POPs may be necessary to present a credible offering with a certain strategy, as is the case with 24-hour opening for supermarkets. A POP might also be designed to negate a competitor's point of distinction. Weight Watcher's food range, for example, seeks to create parity with regard to taste, thereby negating the taste POD of its competitors and leading customers to base their selection on Weight Watcher's POD (namely, calorie and control of fat content). An SCA is analogous to a POD, whereas a KSF can be analogous to either a POP or a POD.

What Business Managers Name as Their SCAs

Managers of 248 distinct businesses in the service and high-tech industries were asked to name the SCAs of their business.[2] The objectives were to identify frequently employed SCAs, to confirm that managers could articulate them, to determine whether different managers from the same businesses would identify the same SCAs, and to find how many SCAs would be identified for each business. The responses were coded into categories. The results, summarised in Figure 8.2, provide some suggestive insights into the SCA construct.

The wide variety of SCAs mentioned, each representing distinct competitive approaches, is shown in the figure. Of course, the list did differ by industry. For high-tech firms, for example, name recognition was less important than technical superiority, product innovation, and installed customer base. The next two chapters

	High-Tech	Service	Other	Total
1. Reputation for quality	26	50	29	105
2. Customer service/product support	23	40	15	78
3. Name recognition/high profile	8	42	21	71
4. Retain good management and engineering staff	17	43	5	65
5. Low-cost production	17	15	21	53
6. Financial resources	11	26	14	51
7. Customer orientation/feedback/ market research	13	26	9	48
8. Product-line breadth	11	23	13	47
9. Technical superiority	30	7	9	46
10. Installed base of satisfied customers	19	22	4	45
11. Segmentation/focus	7	22	16	45
12. Product characteristics/differentiation	12	15	10	37
13. Continuing product innovation	12	17	6	35
14. Market share	12	14	9	35
15. Size/location of distribution	10	11	13	34
16. Low price/high-value offering	6	20	6	32
17. Knowledge of business	2	25	4	31
18. Pioneer/early entrant in industry	11	11	6	28
19. Efficient, flexible production/ operations adaptable to customers	4	17	4	25
20. Effective sales force	10	9	4	23
21. Overall marketing skills	7	9	7	23
22. Shared vision/culture	5	13	4	22
23. Strategic goals	6	7	9	22
24. Powerful well-known parent	7	7	6	20
25. Location	0	10	10	20
26. Effective advertising/image	5	6	6	17
27. Enterprising/entrepreneurial	3	3	5	11
28. Good coordination	3	2	5	10
29. Engineering research and development	8	2	0	10
30. Short-term planning	2	1	5	8
31. Good distributor relations	2	4	1	7
32. Other	6	20	5	31
Total	315	539	281	1,135
Number of businesses	68	113	67	248
Average number of SCAs	4.63	4.77	4.19	4.58

Figure 8.2   Sustainable competitive advantages of 248 businesses

discuss several SCAs in more detail. Most of the SCAs in Figure 8.2 reflect assets or competencies. Customer base, quality reputation, and good management and engineering staff, for example, are business assets, whereas customer service and technical superiority usually involve sets of competencies.

For a subset of 95 of the businesses involved, a second business manager was independently interviewed. The result suggests that managers can identify SCAs with a high degree of reliability. Of the 95 businesses, 76 of the manager pairs gave answers that were coded the same and most of the others had only a single difference in the SCA list.

Another finding is instructive – the average number of SCAs per business was 4.58, suggesting that it is usually not sufficient to base a strategy on a single SCA. Sometimes a business is described in terms of a single competency or asset, implying that being a quality-oriented business or a service-focused business explains success. This study indicates, however, that it may be necessary to have several assets and competencies.

Strategic Options – Routes to an SCA

As noted in Chapter 1, even given the specification of a product-market investment plan, a business strategy will still involve choices that can usefully be conceptualised

Figure 8.3   Strategic options

and labelled as strategic options. A *strategic option* is a particular value proposition for a product market with supporting assets and competencies and functional area strategies and programmes. The value proposition can involve social, emotional and self-expressive benefits as well as functional benefits. Most successful strategies involve more than one strategic option. For example, Hugo Boss combines a prestige strategy with one based on quality and style. Thus, a strategic option is a building block for a business strategy and a business strategy can be viewed as a set of integrated strategic options.

Figure 8.3 lists some of the strategic options that will be discussed in the coming chapters. Chapter 9 will introduce the quality option, as well as others related to a product attribute, product design, product line breadth, corporate social responsibility, and brand equity, Chapter 10 describes the value, focus, innovation, and customer relationship options, and Chapter 11 considers the global option in detail. Of course, each option will have many variants depending on the industry and context. This list is far from complete, but the descriptions of these options will provide insights into others as well.

THE ROLE OF SYNERGY

Synergy between business units can provide an SCA that is truly sustainable because it is based on the characteristics of a firm that are probably unique. A competitor might have to duplicate the organisation in order to capture the assets or competencies involved. A core element in the GE strategic vision was to achieve synergy across many businesses.[3] GE's Jack Welch called it 'integrated diversity'. The concept was that a GE business can call on the resources of the firm and of other GE businesses to create advantage. For example, the SCAs of General Electric in the CT scanner (an X-ray-based diagnostic system) business are in part based on its leadership in the X-ray business, in which it has a huge installed base and a large service network and in part based on the fact that it operates other businesses involving technologies used in CT scanners. A cornerstone of the IBM strategy under Lou Gerstner was to create synergy by pushing core technologies across more product lines.[4] The intent was to leverage the IBM size, scale, and technologies. This vision was a far cry from that of Gerstner's predecessors, who planned to break IBM up into autonomous business units.

Sony exploits the synergy of its many product groups by showcasing them together in Sony Centre outlets. Synergy means that the whole is more than the sum of its parts. In this context, it means that two businesses (or two product-market strategies) operating together will be superior to the same two businesses operating independently. In terms of products, positive synergy means that offering a set of products will generate a higher return over time than would be possible if each of the products were offered separately. Similarly, in terms of markets, operating a set of markets within a business will be superior to operating them autonomously. As a result of synergy, the combined businesses will have one or more of the following:

- increased customer value and thus increased sales
- lower operating costs
- reduced investment

Generally the synergy will be caused by exploiting some commonality in the two operations, such as:

- customers and sometimes customer applications (potentially creating a systems solution)
- a sales force or channel of distribution
- a brand name and its image
- facilities used for manufacturing, offices, or warehousing
- R&D efforts
- staff and operating systems
- marketing and marketing research

Synergy is not difficult to understand conceptually but it is slippery in practice, in part because it can be difficult to predict whether synergy will actually emerge. Often two businesses seem related, and sizeable potential synergy seems to exist but is never realised. Sometimes the perceived synergy is merely a mirage or wishful thinking, perhaps created in the haste to put together a merger. At other times, the potential synergy is real, but implementation problems prevent its realisation. Perhaps there is a cultural mismatch between two organisations, or the incentives are inadequate. The material on implementation in Chapter 16 is directly relevant to the problem of predicting whether potential synergy will be realised.

Alliances

Obtaining instant synergy is a goal of alliances. Sainsbury's alliance with Skype, for example, has provided customers with the convenience of being able to purchase free or inexpensive worldwide Internet calls when they shop. This alliance takes advantage of Sainsbury's distribution ability to deploy Skype's leadership in the nascent VOIP market. Nokia has partnered with Sony Ericsson in its attempts to bring broadcast TV to the mobile phone. This alliance seeks to combine Nokia's strength in the manufacture and marketing of mobile phones with Sony's competence in miniaturisation to build a leadership position in an emerging market. Yahoo formed an alliance with BT to launch a cobranded broadband service in the UK. Chapter 11, Global Strategies, covers the difficult process of putting together alliances and joint ventures and making them work.

Core Assets and Competencies[5]

A firm's asset or competency that is capable of being the competitive basis of many of its businesses is termed a core asset or competency and can be a synergistic advantage. Prahalad and Hamel suggest a tree metaphor, in which the root system is the core asset or competency, the trunk and major limbs are core products, the smaller branches are business units, and the leaves and flowers are end products. You may not recognise the strength of a competitor if you simply look at its end products and fail to examine the strength of its root system. Core competence represents the consolidation of firm-wide technologies and skills into a coherent thrust. A core asset, such as a brand name or a distribution channel, merits investment and management that span business units. Consider, for example, the core competencies of Volvo in car safety, Phillips in the design of consumer electronics, Black & Decker in small motors and Molton Brown in luxury lifestyle goods. Each of these competencies underlies a large set of businesses and has the potential to create more. Each of these firms invests in competence in a variety of different ways and contexts. Each would insist on keeping its primary work related to the core competency in-house. Outsourcing would risk weakening the asset, and each firm would rightfully insist that there is no other firm that could match its state-of-the-art advances.

Capabilities-Based Competition

Capabilities-based competition suggests that the key building blocks of business strategy are not products and markets but, rather, competencies in business processes.[6] Investment in building and managing a process that outperforms competition and can be applied across businesses can lead to a sustainable advantage. Therefore, strategy development must identify the most important processes within the organisation, specify how they should be measured, identify target performance levels, relate performance to achieving superior customer value and competitive advantage, and assign crossfunctional teams to implement them. One such process is the new product development and introduction process. The tense relationship between retailers and brand owners is often attributed to retailer brands and the threat they present to the price and quality expectations of other brands. However, a significant additional tension arises around the demonstrated ability of retailers to identify new product opportunities and exploit them very quickly. The twelve weeks that it can take a retailer to develop and launch a new product provides them with a real advantage when compared with the up to 18 months that a manufacturer brand owner might take.[7] Another is in the management of direct and indirect costs. As demonstrated by Ryanair, this capability has the potential to drive an overall business strategy. Tesco has used its supply chain management skills to drive costs out its business model and to enhance its competitiveness in the marketplace. One of the capabilities that Henkel deploys is its ability to successfully manage global brands such as Sellotape and Persil as well as local/regional brand's such as Somat or Flink.

Developing superior capabilities in key processes involves strategic investments in people and infrastructure to gain advantage. True process improvement does not occur without control and ownership of the parts of the process. Thus, the virtual corporation, which draws pieces from many sources in response to the organisational task at hand, is not a good model for capabilities-based competition.

STRATEGIC VISION VERSUS STRATEGIC OPPORTUNISM

There are two very different approaches to the development of successful strategies and sustainable competitive advantages. Each can work, but may require very different systems, people, and culture. Strategic vision takes a long-term perspective;

the focus is on business strategies that are expected to be successful over a long time period. Strategic opportunism emphasises strategies that make sense today. The implicit belief is that the best way to have the right strategy in place tomorrow is to have it right today.

Strategic Vision

To manage a strategic vision successfully, a firm should have four characteristics:

- *A clear future strategy* with a core driving idea and a specification of the competitive arena, functional area strategies, value proposition, and competitive advantage that will define the business.
- *Buy-in throughout the organisation.* There should be a belief in the correctness of the strategy, an acceptance that the vision is achievable and worthwhile, and a real commitment to making that vision happen.
- *Assets, competencies, and resources to implement* the strategy should be in place, or a plan to obtain them should be under way.
- *Patience.* There should be a willingness to stick to the strategy in the face of competitive threats or enticing opportunities that would divert resources from the vision.

A strategic vision provides a sense of purpose. Ryanair's commitment to building a truly low-cost airline that can compete with and beat the traditional leaders in the airline industry has the potential to inspire. In contrast, it is hard to get energised to increase ROI by 2 points or sales by 10 % so shareholders will be wealthier. Strategic vision also provides the rationale for investment that may require years to achieve a payoff. Aldi's dedication to a price-value, no-frills position throughout its years of operations has enabled it to develop effective processes and resources that allow them to follow this vision. Managing a strategic vision requires a certain kind of organisation and management style, as summarised in Figure 8.4. A strategic vision is based on a forward-looking, long-term perspective – the planning horizon extends into the future two, five, or more than 10 years, depending on the business involved. The goal of the supporting information system and analysis effort is thus to understand the likely future environment. Experts who have insights into key future events and trends can be helpful. Scenario analysis, technological forecasting, and trend analysis should be part of the analysis phase of strategy development.

The organisation needs to be capable of building assets that may not have immediate payoff. A top-down, centralised structure with a reward system that supports the vision is helpful, as is a strong, charismatic leader who can sell the vision to relevant constituencies inside and outside the organisation. Many CEOs have played this role: Willie Walsh at Aer Lingus, James Dyson at Dyson, Steve Jobs at Apple, Stuart Rose at Marks & Spencer and Greg Dyke at the BBC.

Identifying with themes and projects can also leverage and drive a strategic vision. For example, France Telecom's research-and-development centre launched an

Organisational Characteristics	Strategic Vision	Strategic Opportunism
Perspective	• Forward-looking	• Present
Strategic Uncertainties	• Trends affecting the future	• Current threats and opportunities
Environmental Sensing	• Future scenarios	• Change sensors
Information System	• Forward-looking	• On-line
Orientation	• Commitment	• Flexibility
	• Build assets	• Adaptability
	• Vertical integration	• Fast response
Leadership	• Charismatic	• Tactical
	• Visionary	• Action oriented
Structure	• Centralised	• Decentralised
	• Top-down	• Fluid
People	• Eye on the ball	• Entrepreneurial
Economic Advantage	• Scale economies	• Scope economies
Signaling	• Strong signals sent to competitors	• Surprise moves

Figure 8.4   Organisational differences

original project called 'Studio Creatif', which was dedicated to examining and producing concepts for new telecommunications services and to stimulate test products and services with users in all fields. This allowed them to develop prototypes that were viewed by customers and the media as new and enthusiastic personal and professional media and communication systems.

A strategic vision can take many forms. Innocent Drinks wants to help people to do something healthy. Nokia was guided by a vision to lead the development and commercialisation of telecommunications and this enabled them to establish a leadership position in mobile phone technology. Barnardos, the children's charity, seeks to assist vulnerable young people to transform their future and achieve their potential.

Strategic Stubbornness

The risk of the strategic vision route, as suggested by Figure 8.5, is that the vision may be faulty and its pursuit may be a wasteful exercise in strategic stubbornness. There are a host of pitfalls that could prevent a vision from being realised. Three stand out.

Implementation Barriers

The picture of the future may be substantially accurate but the firm may not be able to implement the strategy required. An underestimation of the nature and scope of the challenge of Chinese and Indian firms is likely to be the root of many company's problems in the early twenty-first century just as the arrival of the Internet economy

	Strategic Approach	Strategic Risk
Focus on Future	Strategic vision	Strategic stubbornness
Focus on Present	Strategic opportunism	Strategic drift

Figure 8.5   Vision versus opportunism

was in the 1990s. Many managers view China and India as sources of cheap competition however these economies are increasingly driven by educated workers with skills that will allow these growing nations to compete with European on US firms in a broader fashion.

Faulty Assumptions of the Future

The vision might be faulty because it is based on faulty assumptions about the future. For example, the concept of customer loyalty cards and programmes used by retailers like Tesco and Boots was hoped to encourage brand loyalty and customer retention. However, while many retailers spend a small fortune on the programmes there is little evidence that the financial gains and brand loyalty that they expected have materialised, with the main benefit emerging in the form of an improvement in the quality and quantity of data about customer purchases and behaviour.

A Paradigm Shift

A third problem occurs when there is a paradigm shift. For example, changes in technology might cause the nature of a business to change. Thus, computers changed from mainframes to minicomputers, personal computers, portables, workstations, and servers. In the semiconductor industry, the vacuum-tube business first gave way to transistors and then, in sequence, to semiconductors, integrated circuits and microprocessors. In both cases, each new paradigm brought with it a remarkable change in the cast of characters. It was extremely rare for a leader in one paradigm to be a leader in the next. In fact, it was common to see industry leaders fade sharply in the face of the new paradigms.

New operating models can also change the paradigm. Napster and other online music sites changed the way people listened to music and the formats in which they were willing to accept the product. For example the album may no longer be a relevant way to sell music to format. Following on from this Apple changed the way portable music is stored and listened to with the introduction of the iPod. This has reduced the power of traditional music companies and left bricks and mortar music stores with a challenge to maintain relevance. websites like daft.ie, Rentamatic.co.uk and propertyworld.com changed the way people look for property to buy and rent and challenged newspaper listings and reduced the role of estate and letting agents as sources of information. The emergence and popularity of the fairtrade movement has forced supermarkets not only to stock fairtrade products but to examine how they source their products. In each case, it is no coincidence that the new paradigm has been dominated by new entrants or by incumbents that had been considered insignificant niche players by the leading companies. This movement of industry profits and firm value away from an established way of doing business has been termed 'value migration' by management consultant Adrian Slywotzky.[8]

Why Are Organisations Stubborn?

Organisational stubbornness, which is especially prevalent among successful firms, has several causes. First, there is the ironic penalty of success. Success should tend to provide resources that can be used to create a new-paradigm business. However, success instead tends to reinforce the old vision and efforts to refine it by reducing costs and improving service. The result is that operational improvements often mask the fundamental shifts. Kenichi Ohmae has observed that Japanese firms have a 'winning by working harder' obsession that has not only discouraged change, but also made whole industries unprofitable.[9] For example, Japanese firms have created enormous overcapacity in shipbuilding, automobiles, and other industries and have engaged in destructive price competition in order to 'win'. A common response when a company rejects a new paradigm is for employees to leave and establish a start up to take advantage of the new paradigm. For example, Philleas Fogg snacks were launched by four executives from the Tudor Crisps company. The opportunity to enter the adult savoury snack market was not taken by Tudor when presented to them by their own employees. So they left the firm and created their own range of products, which today is one of the most successful brands in the UK market.

Second, and closely related, the new paradigm will probably require a different organisation, and, in particular, a different culture. It is not easy to change a culture, especially when an organisation has successfully developed and nurtured that culture to suit the old vision. The strength of the existing culture and the difficulty of change were two key reasons that business transformation at British Airways and marks and spencer occurred after financial losses.[10]

Third, why participate in killing the golden goose? Any new-paradigm success will often directly cannibalise the old-vision business. There is also the possibility that the new paradigm can't be seen for the success of the existing one. James Dyson originally attempted to sell his idea for a revolutionary vacuum cleaner to the major incumbents in the market. One of the reasons why they rejected the proposal was that the Dyson product was bagless and the incumbents had substantial revenues from the sales of vacuum cleaner bags.

The power of a vision is based on the commitment that accompanies it. This commitment, together with a focus on the future instead of the past, can result in pursuing a faulty vision beyond the point at which the probability of success is high. The trick is to maintain commitment and patience in the face of adversity, while at the same time not allowing a failed vision to use up resources on a futile attempt at a miracle recovery.

Strategic Opportunism

Strategic opportunism is driven by a focus on the present. The premise is that the environment is so dynamic and uncertain that it is not feasible to aim at a future target. Unless a business is structured to have strategic advantages in the present, it is unlikely to be strategically successful in the future. Strategic opportunism provides several advantages. One is that the risk of missing emerging business opportunities is reduced. Firms such as Tesco in gourmet foods, Kellog's in cereal brands and Weight Watchers in weight loss all seek emerging niche segments and develop brands tailored to speciality markets. Thus Tesco's Finest brand, Kellog's Nutri-Grain bars and Weight Watchers range of ready meals and deserts are all designed to appeal to a current popular trend or taste.

Strategic opportunism also tends to generate a vitality and energy that can be healthy, especially when a business has decentralised R&D and marketing units that generate stream of new products. Within easyGroup, for example, new businesses opportunities are continuously identified and evaluated with respect to their prospects. HP is another firm that believes in decentralised entrepreneurial management. These decentralised firms are often close to the market and technology and are willing to pursue opportunities.

Strategic opportunism results in economies of scope, with assets and competencies supported by multiple product lines. For example, Adidas applies its brand assets and competencies in product design and customer sensing to a wide range of product markets. Its strategy revolves around marketing sports footwear, apparel and accessories for running, basketball, football, tennis and training. It focuses its attention on innovative footwear and uses the opportunity of celebrity sponsorship to promote its range. This association with high-profile individuals, a superior product design and one of the world's most widely recognised brand names allows them to develop strong emotional ties and relationships with customers.

As Figure 8.4 suggests, the prototypical business driven by strategic opportunism is very different from a business guided by a strategic vision. The strategic uncertainties are very different. What trends are most active and critical now? What is the current driving force in the market? What are the strategic problems facing the business that need immediate correction? What technologies are ready to be employed? What are current strategic opportunities and threats? What are competitors doing in the market and in the lab? What strategy changes are occurring or will soon occur?

The supporting information system and analysis are also different. To support strategic opportunism, companies must monitor customers, competitors and the trade to learn of trends, opportunities, and threats as they appear. Information gathering and analysis should be both sensitive and online. Frequent, regular meetings to analyse the most recent developments and news may be helpful. The organisation should be quick to understand and act on changing fundamentals. The hallmark of an organisation that emphasises strategic opportunism is strategic flexibility and the willingness to respond quickly to strategic opportunities as they emerge. The organisation is adaptive, with the ability to adjust its systems, structure, people, and culture to accommodate new ventures. The strategy is dynamic, and change is the norm. New products are being explored or introduced and others are de-emphasised or dropped. New markets are entered and disinvestment occurs in others. New synergies and assets are being created. The people are entrepreneurial, sensitive to new opportunities and threats, and fast to react.

Strategic Drift

The problem with the strategic opportunism model is that, as suggested by Figure 8.5, it can turn into strategic drift. Investment decisions are made incrementally in response to opportunities rather than directed by a vision. As a result, a firm can wake up one morning and find that it is in a set of businesses for which it lacks the needed assets and competencies and that provide few synergies. At least three phenomena can turn strategic opportunism into strategic drift. First, a short-lived, transitory force may be mistaken for one with enough staying power to make a strategic move worthwhile. If the force is so short-lived that a strategy does not pay off or does not even have a chance to get into place, the result will be a strategy that is not suitable for the business or the environment.

Second, opportunities to create immediate profits may be rationalised as strategic when, in fact, they are not. For example, an instrumentation firm might receive many requests from some of its customers for special-purpose instruments that could conceivably be used by other customers but that have little strategic value for the company. Such opportunities might result in a sizeable initial order but could divert research-and-development resources from more strategic activities. Third, expected synergies across existing and new business areas may fail to materialise owing to implementation problems, perhaps because of culture clashes or because the synergies were only illusions in the first place. A drive to exploit core assets or competencies might not work. As a result, new business areas would be in place without the expected sustainable advantages.

Strategic drift not only creates a business without needed assets and competencies but it can also result in a failure to support a core business that does have a good vision. Without a vision and supporting commitment, it is tempting to divert investment into seemingly sure things that are immediate strategic opportunities. Thus, strategic opportunism can be an excuse to delay investment or divert resources from a core vision.

One example of strategic drift is a firm that designed, installed, and serviced custom equipment for steel firms. Over time, steel firms became more knowledgeable and began buying standardised equipment mainly on the basis of price. Gradually, the firm edged into this commodity business to retain its market share. The company finally realised it was pursuing a dual strategy for which it was ill suited. It had too much overhead to compete with the real commodity firms, and its ability to provide upscale service had eroded to the point that it was now inferior to some niche players. Had there been a strategic vision, the firm would not have fallen into such a trap.

Another is a discounter that did well when operating a limited product line in a local market with a low-cost message. The customer value was clear and the hands-on management style was effective. However, when the firm expanded its geographic and product scope even going into groceries, the management systems were no longer adequate and the value proposition become fuzzy as well. It had drifted into a business requiring assets and competencies it did not have.

Vision Plus Opportunism

Many businesses attempt to have the best of both worlds by engaging in strategic vision and strategic opportunism at the same time. Strategic opportunism can supplement strategic vision by managing diversification away from the core business and by managing the route to achievement of a firm's vision. Thus, if Rolex's vision is to exploit brand associations by extending its name to other product categories, strategic opportunism can describe the process of selecting the extensions and the order in which they are pursued.

The combination can and does work. However, there are obvious risks and problems. One is that strategic vision requires patience and investment and is vulnerable to the enticements represented by the more immediate return that is usually associated with strategic opportunism. It is difficult to maintain the persistence and discipline required by strategic vision in any case, even without the distractions of alternative strategies that have been blessed as part of the thrust of the organisation. The organisational problems are worse. It is difficult for one organisation to use both approaches well because the systems, people, structure, and culture that are best for one approach are generally not well suited to the other. To create an organisation that excels at or even tolerates both is not easy.

A DYNAMIC VISION

An attractive strategy is to have a *dynamic* vision that can change in anticipation of emerging paradigm shifts. This is a difficult goal, and few managers and firms have been able to pull it off. But the payoff is huge. And some firms, such as the largest steel firm in the US, Nucor, have succeeded. In the 1970s, facing price pressures from fully integrated steel firms plus efficient Japanese brands, Nucor developed a strategy of producing joists (higher value products used in construction) in rural minimills that employed nonunionised labour and used scrap steel as raw material. For a decade, this model made Nucor a strategic and financial success. By the mid-1980s, however, others had started to copy the strategy, scrap steel was no longer as plentiful, and aluminum had made serious inroads into traditional steel markets. In response to these changes, Nucor again reinvented the paradigm by focusing on flat-rolled, up-market products, using a scrap-steel substitute, and drawing on iron ore in Brazil and a processing plant in Trinidad.[11]

Microsoft has had similar success, although they did not abandon the old vision but rather augmented it with a new direction. Microsoft's focus progressed from operating systems to applications to the Internet. Other firms such as News International, the BBC and Tesco have all adopted a dynamic vision in their strategy, which has left them well positioned to engage with the net age.

How do you change a vision? Certainly it requires a will to change, an ability to anticipate paradigm shifts and create the new vision via an insightful and forward looking strategic analysis, and an ability to change the organisation and particularly the culture. The strategic analysis phase has already been covered. The organisational elements will be discussed in Chapter 16. The next two sections will discuss two perspectives that provide paths relevant to changing a vision: strategic intent and strategic flexibility.

Strategic Intent

Hamel and Prahalad have suggested that some firms have strategic intent, which couples strategic vision with a sustained obsession with winning at all levels of the organisation.[12] They note that this model explains the successful rise to global leadership of companies such as Canon, Komatsu, Samsung and Honda. Thus, Canon was out to 'beat Xerox' Komatsu to 'encircle Caterpillar' and Honda to become a 'second Ford'.

A strategic intent to achieve a successful strategy has several characteristics in addition to strategic vision and an obsession with success. First, it should recognise the essence of winning. Coca-Cola's strategic intent has included the objective of putting a coke within 'arm's reach' of every consumer in the world because distribution and accompanied visibility are the keys to winning. LG's strategic intent is to become one the worlds top three home electronics players by 2010. The essence of this success is to be recognised as a global brand. LG intends to use mobile phone handsets to drive its global brand building activity. In order to build its position in the handset market LG have identified speed to market as the essential ingredient and pursue this with vigour.[13]

DIRECT LINE

In 1990 Royal Bank of Scotland developed a single motor insurance company called Direct Line which sold products more cheaply than competitors by cutting out brokers. since its founding it has grown from a single product into a superbrand, selling several different products with profits increasing from £26 million in 1996 to £355 million in 2003. The motor insurance market in the UK is particularly competitive and when Direct Line was established there were a number of competitors including insurance companies, other direct operators and Internet insurance brokers. But it is clear that Direct Line had a strategic intent to succeed in the motor insurance market. Its goal was not to establish sales using lower cost media; instead the company demonstrated a high level of commitment to building an insurance super brand that customers could recognise. In fact it is not only higher sales and lower costs that differentiate Direct Line from its competitors; it is also an investment in high-cost brand building communication. As Direct Line had no physical outlets or sales force the strategy behind Direct Line's success was to use a powerful advertising campaign which represented a tangible aspect of the service to customers. This campaign centred on the Red Phone device, which is used in all of the company's communications. This campaign was highly successful and not only built brand awareness for the company quickly but also captured customers' imaginations. Combined with an effective IT system, the result was growing profit and market share.[14]

Second, strategic intent involves stretching an organisation with a continuing effort to identify and develop new SCAs or to improve those that exist. Thus, it has a dynamic, forward-looking perspective. What will our advantage be next year and two years after that? Consider the social networking sites such as MySpace.com and Bebo.com which have come to the fore in recent years. These sites have emerged from the Internet revolution, fuelled by a desire amongst young people to commune and their willingness to interact and shape that community. All of this is taking place at a time when media consumption is becoming increasingly individual. The customer value propositions of both sites have led them to great success and consequently their revenues from advertising and other marketing deals have soared. But how will these sites fair as the current demographic cohort ages? Their attractiveness to advertisers is the ability to target individuals, how will consumers respond to this targeting? Will concerns for the safety of young people lead parents to prevent their children from using these sites? These sites have an SCA right now but maintaining these going forward will require skilful negotiation.

Third, strategic intent often requires real innovation, a willingness to do things very differently. Anglo-Irish Bank entered the financial services market in Ireland as a specialist in business banking, focusing on providing a rapid solution to customers borrowing needs. Its commitment to a speedy response caught incumbent business banks unawares and contributed to their success.

An obsession with winning can be created even without a competitor. Peter Johnson told how he created a phantom competitor when running Trus Joist, a maker of structural components for buildings, which had a patent-based monopoly.[15] The phantom competitor developed low-cost options and generated creative options for breaking into the business. As a result, Trus Joist was stimulated to innovate in an adjacent market. Strategic intent provides a long-term drive for advantage that can be essential to success. It provides a model that helps break the mould, moving a firm away from simply doing the same things a bit better and working a bit harder than the year before. It has the capability to elevate and extend an organisation, helping it reach levels it would not otherwise attain.

Strategic Flexibility

Strategic intent usually represents a commitment to attaining an SCA. However, in some dynamic industries, an SCA can be a moving target that is difficult to attain proactively because there are too many uncertainties to make the necessary predictions about customer needs, technology, competitive posture, and so on. In those contexts, the answer is to attain strategic flexibility, so that the business will be ready when a window of opportunity arises. Strategic flexibility (the ability to adjust or develop strategies to respond to external or internal changes) can be achieved in a variety of ways, including participating in multiple product-markets and technologies, having resource slack, and creating an organisational system and culture that supports change.

Participation in multiple product-markets or technologies means that the organisation is already 'on the ground' in different arenas. Thus, if it appears that demand will shift to a new product-market or that a newer technology will emerge, the organisation can just expand its current product-market rather than start from zero with all the risks and time required. An organisation may also participate in business areas with weak returns in order to gain the strategic flexibility to deal with possible market changes. For example, in 2005 News International purchased MySpace.com, for US$580 million and ING Entertainment, a gaming site, for US$650 million. While these sites were modestly profitable at the time they were acquired, their profits did not justify the premium paid. However, for News International they provided two steeping stones to building presence and revenues in the online world.[16]

Investing in underused assets provides strategic flexibility. An obvious example is maintaining liquidity (as with Toyota's €36 billion cash hoard) so that investment can be funnelled swiftly to opportunity or problem areas. Maintaining excess capacity in distribution, organisational staffing, or research and development can also enhance a firm's ability to react quickly.

An organisational culture that supports change will create strategic flexibility. A change-enhancing culture starts with being good at detecting opportunities and threats, perhaps drawing on the external information system described in Chapter 6. It will also include an entrepreneurial style, supported by organisational structures and reward systems, which encourages managers to exploit opportunities with action-oriented strategies. There has to be some ability to tolerate a 'ready, fire, aim' mentality.

A Note of Caution

A strategic vision requires real persistence in the face of tempting distractions. It also requires discipline and eye-on-the-ball focus. Visions that are excessively dynamic are no longer visions at all. There is a very real risk of capsising when trying to catch the wave.

THE MISCONCEPTIONS OF BUSINESS LOSERS

An analysis of some egregious business blunders revealed four fatal misconceptions:[17]

- Labour costs are killing us. In fact the labour content is often only a small percentage of value added. Furthermore, the most efficient factories have more costly labour input; they just use and motivate it better.

- You can't make money at the low end. Actually last year's low end from radios to semiconductors often forms the technological, manufacturing and marketing basis for next year's high end.

- We can't sell it. Firms often attempt to sell new and innovative products using marketing methods familiar to them rather than approaches attuned to the innovation.

- It's cheaper to buy it (a new business area) than grow it. Treating businesses as stand-alone units to be bought or sold discourages unit synergy, diverts attention to external investment (the grass is always greener on the other side), and treats investment needed for survival as just another capital budgeting decision.

KEY LEARNINGS

- To create an SCA, a strategy needs to be valued by the market and supported by assets and competences that are not easily copied or neutralised by competitors. The most common SCAs are quality reputation, customer support, and brand name.

- Synergy is often sustainable because it is based on the unique characteristics of an organisation.

- Strategic opportunism focuses on the present and emphasises current opportunities and strategic choices, whereas strategic vision has a long-term perspective and avoids changes in strategy. Opportunism can lead to strategic drift, while a vision-based approach can lead to strategic stubbornness.

- Strategic intent couples strategic vision with a sustained obsession. Strategic flexibility provides a way for organisations to exploit strategic opportunities and manage strategic problems.

FOR DISCUSSION

1. What is a sustainable competitive advantage? Identify SCAs for BMW, Nestle, UBS and T-mobile.

2. Pick a product class and several major brands. What are each brand's points of parity and point of difference? Relate POPs to KSFs, and the POD to SCAs.

3. What is synergy? What are the sources of synergy? Give examples. Why is it so elusive?

4. What is strategic vision and how does it differ from strategic opportunism? What are strategic drift and strategic stubbornness and why do they occur? Can you name any examples besides those mentioned in the chapter? Were faulty strategic decisions the real problem or was there a deeper organisational flaw? What is a dynamic vision and is it feasible?

5. Compare strategic vision with strategic intent. Illustrate with examples.

6. Illustrate strategic flexibility with examples..

NOTES

1. Kevin Lane Keller (2003) *Strategic Brand Management*, 2nd edition, Upper Saddle River, NJ, Prentice-Hall, pp. 131–6.

2. David A. Aaker (1989) Managing assets and skills: the key to a sustainable competitive advantage. *California Management Review*, Winter, pp. 91–106.

3. Noel M. Tichy (1993) Revolutionise your company. *Fortune*, 13 December, pp. 114–18.

4. Louis V. Gertner, Jr. (2002) *Who Says Elephants Can't Dance?* Harper Business, New York.

5. This book uses the phrase 'core assets and competencies', which is an extension of the term 'core competencies' used in the article by C. K. Prahalad and Gary Hamel, 'The core competence of the corporation', *Harvard Business Review*, May–June 1990, pp. 79–91.

6. George Stalk, Philip Evans, and Lawrence E. Shulman (1992) Competing on capabilities: the new rules of corporate strategy. *Harvard Business Review*, March–April, pp. 57–69.

7. Claire Murphy (2006) Asda grows label-conscious. *Marketing*, 17 May, p.14.

8. Adrian J. Slywotzky (1996) *Value Migration*, Harvard Business School Press, Boston.

9. Kenichi Ohmae (1989) Companyism and do more better. *Harvard Business Review*, January–February, pp. 125–132.

10. Michael L.Tushman and Charles A. O'Reilly (1997) *Winning through Innovation: A Practical Guide to Leading Organisational Change and Renewal*, Harvard Business School Press, Boston.

11. Adrian J. Slywotzky (1996) *Value Migration*, Harvard Business School Press, Boston.

12. Gary Hamel and C.K. Prahalad (1989) Strategic intent. *Harvard Business Review*, May–June, pp. 63–76.

13. Korea's LG: The Next Samsung (2005) *Business Week Online*, 13 January. http://www.businessweek.com/technology/content/jan2005/tc20050113_3581_tc024.htm?chan=search

14. http://www.directline.com/; Nigel Robinson and Dom Boyd "Direct Line: How a red-phone grew a super product into a super brand", IPA Effectiveness Awards, Institute of Practitioners in Advertising, London, 2004.

15. Peter T. Johnson (1988) Why I race against phantom competitors. *Harvard Business Review*, September–October, pp. 106–12.

16. Old mogul, new media. *The Economist*, 19 January 2006.

17. Adapted from Thomas A. Stewart (1990) Lessons from US Business Blunders. *Fortune*, 23 April 23, pp. 128–38.

CHAPTER NINE

Strategic Options: Quality and Brand Equity

If you don't have a competitive advantage, don't compete.
—*Jack Welch, GE*

You can't depend on your eyes when your imagination is out of focus.
—*Mark Twain*

If all Coca Cola's assets were destroyed overnight, whoever owned Coca Cola could walk into a bank the next day and get a loan to rebuild everything.
—*Curtis Carlton, Coca Cola*

A business strategy, as defined in Chapter 1, involves four components: the product-market investment decision, the customer value proposition, the organisation's assets and competencies and functional strategies and programmes. For a given industry and organisational context, a strategist will have innumerable ways to compete. Alternative markets, submarkets, product extensions and new product arenas can always be considered. A bewildering variety of customer value propositions, each with its own nuances and spins, will represent strategy variants. Hundreds of conceivable assets and competencies can be developed, nurtured, exploited, and combined, and there are potentially thousands of viable functional strategies and programmes.

Usually, however, business strategies cluster around a limited number of strategic options – particular value propositions for a product market, supported by assets and competencies and functional strategies and programmes. Common strategic options include quality, brand equity, focus (on a product or market), value, innovation, customer relationships, or being global. Each of these options needs to be adapted to a given context, but all should offer a clear value proposition to customers and be supported by assets and competencies and functional strategies and programmes.

Understanding these strategic options will help guide you in evaluating and developing business strategies. To succeed, you will need to be creative and cast a wide net;

having a set of potentially viable options can help make sure that you consider all of the promising alternatives. In addition, when you have a sense of the available choices, you will be more thorough and realistic in appraising whether a proposed strategic option is likely to succeed. Finally, knowing the keys to success of the various options will enhance the development of programmes to implement a business strategy.

A business may select more than one strategic option – choosing to walk and chew gum at the same time, so to speak. It is not an either/or situation. In fact, most successful strategies will represent an integration of several strategic options. A solid understanding of each, however, can guide you not only in deciding which to include but also in specifying their respective roles and priorities in the overall strategy. Which should be dialled up? How should various options interact? The way they combine can be a key to success.

BUSINESS STRATEGY CHALLENGES

Which strategic option or set of options should form the basis for a business strategy? To answer this question, each option should be challenged with respect to whether it contains a real and perceived value proposition and whether it is relevant, sustainable, and feasible. The goal of this analysis is to identify not only the potential impact of the strategic option, but also its limitations and feasibility.

Is There a Real Customer Value Proposition?

A successful business strategy needs to add value for the customer and this value needs to be real rather than merely assumed. For example, the British supermarket chain, Iceland, tried to develop its product line by stocking only organic own labels but this backfired as its core market was not could not afford these products. Bic tried to apply its familiar brand name to a disposable underwear product line but the Bic brand name, which is synonymous with stationery and lighters, did not extend well to this new product line and it failed. Value is more likely to be real if it is driven from the customer's perspective rather than from that of the business operation. How does the point of differentiation affect the customer's experience of buying and using the product? Does it serve to reduce cost, add performance, or increase satisfaction? The concepts of unmet needs and customer problems, outlined in Chapter 3, are relevant. Does market research confirm that value is added from the customer's perspective?

Is There a Perceived Customer Value Proposition?

Further, the value proposition must be recognised and perceived as worthwhile by the customers. Delivering a value proposition is pointless unless customers know about it and believe it. For example, customers may be unaware that the online customer bidding website eBid offers free selling to customers, or that phone calls made over Skype are free. This may occur because customers have not have been exposed to the information because the information was not packaged in a memorable and believable way, or because the attribute or service was not considered to be relevant or of value.

The perceived value problem is particularly acute when the customer is not capable of judging the added value easily. Customers, for example, cannot evaluate airline safety or the skill of a dentist without investing significant time and effort. Instead the customer will look for signals, such as the appearance of the aircraft or the professionalism of the dentist's front office. The firm's task, then, is to manage the signals or cues that imply added value.

Is the Strategy Relevant to Customers?

A business has to make what customers want to buy. The product or service has to be considered relevant to the markets in which the business chooses to compete. As noted in the discussion of relevance in Chapter 5, it is pointless to produce the best readymade meals if customers are interested in fresh food. If a business has a value proposition that is of secondary interest to customers they may look elsewhere even if the business is executing its value proposition effectively. If the products are considered passé or inferior, the business will lack relevance.

Is the Strategy Sustainable?

The strategy's point of difference from competitors needs to be not only perceived but sustainable. This is often a tough challenge, because most points of differentiation are easily copied. One route to a sustainable advantage is to own an important product dimension, perhaps with the aid of a branded differentiator. The Philips CoolSkin range of electric razors incorporates a Nivea lotion dispenser that reduces friction and ensures a closer shave. Philips successfully employed this branded differentiator in order to attract wetshavers who had not previously considered electric razors.[1] A second route would be creating a programme of continuous investment and improvement that enables the strategy to remain a moving target, always ahead of competitors or poised to leapfrog them. Third, a business could create points of differentiation that are based on unique assets and competencies of the organisation, which are inherently difficult to copy.

Overinvestment in a value-added activity may pay off in the long run by discouraging competitors from duplicating a strategy. For example, competitors might be deterred from developing a service backup system that is more extensive than current customers expect. The same logic can apply to a broad product line. Some elements of that line might be unprofitable, but still might be worth retaining if they plug holes that competitors could use to provide customer value.

Is the Strategy Feasible?

It is one thing to create the perfect strategy with respect to customers, competitors, and the marketplace. It is another to execute that strategy effectively. The strategy may require assets and capabilities that are currently inadequate or do not exist and programmes to develop or upgrade them may turn out to be unrealistic. Alliance partners to fill the gap may be difficult to find or to work with. Further, an objective analysis of the customer trends, competitor strengths, or market dynamics may reveal that any strategic success will be shortlived.

STRATEGIC OPTIONS

There are an infinite number of business strategy variants in any context but certain strategic options tend to be used most often. In this chapter and the two that follow, seven of these options – quality, brand equity, value, focus, innovation, customer relationships and being global – will be discussed in some detail. Each is frequently employed, has led to performance successes and is associated with a body of knowledge and experience. Further, the resulting analysis of these few will provide a feel for the types of issues and questions associated with any strategic option.

A snapshot of some of the other strategic options that can be considered follows, to provide a glimpse of the scope of choices available to the business strategist. The ultimate goal of developing brilliant strategies will be reached only when brilliant options are considered. It does little good to be an expert at selecting among mediocre alternatives.

Product Attribute

If a product or service attribute is central to the purchase and use of an offering, one strategic option is to dominate or even own that attribute. Rolex, the Swiss watchmaker has long dominated the prestige end of the watch market and has strong credibility in this space. Nivea has a historical position as a leader in the skincare market and has been able to use this to successfully enter and achieve a leadership position in the rapidly developing men's skincare market. In each case, the attribute is relevant to customers, and the brands are clearly positioned on that attribute.

If such an option is to be viable over time, it needs to be protected against competitors. Having patent protection is one route. Nestlé have created a strong position in the coffee market based on an expanding number of patents on its coffee products like Nespresso. Rolex have taken another route and developed an investment programme in order to support a design process that can take up to five years and maintain a competitive edge in the market through delivering on its brand promise of quality and prestige.

Another route to owning an attribute over time is to brand it and then actively manage that brand and its promise. For example, in 1999, the Westin Hotel Chain created the 'Heavenly Bed', a customer designed mattress set (by Simmons) that became a branded differentiator for the chain. The Heavenly Bed was meaningful in that it addressed the fundamental purpose of a hotel room – to provide a good night's sleep. It also had an impact. During the first year of its life, hotel sites that featured the Heavenly Bed had a 5% increase in customer satisfaction, noticeably improved perceptions of cleanliness, room décor, and maintenance, and increased occupancy. Westin has actively managed the Heavenly Bed brand. The bed can now be purchased, and the concept has been extended into the Heavenly Bath, giving core loyal customers another reason to believe and to talk about Westin to friends.

Product Design

An offering can appeal to a person's aesthetics, providing substantial self-expressive as well as functional benefits. Clothing brands like Prada, Gucci or Diesel most clearly pursue such a strategy with particular brands offering the expression of personal taste and style. In the car market iconic marques such as the Mini or the Citroen C3 Pluriel offer buyers the opportunity to make statements about themselves and their style values.

Pursuing a design option requires the firm to really have a passion for design and to support a home for a creative design team. Creating such a culture and infrastructure is a key to success for firms like Dyson, Bang & Olufsen and Lush handmade cosmetics. Because achieving a home for design can be difficult, another route is to create an alliance with a design firm, which allows access to best-of-breed designers when needed. Outsourcing can succeed if the firm manages the alliance properly and establishes exclusive ownership of the output.

Product Line Breadth

A compelling value proposition can be based on product-line breadth. Tesco.Com has become one of Britain's leading online retailers using a wide range of products like food, drink, flowers, entertainment, banking and insurance to contact lenses, gas, electricity and legal advice. Ebookers, Europe's leading online travel retailer, offers a wide range of travel products including hotel reservations, flights, car hire and sports packages, allowing customers to book their complete holiday experience through one agent.

Especially in the business-to-business space, many firms are trying to move from being component suppliers to being systems solution players. One reason is that a systems-based organisation will be more likely to control the customer relationship. Another is a need to capture greater margins, because components can tend to become commodities. Simply bundling products, though, is rarely enough. To deliver value to the customer, a firm must offer not only product breadth but a systems orientation and expertise.

Corporate Social Responsibility

Ikea has supported world causes like UNICEF for children's rights in India, the WHO for immunisation programmes and environmental causes like Global Forest Watch. German company Bayer collaborates with National Geographic to focus on the development of new sources of water supply; they have also committed to a Youth Environmental Program and Global Compact initiative for Human Rights. Boots supports Cancer Research UK with their SunSmart Campaign and fundraises for Breast Cancer Care and Children in Need. In each case these firms have used their involvement with society both to express their corporate values and to enhance their corporate image.

Chief executives believe that corporate social responsibility (CSR) can pay off. In one survey, more than 90% thought that socially responsible management creates shareholder value.[2] In another study, 300 firms judged to have high commitment to CSR had a slightly higher stock return during a two-year period beginning in October 2000.[3] Perhaps providing a more direct measurement, a UK study compared the marketplace performance of three energy companies. Two of these, BP and Shell, were perceived as environmentally friendly while the third, Esso, had visibly taken the position that renewable energy was not a viable solution and that the Kyoto international accords on the environment were flawed. Greenpeace subsequently attacked Esso with a high-profile 'StopEsso' campaign. A subsequent Greenpeace poll found that the proportion of British gasoline buyers who said they regularly used Esso stations dropped by 7% during the year of the campaign.[4]

There are good reasons why CSR could influence profitability. Many people fundamentally want to have a relationship with good people who can be trusted and they perceive that CSR programmes reflect a firm's values. A strong and visible CSR programme can deliver self-expressive benefits, particularly for the core group of customers who have strong feelings about environmental issues. Nokia, a world leader with respect to CSR, integrates various socially responsible programmes into their business, including community initiatives like the International Youth Foundation and environmental initiatives like their Eco Declaration, which details the materials used in the products and assists in its ultimate recycling and disposal. A CSR programme can also be defensive; in that it can help a firm deal with an accident or criticism by activists based on social responsibility issues.

Ad hoc programmes, though, are not the way to pursue CSR. Rather, the programmes need to be focused, meaningful, consistent over time and hopefully branded. All firms will give lip service and some resources toward CSR. The firms that stand out, such as BP, Cadbury and Boots have devoted considerable amounts of their company profits to social improvements.

There are challenges in pursuing a CSR strategy. One, perhaps the most serious, involves creating unreasonable expectations. If a firm is visible and active with regard to CSR, people will expect it to be flawless. Given the complexity of the issues, however, a firm can be making strides and still be criticised. Large energy firms such as BP can make significant investments in renewable energy relative to its competitors, for example, but some may correctly point out that the investment is still small relative to BP's size. Sports goods firms like Adidas can make progress in addressing the labour practices of its offshore suppliers, but still draw fire because problems remain. Another challenge is to make CSR programmes visible and relevant to customers, many of whom will find a firm's CSR activities too far removed from its offering's attributes and benefits.

This list of strategic options could be extended in any given context. For now, in the balance of this chapter and in the next two, we will explore seven options in more detail: quality, brand equity, value, innovation, focus, customer relationships and being global.

THE QUALITY OPTION

Perceived quality can be the driver of a business strategy as the Lexus case shows.

Lexus – A Passion for Excellence

In 2006 Lexus topped the JD Power & Associates UK Customer Satisfaction study for the sixth year in a row. The same survey identified Lexus as the industry leader in quality and reliability, service satisfaction and vehicle appeal. In recent years similar results have been achieved in other markets, including the US and Germany. These successes exemplify an incredible quality performance over a long time period.[5] Among the many reasons behind the Lexus achievement, several stand out. First, the

Lexus concept was based on quality from its inception. Toyota launched Lexus in the early 1980s as a brand that would take automobile design, manufacturing, and retailing to a new level. Second, the brand delivered on the concept as Lexus drew on assets and competencies developed by Toyota to make cars that were more reliable and had fewer defects. Third, a new-dealer network offered the potential to break from industry norms and provide a pleasant buying experience. Fourth, the positioning of the Lexus brand (with the classic 'relentless pursuit of perfection' tagline) delivered the quality message consistently over the years. The challenge facing Lexus now is that despite its success with a quality mission and message, it has failed to develop much personality in comparison to BMW, Mercedes and Jaguar. When the latter brands gradually closed the quality gap over the years, the Lexus message became less compelling. In response, Lexus belatedly has tried to inject some emotional and self-expressive benefits, as demonstrated by its modified tagline 'the passionate pursuit of perfection'. It has not been an easy task.

A quality strategy means that the brand – whether it is for hotels, cars, or clothing – will be perceived as superior to other brands in its reference set. The point of superiority is not limited to an attribute or service but spans the offerings, delivering exceptional quality across products and individual attributes. Usually, such superiority will be associated with a price premium.

The reference set could be premium offerings, for example BMW is compared with Mercedes, Lexus and Jaguar. A brand may also be superior within a reference set of value brands. Thus, Asda may be regarded as higher in quality than other discount retailers, although no one would confuse it with Waitrose or Harrods Food Hall. It will simply be judged on a different set of criteria, including ease of parking, waiting time at checkout, courtesy of the checkout person, and whether desired items are in stock.

Customers will define superiority. In nearly all contexts, a single overall indicator of quality exists, is relevant to customers, and in fact drives other, more specific dimensions of performance. To understand what drives perceived quality and to actively manage it, however, you will need to determine the underlying dimensions in any given context.

Figure 9.1 lists several dimensions of quality that are often relevant. Of course, each of these dimensions has multiple components (for example, performance for a

---

1. **Performance.** What are the specifications? How well is the task performed? Does the lawn mower cut grass well? Does the bank handle transactions with speed and accuracy?

2. **Conformance to specifications.** Does the product or service perform reliably and provide customer satisfaction?

3. **Features.** Does the airline offer the latest movie technology, the most comfortable seats, and the best frequent-flier plan?

4. **Customer support.** Does the firm support the customer with caring, competent people and efficient systems?

5. **Process quality.** Is the process of buying and using the product or service pleasant, rather than frustrating and disappointing?

6. **Aesthetic design.** Does the design add pleasure to the experience of buying and using the product or service?

Figure 9.1 Dimensions of quality

printer will involve attributes such as speed, resolution, and capacity). Further, the list itself will depend on the context. The dimensions of quality in a service or software context will differ from those in a product context.

In a service context – such as a bank, restaurant, or amusement park – research has shown that quality is based in large part on the perceived competence, responsiveness, and empathy of the people with whom customers interact.[6] A successful organisation therefore must deliver consistently on those dimensions. Delivering service quality, however, also means managing expectations. If expectations are too high, the service experience might be unsatisfactory even if it is at a high level. Generating clarity about the service promise, whenever possible, will thus be helpful.

Negative experiences are more salient than positive ones so avoiding them is often as important as creating positive ones. The challenge is to seek points of annoyance and attempt to reduce their incidence and intensity. For example, in order to make even waiting in line at their respective locations bearable, Disney provides entertainment with its delightful characters. In the software and information-products industry, the products need to work, but perceptions of quality are often driven by three other factors as well. First, the experience should not be frustrating: the product should be easy to install and use, even for those who are new to it. Second, the performance of the customer support centre is crucial. A good support experience will not only decrease user frustration but also help create a personal relationship by exhibiting concern and competence. Third, software users do not want to be left behind. They want a continuous stream of novel features and upgrades – not merely cosmetic changes, but real improvements that work.[7]

One trend is a greater emphasis on the *process* that customers experience rather than the output of the experience because often the output is harder to differentiate. Any part of the total customer-facing process may receive a quality focus, including the customer's information-gathering, transaction, and post-purchase experiences. One result can be the creation of branded features (such as Amazon's One-Click buying) or offering a simplified, less frustrating buying experience. Leading European retailers such as Boots, Carrefour, Metro Group and Sainsbury's now offer customers the opportunity to self-scan their purchases, reducing queuing time at checkouts.

Understanding what drives quality in a given segment is a critical step in creating a quality programme and monitoring its effectiveness. One risk in focusing on specific dimensions, however, is that the resulting measures can be counterproductive. For example, a company sought to improve the quality of its phone service by measuring the percentage of calls answered after the first ring. Unfortunately, the pressure to answer promptly caused agents to become abrupt and impatient with callers, and thus customer satisfaction suffered. The saying 'be careful what you wish for' is especially true in performance measurement.

Perceived Quality and Financial Performance

Perceived quality is a powerful construct. Image studies regularly show that customers who attribute high quality to a brand also will believe that it excels on a wide variety of attribute dimensions. Not surprisingly, quality is also associated with brand choice, in studies of the car market, customers' quality perceptions of automobiles, has found that its results influenced 40% of buyers.[8] Most important of all, though, perceived quality

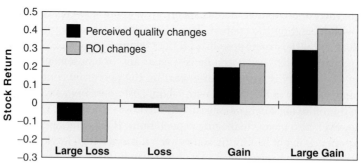

Figure 9.2   Perceived quality and stock return

has been found to be related to financial performance. An analysis of a database of some 3000 businesses found that firms in the highest twentieth percentile with respect to perceived quality averaged twice the ROI of those in the bottom twentieth percentile.[9] Perceived quality was found to affect ROI directly because the cost of retaining customers is reduced and indirectly because it allows a higher price to be charged and enhances the market share. The finding of higher market share suggests that a quality strategy does not have to involve a focus on narrow, ultra-high premium niches.

Perceived quality has also been shown by Aaker and Jacobson to drive stock return, a measure that truly reflects long-term performance.[10] They analysed annual measures of perceived quality obtained from the Total Research EquiTrend database for 35 brands for which brand sales were a substantial part of firm sales. The impact on stock return of perceived quality, they found, was nearly as strong as the impact of ROI. Given that ROI is an established and accepted influence on stock return, the performance of perceived quality is noteworthy. It means that investors are able to detect and respond to programmes that affect intangible assets such as perceived quality. Figure 9.2 shows the dramatic relationship between perceived quality and stock return.

Total Quality Management

To pursue a quality strategic option successfully, a business must distinguish itself with respect to delivering quality to customers. To accomplish this goal, it needs a quality-focused management system that is comprehensive, integrative, and supported throughout the organisation. Such a total quality management (TQM) system[11] should incorporate a host of tools and precepts, including the following:

- The commitment of senior management to quality, as evidenced by a substantial time commitment and an emphasis on TQM values.
- Cross-functional teams empowered to make changes by initiating and implementing quality improvement projects.
- A process (rather than results) orientation. The goal is not a one-time quality enhancement but to develop processes that will lead to quality improvements on an ongoing basis. Teams should use problem-solving tools and methods to develop programmes.

- A set of systems, such as suggestions systems, measurement systems, and recognition systems.
- A focus on the underlying causes of customer complaints and areas of dissatisfaction.

One approach used in TQM is to explore a problem in depth by repeatedly asking, 'why?' This process has been dubbed the 'five whys'.

- The tracking of key quality measures – including customer satisfaction, the ultimate quality measure.
- The involvement of suppliers in the system through supplier audits, ratings, and recognition, as well as joint team efforts.

Signals of High Quality

Most quality dimensions, such as performance, durability, reliability, and serviceability, are difficult if not impossible for buyers to evaluate. As a result, consumers tend to look for attributes that they believe indicate quality. The fit-and-finish dimension can be such a quality signal. Buyers assume that if a firm's products do not have good fit and finish they probably will not have other, more important attributes. An electronics firm, for example, found that its speed of responding to information requests affected its perceived product quality. In pursuing a quality strategy it is usually critical to understand what drives the perception of quality and then focus on small but visible elements. Research has shown that in many product classes, a visible key dimension can be pivotal in affecting perceptions about more important dimensions that are very difficult to judge.[12] Some examples for different markets are as follows:

- *Broadband suppliers.* A professional attitude on the part of the installation team means quality.
- *Tomato juice.* Thickness means high quality.
- *Cleaners.* A lemon scent can signal cleaning power.
- *Supermarkets.* Produce freshness means overall quality.
- *Cars.* A solid door-closure sound implies good workmanship and a safe body.
- *Clothes.* Higher price means higher quality.

QUALITY AT SHERATON

A team of two dozen people developed a service improvement programme at Sheraton labelled the Sheraton Guest Satisfaction System.[13] The system has several elements:

- Customer-satisfaction goals. Employees are expected to be friendly, acknowledge a guest's presence, answer guests' questions, and anticipate their problems and needs. Staff performance in these areas is measured, and good employees are rewarded with prizes and recognition.

- Hiring. Responses to videos of potentially problematic incidents help personnel select staff who really empathise with people.
- Training. A series of training programmes that include role-playing exercises help staff cope with difficult situations.
- Measurement. Quarterly reports are based on guest questionnaires that rate factors such as bed comfort and room lighting, as well as interactions with employees.
- Ongoing meetings. Performance is assessed, problems are corrected, and improvement programmes are developed.
- Rewards. The top-performing and most improved hotels each quarter become members of Sheraton's 'Chairman's Club.'

In the service context, the most important attributes, such as the competence of those providing the service, are extremely difficult to evaluate – consider, for example, how true this is for surgeons, librarians, airline pilots, dentists, or bankers. Customers cope by looking at those dimensions that are easily evaluated, such as the physical appearance of personnel, a facility or waiting time. The chairman of one airline was quoted as saying, 'Coffee stains on the flip-down trays mean [to the passengers] that we do our engine maintenance wrong.'[14] It is thus crucial to understand not only what customers believe is important with respect to quality but also what drives those perceptions.

THE BRAND EQUITY OPTION

Lynx

'How do you turn a £2.19 deodorant into a youth icon? Then, how do you keep it there for 17 years. Just ask Lynx.'[15] Lynx, marketed as Axe in Europe, is Europe's number one deodorant for men; it is Lever's leading male grooming brand and is sold in more than 50 countries. The success of Lynx is down to its ability to capture a particular emotion amongst its target market of young men. Lynx recognised that these young guys were more interested in the confidence smelling well gave them when meeting girls than in the functional benefits of freshness that other deodorant brands offered. Thus Lynx adopted simple message: use Lynx and get the girl.[16] To execute this theme Lynx have used both product innovation and advertising to create and sustain their brand equity. Product innovation at Lynx is simple, they offer six varieties of deodorant and introduce a new one each year with the weakest from the previous year being culled. With constant product innovation, new users and old have ongoing opportunities to engage and reengage with the brand.[17]

In advertising terms Lynx have created some of the most iconic advertising of the past twenty years. Although the creative side of Lynx advertising is a vital part of the story, the advertising strategy is probably more so. Following its introduction in 1985

Lynx used advertising themes that reflected the view of masculinity that prevailed society at the time. The advertising themes were of man as hero and conqueror and were responsible for the enormous success of the brand at the start of its life. The man got the girl but he did so in a heroic fashion. However, research in the early 1990s showed that Lynx was in danger of becoming the Brut of the 1990s.[18] That is a brand whose understanding of masculinity was far from current and which had become a burden. The response from Lynx and its advertising agency was to seek to monitor and update their understanding of masculinity as it evolved. This led Lynx to commercials that mirrored the 'new Lads' culture of the mid-to-late 1990s, the emergence of 'lads with girls' culture of the late 1990s and more recent themes such as seduction. Prior to the England versus Sweden game in the 2006 World Cup, Lynx launched its 'Billion' commercial. The ad featured an uncountable number of young women running, swimming and climbing to get to a guy alone on a beach spraying himself with two cans of Lynx. The closing headline 'spray more, get more' reflected the current interpretation of 'use Lynx get, the girl'. The ad was then featured on the Lynx website and a variety of other websites and became a phenomenon over the summer of 2006.

The benefits of these efforts have been a brand that was launched at a 50 % price premium and has managed to maintain that premium. In addition, in econometric modelling, Lynx outsells own brand products more than three times with its price premium retained, if the price was reduced to that of own label brands its brand equity would allow it to outsell the own labels 4.7 times.[19] The youth target market presents a particular challenge as the market must be recaptured every five years or so. In 1990 Lynx was used by 32.7 % of 15–19 year olds; in 1996 by 72.1 % and in 2001 by 81.5 %;[20] in each case there was a different cohort of users and in each case a very high level of penetration.

The Lynx case demonstrates the strategic value that building and maintaining brands and creating brand equity confer on the owners of a business. Branding represents one of the central tenets of marketing and so various definitions of a brand appear in marketing texts.[21] One defines a brand as 'a name term, sign, symbol or design or combination of them, which is intended to identify the goods of one seller or group of sellers and to differentiate them from those of competitors'.[22] This and other definitions generally fail to capture the essence of what branding involves or achieves. Inevitably couched in abstract and lifeless language they focus primarily on the ingredients of the brand and as such fail to capture the essence of branding. The development of brand image involves the marketer in breathing life into an innate product, thereby endowing it with a distinct personality and human characteristics in the eyes of the consumer. Branding results in an invisible yet magnetic relationship between brand and consumer which must of necessity involve the brand in the world of the consumer. The concept of brands as social signals is now well accepted with congruity between brand and user self-image regarded as a key motivational factor in consumer choice. So much so that it has been suggested that brands are part of consumers and consumers are part of brands.[23] The case of Lynx demonstrates how a brand can become integral to the life of a consumer. The value of this in the creation of competitive advantage is best understood through the concept of brand equity.

Figure 9.3   Sources of brand equity

Brand equity as a strategic option puts the creation of brand equity, or the building of strong brands, to the fore. Brand equity refers to the set of brand assets and liabilities linked to a brand, its name and symbol, that add to or subtracts from the value provided by a product or service to a firm and/or to that firm's customers.[24] When brands with high brand equity are thought of, a number of obvious examples come to mind, Coca-Cola, Nokia, Disney each are large brands which provide consumers with clear expectations, certainty of deliverables and for their owners they provide the reward of an enviable price premium. In Figure 9.3, the sources of brand equity are highlighted and discussed in the following sections.

Sources of Brand Equity

Brand Awareness

Brand awareness refers to the strength of a brands presence of a brand in the memory of a consumer. Brand awareness can create a reason to buy as well as a basis for a customer relationship. It is remarkable how much familiarity can influence. Taste tests of food and drink brands show that a recognised name can positively effect evaluations even if the consumer has never purchased or used the brand. Brand awareness can signal presence, commitment, and substance – attributes that can be very important, to industrial buyers of big-ticket items as well as consumer buyers of durable goods. The logic is that if a brand is recognised, there must be a reason.

Marketers usually consider two main measures of awareness: prompted and unprompted awareness. The former refers to consumers' ability to recognise the name of a brand from a list of brand names; the latter to their ability to recall the brand name when asked to identify brand in a category – for example which brands of ladies' perfume or champagne can you recall? The answers to these questions are important for marketers, particularly unprompted awareness. Consider business travellers who visit an airport duty-free shop to buy perfume for their mothers. The choice is vast, there are literally hundreds of options. How do consumers solve this problem? Most customers have a small number of brands that they can recall on an unprompted basis in each category, this is their consideration set for that category. The likelihood is that without significant external intervention the brand purchased will come from that consideration set.

It can be very difficult to dislodge a brand, or to enter the consideration set for a category, where one or a number of brands has achieved a dominant awareness level. For example, when Cadbury's Boost was launched to target what manufacturers refer to as the gutfill market it had a difficult time competing against existing mature brands in this sector like Mars and Snickers, which at the time had dominant brand awareness as hunger-buster snacks. Thus brand awareness can provide a brand owner with a durable and sustainable advantage.

Brand awareness also provides a strong base around which to develop a brand through attaching other associations. For example, the fastest growing prepackaged cheese brand in the UK, Cheesestrings, used advertising and a branded website to introduce a healthy association to the brand. The new message emphasised its 100% cheese content and the absence of sugar and preservatives in the product. The frozen food category has suffered as consumer preferences have switched to fresh foods. One of the leading brands in the category, Findus, has approached the problem by emphasising the positive health aspects of its ranges. For example, that freezing preserves the freshness of its foods and the absence of GMO's provide reassurance on the health benefits of its products. The advantage of such associations is that they expand the appeal of the brand.

Brands with high awareness tend to be liked and thus purchased more frequently. Remaining with the theme of health awareness, brands in categories that have had long term association with health such as mineral water, fruit juice and soya-based products have benefited from this market trend.

Historically brand awareness was built through advertising, particularly through TV, radio and press. The Carlsberg 'Danes don't want to see it leave' and 'Carlsberg don't do…' campaigns do not refer to any particular attribute of the brand but have raised considerable awareness for the Carlsberg brand.

While these media are still popular, the emergence of new promotional tools and the fragmentation and clutter of media channels makes the task of building brand awareness more formidable. Even for giant brands like Philips, Nestlé and Virgin, which have a broad product and sales base, maintaining visibility is a challenge. The key is to become skilled at operating outside the normal media channels by using event promotions, publicity, sampling, and other attention grabbing antics which are now broadly referred to as 'buzz marketing'. One example of this is the Adidas' 'impossible is nothing' campaign featuring six of Adidas' top celebrity endorsers including Muhammad Ali and David Beckham. They used large outdoor media in Athens during the 2004 Olympic period, set up 100-foot tall streaming video wall projections on historical buildings in London and Paris, and in specific London tube stations every media unit on platforms was used so onlookers were faced with the campaign logo 'Nothing is Impossible' no matter were they looked. This allowed Adidas to increase their awareness levels much more effectively than if they had relied only on mass media advertising.

Sponsorship is also an important tool in awareness building. B&Q's sponsorships of sailing's Ellen MacArthur in order to build awareness of their brand in France were sailing is a very popular pastime. Within three years MacArthur had secured second place in the Vendée Globe round the world race and B&Q had benefited with free publicity valued in the region of €120 million.[25]

Perceived Quality

The issue of quality was dealt with earlier in this chapter, at this point the focus will be on how quality perceptions affect customer behaviour. For many people quality provides a strong reason to buy. Kobe beef, Dom Perignon champagne, Macallan whiskey and Padron cigars all share a common trait, they are generally regarded as being the best quality brands in their respective categories. For this reason they are priced at a premium, available only selectively and are heavily in demand. Quality does not have to mean the absolute best but may also refer to a best in class. Toyota produces cars for the mass market but their quality and reliability relative to their price have made them world leaders and provided a strong reason to choose them above other brands.

The pursuit of quality in certain categories has led to communities forming around the advancement of quality. In the chocolate market Seventypercent.com, referring to the high cocoa content of quality chocolate, provides chocolate fans with the opportunity to review products, discuss trends and purchase fine products.

Quality is successfully employed by many brands, such as Singapore Airlines, Honda and Samsonite, as a basis for differentiation or positioning. Bose has used sound quality as the basis for its differentiation. Employing the twin tracks of a strong commitment to research and heavy investment in the brand and its promise, Bose has used quality to achieve a leadership position in its field. Quality relates to its technology, which uses research based on how the ear responds to sound, its manufacturing, which produces sleek, flawless products and its commitment to producing only those products that can deliver significantly better performance than competitors. This commitment to quality has allowed Bose to become a trusted consumer brand with high repurchase intent. In 2006 Forrester Research ranked Bose as the most trusted consumer brand in the US ahead of other brands such as Apple and Sony.[26] A brand which has a high quality perception will also more easily support extensions. Samsonite has a strong reputation for quality in the luggage market and has used this to expand its franchise to travel products, including a wider range of bags, wallets and personal items. In a crowded channel environment, high quality products may also be more likely to be listed by retailers, other distributors or sought out online by consumers.

Brand Associations

The third component of brand equity is the associations the consumer makes with a brand. Associations are important as they provide consumers with a connection to the brand that they can use to recall the brand. Associations can be any aspect of the brand that the consumer relates with the brand including functional attributes such as safety (Britax car seats), design (Dyson, Honda), brand symbols (Puma), brand terms, ('because I'm worth it') usage situations (Dom Perignon for celebrations).[27] One common error in brand building is to overemphasise functional benefits that may limit the ability of the brand to extend into other areas as well as providing competitors with a target which they can use to attack the brand.[28] Aaker has suggested that brands wanting to create a positive overall identity might promote associations which include functional benefits but also emotional (Diesel's association with youthfulness, tribalism and Italian design) and self-expressive benefits (the elegance and sophistication of Grey Goose vodka), organisational intangibles (Dyson's expertise in design and innovation), brand personality (L'Oréal's – because I'm worth it) and symbolic representations of the brand (Puma's leaping cat). The value of this wider view of brand associations lies in the greater opportunity it provides for a consumer to develop a positive relationship with the brand and the potential it provides to extend the brand into other areas.

Associations are created using a variety of elements of the marketing mix. Diesel for example, has a long-term commitment to abstract and creative advertising. The iconic chocolate bar, Bounty, sponsors the Love Island reality TV shown in the UK and Ireland in order to reinforce its association with tropical paradise. Such an association provides the brand both with a useful point of differentiation and through the related association of tropical paradise with indulgence, an important motivation to buy chocolate.

Brand Loyalty

Brand loyalty is a measure of the commitment a consumer has to rebuying the brand in the future. Brand such as Toyota, Apple and Google have legendary levels of loyalty. For the owners of these brands the benefits are great. Foremost is the disincentive loyalty provides for new competitors to enter. A loyal customer base also provides marketing economies. It has been estimated that the costs of attracting a new customer can be up to six times of retaining an existing one.[29]

One of the most important aspects of brand loyalty is the role which loyal consumers play in promoting the brand to other consumers, through word-of-mouth communications about the brand. The recommendation of a knowledgeable friend can have a much higher level of credibility than advertising by a firm. With this in mind Frederick Reichheld has suggested that firms should measure this activity by asking customers how likely they would be to recommend a brand to a friend and calculating the 'net-promoter score'.[30] The management value of this score is that increasing the net promoter figure can lead to higher growth for the firm and so provides a useful performance metric.

Brand loyalty is also important in gaining support from retailers. The essence of retail is to maximise stock turnover. Brands with a high level of loyalty such as Fairy, Nescafe, Colgate and Andrex provide retailers with an assurance of turnover and drives their willingness to list these products. Extensions of brands with high loyalty are also more likely to be attractive to supermarkets.

From the consumer perspective brand loyalty is also important. Think of the brand of toothpaste you use, when you go to buy toothpaste how much time to spend deciding about the brand? Unless you have a specific need (such as sensitive teeth) chances are that you don't spend a great deal of time. Now think of all of the other products that you buy regularly but don't really think about. Consumers use loyalty and routine to reduce the amount of time they have to spend thinking about making purchases for some products in order to free up time to think about other things. Think again of your experience of the supermarket. How many people are stationary in front of the toothpaste? How many are dawdling in the wine aisle?

The Financial Benefits of Brand Equity

Placing a value on brands is difficult and contestable. What is not is less disputable is the contribution that brands make to the financial wellbeing of the firm. Brand contribute to the value of the firm in four ways:[31]

- *Increasing cash flow.* Brands with high equity can charge higher prices and increase their cash flow. Greater certainty over demand also allows them to purchase materials and plan manufacturing more effectively, thus reducing costs.
- *Accelerating cash flows.* New product introductions from strong brands are adopted more quickly and thus their cash flow is accelerated.
- *Adding to the long term value of the business.* Strong brands tend to have long and certain lives as revenue generators. This enhances the continuing value of cash flow and the value of the business.
- *Lowering the costs of capital.* As the cash flow of the branded business is more certain, its cost of capital is reduced.

Building and Maintaining Strong Brands

The creation of brand equity requires strategy, investment and commitment. In the previous discussion we have considered how brand equity might be created. It is also important to understand how to maintain that equity once it is created. A number of techniques exist but the most prominent is the Brand Report Card developed by Kevin Keller.[32] This management tool looks at the management actions required to create brand equity and identifies the qualities of strong brands.

The Brand Delivers Benefits Customer Truly Desire

Ryanair and easyJet can be thought of in many ways, but above all else their popularity is based on delivering benefits that their customers truly desire: getting from point A to point B, cheaply and easily. This type of fundamental thinking is of value to all marketers. The invitation is to ask if brands truly meet the needs of customers, if unmet needs exist and if so what products are being developed to meet them.

The Brand Stays Relevant

In response to the threats to their brands posed by rising obesity and broader health concerns, companies such as Cadbury, Nestlé and Walkers are innovating with their brands to meet the challenges and to ensure that their brands successfully embrace them. Other brand owners should ask themselves if their brand portfolio makes similar provision for emerging trends and for the type of routine renewal that every brand portfolio requires.

The Pricing Strategy is Based on Customer's Perceptions of Value

There are many reasons why Apple iTunes has been such a fantastic success, one of those lies in its pricing. Firstly, consumers can buy the exact tracks they want at an individual price without buying an entire album. Secondly, the price of tracks is a very acceptable 99 cents in the Eurozone. Managers should ask if the price they charge for their brands are based on similar value perceptions.

The Brand is Properly Positioned

Walkers Sensations was launched in response to the emergence of the high-growth kettle chip market. Although it had many of the characteristics of kettle chips it was positioned as an everyday treat rather than a special treat, as kettle chips were. In addition it was priced at a 20 % premium to ordinary crisps while kettle chips were at a higher premium. Brand owners need to ask if their brands have identified and communicated suitable points of parity and points of difference for their brands.

The Brand is Consistent

The strongest message from the Lynx case study presented at the start of this section is the importance of a consistent brand message over time. Lynx has consistently appealed to the emotions of young men. For other brands the question is whether conflicting messages are being sent.

The Brand Portfolio and Hierarchy Make Sense

For managers the question is whether the brand portfolio offers satisfactory branded coverage of your market. Cadbury's family brand and a number of sub-brands offer consumers a choice from a strong branded portfolio.

The Brand Uses and Coordinates the Full Repertoire of Marketing Activities to Build Equity

Guinness uses a wide repertoire of marketing activities to support its brand including advertising, brand website, sponsorship, promotions and the outstanding Guinness Storehouse visitor centre in Dublin. Brand owners should ask if their brand would benefit from the unique ability of any communications tool not currently being used or from an existing tool being used differently.

The Managers of the Brand Understand what the Brand Means to Customers

Managers of British Airways and Singapore Airlines understand what their brands mean to the business traveller. They understand why their customers pay a premium for their services and they work hard to maintain customer understanding. For other brand owners is there an understanding at all levels of management of why customer value their brands?

The Brand is Given Proper Financial Support and that Support is Sustained over the Long Run

Is the brand and its ongoing maintenance provided with the appropriate levels of financial support?

The Company Monitors Sources of Brand Equity

Companies such as Colgate-Palmolive and Canada Dry have appointed brand equity managers to ensure that a long-term view is taken to the monitoring, reporting and protection of brand equity.[33]

With tools like this the temptation is always to seek to maximise the company's score on each dimension. However, the value of the tool is as a diagnostic rather than a measurement device. Thus its usefulness lies in its ability to highlight the relationship between elements and how a change in one might affect another over time, as much as in the absolute measurement.

The Challenge to Branding

For marketers the benefits of brands are obvious. However, commitment to the development and maintenance of strong brands is not even and there are forces within and beyond the firm placing pressure on brand owners. The first is earnings pressure. The average tenure of the CEO is falling around the world and those who meet shareholder expectation in terms of earnings are more likely to keep their jobs. Cutting the marketing budget, particularly for expensive advertising or brand development activity, is easier and has a more immediate impact on earnings than improving productivity or opening up new markets. Heinz has come in for criticism in this regard as they have reduced marketing spend order to maintain earnings with a resulting perception that their core brand messages are not as clear as they need to be.[34]

Retailers also offer a complex threat to brands. While they obviously require strong brands to encourage consumers to shop in their stores, they are increasingly introducing their own brands and put manufacturer brands under increasingly pressure for margin increases and marketing support. Retailer action in this area is becoming more sophisticated and has moved far on from the time when own label was associated with cheap but nasty products. Many retailers such as Tesco and Marks & Spencer have produced own brand ranges which are of the highest quality and command premium pricing.

Finally, marketers themselves have been guilty of over-reliance on sales promotion techniques. The pressure on brand managers is to drive brand sales and in many categories promotions have become the norm rather than the exception. In 2006 the managing director of Procter & Gamble, UK & Ireland, Gianni Ciserani, noted that brands were under threat from reduced investment in brand building and innovation as a result of pressure to cut prices for consumers and an over reliance on promotions.[35]

While the benefits of a strategic commitment to brand equity are clear, the challenges to sustaining investment in brands are many and growing.

KEY LEARNINGS

- Strategic options – that is, particular value propositions for a product market with supporting assets and competencies and functional strategies and programmes – form the basis for successful business strategies.

- To be successful, strategic options should contain both real and perceived value propositions and be relevant, sustainable, and feasible.
- Among the many possible strategic options can be based on a product attribute, product design, product line breadth, corporate social responsibility (CSR), quality, brand equity, value, innovation, focus, customer relationships, and being global.
- One common strategic option is to create an offering with real and perceived superiority in quality to reference competitors in the eyes of customers. Quality dimensions will depend on the context but could include performance, conformance to specifications, features, customer support and process quality.
- Research has shown that perceived quality drives both ROI and stock return.
- An important strategic option is to build brand equity. Brand equity has four main sources, brand associations, brand awareness, brand loyalty and perceived quality
- Brands with high brand equity provide their owners with competitive and financial benefits.

FOR DISCUSSION

1. Consider three of the following strategic options: product attribute, product design, product-line breadth, corporate social responsibility, brand equity, and quality. For each of these three strategic options, think of two firms not mentioned in the book that have pursued them. Which of the two firms has done better with respect to the five business strategy challenges? Discuss why and how that firm was able to do better.

2. Evaluate the quality strategy of Volkswagen with respect to the business strategy challenges. How might Volkswagen add more personality and emotion to its brand? Think of role models that have achieved a quality reputation and a strong personality.

3. Pick a product or service offering. How would you develop a set of customer survey questions that would measure its quality on an ongoing basis? How would you administer the survey?

4. What are the lessons from the Lynx case for other companies and brand owners?

NOTES

1. David A. Aaker (2004) Hybrids, The heavenly bed and purple ketchup. The Brands Lecture, British Brands Group.
2. Stan L. Friedman (2003) Corporate America's social conscience. *Fortune*, 23 June, p. S6.

3. Ibid.

4. Esso – should the tiger change its stripes? *Reputation Impact*, October 2002, p. 16.

5. Lexus, http://www.lexus-europe.com, 2006.

6. Valarie A. Zeithaml, Leonard L. Berry and A. Parasuraman (1988) Communication and control processes in the delivery of service quality. *Journal of Marketing*, April, pp. 35–48. A. Parasuraman, Leonard L. Berry and Valarie A. Zeithaml (1990) Guidelines for conducting service quality research. *Marketing Research*, December, pp. 34–44.

7. C. K. Prahalad and M. S. Krisnan (1999) The new meaning of quality in the information age. *Harvard Business Review*, September–October, p. 110.

8. Lawrence Ulrich (2003) Toyota, Lexus lead in quality, www.auto.com/industry, 16 June.

9. Robert Jacobson and David A. Aaker (1987) The strategic role of product quality. *Journal of Marketing*, October, pp. 31–44.

10. David A. Aaker and Robert Jacobson (1994) The financial information content of perceived quality. *Journal of Marketing Research*, May.

11. For a summary of total quality management in the US, see the special issue on this subject in *California Management Review*, Spring 1993.

12. A. Parasuraman, Leonard L. Berry, and Valarie A. Zeithaml (1990) Guidelines for conducting service quality research. *Marketing Research*, December, pp. 34–44.

13. David Walker (1989) At Sheraton, the guest is always right. *Ad Week s Marketing Week*, 23 October, pp. 20–1.

14. Tom Peters and Nancy Austin (1985) *A Passion for Excellence*, New York, Random House, p. 77.

15. Michael Kelly and Matthew Gladstone, 'Lever Faberge - Lynx', Advertising Effectiveness Awards, 2002. © 2006 Copyright and database rights owned by WARC

16. Ibid

17. Ibid.

18. Ibid.

19. Ibid.

20. Ibid.

21. The structure and content of this view of branding was provided by Prof. Tony Meenaghan.

22. Philip Kotler (1988) *Marketing Management: Analysis, Planning and Control*, Englewood Cliffs, NJ, Prentice-Hall.

23. J. Lannon and P. Cooper (1983) 'Humanistic advertising - a holistic cultural perspective. *International Journal of Advertising*, 2, 195–213.

24. David A. Aaker (1991) *Managing Brand Equity*, Free Press, New York, p. 15.

25. Ellen McArthur, http://www.redmandarin.com/news/media-articles/sailing-sponsorship-sail-of-the-century.

26. Olga Kharif (2006) Selling sound: Bose knows. *Business Week*, 15 May.

27. David A. Aaaker and Erich Joachimsthaler (2000) *Brand Leadership*, Free Press, London, p. 17.

28. David A. Aaker (1996) *Building Strong Brands*, Free Press, London, p. 25.

29. Frederick F. Reichheld (1995) *The Loyalty Effect*, Harvard Business School Press, Boston MA.

30. Frederick F. Reichheld (2003) The one number you need to grow. *Harvard Business Review*, December.

31. Peter Doyle (2000) *Value Based Marketing*, John Wiley & Sons, Chichester, pp. 229–32.

32. Kevin Lane Keller (2000) The brand report card. *Harvard Business Review*, January-February.

33. Peter Doyle (2002) *Marketing Management and Strategy*, Pearson Education Limited, London, p. 185.

34. Claire Murphy, The Trouble with Heinz, Marketing, 14 June 2006, p. 26–28

35. Joanna Bowery (2006) P&G boss slams innovation-stifling promotions. *Marketing*, 4 May.

CHAPTER TEN

Strategic Options: Value, Focus, Innovation and Customer Relationships

If you want to build a ship, don't drum up the men to gather wood, divide the work, and give orders. Instead, teach them to yearn for the vast and endless sea.
—*Antoine de Saint Exupery*

What matters in the new economy is not return on investment, but return on imagination.
—*Gary Hamel*

Never follow the crowd.
—*Bernard M. Baruch*

*I*n this chapter, we will continue detailing strategic options that are widely used, which have led to success over a long time period, and for which some experience and insight are available. These include the value, innovation, focus and customer relationship options. In each case, although positioning is important, the strategy needs more: commitment, ongoing investment, and programmatic management over time. The culture and values of the organisation need to support the strategy. The soundest strategy from a market-place view will ultimately falter if the organisation is not compatible and supportive.

THE VALUE OPTION

Aldi

Aldi is an international hard discount supermarket chain that was founded in Germany in 1946. Its goal is to provide products at aggressively low prices and it has managed to establish a large market with this tactic. Aldi's price competitiveness stems from a cost-cutting, no-frills strategy. Aisles are left undecorated and it is common to find empty

184

shelves with the products simply placed on a pallet alongside the shelves; once customers have cleared a pallet it is replaced. They have adopted a minimal staffing level,
which is evident from the sometimes long checkout queues in Aldi stores, although an
efficient checkout system means that a long queue may not always mean a longer waiting time than other stores. Stores have no telephone listings to reduce the time spent
on answering the phone and minimising the time that checkouts are left idle. Aldi tries
to keep its stores as small as possible to avoid spending money on high land prices in
urban areas. In most of Europe Aldi does not advertise except in local papers or by
direct mail, although it began advertising in the UK in 2005. With the introduction of
the Euro, customers generally believed that retailers used the changeover to increase
prices of products, but Aldi included before and after prices on products and rounded
the euro price down instead of up like other retailers. This earned it considerable
goodwill amongst customers. Many of Aldi's products are own-brand labelled with the
number of other brands limited. Aldi offer special weekly buys, like 'Thursday buys'
or Sunday buys', with exceptional discounts on clothing, toys, flowers and so forth.
Such strategies appear to be accepted by customers in exchange for the value that they
receive from Aldi. While the Aldi's brand reputation is associated with cheap shops
selling poor quality goods, in countries like Germany Aldi countered and changed this
reputation by introducing cookbooks that used only Aldi products which altered the
public's opinion of Aldi's undeserved reputation. In the UK Aldi faced strong price
competition with British retailers but remains profitable (although still a small player
with only 3 % of the market), due to its commitment to its strategic principles.[1]

easyGroup

The easyGroup was founded in the UK in 1995 with the establishment of easyJet,
a lowfares airline. In 1998, as the airline developed as a brand the easyGroup was
formed. Today the easyGoup is the owner of the easy brand name and franchises in
a dozen industries – mainly in travel, leisure, telecoms and personal finance. In their
own words the easy brand stands for great value, taking on the big boys, for the many
not the few, innovation, simple, entrepreneurial, honest, open and fun. The company
brand, culture and strategy has enabled them to apply generic lessons and organisational capabilities to achieve success across diverse industries. They follow the easy
format of a no-frills strategy to make the product or service cheaper for the customer.
These strategies include using technology to automate customer service and reduce
labour costs and adopting a yield management approach to managing supply and demand. The key to the success of this lies in starting at a low headline grabbing price
and then increasing or decreasing the price depending on the level of demand. For
example, cinemas in the UK have only a 20 % occupancy rate and easyCinema adopted
a strategy of changing the price to meet the demand to improve this occupancy rate,
depending on the time of week, demand for a film and how long the film had been out
for. easyCinema breaks other rules of the cinema industry by encouraging customers
to bring their own food and drinks with them. Traditionally it is very expensive for
customers to buy these in the cinema and this has been a source of customer dissatisfaction. easyJet, the low-fares airline operation, succeeded in displacing a number
of established airlines by attracting the low end budget travellers. The flexibility of

the low-cost strategy leaves easyJet with greater flexibility to cope with crises such as the turbulence that struck the airline industry after September 11. easyJet was able to drop its price without affecting its profit margin. The strategic principles of the easyGroup have allowed them to compete aggressively with industry leaders and achieve phenomenal success across many industries. The company culture has a distinct sense of adventure and innovation with six full-time employees called the New Ventures Team dedicated to identifying new opportunities to expand the easy brand into different markets. easyGroup have specific criteria for examining the potential of new businesses – they decide if the business can be summed up in one word: 'simple'.[2]

Ford and the Experience Curve

Ford introduced the Model T in 1908, and by the mid-1920s it had sold 15 million. It was a car that was reliable, easy to operate, and remarkably inexpensive.[3] The Model T began its life priced at $850 (around $17 000 in modern dollars) but the price fell continuously until in 1922 it cost less than $300. As a result, the demand for automobiles expanded, affecting the work and lifestyle of the time. The car could be value priced because of the mass production that Ford pioneered. Model Ts all used the same chassis, were almost all the same colour (black) and were designed to be easy to build. As a result, production costs declined according to an 85% experience curve (that is, costs fell roughly 15% every time cumulative production doubled). Figure 10.1 presents the pattern. The experience curve effect was created in part because of the building of the huge River Rouge plant, a reduction in the proportion of management staff (from 5% to 2% of all employees), extensive vertical integration, and the creation of the integrated, conveyor-driven mechanised production process.

In the early 1920s, however, consumers began to request heavier, closed-body cars that offered more comfort. The Model T design could not be adapted and, in 1927, Ford had to shut down operations for nearly a year to retool. The focus on cost reduction and exploiting the experience curve, it turned out, limited the company's ability to respond to changing times and competition. The standardised product, extensive vertical integration, and single-minded devotion to production improvements

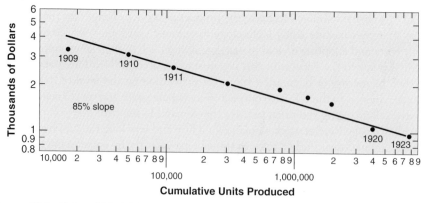

Figure 10.1   Price of Model T, 1909–23 (average list price in 1958 dollars)

had clear experience-curve advantages but they also tended to create an organisation whose goals and thrust were intimately involved with preserving the status quo, the existing product. There is no free lunch.

In nearly every market, from kitchen appliances to cars to toothpaste to booksellers to financial services, there will be a segment that is motivated by price. Even in high-end markets such as luxury cars there can be radical price differences, between brands. Significant price differences also exist in single product ranges with entry level and range topping models sometimes differing by up to 100%. Whether it comprises 10% or 80% of the market, the price segment will usually be a significant one. Ignoring the value segment can be risky because even healthy markets can evolve into situations where price grows in importance. In consumer electronics, appliances, and other product arenas, competitors have created overcapacity, causing a need to create or maintain a critical mass in the market. Powerful retailers with their own brands as competitive tools are another potential contributing force. Thus, ignoring the value segment may not be an option. It may be necessary to participate, perhaps with a value brand or as a private label supplier, in order to maintain scale economies.

As Figure 10.2 suggests, to compete successfully in the value arena it is necessary to:

- have a cost advantage (or at least avoid a cost disadvantage)
- make sure the quality perception does not erode to the point that the offering is considered unacceptable, and
- create a cost culture in the organisation

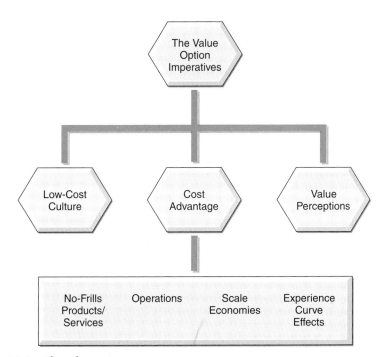

Figure 10.2   The value option

Creating a Cost Advantage (or Avoiding a Cost Disadvantage)

Although there is a tendency to think of low cost as a single approach, there are actually many dimensions to cost control and thus many routes to a cost reduction. The successful low-cost firms are those that can harness multiple approaches, including the use of no-frills products/services, operational efficiency, scale economies and the experience curve.

No-Frills Product/Service

One direct approach to low cost is simply removing all frills and extras from a product or service. Budget hotels like Jury's Inn and Hotel Formule 1 provide a service with limited extras and amenities. No-frills airlines like BMI Baby, Ryanair and easyJet follow a similar strategy offering no-frills services at a lower cost. Supermarket chains such as Tesco with their 'Value Lines', KwikSave and Iceland all provide own-label brands that offer a cheap, basic alternative to branded products. These products are adequate for consumers but may lack the aesthetic appeal of popular branded products and are generally not supported in a marketing sense. Value furniture retailer Ikea use self-service warehouses and self-assembly strategies to create sustainable cost advantages.

A major risk, especially in the service sector, is that competitors will position themselves against a no-frills offering by adding just a few features. In the low cost airline market in the US JetBlue has made strong inroads by offering budget fares but offering inflight services such as snacks and inflight TV. The result of such strategies can be a feature and price war.

Operations

Enduring cost advantages can also be created through efficiencies in operations. They can be based on government subsidies, process innovation, distribution efficiency (like Tesco's supply-chain management system), access to target markets (Internet banking services appealing to young to middle-aged professionals and bringing them out of banks), outsourcing competencies and the management of overheads.

To obtain significant operational economies it is useful to examine the value chain and look for inherently high-cost components that could be eliminated or reduced by changing the way that the business operates. The best example is the disintermediation of channel members. By selling directly, and by cutting out brokers, companies like Direct Line, a single-product UK motor insurance company, was able to sell to customers more cheaply. Online selling of products like books, music, clothes and food eliminate the need for physical stores thereby reducing costs.

Another place to find operations-based cost savings is in the interface with a supplier or customer. Zara links its stores, warehouses and design centres by computer to ensure an efficient design and supply system. In the US, Procter & Gamble (P&G) realised that retailers were buying products and shipping them across country, or storing them for months just to take advantage of short-term price deals, leading to grossly inefficient ordering and warehousing practices.[4] In response, P&G embarked on an ongoing partnership with Wal-Mart to optimise the system. One result was a continuous replenishment system for reordering, shipping, and restocking that would minimise shipping and warehouse costs, inventory, and out-of-stock conditions. Another was a revision of the trade discount policy to remove incentives to engage in unproductive gaming of promotions. Ten years after the partnership programme began, stockkeeping units were down 25%, sales staffing was down 30%, inventory was down 15%, and the programme was expanded to all major P&G customers.

Making operations more efficient can be a battle. Firms successful at reducing costs plan and implement incremental improvements over time. The devil is in the details. Each component of operations needs to be considered an opportunity. Banks in an effort to reduce the number of customers visiting their premises introduced service improvements like telephone and Internet banking, which provide convenience for customers and reduce costs for banks. Utility companies like Vodafone and O2 eliminated pay-over-the-counter billing and introduced mandatory direct debits for new customers to reduce transaction costs for them. These are all small improvements aimed at advancing the cost position. Continuous improvement in efficiency, as companies like Ryanair strive for by charging customers for baggage to discourage them from bringing extra luggage and improve the efficiency of check-ins, can create an ongoing competitive advantage.

There is always resistance to change, especially to major shifts in processes and perspectives. So a change agent is often needed. The catalyst can be a person who comes in and makes sure that cost reduction is a priority and that all aspects of the organisation are involved, or sometimes it can be an acquisition. A merger or acquisition can reduce costs not only by eliminating redundancies but by removing barriers to change. The result can be a much leaner operation than was once in place.

Scale Economies

The scale effect reflects the natural efficiencies associated with size. Fixed costs such as advertising, sales force overheads, R&D, staff work, and facility upkeep can be spread over more units. Furthermore, a larger operation can support specialised assets and activities (such as market research, legal staff, and manufacturing engineering operations) dedicated to a firm's needs. During its early days, Amazon maintained that the fixed costs of warehousing and technology would ultimately create a sustainable cost advantage, but only when the scale of its operations reached billions of dollars. The firm was ultimately proved correct.

An empirical study of the performance of 109 food, beverage, and consumer products companies of different sizes demonstrates the phenomenon of scale economies.[5] Figure 10.3 shows the financial performance of small firms (49 firms with sales

	Small	Tweeners	Large
Operating-profit growth rate	(2.8%)	3.4%	9.6%
Return on assets	7.1%	9.0%	15.7%
Shareholder return over five years	(1.2%)	3.8%	6.2%

Figure 10.3   Financial performance by firm size

FOCUS

Shouldice Hospital

Shouldice Hospital near Toronto only does hernia operations.[6] Since its founding in 1945, nearly 300 000 operations have been conducted, with a 99 % success rate. Measured by how often repeat treatment is needed, Shouldice is 10 times more effective than other hospitals. The surgical procedure used is branded as the Shouldice Technique. The experience of the doctors and staff is appealing but so are the Shouldice setting and its recovery programme. Located on a country estate, the hospital has a calming ambience and facilities tailored to needs of recovering hernia patients.

Patients walk to watch TV, to eat, and even to and from the operating room, because walking is good therapy for hernias. There is thus no need to deliver food to rooms, or to have wheelchair facilities. The length of a hospital visit at Shouldice is around half the norm elsewhere. No general anaesthesia is administered, because local anaesthesia is safer and cheaper for hernia operations.

By concentrating on one narrow segment of the medical market, Shouldice has developed a hospital that is proficient, inexpensive, and capable of delivering an extraordinary level of patient satisfaction. Ex-patients are so pleased that the Shouldice Hospital annual reunion attracts some 1 500 'alumni.'

O'Brien's Sandwich Bars

The O'Briens Sandwich Bars franchise was established by Brody Sweeney in 1988. In 2006 there were 270 outlets in 13 countries including Ireland, the UK and Singapore. The secret to the success of the franchise has been its focus on the sandwich and its accompaniments. Over time growth in franchise sales has been driven by refinement of this concept without a loss in focus. The Guilt Free Food concept at O'Brien's has seen them addressing the health concerns of convenience food consumers by identifying low fat and low GI sandwich and other innovative food options. In addition, they have developed their range of beverages to include fresh fruit smoothies and a variety of organic foods. Reflecting the focus strategy, and the ability of this firm to actively manage and maintain its focus, a pre-existing strong commitment to social responsibility has been expanded with a move to offer fair-trade tea and coffee.

Castrol Motor Oil

Castrol Motor Oil is a very successful global brand in the shadow of European competitors such as Esso, Shell, Elf, and private-label brands from power retailers. There are two keys to Castrol's strategy. First, it focuses on male car owners who change their own oil. Castrol has no distribution in service stations but that is not a liability for its chosen segment. The brand personality and communication efforts used by Castrol to match its macho, independent customer profile are very different from those needed by the major players in order to reach a broader market. For example its website has a very strong reporting feature on the Grand Prix season and other motor sports popular with European car enthusiasts. Second, Castrol engages in a very dynamic product and package policy, creating niche offerings and keeping retailers off balance.

A focus strategy concentrates on one part of the market or product line and can emerge in virtually any arena. Gucci, Prada and Armani designers and Hotel Goldner Hirsch in Austria focus on the upscale segment. A car-parts manufacturer may focus on supplying large volume customers only or just a single company. Bailey's has sought to expand it's appeal from special occasions but keep its focus on being a treat, by sponsoring TV shows like *Sex in the City* on LivingTV with the slogan 'girls' night in'. The clothing retailer Evans is focused on designer plus sizes for women and providing a positive shopping environment for its customers. In order to enhance the buying environment each sales person attend a 'fit to flatter' training programme where they are trained to match garments to particular body shapes.

Focus strategies concentrate resources, provide a way to compete when resources are limited, and add credibility to a positioning strategy (see Figure 10.4).

Concentrating Resources and Energy

Because a focus strategy by its nature tends to avoid strategy dilution or distraction, it is more likely to lead to a sustainable advantage. When internal investments, programmes and culture have all been directed toward a single end and there is buy-in on the part of everyone in the organisation, the result will be assets, competencies, and functional strategies that match market needs. In most cases, expansion of the product line or market results in compromises and a diluted ability to deliver on the business model. For example, easyGroup's product portfolio is so diverse ranging from an airline, pizza delivery service to watchmakers, it may create confusion over what the brand actually means to consumers. Each sub-brand in the group is cannibalised by the diversity of the other brands. One reason is the strategic and operational advantages of focusing. Product focus can result in technical superiority. In most businesses, the key people have expertise or interest in a limited product arena. Those who are the driving force behind a fashion firm, for instance, may be interested primarily in women's high fashion. A bookstore may be established by someone who is interested in reading and literature. When the products of a firm capture the imagination of its

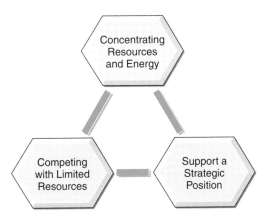

Figure 10.4   A focus strategy

key people, the products tend to be exciting, innovative, and high quality. As the product line broadens, however, the products tend to be me-too products, which do not provide value and detract from the base business. In such situations, the willpower to maintain focus by resisting product expansion may pay off. The potential of enhancing an SCA by using a focus strategy must be balanced by the fact that it naturally limits the potential business. As a result, profitable sales may be missed. Furthermore, the focused business will often have to compete with larger companies that will enjoy scale economies. Thus, it is crucial for the focus to be closely tied to a strategy with meaningful SCAs. Because of the appeal of a larger business and the perceived need to increase scale, it can take discipline to stick to a focus strategy.

Competing with Limited Resources

A business that simply lacks the resources to compete in a broad product market must focus in order to generate the impact needed to compete effectively. Such a limitation can occur, for example, when an automobile or airplane manufacturer faces heavy product development and tool costs, or a consumer products firm cannot afford to support multiple brands.

A focus strategy provides the potential to bypass competitors' assets and competencies. For example, in the fast-moving consumer goods (FMCG) industry (such as cereals, detergents and personal care) the ability to establish brand names and distribute branded products is a key success factor. However, firms can also do well by focusing on private-label manufacture, in which cost-control considerations dominate. These firms insulate themselves from the major manufacturers, who would compromise their own brands by producing private labels.

Although the payoff of a small niche may be less than that of a large, growing market, the competition may often also be less intense. The majority-fallacy concept states that appraisals of large, attractive segments overlook or minimise the likelihood that many competitors will be attracted to the segment resulting in destructive overcapacity. A more modest product-market scope involving smaller market potential may thus be a preferable choice.

Supporting a Strategic Position

A focus strategy may also provide a positioning tool. The association of a business with a narrow product line, segment, or geographic area can serve to provide a useful identity. For example, Brown Thomas department store in Dublin competes at the higher -priced end of the market and consequently appeals to a very narrow segment. Any effort to compete in a broader product market, even if feasible, would risk damaging the exclusive image it has developed for its existing stores. Narrow Aisle, based in the UK, is known as a manufacturer specialising in forklift trucks for narrow aisle warehouses.

A focus strategy can translate into a value proposition for customers that supports the strategic positioning. First, a focused firm will have more credibility than a firm that makes a wide array of products, as demonstrated by Shouldice Hospital in hernia surgeries and O'Brien's Sandwich bar in sandwiches. If you are really interested in the best, you will go to a firm that specialises in and has a passion for the business. Second, the bond between the loyal user and the brand will tend to be greater when the brand is focused. The popularity of Ann Summers underwear parties for women and the Innocent 'Fruitstock' festival would not happen without a focus strategy.

INNOVATION

Nokia

With its sharp designs, rapid model changes and feature additions based on a close monitoring of customer needs, Nokia was voted tenth most innovative company in the world in 2005 by the Boston Consulting Group. Although its position is under challenge from manufacturers like Sony Ericsson and Samsung, it remains the world's number-one manufacturer of mobile phones, selling in 130 countries. It is the world's largest telecommunications equipment manufacturer and sold 265 million handsets worldwide in 2005. Nokia have the advantage of outstanding loyalty from its traditional customers, together with a reputation for reliability and user-friendliness, which has resulted in one third of all mobile phones used in the world being manufactured by Nokia. Nokia's corporate culture is directed by 'The Nokia Way', which emphasises speed, flexibility, openness and employee participation. They are a progressive and forward thinking company and invest heavily in research and development in order to ensure they are 'first to market' with new technology. One of Nokia's problems is its difficulty in competing against electronics giants like Sony Ericsson and Samsung with their unparalleled expertise in technologies like digital photography and LCD displays. As these technologies became more and more important in modern phones, the gap between Nokia and its rivals became more apparent. Nokia's global share fell from 38 % in 2003 to under 30 % in 2004 due to Nokia's failure to keep up with consumers preferences for clamshell phones. Nokia's strategic aim was to position the brand as the personal brand of mobile phone technology. Their response was to focus more on innovative design and the concept of a 'fashion' phone and they introduced their first clamshell design followed by nine more models over the duration of a year, including mid-range and top-range handsets with digital cameras and colour, at the top end of the market. In 2003 Nokia launched the N-Gage handset, which is a high-end mobile gaming device, to compete against Sony PlayStation and Nintendo. When these failed to make the desired impact on their sales they launched the N-Series, a new range of multimedia computer phones, which allow customers to access more advanced video and camera functions and receive broadcast TV and MP3 music storage. They also launched a nonmobile device, the Nokia 770 Internet Tablet which is a mobile Internet and browser device. Nokia also developed the more sophisticated E-Series 'smartphones', which are designed for corporate customers. They now occupy a dominant position in the smartphone market with the Series 60 platform. Such is Nokia's devotion to expanding its business into new innovative areas that an investment division called BlueRun Ventures has been established and researches and develops new business areas outside Nokia's core business market's, for example in broadband, IP networks and other communications related services.[7]

Sony

Sony is one of the strongest brands not only in Japan, but throughout the world. In the US, the Harris Poll each year since 1995 has asked people to name what they believe are the top three product or service brands. In 2002, Sony was the most often-named brand for the third year in a row; during the seven years of measurement, Sony has never placed lower than third.[8]

One reason behind Sony's brand strength is its disciplined focus on innovation, as it strives continuously to deliver astonishing technology. Sony marketing executive T. Scott Edwards has noted that the Sony 'value proposition is innovation. Part of innovation is constantly providing consumers with news. Primarily we do that with new products.'[9] Sony France once had a tagline, 'If you can dream it, we can make it.' This captured the innovative spirit of the organisation.

Rather unique among Japanese firms, the Sony corporate brand is supported by a host of strong product brands. Some of these brands, such as Walkman, Handycam, and Aibo (a personal entertainment robot) have helped define a product category that is associated with Sony. Others, such as Trinitron and Wega (television), Xplod (mobile entertainment), Playstation (games), Clie (handheld PDA), Cyber-shot (digital camera), and VAIO (notebook computer) represent significant relevant product advances that are owned by the Sony brand. For example, in 2003 VAIO became (along with PowerBook) one of the strongest brands in the portable computer space despite being a late entry in part because of its dramatic design.[10]

The support that these brands received from and delivered to the Sony brand has been documented by the Dentsu advertising agency. The agency asked a sample of Japanese in 2000 about the extent to which they agreed with two statements: 'The brand contributes toward Sony's image' and 'I would choose it because it's a Sony.' The sub-brands PlayStation, Handycam, VAIO, and Walkman demonstrated a strong two-way flow of influence, supporting the Sony image, while the corporate brand helped make the sub-brand more attractive. For other sub-brands, however, the influence was neither always symmetrical nor strong. Aibo contributed to the Sony brand but relied less on the Sony connection for its own worth. Trinitron and Clie, in contrast, drew on the Sony brand strength but were relatively low on helping to support the Sony brand. Sony Life, an insurance brand used in the Japanese market that does not fit the Sony image or identity, was perceived as disconnected from the Sony brand in that it neither helped nor benefited from the corporate brand name.

Innovation may be the most widely used business strategy option. It is hard to find a firm that does not want to be truly creative in ways that touch the customer. Innovation is a sought-after ability because it goes to the heart of the offering – how can the product and its delivery to customers be improved so that the value proposition and point of differentiation are enhanced? For most firms, innovation means incremental improvement. They offer the same product or service, but add elements through creative engineering supported by investments. Nokia's mobile phones, such as the Nokia 9210, Nokia 7200 to the Nokia 9500 while improvement on earlier models still share the same basic functions of earlier products, and customers regard the improvements as incremental. Some firms, however, occasionally engage in disruptive innovation (a concept introduced in Chapter 6) by creating new products that define new product categories or subcategories. Both Sony and Nokia have been able to do this several times, an accomplishment that sets them apart from most companies.

While many firms strive for innovation, not all achieve it. Success requires a true commitment to innovation that survives pressures for short-term results. This commitment must be well managed so that the right people are given the right environment. Further, the organisation must be competent at turning innovation (whether it comes from R&D, marketing, the customer, or wherever) into commercial products and must be willing to take chances and be wrong.

The stimulation of strong competitors is often behind many innovative firms. Two of the 11 firms in the Collins list of 'good to great' companies that prospered by innovating were pushed by strong competitors. Nucor found new methods of steel production in the face of aggressively priced foreign suppliers. Kimberley-Clark sold off its mills and decided to compete directly with P&G in branded paper products by innovating behind brands like Huggies and Kleenex.[11] Companies producing women's cosmetic products like Clinique and Lancome are constantly under pressure from competitors and customers alike to produce innovations in their main product categories.

Innovation and the Value Proposition

Innovation provides value to customers along several dimensions. An incremental innovation usually enhances the value proposition by providing a new or improved attribute or feature. The confidence in purchasing the product or service, as well as the satisfaction in using it, will thus be enhanced. The value to the customer goes beyond the specific benefits, however, because an organisation perceived as innovative is usually seen to have other desirable characteristics that can affect purchase and loyalty. An innovative firm, for example, is often seen as having credibility in its product arena, which translates into trust and confidence. In some contexts, there are even prestige and self-expressive benefits in being seen as the innovator.

Firms such as Apple that create new categories or subcategories (as opposed to incremental improvements) are likely to generate additional benefits. First, the perception of being innovative is likely to be stronger. Second, to the extent that a new product category or subcategory is defined, the innovation has the potential to affect whether competitor brands will be considered relevant. Apple demonstrated this capability by defining the iPod space. Third, such innovations can generate first mover positions, giving the firm a perception of authenticity and the powerful associations that accompany it. The first-mover advantage is worth exploring further.

The First-Mover Advantage

As noted in the preceding paragraph, innovation can create a first-mover advantage. Competitors will be playing catch-up technologically. If they copy the innovation they risk being left behind again as advancements continue. In the meantime, the innovator can create customer loyalty based on several factors. One of these is simple familiarity; if the first mover's product or service is satisfactory, there may be no incentive to try something different. Alternatively, a customer may have been enticed or required to make a long-term commitment to the product or service. It then becomes not just risky, but expensive and inconvenient to change. To capture a first-mover advantage it is important to hit the market first and invest to build position. High initial prices may be an attractive way to capture margin and recover development costs but a low-price strategy may serve to build share and thus construct a more daunting barrier to followers. Followers will have the benefit of seeing the innovation, but will often need to create a significantly better offering to have a chance of dislodging the first mover among its user base. Making that user base as large as possible maximises the challenge.

RESEARCH ON EARLY MARKET LEADERS

It turns out that true market pioneers often do not survive – frequently because they entered before the technology was in place, or because they got blown away by larger competitors.[12] In contrast, Golder and Tellis found that early market leaders (that is, firms which assume market leadership during the early product growth phase) had a minimal failure rate, an average market share almost three times that of market pioneers, and a high rate of market leadership.[13] The authors noted that successful early market leaders tended to share the following characteristics:

- Envisioning the mass market. While pioneers such as Ampex in video recorders or Chux in disposable diapers charged high prices, the early market leaders (Sony and Matsushita in video recorders, or P&G in diapers) priced their offerings at a mass-market level. Timex in watches, Kodak in film, Gillette in safety razors, Ford in automobiles, and L'eggs in women's hosiery all used a vision of the mass market to fuel their success.

- Managerial persistence. The technological advances of early market leaders often took years of investment. P&G needed a decade of research to create the successful Pampers entry, and the Japanese firms spent twice as long developing the video recorder.

- Financial commitment. The willingness and ability to invest is a crucial factor when the payoff is in the future. For example, when Rheingold Brewery introduced Gablinger's light beer, it had a promising start, but financial downturns in other sectors caused the firm to withdraw resources from the brand. In contrast, Philip Morris invested substantially in Miller Lite for five years in order to achieve and retain a dominant position.

- Relentless innovation. It is clear that long-term leadership requires continuous innovation. Gillette learned its lesson in the early 1960s when the UK firm Wilkinson Sword introduced a stainless steel razor blade that lasted three times longer than Gillette's carbon steel blade. Gillette, after experiencing a sharp market share drop, returned to its innovative heritage and developed a new series of products.

- Asset leveraging. Early market leaders often also hold dominant positions in a related category, allowing them to exploit their distribution clout and a powerful brand name to achieve shared economies. Diet Pepsi and Coke's Tab, for example, were able to use distribution and branding advantages to take over the diet cola market from the pioneer, Royal Crown Cola.

- Follower advantages. Some firms deliberately engage in follower strategies in order to achieve reduced R&D investment, to make sure of the product's acceptance, and to learn about how customers buy and use the product. The follower can make sure the timing is right. Recall, for example, how Apple's Newton PDA was premature and struggled, whereas later competitors found a ready market.

THE CUSTOMER RELATIONSHIP OPTION

Manchester City Football Club is world renowned for the support they receive from their fans. Like all football clubs they face the problems of spiralling wages and transfer fees and the consequent need to maximise their revenue. When the club rejoined the premiership in 2003 it began to manage its customer relationships in a more sophisticated fashion to meet its financial challenges. Entry to the City of Manchester Stadium is by a RFID smart ticket through unmanned turnstiles. Fans can book tickets for games by phone or Internet and have them credited to their smartcard, known as a Citycard. This technology allows the club to see who is attending which games, what merchandise they buy and to communicate with them by email or SMS. The club has used this system to boost revenues in two ways. Firstly, it noted that many hardcore fans entered the ground less than thirty minutes before kick-off and so could not visit the club's merchandise store as it was on the opposite side of the ground to their seats. To remedy this, a mobile store was positioned to allow them to buy before merchandise games. A second initiative was a ticket buyback scheme that allowed the club to buy unused tickets back from fans and to re-sell them, generating approximately £500 000 per season.[14]

This example demonstrates how the management of customer relationships is becoming increasingly influenced by technology and the ambition of managing the customer as an individual. In recent years this process has come to be known as customer relationship management or CRM.

Customer Relationship Management (CRM)

The core principle of CRM is that greater profitability can be enjoyed if lasting and mutually beneficial relationships can be created between firms and their customers. While the promotion of loyalty or relationships has always been to the fore of business thinking, two trends have been to the fore in promoting the emergence of CRM. The first is the research of leading marketing thinkers such as Fred Reichheld, Don Peppers and Martha Rogers who promote the view that costs can be reduced and profits maximised if customers are marketed to directly. The second is IT advances such as database management and data mining. The ability of these tools, and the possibility of web based interactivity supporting mass customisation, has forced CRM to the fore in recent years.

While its practice is much debated, five core stages of the CRM process can be identified:

1. *Identify customers and create a database.* The starting point for CRM is to create, integrate and maintain an effective database of actual or potential customers. Very often firms will have multiple sources of information about customers; this should be integrated into a single system. Ideally the database should have a variety of information such as a customer purchase history, contact details, segment descriptor details and a history of the customer's responses to previous marketing efforts.[15] There are many vehicles for gathering customer information such as company and brand websites, with the advance of personal communications the mobile phone has become popular. For example, lingerie company Gossard used a 10-second slot after a TV advertisement inviting customers to text a number in exchange for a small discount on one of its lines. After customers sent their text messages they received a bounce back asking them for name, address and postcode to receive the voucher. This allowed Gossard to build a database of active customers which was targeted for a new product and which yielded a six months sales target in just six weeks.[16]

2. *Segment customers.* With the creation of a database, marketers segment customers based on customer profitability and other bases appropriate to their business. One of the benefits arising from the volume and quality of information that can be brought together in the customer identification and database creation stage is that segmentation can be based more on predictive variables than descriptive ones. Thus marketers can match customers with appropriate levels of investment with the most profitable customers in the future receiving one set of communications and other groups such as low profit and dormant customers receiving communications appropriate to their status. CPP are a card protection provider with a database of about seven million customers about which they knew little. For CPP, key customer outcomes are response to offer to purchase, cancellation during cooling off period, cancellation at the end of the year or cancellation within three years. CPP built a scorecard based on product usage factors, such as claims history, that allowed them to predict buying and cancellation behaviour and to target segments appropriately.[17]

3. *Interact with customers and build relationships.* Having identified the customers who are most valued the next stage is to develop a relationship with them with the objective of securing the benefits of reduced defection, improved customer profitability or extending the life of customer relationships. At this stage of the CRM process the task is to deliver a high level of satisfaction. Russ Winer[18] suggests a number of ways to drive satisfaction and build relationships:

- **Customer service.** The need for customer service to resolve problems as they arise is well established. Most firms have established routines for dealing with customer problems, some of these, such as at Ritz-Carlton, are significant sources of competitive advantage. CRM can play a role in supporting these efforts, but a bigger role in anticipating and resolving problems before they occur. British Gas faces a customer problem in that the average user thinks about utilities for about three hours per year and then only when a problem arises. In order to create a dialogue with its customers, British Gas has created an e-magazine, house.co.uk, which provides customers with information about dealing with common and easy to solve problems and managing bills, two of the major causes of customer problems.[19]

- **Customisation.** In essence customisation is creating products for individuals. WeightWatchers offers an online, personalised weight loss service. Using information members gave them regarding food preferences, individual eating plans are created. Customers indicate their preferred day to enter their weight each week and on the day prior a reminder email is sent. If weight is being lost too quickly a message is sent suggesting they slow down. Each member also benefits from personal weight loss charts.[20] While there will be clear economies here for WeightWatchers the personalisation of service offers the customer an enhanced service, with the communications devices supporting the relationship on an ongoing basis.

- **Community creation.** Creating a community around a company or brand and deepening the relationship between the brand and the customer can make defection to competitors more difficult. Increasingly, companies are recognising the value of community websites for information about product problems and development opportunities. The Mazda MX-5 is an iconic sports car, which had a number of unofficial clubs and websites devoted to it. Mazda launched its own website which allowed owners to interact with Mazda staff, as well as providing news about the car and a forum for interaction with other owners. In 2005 Mazda re-launched its website with the objective of increasing the level of activity on the site. Through more frequent updating and closer monitoring of the forums the number of unique visitors to the site rose by 150% with membership growth of 10% per month. Mazda's ambition is to use this deeper interaction to provide a better experience of the brand to its most loyal customers.[21]

- **Loyalty programmes.** The best known loyalty programmes are those run by airlines and supermarkets. In essence the customer is rewarded for repurchase. These schemes have been coming in for criticism in recent years as the schemes become generic and consumers have wallets full of loyalty cards. Virgin Holidays have overcome this criticism by offering those who book three holidays with them membership of their Frequent Virgin Club and providing them with 10% discounts, preferential treatment at resorts as well as member parties. Despite having to pay for them, these parties are regularly sold out.[22]

4. *Establish metrics.* As CRM offers an alternative approach to marketing, additional metrics are required. Two major categories of measures are appropriate. The first is lifetime customer value (LTCV). This is calculated by multiplying the average revenue per user by the average length of time a customers remains with firm, less the costs of acquiring and maintaining that customer. The figure is a key management metric as are each of its components. The second metric is customer share which is the percentage of a customer's total requirement over a period of time that the company fills. This figure is arrived at by calculating what a customer will spend on the category over a time period and dividing it by LTCV. This metric put the activities and achievement of the firm in context.

5. *Privacy concerns.* There is growing concern, particularly in Europe, regarding the information with companies retain on customers. This concern has the potential to reduce the confidence that customers have in brand and companies. It has also attracted the attention of government and regulatory bodies. In the EU the primary pieces of legislation are the Data Protection Directive, the Privacy and Electronic Communications Regulations Directive, as well as a variety of national regulations, which combine to create a somewhat unclear landscape for CRM activities.

Dealing with Problems with CRM

The growth phase for CRM in the 1990s saw large sums being spent on CRM software that promised to deliver 360-degree views of the customer as well as providing seamless support for field sales staff. In practice, many of these projects ran wildly over time and budget and perhaps only 50 % of these projects ever delivered what they promised. However, the need to understand and build relationships with customers remains. Four risks to be avoided for CRM success have been suggested:[23]

1. *Implementing CRM before creating a customer strategy.* Customer relationship management is not a strategy; it is a tool that supports a strategy. In order for CRM to be effective a company must have a customer strategy in place. The Irish Post Office, An Post, identified a need to have a clearer understanding of who its customers were and how they were buying in order to create communication with them. It implemented a CRM system that allowed them to pinpoint particular communications issues (such as dealing with complaints) and to resolve them.[24]

2. *Installing CRM technology before creating a customer-focused organisation.* The installation of a CRM system should be the final piece in a strategic and organisational jigsaw in which metrics, structures and incentives are all

faced towards the customer relationship. Without organisational and cultural support, CRM is likely to fail. One example of this kind of alignment is in the appointment of CCOs or Chief Customer Officers. Coca-Cola, Intel and HP and Campbell Soup have all appointed CCOs to ensure that the voice of the customer is heard at board level as well as ensuring that the culture and structures of the organisation are suitably aligned towards the needs of the customer.[25]

3. *Assuming more CRM technology is better.* For many firms the allure of CRM providers and the continuing development of CRM technology leads to the assumption that greater investment in technology will lead to better customer relationships. However, a better approach is to examine those situations where technology can play a role and where some other form of relationship building such as phone calls or thank you notes can play a role. Merlin Stone, a leading CRM thinker, has suggested that firms committed to the successful management of relationships with their customers spend time learning about the type of interactions and relationships which customers want to have with them and react accordingly, whether with or without technology.

4. *Stalking Customers, not wooing them.* Customers are being invited to have relationships with companies and brands every day. There may be an unrealistic expectation about what customers are willing or able to engage in.[26] Kodak is a well-established brand in the film market and has used CRM for a number of years to allow digital camera users to get the most out of their cameras. Upon registration at the Kodak website, new members receive an email every two weeks for 12 weeks to provide them with the basics of digital photography. Following this a monthly email is sent which Kodak themselves describe as 'useful, but not too intrusive.'[27] This approach to CRM may do a better job of convincing customers of the value of a relationship than a more aggressive approach.

KEY LEARNINGS

- A value position needs to be communicated effectively and supported by a cost advantage, which can be based on a no-frills offering, operations, scale economies, and/or the experience curve.
- A focus strategy avoids diluting or distracting from the implementation of strategy, provides a way to compete when resources are limited, can contribute to a positioning strategy, reduces competitive pressures, and can connect with customers. Following a focus strategy requires discipline to avoid expanding the offering.
- Innovation can generate a value proposition, enhance credibility, be prestigious, and create a first-mover advantage.
- CRM can provide sustainable advantage if managed pragmatically.

FOR DISCUSSION

1. Compare the value strategies of Aldi and easyGroup. How are they similar? How are they different? What are the bases for the value proposition in each case? Why has the advantage been sustainable?

2. Develop expansion options for Shouldice Hospital and/or O'Briens Sandwich Bars.

3. Have Shouldice Hospital and O'Briens generated first-mover advantages? How? What is to stop others from following them? Where do you see the primary competition for Shouldice and O'Brien's coming from?

4. Compare and contrast the innovation strategies of Nokia and Virgin. Which has engaged in disruptive innovation (introduced in Chapter 6)? Which is better described as having sustaining innovations?

NOTES

1. http://www.aldi.com/; http://biz.yahoo.com/ic/54/54910.html; "Aldi", Wikipedia, http://en.wikipedia.org/wiki/Aldi.

2. www.easy.com; Jackson Mahr, "easyGroup" Brandchannel.com, http://www.brandchannel.com/features_profile.asp?pr_id=236; INSEAD Knowledge Pass the Popcorn: What Should easyJet DO Next? http://knowledge.insead.edu/abstract.cfm?ct=12547.

3. William J. Abernathy and Kenneth Wayne (1974) Limits of the Learning Curve. *HarvardBusiness Review*, September–October, pp. 109–19. Figure 10.1, which is used with permission, is sourced from this article.

4. Material is drawn in part from Lawrence D. Milligan (1997) Keeping it simple, the evolution of customer-business development at Procter & Gamble. Remarks made at the American Marketing Association Doctoral Symposium, Cincinnati, July 1997.

5. Swandler Pace & Co. (1997) Does size really matter? *Research Note*, 10(3).

6. William H. Davidow and Bro Utal (1989) Service companies: focus or falter. *Harvard Business Review*, July–August, pp. 77–85.

7. www.Nokia.com; http://research.nokia.com; "Nokia" http://en.wikipedia.org/wiki/Nokia.

8. Humphrey Taylor (2002) Sony retains number one position in the Harris Poll annual 'Best Brand' survey for third year in a row. Harris Poll, July. http://www.harrisinteractive.com/harris_poll/index.asp?PID=311.

9. Kenneth Hein (2002) When is enough enough? *Brand Week*, p. 27.

10. According to research conducted by Techtel in 2003.

11. Jim Collins (2003) *Good to Great*, HarperBusiness, New York, Chapter 2.

12. Peter N. Golder and Gerard J. Tellis (1993) Pioneer advantage: marketing logic or marketing legend?' *Journal of Marketing Research*, May, pp. 158–70.

13. Gerard J. Tellis and Peter N. Golder (1996) First to market, first to fail? Real causes of enduring market leadership. *Sloan Management Review*, Winter, pp. 65–75.

14. David Murphy (2006) Premier league CRM. *Marketing Direct*, 10 April.

15. Russell S. Winer (2001) A framework for customer relationship management. *California Management Review*, 43(4).

16. David Murphy (2004) Data capture: new generation data capture. *Direct Response*, 30 June.

17. Sean Kelly (2003) Data clinic: technique – using data mining for market segmentation. *Direct Response*, 30 January.

18. Russell S. Winer (2001) A framework for customer relationship management. *California Management Review*, 43(4) summer.

19. Charlotte Goddard (2003) Personalisation Masterclass: the revolution masterclass on personalisation. *Revolution UK*, 1 November.

20. Brand engagement, *Marketing*, 5 July 2006.

21. Rob McLuhan (2005) Loyalty marketing: relationship builder. *Marketing Direct*, 26 September.

22. Darrell K. Rigby, Frederick F. Reichheld and Phil Schefter (2002) Avoid the four perils of CRM. *Harvard Business Review.*

23. Guy Tweedie (2006) 'Data clinic: technique – fighting back on the CRM failure culture, *Direct Response*, 14 June.

24. Dale Buss (2002) The new CCO: Delivering customer care, *Brandchannel.com*, 3 June.

25. Susan Fournier, Susan Dobscha and David Glen Mick (1998) Preventing the premature death of relationship marketing, *Harvard Business Review, January-February.*

26. Kim Benjamin (2005) Kodak case study: picture perfect. *Marketing Direct*, 21 July.

CHAPTER ELEVEN

Global Strategies

Most managers are nearsighted. Even though today's competitive landscape often stretches to a global horizon, they see best what they know best: the customers geographically closest to home.
—*Kenichi Ohmae*

A powerful force drives the world toward a converging commonality, and that force is technology... The result is a new commercial reality – the emergence of global markets for standardised consumer products on a previously unimagined scale of magnitude.
—*Theodore Levitt*

My ventures are not in one bottom trusted, nor to one place.
—*William Shakespeare,* The Merchant of Venice

M*any* firms find it necessary to develop global strategies in order to compete effectively.

A global strategy is different from a multidomestic or multinational strategy, in which separate strategies are developed for different countries and implemented autonomously. Thus, a retailer might develop different store groups, in several countries, that are not linked and that operate autonomously. A multidomestic operation is usually best managed as a portfolio of independent businesses, with separate investment decisions made for each country.

A global strategy, in contrast, represents a worldwide perspective in which the interrelationships between country markets are drawn on to create synergies, economies of scale, strategic flexibility, and opportunities to leverage insights, programmes, and production economies.

A global strategy can result in strategic advantage or neutralisation of a competitor's advantage. For example, products or marketing programmes developed in one market might be used in another. Or a cost advantage may result from scale economies generated by the global market or from access to low-cost labour or materials.

Operating in various countries can lead to enhanced flexibility as well as meaningful sustainable competitive advantages (SCAs). Investment and operations can be shifted to respond to trends and developments emerging throughout the world or to counter competitors that are similarly structured. Plants can be located to gain access to markets by bypassing trade barriers. Even if a global strategy is not appropriate for a business, making the external analysis global may still be useful. Knowledge of competitors, markets, and trends from other countries may help a business identify important opportunities, threats, and strategic uncertainties. A global external analysis is more difficult, of course, because of the different cultures, political risks, and economic systems involved.

A global strategy requires addressing a set of issues that include the following:

- Should the firm become global by entering new countries?
- What countries should be entered and in what sequence?
- To what extent should products and service offerings be standardised across countries?
- To what extent should the brand name and marketing activities (such as brand position, advertising, and pricing) be standardised across countries?
- How should the brand be managed globally?
- To what extent should strategic alliances be used to enter new countries?

Each of these issues will be explored in turn. The next section, in which the motivations for global strategies are presented, will be followed by discussions of how to select which countries to enter, standardisation versus customisation, global brand management, and the use of alliances in developing global strategies.

MOTIVATIONS UNDERLYING GLOBAL STRATEGIES

A global strategy can result from several motivations in addition to simply wanting to invest in attractive foreign markets. The diagram of these motivations shown in Figure 11.1 provides a summary of the scope and character of global strategies.

Figure 11.1   Global strategy motivations

Obtaining Scale Economies

Scale economies can occur from product standardisation. The Ford world-car concept, for example, allows product design, tooling, parts production, and product testing to be spread over a much larger sales base. Standardisation of the development and execution of a marketing programme can also be an important source of scale economies. Consider Coca-Cola, which since the 1950s has employed a marketing strategy – the brand name, concentrate formula, positioning, and advertising theme – that has been virtually the same throughout the world. Only the artificial sweetener and packaging differ across countries.

Scale economies can also occur from standardisation of marketing, operations and manufacturing programmes. Brands that share advertising (even when it is adjusted for local markets) spread the production and creative effort over multiple countries and thus a larger sales base. A firm similarly benefits when fixed costs involving IT and production technologies can be distributed over countries.

Desirable Global Brand Associations

Brand names linked to global strategies can have useful associations. For customers and competitors, a global presence automatically symbolises strength, staying power, and the ability to generate competitive products. Such an image can be particularly important to buyers of expensive industrial products or consumer durables such as cars or computers because it can lessen concern that the products may be unreliable or rendered obsolete by technological advances. Japanese firms such as Yamaha, Sony, Canon, and Honda operate in markets in which technology and product quality are important, and they have benefited from a global brand association.

Access to Low-Cost Labour or Materials

Another motivation for a global strategy is the cost reduction that results from access to the resources of many countries. Substantial cost differences can arise with respect to raw materials, research-and-development talent, assembly labour, and component supply. Thus, a computer manufacturer may purchase components from South Korea and China, obtain raw materials from South America and assemble in Mexico and five other countries throughout the world in order to reduce labour and transportation costs. Access to low-cost labour and materials can be an SCA, especially when it is accompanied by the skill and flexibility to change when one supply is threatened or a more attractive alternative emerges.

Access to National Investment Incentives

Another way to obtain a cost advantage is to access national investment incentives that countries use to achieve economic objectives for target industries or depressed areas. Unlike other means to achieve changes in trade, such as tariffs and quotas, incentives are much less visible and objectionable to trading partners. Thus, the British government has offered Japanese car manufacturers a cash bonus to locate a plant in the UK. The governments of Ireland, Brazil and a host of other countries offer cash, tax breaks, land, and buildings to entice companies to locate factories there.

Cross-Subsidisation

A global presence allows a firm to cross-subsidise, to use the resources accumulated in one part of the world to fight a competitive battle in another.[1] Consider the following:

One firm uses the cash flow generated in its home market to attack a domestically oriented competitor. For example, in the early 1970s, Michelin used its European home profit base to attack Goodyear's US market. The defensive competitor (Goodyear) can reduce prices or increase advertising in the US to counter, but by doing so, it will sacrifice margins in its largest markets. An alternative is to attack the aggressor in its home market, where it has the most to lose. Thus, Goodyear carried the fight to Europe to put a dent in Michelin's profit base.

The cross-subsidisation concept leads to two strategic considerations:[2]

- To influence an existing or potential foreign competitor, it is useful to maintain a presence in its country. The presence should be large enough to make the threat of retaliation meaningful. If the share is only 2 % or so, the competitor may be willing to ignore it.

- A home market may be vulnerable even if a firm apparently controls it with a large market share. A high market share, especially if it is used to support high prices and profits, can attract foreign firms that realise the domestic firm has little freedom for retaliation. A major reason for the demise of the US consumer electronics industry was that US firms were placed at a substantial disadvantage compared with global competitors that had the option to cross-subsidise.

INDICATORS THAT STRATEGIES SHOULD BE GLOBAL

- Major competitors in important markets are not domestic and have a presence in several countries.

- Standardisation of some elements of the product or marketing strategy provides opportunities for scale economies.

- Costs can be reduced and effectiveness increased by locating value added activities in different countries.

- There is a potential to use the volume and profits from one market to subsidise gaining a position in another.

- Trade barriers inhibit access to worthwhile markets.

- A global name can be an advantage and the name is available worldwide.

- A brand position and its supporting advertising will work across countries and has not been preempted.

- Local markets do not require products or service for which a local operation would have an advantage.

Dodge Trade Barriers

Strategic location of component and assembly plants can help gain access to markets by penetrating trade barriers and fostering goodwill. Locating final-assembly plants in a host country is a good way to achieve favourable trade treatment and goodwill because it provides a visible presence and generates savings in transportation and storage of the final product. Thus, Caterpillar operates assembly plants in many of its major markets, including Europe, Japan, Brazil, and Australia, in part to bypass trade barriers. An important element of the Toyota strategy is to source a significant portion of its car cost in the United States and Europe to deflect sentiment against foreign domination.

Access to Strategically Important Markets

Some markets are strategically important because of their market size or potential or because of their raw material supply, labour cost structure, or technology. It can be important to have a presence in these markets even if such a presence is not profitable. Because of its size, the US market is critical to those industries in which scale economies are important, such as automobiles or consumer electronics. It is likely that the growing middles classes of India and China will soon make them similarly important. Sometimes a country is important because it is the locus of new trends and developments in an industry. A firm in the fashion industry may benefit from a presence in countries that have historically led the way in fashion. Or a high-tech firm may want to have operations in a country that is in the forefront of the relevant field.

Sometimes adequate information can be obtained by observers but those with design and manufacturing groups on location will tend to have a more intimate knowledge of trends and events.

WHAT COUNTRY TO ENTER?

Once a firm has decided to become global, deciding what country or countries to enter – and in what sequence – is a key challenge. Entering any new market can be risky and take away resources that could be used to make strategic investments elsewhere. A frequently unforeseen consequence of global expansion is that healthy markets, especially the home market, are put at risk by this diversion of resources. It is thus important to select markets for which the likelihood of success will be high and the resource drain minimised.

Market selection starts with several basic dimensions:

- Is the market attractive in terms of size and growth? Are there favourable market trends? For many companies, China and India often appear attractive because of their sheer size and growth potential.
- How intense is the competition? Are other firms well entrenched with a loyal following, and are they committed to defending their position? When Tesco was first considering entering the continental European market it found that expansion to France was unattractive because of the established competition,

whereas Eastern European countries had much less formidable competition. As a result, Hungary was the first country in continental Europe that Tesco entered.[3]

- Can the firm add value to the market? Will the products and business model provide a point of differentiation that represents a relevant customer benefit? Tesco has developed an Internet-based home delivery system for grocery retailers that adds value in many markets, including the US.[4]

- Can the firm implement its business model in the country or do operational or cultural barriers exist? How feasible is any adaptation that is required? Marks & Spencer, a UK retailer spanning food, clothing, and general merchandise, attempted to export its offerings and the look and feel of its stores to the Continent, only to find that these offerings had little appeal to Europeans.

- Can a critical mass be achieved? It is usually fatal to enter countries lacking the sales potential needed to support the marketing and distribution effort needed for success.

  Understanding the four types of distance between a firm and the target country can be helpful in making these judgements, particularly the last two.[5] Geographic distance includes not only the physical distance but whether there is a common border, sea or river access, or a different climate. Administrative distance involves government policies, as well as possible restrictions on trade, monetary weakness, or political hostility. Cultural distance refers to dissimilar languages, ethnicities, religions and social norms. Economic distance means disparities in consumer incomes, national infrastructure, and the costs of natural and human resources.

These multiple forms of distance, particularly cultural and administrative distance, help explain why firms attracted to China's enormous potential are finding it difficult to enter successfully. In one survey, more than half of the firms admitted that their business performance in China had been 'worse than planned'.[6] Culturally, the language problem, the importance of personal connections, and consumer preferences for home-country brands all affect the success of foreign entrants into China. Administrative barriers such as market access restrictions, high taxes, and customer duties also inhibit entering firms.

A strategy of entering countries sequentially has several advantages. It reduces the initial commitment, allows the product and marketing programme to be improved based on experience in preceding countries, and provides for the gradual creation of a regional presence. Other factors, however, argue that global expansion should be done on as wide a front as possible. First, economies of scale, a key element of successful global strategies, will be more quickly realised and will be a more significant factor. Second, the ability of competitors to copy products and brand positions – a very real threat in most industries – will be inhibited because a first-mover advantage will occur in more markets. Third, standardisation, a topic to which we now turn, is more feasible.

STANDARDISATION VERSUS CUSTOMISATION

Standardised brands gained widespread credence as a strategy because of Ted Levitt's classic 1983 Harvard Business Review article, 'The globalisation of markets', which gave three reasons why it would succeed.[8] First, the forces of communication, transport and travel were breaking down the insulation of markets, leading to a homogeneity of consumer tastes and wants. Second, the economics of simplicity and standardisation – especially with respect to products and communication – represented compelling competitive advantages against those who held on to localised strategies. Third, customers would sacrifice preferences in order to obtain high quality at lower prices. The article provided an academic underpinning to the logical premise that standardisation should be the goal of a global business. Pringles, Visa, MTV, Sony, Dove, Unilever, Danone, BP, DeBeers, Nike, McDonald's, Pantene, Disney and IBM are the envy of many brand builders because they seem to have generated global businesses with a high degree of similarity in terms of brand, position, advertising strategy, personality, product, packaging, and look and feel. Pringles, for example, stands for 'fun', a social setting, freshness, less greasiness, resealability and the whole-chip product everywhere in the world. Further, the Pringles package, symbols, and advertising are almost the same globally. Disney's brand of magical family entertainment is implemented by theme parks, movies, and characters that are remarkably consistent across countries. These 'standardised' brands are often not as identical worldwide as one might assume. McDonald's has disparate menus, advertising, and retail architectures in various countries. Pringles uses different flavours in different countries, and advertising executions are tailored to local culture. Heineken is the premium beer to enjoy with friends everywhere – except at home in the Netherlands, where it is more of a mainstream beer. Visa even has had different logos in some countries (such as Argentina) and Coke has a sweeter product in areas like southern Europe. Regardless of these variations, brands that have moved toward the global end of the local global spectrum demonstrate some real advantages.

A standardised brand can achieve significant economies of scale. For example, when IBM decided to exchange some three dozen advertising agencies for one in order to create a single global campaign (even if it needed some adapting from market to market), one motivation was to achieve efficiencies. The task of developing packaging, a website, a promotion or a sponsorship will also be more cost-effective when spread over multiple countries. Economies of scale across countries can be critical for sponsorships with global relevance, such as the World Cup or the Olympics. Perhaps more important though, is the enhanced effectiveness that results from better resources. When IBM replaced its roster of agencies with Ogilvy & Mather it immediately became the proverbial elephant that can sit wherever it wants. As the most important O&M client, it gets the best agency talent from top to bottom. As a result, the chances of a well-executed breakout campaign are markedly improved. Cross-market exposure produces further efficiencies. Media spillover, where it exists, allows the standardised brand to buy advertising more efficiently. Customers who travel can get exposed to the brand in different countries, again making the campaign work harder. Such exposure is particularly important for travel-related products such as credit cards, airlines, and hotels.

A standardised brand is also inherently easier to manage. The fundamental challenge of brand management is to develop a clear, well-articulated brand identity (what you want your brand to stand for) and to find ways to make that identity a driver of all brand-building activities. The absence of multiple strategies makes this task less formidable with a global brand. In addition, simpler organisational systems and structures can be employed. Visa's 'worldwide acceptance' position is much easier to manage than dozens of country-specific strategies.

The key to a standardised brand is to find a position that will work in all markets. Sprite, for example, has the same position globally – honest, no hype, refreshing taste. It is based on the observation that kids everywhere are fed up with hype and empty promises and ready to trust their own instincts. The Sprite advertising tagline ('Image is nothing. Thirst is everything. Obey your thirst.') resonates around the world.

Several generic positions seem to travel well. One is being the 'best', the upscale choice. High-end premium brands such as Mercedes, Montblanc, Heineken and Tiffany's can cross geographic boundaries because the self-expressive benefits involved apply in most cultures. Another is the country position. For example, the 'American' position of brands such as Coke, Levi's, Baskin-Robbins, KFC and Harley-Davidson will work everywhere (with the possible exception of the US). A purely functional benefit such as Pampers' dry, happy baby can also be used in multiple markets. Not all brands that are high-end or American or have a strong functional benefit, however, can be global.

Standardisation can come from a centralised decision to create a global product. Canon, for example, developed a copier that had a common design throughout the world in order to maximise production economies. Unfortunately, the copier could not use the standard paper size in Japan, resulting in substantial customer inconvenience. The risk inherent in a truly global standardisation objective is that the result will be a compromise. A product and marketing programme that almost fits most markets may not be exactly right anywhere; such a result is a recipe for failure or mediocrity.

Another strategy is to identify a lead country – a country whose market is attractive because it is large or growing or because the brand has a natural advantage there. A product is tailored to maximise its chances of success in that country, then exported to other markets (perhaps with minor modification or refinements). A firm may have several lead countries, each with its own product. The result is a stable of global brands, with each brand based in its own home country. Nissan has long taken this approach, developing a corporate fleet car for the UK, for example, and then offering it to other countries. Lycra, a 35-year-old ingredient brand from Du-Pont, has lead countries for each of the product's several applications all under the global tagline 'Nothing moves like Lycra.' Thus, the Brazilian brand manager is also the global lead for swimsuits, the French brand manager does the same for fashion, and so on.

Global Leadership Not Standardised Brands

The fact is that a global brand is not always optimal or even feasible. Yet, attracted by the apparent success of other brands, many firms are tempted to globalise their own brand. Too often the underlying reason is really executive ego and a perception that globalisation is the choice of successful business leaders. Such decisions are often implemented by a simple edict – that only global programmes are to be used. The consolidation of all advertising into one agency and the development of a global advertising theme are typically cornerstones of the effort. Even when having a standardised brand is desirable, though, a blind stampede toward that goal can be the wrong course and even result in significant brand damage. There are three reasons.

First, economies of scale and scope may not actually exist. The promise of media spillover has long been exaggerated and creating localised communication can sometimes be less costly and more effective than adapting 'imported' executions. Further, even an excellent global agency or other communication partner may not be able to execute exceptionally well in all countries.

Second, the brand team may not be able to find a strategy to support a global brand, even assuming one exists. It might lack the people, the information, the creativity, or the executional skills and therefore end up settling for a mediocre approach. Finding a superior strategy in one country is challenging enough without imposing a constraint that the strategy be used throughout the world.

Third, a standardised brand simply may not be optimal or feasible when there are fundamental differences across markets. Consider the following contexts where a global brand would make little sense:

- *Different market share positions.* Ford's European introduction of a people carrier, the Galaxy, into the UK and Germany was affected by its market share position in each country. As the number-one car brand in the UK with a superior quality image, Ford sought to expand the Galaxy's appeal beyond soccer moms to the corporate market. So the UK Galaxy became the 'non-van,' and its roominess was compared to first-class airline travel. In Germany, however, where Volkswagen held the dominant position, the Galaxy became the 'clever alternative'.

- *Different brand images.* Honda means quality and reliability in the US, where it has a legacy of achievement based on the J. D. Powers ratings. In Japan, however, where quality is much less of a differentiator, Honda is a car-race participant with a youthful, energetic personality.

- *Preempted positions.* A superior position for a chocolate bar is to own associations with milk and the image of a glass of milk being poured into a bar. The problem is that different brands have preempted this position in different markets (for example, Cadbury in the UK and Milka in Germany).

- *Different customer motivations.* In Finland, after finding that users were apprehensive about perceived machine complexity, Canon became the copier that empowered the user, making him or her the boss. In Germany and Italy, however, more traditional attribute-oriented messages did better.

- *Names and symbols may not be available or appropriate everywhere.* The Ford truck name Fiera means 'ugly old woman' in some Spanish speaking countries. Procter & Gamble's Pert Plus needed to be sold as Rejoy in Japan, Rejoice in much of the Far East, and Vidal Sassoon in the UK because the Pert Plus name had been preempted. A global business strategy is often misdirected. The priority should be developing nonstandardised brands (although such brands might result) but standardised brand *leadership,* strong brands in all markets. Effective, proactive global brand management should utilise the people, systems, culture, and structure of an organisation to allocate brand-building resources globally, create global synergies, and develop a global brand strategy that will coordinate and leverage the strategies in individual countries.

GLOBAL BRAND MANAGEMENT

A study of some 50 global firms, conducted by David Aaker and Erich Joachimst-haler and extended by the Dentsu advertising agency, concluded that an effective global brand management system needs to address four challenges – developing a communication system to facilitate the sharing of insights and experiences, creating a global brand planning system, form an organisational structure that will resist the 'I am different' syndrome, and finding ways to achieve brilliance in brand-building (see Figure 11.2).[9]

Global Brand Communication System

A cross-country communication system that shares insights, methods and best practices is the most basic and nonthreatening element of global brand management. A customer insight that may be obvious in one country might be more subtle and difficult to access in another. For most companies, a cross-country system includes a person or small team that identifies and disseminates experiences, supplemented by global meetings where involved managers can exchange experiences (both formally and informally). Intranets often play an active role in the process, with the principal challenges being how to encourage people to express their experiences and preventing information overload. Mobil (now Exxon) addressed these challenges by having

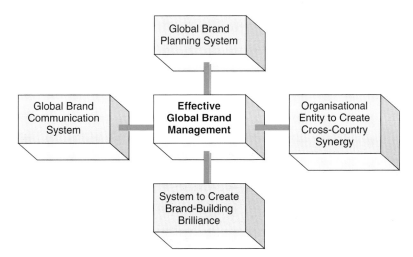

Figure 11.2   Effective global brand management

each intranet sponsored by a senior manager and directed by a leader/facilitator who provides the necessary energy, ideas, and continuity.

Global Brand Planning System

Every country manager needs to use the same vocabulary and planning template when developing strategies. Without this commonality, there is little chance of creating synergy across countries. The planning template should include some basic elements of strategic analysis, self-analysis, a business strategy, tactical plans, goals and measurement.

Organisational Brand Planning Structure

The goal of achieving significant global synergies is usually inhibited by local biases usually supported by a well-established decentralised structure and culture. Country managers often believe that context is unique, so consumer insights and best practices from other markets do not apply. They further believe that others lack the background to understand the subtle ways in which their country differs from others. To have any hope of creating synergy and leveraging programmes to achieve market success in the face of such biases, someone or some group needs to be in charge of the global brand. A global brand manager serves this role in some firms. There might also be a global brand team, with cross-country representation that can play either a leadership or supporting role.

Whether the global brand is represented by a person or a team, the people involved need three key ingredients for success, or at least access to these ingredients. The first is an in-depth knowledge of the local markets, including trends, competitor dynamics, segmentation, and customer motivations. The second is an understanding of the product or service, its underlying technology, and how the offering might be extended. The third is real authority and resources, as well as the ability to participate in the development of country-specific business strategies.

DYSFUNCTIONAL GLOBAL BRAND MANAGEMENT STYLES

When the centralised brand group lacks one or more of the three success ingredients, the brand management process is at risk of falling into one of the following models:

- Uninformed dictator model. In this model, a person with organisational power (sometimes the CEO) becomes a convert to brand power and standardisation. This reborn brand champion, however, lacks market and/or product knowledge and, most importantly, patience. As a result, he or she is prone to make arbitrary decisions without research or analysis. Perhaps, for example, a hasty decision is made to change a brand name or position after an acquisition, or whenever a brand appears inconsistent across markets. If such a decision damages the brand (or even if it is not supported within the organisation) the ability and willingness of employees to support the brand going forward can be affected as well.

- Brand bureaucracy model. The brand group in this model lacks adequate market knowledge and is seriously deficient in authority and/or resources. The team becomes little more than a logo cop charged with making sure that the visual presentation is correct and perhaps sending out forms to be filled in by the business units. This model can work for a while, especially when the visual presentation is clearly confused across markets. But over time, the team is often ignored as others recognise its lack of influence.

- All hat, no cattle model. This expression comes from the old American West popularised by cowboy movies where people with no resources (cattle) talk big (and wear 'big' hats) while others with thousands of head of cattle talk softly. In much the same way, management sometimes decides that brands are important but fails to provide the brand team with enough authority and/or resources. As a result, regardless of how capable the people are or how much market and product knowledge they have, the brand team cannot influence autonomous business units, hire outside brand experts, or really do anything of significance. As a result, the organisation gets frustrated or suspects that top management is only giving lip service to the brands. This model is all too common in Japanese firms.

- Anarchy model. In the anarchy model, the organisation has an extremely decentralised structure, with little guidance or cross-country communication. Market understanding, product knowledge, and strategic talent are sprinkled unevenly throughout the organisation. Some business units will do well, but the organisation as a whole will be underleveraged, and most countries will be vulnerable to underperformance.

The global brand manager or team can influence country strategies in a variety of ways. The best approach in a particular case will depend on the maturity of the global operation and the extent to which the decentralised culture is ingrained. At one extreme is the centralised command-and-control model, where external analysis and strategy are centralised and the country mangers are simply implementers. At the other is the anarchy model, one of five dysfunctional models described in the insert. In between are the service provider, consultant, and facilitator models.

- *Service provider model.* The central brand group will be a partner and service provider. It will select and manage the single advertising agency, for example, but the objectives for the communication will be initiated from the country and be jointly determined. The centralised group will control some of the brand-building budget, perhaps including sponsorships and corporate advertising.

- *Consultative model.* The central brand group learns about the markets, competitors, and customers and develops insights and brand options. It would then meet with the business units, provide insights, and make suggestions as to what brand strategy should be considered and what brand-building programmes are likely to be effective.

- *Facilitator model.* The central group becomes a facilitator in helping the business units work within a defined brand management process to develop sound strategies and would have less responsibility for knowing the markets and making strategy suggestions. Least threatening, this model is usually the best choice when introducing global brand management into an organisation.

Delivering Brilliance in Brand Strategy Implementation

Global brand leadership, especially in these days of media clutter, requires implementation brilliance – 'good enough' is *not* good enough. The dilemma is how to achieve brilliance in local markets while still gaining synergy and leverage as a global organisation. Here are some guidelines:

- Consider what brand-building paths to follow for example, advertising versus sponsorship, retail presence, or promotions. The genius may not be in execution per se but in the selection of the vehicles.

- Get the best and most motivated people to work on the brand. Some agency-client tension can be helpful in this regard; Audi, for instance, uses multiple agencies.

- Develop multiple options. In general, the more attempts you make at brilliance, the higher the probability that it will be reached. Procter & Gamble finds exceptional ideas by empowering its country brand teams to develop breakthrough brand-building programmes. When one is found (such as Pantene Pro-V's 'Hair so healthy it shines'), it is rolled out country by country.

- Measure the results. Measurement drives excellence, and a global brand measurement system is fundamental to excellence.

STRATEGIC ALLIANCES

Strategic alliances play an important role in global strategies because it is common for a firm to lack a key success factor for a market. It may be distribution, a brand name, a sales organisation, technology, R&D capability, or manufacturing capability. To remedy this deficiency internally might require excessive time and money. When the uncertainties of operating in other countries are considered, a strategic alliance is a natural alternative for reducing investment and the accompanying inflexibility and risk.

For example, IBM, which has relatively few alliances in the United States, has teamed up with just about everyone possible in Japan.[10] It has links with Ricoh in distribution of low-end computers, with Nippon Steel in systems integration, with Fuji Bank in financial systems marketing, with OMRON in integrated computer manufacturing, and with NTT in value-added networks. There is even a book in Japanese entitled *IBM's Alliance Strategy in Japan.* As a result, IBM is considered a major insider in the Japanese market, and it competes across the board in all segments and applications.

Strategic alliance is thus becoming a key part of global competition. Kenichi Ohmae, a Japanese management guru, has said that: Globalisation mandates alliances, makes them absolutely essential to strategy. Uncomfortable, perhaps – but that's the way it is. Like it or not, the simultaneous developments that go under the name of globalisation make alliances – entente – necessary.[11]

A strategic alliance is a collaboration leveraging the strengths of two or more organisations to achieve strategic goals. There is a long-term commitment involved. It is not simply a tactical device to provide a short-term fix for a problem – to outsource a component for which a temporary manufacturing problem has surfaced, for example. Furthermore, it implies that the participating organisations will contribute and adapt needed assets or competencies to the collaboration and that these assets or competencies will be maintained over time. The results of the collaboration should have strategic value and contribute to a viable venture that can withstand competitive attack and environmental change.

A strategic alliance provides the potential for accomplishing a strategic objective or task – such as obtaining distribution in Italy – quickly, inexpensively, and with a relatively high prospect for success. This is possible because the involved firms can combine existing assets and competencies instead of having to create new assets and competencies internally.

Forms of Strategic Alliances

A strategic alliance can take many forms, from a loose informal agreement to a formal joint venture. The most informal arrangement might be simply trying to work together (selling our products through your channel, for example) and allowing systems and organisational forms to emerge as the alliance develops. The more informal the arrangement, the faster it can be implemented and the more flexible it will be. As conditions and people change, the alliance can be adjusted. The problem is usually commitment. With low exit barriers and commitment, there may be a low level of strategic importance and a temptation to back away or to disengage when difficulties arise.

A formal joint venture involving equity and a comprehensive legal document, on the other hand, has very different risks. When equity sharing is involved, there is often worry about control, return on investment, and achieving a fair percentage of the venture. A major concern is whether such a permanent arrangement will be equitable in the face of uncertainty about the relative contributions of the partners and the eventual success of the endeavour. Also, one or more of the firms involved may tend to drag their heels and the venture may lose a window of opportunity. Another concern is that equity positions and the accompanying limits on each partner's contribution can result in a lack of needed flexibility as conditions change. Furthermore, the parties involved may rely excessively on legal documents to preserve the health of the alliance.

Motivations for Strategic Alliances

Strategic alliances can be motivated by a desire to achieve some of the benefits of a global strategy, as outlined in Figure 11.1. For example, a strategic alliance can:

- *Generate scale economies.* The fixed investment that Toyota made in designing a car and its production systems was spread over more units because of a joint venture with GM in California.
- *Gain access to strategic markets.* The Japanese firm JVC provided VCR design and manufacturing capability but needed a relationship with Thompson to obtain help in accessing the fragmented European market.
- *Overcome trade barriers.* Inland Steel and Nippon Steel jointly built an advanced cold-steel mill in the US. Nippon supplied the technology, capital, and access to Japanese auto plants in the US. In return, it gained local knowledge and, more important, the ability to get around import quotas.

Perhaps more commonly, a strategic alliance may be needed to compensate for the absence of or weakness in a needed asset or competency. Thus, a strategic alliance can:

- *Fill out a product line to serve market niches.* Ford, General Motors, and Chrysler have, for example, relied on alliances to provide key components of its product line. Ford's long-time relationship with Mazda has resulted in many Ford models, as well as access to some Far East markets. When Mazda decided not to build a minivan, Ford turned to Nissan for help. One firm simply cannot provide the breadth of models needed in a major market such as the US.
- *Gain access to a needed technology.* While JVC gained access to the European market, its European partner accessed a competitive VCR source.
- *Use excess capacity.* The GM/Toyota joint venture used an idle GM plant in California.
- *Gain access to low-cost manufacturing capabilities.* GE sourced its microwave ovens from Samsung in South Korea.
- *Access a name or customer relationship.* NGK bought an interest in a GE subsidiary whose product line had become obsolete in order to access the GE name and reputation in the US electrical equipment market. A US injection moulder joined with Mitsui in order to help access Japanese manufacturing operations in the US that preferred to do business with Japanese suppliers.
- *Reduce the investment required.* In some cases, a firm's contribution to a joint venture can be technology, with no financial resources required.

The Key: Maintaining Strategic Value for Collaborators

A major problem with strategic alliances occurs when the relative contribution of the partners becomes unbalanced over time and one partner no longer has any proprietary assets and competencies to contribute. This has happened in many of the partnerships involving US and Japanese firms in consumer electronics, heavy machinery, power-generation equipment, factory equipment and office equipment.[12] The result, when the US company has become deskilled or hollowed out and no longer participates fully in the venture, can be traced in part to the motivation of the partners. Japanese firms are motivated to learn skills; they find it embarrassing to lack a technology and they work to correct deficiencies. Firms from the US are motivated to make money by outsourcing elements of the value chain in order to reduce costs. They start by outsourcing assembly and move on to components, to value-added components, to product design and finally to core technologies. The US partner is then left with just the distribution function, whereas the Japanese firm retains the key business elements such as product refinement, design, and production.

Hamel, Doz and Prahalad studied 15 strategic alliances and offered suggestions as to how a firm might protect its assets and competencies from its alliance partner.[13] One approach is to structure the situation so that learning takes place and access to missing competencies and assets occurs. Compare, for example, the joint Toyota/GM manufacturing facility, where GM is involved in the manufacturing process and its refinements, to Chrysler's effort to sell a Mitsubishi car designed and manufactured in Japan. In the latter case, Mitsubishi eventually developed its own name and dealer network and now sells its car directly. When the motivation for an alliance is to avoid investment and achieve attractive short-term returns instead of to develop assets and competencies, the alliance will break down.

Another approach is to protect assets from a partner by controlling access. Many Japanese firms have a coordinated information transfer. Such a position avoids uncoordinated, inappropriate information flow. Other firms put clear conditions on access to a part of the product line or a part of the design. Motorola, for example, releases its microchip technology to its partner, Toshiba, only as Toshiba delivers on its promise to increase Motorola's penetration in the Japanese market. Still others keep improving the assets involved so that the partner's dependence continues. Of course, the problem of protecting assets is most difficult when the asset can be communicated by a drawing. It is somewhat easier when a complex system is involved – when, for example, the asset is manufacturing excellence.

The problem of protection is reduced substantially when the two partners bring complementary assets into the alliance that are core competencies of each and are the bases of other business areas. Thus, the danger that one will wither is low. Clintee International formed a joint venture between Baxter (a health-care giant) and Nestlé (the food and nutrition products firm) and realised more than $400 million in sales just three years later. Baxter was strong in the parenterals business, which included products that delivered nutrition intravenously or through a catheter, and it had experience with medical markets, mainly in the US. Nestlé had a strong background in basic nutrition, a growing interest in adult nutrition products, a strong research-and-development capability and a presence in world markets. Neither firm was likely to see its core strengths dissipated in the context of the joint venture.

Making Strategic Alliances Work

Even if an alliance is strategically sound, a host of operational problems can arise. One study of 37 joint ventures uncovered a variety of management problems.[14] In one case, the partners differed in terms of priorities for short-term versus long-term objectives. In another, a British firm could not understand a US partner's obsession with numbers and analysis. In still another, a sensitive decision about the location of a new plant became political. With strategic alliances, at least two sets of business systems, people, cultures, and structures need to be reconciled. In addition, the culture and environment of each country must be considered. The Japanese, for example, tend to use a consensus building decision process that relies on small group activity for much of its energy; this approach is very different from that of managers in the US and Europe.

Furthermore, the interests of each partner may not always seem to be in step. Many otherwise well-conceived alliances have failed because the partners simply had styles and objectives that were fundamentally incompatible. There are several keys to making a collaboration work. Perhaps the most important is that it be well planned to provide ongoing mutual benefit. Partners should make sure they have real assets and competencies that combine to provide strategic advantage.

These assets and competencies should continue to be relevant to the venture and to be maintained by the partners over time. If there is a significant ongoing strategic motivation reinforced by success, problems are more likely to be manageable. When a joint venture is established as a separate organisation, research has shown that the chances of success will be enhanced if:

- The joint venture is allowed to evolve with its own culture and values – the existing cultures of the partners will probably not work even if they are compatible with each other.

- The management and power structure from the two partners is balanced.

- Venture champions are on board to carry the ball during difficult times. Without people committed to making the venture happen, it will not happen.

- Methods are developed to resolve problems and to allow change over time. It is unrealistic to expect any strategy, organisation, or implementation to exist without evolving and changing. Partners and the organisation thus need to be flexible enough to allow change to occur.

Alliances are a widespread part of business strategy (the top 500 global businesses have an average of sixty major alliances each) but need to be actively managed. One study of some 200 corporations found that the most successful at adding value through alliances employed staff who coordinated all alliance-related activity within the organisation.[15] This function would draw on prior experiences to provide guidance to those creating and managing new alliances. IBM subsidiary Lotus, for example, has 'thirty- five rules of thumb' to manage alliances from creation to termination. The dedicated alliance staff would also increase external visibility (an alliance announcement has been found to influence stock price), coordinate internal staffing and management of alliances, and help identify the need to change or terminate an alliance.

KEY LEARNINGS

- A global strategy considers and exploits interdependencies between operations in different countries.
- Among the motivations driving globalisation are obtaining scale economies, accessing low-cost labour or materials, taking advantage of national incentives to cross-subsidise, dodging trade barriers, accessing strategic markets, and creating global associations.
- A brand with extensive commonalities across countries can potentially yield economies of scale, enhanced effectiveness because of better resources involved, cross-market exposure, and more effective brand management.
- The selection of a country to enter should involve an analysis of the attractiveness of the market and the ability of the firm to succeed in that market.
- A standardised brand is not always optimal. Economies of scale may not exist, the discovery of a global strategy (even assuming it exists) may be difficult, or the context (for example, different market share positions or brand images) may make such a brand impractical.
- Global brand management needs to include a global brand communication system, a global brand planning system, a global management structure, and a system to encourage excellence in brand building. The brand group can operate under a command-and-control, service provider, consultative, or facilitator style.
- Strategic alliances (long-term collaboration leveraging the strengths of two or more organisations to achieve strategic goals) can enable an organisation to overcome a lack of a key success factor, such as distribution or manufacturing expertise.
- A key to the long-term success of strategic alliances is that each partner contributes assets and competencies over time and obtains strategic advantages.

FOR DISCUSSION

1. Pick a product or service that is offered in a limited number of countries. Assess the advantages of expanding to a more global presence.

2. For a particular product or service, how would you evaluate the countries that would represent the best prospects? Be specific. What information would you need, and how would to obtain it? Prioritise the criteria that would be useful in deciding which countries to enter.

3. What is the advantage of a global brand team? What are the problems of using a team to devise and run the global strategy? When should a team lead, and when should it take on a supporting role? Would your answer differ for BP versus P&G? Why?

4. For a firm such as Royal Bank of Scotland, Danone or Renault, how would you go about creating blockbuster brand-building programmes – for example, sponsorships, promotions, or advertising? How would you leverage those programmes?

5. Select a company. How would you advise it to find an alliance partner to gain distribution into China? What advice would you give regarding the management of that alliance?

NOTES

1. Gary Hamel and C. K. Prahalad (1985) Do you really have a global strategy? *Harvard Business Review*, July–August, pp. 139–48.

2. Ibid.

3. Victoria Griffith (2002) Welcome to your glocal superstore. *Strategy and Business*, 26, p. 95.

4. Ibid.

5. Pankaj Ghemawat, 'Distance Still Matters,' *Harvard Business Review*, September 2001, pp. 137–147.

6. Ghemawat, op. cit., p. 144.

7. The material in this section draws from David A. Aaker and Erich Joachimsthaler *Brand Leadership*, New York, The Free Press, Chapter 10.

8. Theodore Levitt, (1983) The globalisation of markets. *Harvard Business Review*, May–June, pp. 92–102.

9. David A. Aaker (with Erich Joachimsthaler) (1999) The lure of global branding. *Harvard Business Review*, November–December.

10. Kenichi Ohmae (1989) The global logic of strategic alliances. *Harvard Business Review*, March–April, pp. 143–54.

11. Ibid.

12. David Lei and John W. Slocum, Jr. (1992) Global strategy, competence-building and strategic alliances. *California Management Review*, Fall, pp. 81–97.

13. Gary Hamel, Yves L. Doz and C. K. Prahalad (1989) Collaborate with your competitors – and win. *Harvard Business Review*, January–February, pp. 133–9.

14. J. Peter Killing (1986) How to make a global joint venture work. *Harvard Business Review*, March–April, pp. 78–86.

15. Jeffrey H. Dyer, Prashant Kale and Harbir Singh (2001) How to make strategic alliances work, *MIT Sloan Management Review*, Summer, pp. 37–43.

CHAPTER TWELVE

Strategic Positioning

If you are first you are first. If you are second you are nothing.
—*Bill Shankly*, Liverpool Football Club

Standing in the middle of the road is very dangerous; you get knocked down by the traffic from both sides.
—*Margaret Thatcher*

The secret of success is constancy of purpose.
—*Benjamin Disraeli*

S trategic position, the face of the business strategy, specifies how the business aspires to be perceived (by its customers, employees, and partners) relative to its competitors and market. Strategic initiatives and communication programs are driven by strategic position, and it is the guiding beacon for organisational culture and values. For all of these reasons, it is crucial to get the strategic position right. In particular, as suggested by Figure 12.1, a strategic position should be:

- *Strategic.* It should reflect a long-term effort to gain advantage in the market over competitors, and it should not be changed until the strategy itself is changed. In contrast, an advertising campaign and a tagline reflect a communications objective, which is tactical and may change within the life of a business strategy.
- *The face of the business strategy.* Unlike an image, which reflects current associations held by customers, the strategic position is under the control of the firm. Indeed, the strategic position is too important to be left in the hands of customers, who lack knowledge of the business strategy going forward. Positioning should reflect business strategy.
- *Defined relative to competitors and to the market.* Because the business does not exist in a vacuum, it must not only decide what its scope should be but have a point of differentiation from its competition. If a desired strategic

225

position of innovation has been adopted by competitors, the business must create a spin on innovation that is ownable and differentiated – for example, innovation that provides customer benefit (rather than merely stretching technological boundaries).

- *Logically and/or emotional resonant with customers and relevant to the market.* A strategic position that is liked and admired can fail if it ceases to be meaningful.

THE ROLE OF THE STRATEGIC POSITION

The need to articulate a strategic position introduces discipline and clarity into the strategy formulation process. The ultimate strategy is usually more precise and elaborate as a result. The strategic position has other, more explicit, roles to play as Figure 12.1 indicates.

One role is to drive and guide strategic initiatives throughout the organisation, from operations to product offering to research-and-development project selection. The overall thrust captured by the strategic position should imply certain initiatives

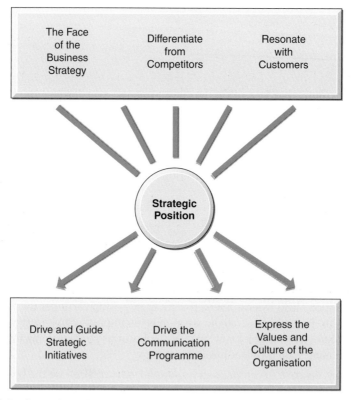

Figure 12.1   Strategic positions

and programmes. For example, given that we want to be an e-business firm, what tools and programmes will customers expect from us? Initiatives and programmes that do not advance the strategic position should be dialled down or killed.

A second role is to drive the communication programme. A strategic position that truly differentiates the product and resonates with customers will provide not only punch and effectiveness to external communication, but consistency over time because of its long-term perspective.

A third role is to support the expression of the organisation's values and culture to employees and business partners. Such internal communication is as vital to success as reaching out to customers. Lynn Upshaw, a San Francisco communication consultant, suggests asking employees and business partners two questions:

- Do you know what the business stands for?
- Do you care?

Unless the answers to these questions are 'yes', that is, employees and business partners understand and believe in the business strategy, the strategy is unlikely to fulfil its potential. Too many businesses drift aimlessly without direction, appearing to stand for nothing in particular. Lacking an organisational sense of soul and a sound strategic position, they always seem to be shouting 'on sale', attached to some deal, or engaging in promiscuous channel expansion.

The strategic position for a business is analogous to the core identity (and related aspirational associations) for a brand, as described in the books *Building Strong Brands* and *Brand Leadership*.[1] In some cases the two concepts are identical, but in others a strategic position can be broader as it applies to a business strategy rather than a brand strategy. Strategic position can dramatically affect the prospects of a business, as demonstrated by the experiences of Virgin Atlantic Airlines, IBM, and Ryanair.

Virgin Atlantic Airlines

In 1970, Richard Branson and a few friends founded Virgin as a small mail-order record company in London, England. By the mid-1980s, this modest beginning had led to a chain of record shops and the largest independent music label in the UK, with artists as diverse and important as Phil Collins, the Sex Pistols, Boy George and the Rolling Stones. The 1990s saw the retail business grow to include over 100 Virgin 'megastores' sprinkled around the world. Many, such as the Times Square store, made a significant brand statement with their signage, size, and interior design.

In February 1984, Branson, who found air travel boring and unpleasant, decided to start Virgin Atlantic Airlines to make flying fun and enjoyable for all classes, not just first-class passengers. Defying the odds (and vigorous attempts by British Airways to crush it), Virgin has prospered. By the end of the 1990s, it had become the number two airline in most of the markets and routes it served. Not only that, it enjoyed the same consumer awareness and reputation as much larger international carriers including service-oriented airlines such as Singapore Airlines, which is consistently rated high with respect to trust, innovation, and service. Virgin Atlantic's success is due in part to its strategic positioning along several dimensions: service quality, value for money, being the underdog and an edgy personality.

Extraordinary Service Quality

There are thousands of moments of truth in the airline business when the customer experiences service quality (or the lack of it) first hand. In this context Virgin has performed extraordinarily, not only delivering on the basics but often dazzling with original 'wow'-type experiences. Virgin pioneered sleeper seats in 1986 (British Airways followed nine years later with the cradle seat), limo service at each end of the flight (or motorcycle service for those flying light), in-flight massages, child safety seats, individual TVs for business class passengers, drive-through check-in at the airport, and new classes positioned above the normal service levels of coach and business class. It offers first-class passengers a new tailor-made suit to be ready at their destination, masseurs or beauty therapists and a facility to shower, take a Jacuzzi and even nap.

Value for Money

Virgin Atlantic's Upper Class is priced at the business-class level but equivalent to many other airlines' first-class service. Mid Class is offered at full-fare economy prices, and most Virgin Economy tickets are available at a discount. While this lower price point offers a clear consumer advantage, however, Virgin does not emphasise the price position in its promotion. Cheapness *per se* is not the message at Virgin.

The Underdog

Virgin's business model is straightforward. The company typically enters markets and industries that have large, established players (such as British Airways, Coca-Cola, Levi Strauss, British Rail and Smirnoff) that can be portrayed as being somewhat complacent, bureaucratic and unresponsive to customer needs. In contrast, Virgin presents itself as the underdog who cares, innovates, and delivers an attractive, viable alternative to customers. When British Airways attempted to prevent Virgin from gaining routes, Virgin painted British Airways as a bully standing in the way of an earnest youngster who offered better value and service. Virgin, personified by Branson, is the modern-day Robin Hood, the friend of the little guy.

The Virgin Personality

The Virgin brand has a strong, perhaps edgy personality largely reflecting its flamboyant service innovations and the values and actions of Richard Branson. Virgin as a person would be perceived as someone who:

- flaunts the rules
- has a sense of humor that can be outrageous at times
- is an underdog, willing to attack the establishment
- is competent, always does a good job, and has high standards

Interestingly, this personality spans several unrelated characteristics: rulebreaker, fun-loving, feisty, and competent. Many businesses would like to do the same but feel that they must choose between such personality extremes. The key is not only the personality of Branson himself but also the fact that Virgin has delivered on each facet of this personality.

Virgin is a remarkable example of how the right strategic position can allow a business to stretch far beyond what would be considered its acceptable scope of operations. Rather than restrict itself to records and entertainment, Virgin has used its strategic position to extend from record stores to airlines, colas, condoms, and dozens of other categories. The Virgin Group comprises some 100 companies in 22 countries, including a discount airline (Virgin Express), financial services (Virgin Direct), a cosmetics retail chain and direct sales operation (Virgin Vie), several media companies (Virgin Radio, Virgin TV), a rail service (Virgin Rail), soft drinks and other beverages (Virgin Cola, Virgin Energy, Virgin Vodka), a line of casual clothing (Virgin Clothing, Virgin Jeans), a new record label (V2 Records) and even a bridal store (Virgin Bride). In each business, the strategic position works to provide differentiation and advantage.

In fact, the decision to extend Virgin, a business then associated with rock music and youth, to an airline could have become a legendary blunder if it had failed. However, because the airline was successful and was able to deliver value with quality, flair, and innovation, the master Virgin brand developed associations that were not restricted to a single type of product. The elements of the Virgin strategic position – extraordinary service quality, value for money, the underdog personality, uniqueness – work over a large set of products and services. It has become a lifestyle brand with an attitude whose powerful relationship with customers is not solely based on functional benefits within a particular product category.

Virgin's success has been driven in part by pure visibility, largely based on publicity personally generated by Richard Branson. Realising that Virgin Atlantic could not compete with British Airways in advertising expenditures, he used publicity stunts to create awareness and develop associations. When the first Virgin Atlantic Airlines flight took off in 1984 with friends, celebrities, and reporters on board, Branson appeared in the cockpit wearing a vintage First World War leather flight helmet. The onboard video (a prerecorded tape of course) showed the 'pilots' – Branson and two famous cricket players – greeting the passengers from the cockpit.[2]

Branson's publicity efforts have not by any means been limited to Virgin Atlantic. For the launching of Virgin Bride, a company that arranges weddings, he showed up in a wedding dress. At the 1996 opening of Virgin's first US megastore in New York's Times Square, Branson (a balloonist holding several world records) was lowered on a huge silver ball from 100 feet above the store. These and other stunts have turned into windfalls of free publicity for Virgin, helping the brand in all contexts. Branson has fully mastered his role. By employing British humour and the popular love of flouting the system, he has endeared himself to consumers. By never deviating from the core brand values of quality, value for money, being the underdog and having an edgy personality, he has gained their loyalty and confidence. Evidence of this high level of trust in Branson and Virgin abound. When BBC Radio asked 1 200 people whom they thought would be most qualified to rewrite the Ten Commandments, Branson came in fourth, after Mother Teresa, the Pope, and the Archbishop of Canterbury. When a British daily newspaper took a poll on who would be most qualified to become the next mayor of London, Branson won by a landslide. The challenge for a business that is built on a track record of success and functional innovation like Virgin's is formidable. The next battle could always be its Waterloo and Virgin may indeed meet this fate with its Virgin Rail business. With nearly 30 million annual trips, the rail business is highly visible and the ability to deliver high-quality performance is not entirely in Virgin's control. Passengers whose expectations were based on Virgin Atlantic Airways were disappointed with mediocre service and late or cancelled trains. In retrospect, such a risky venture would have been better off under another name to provide some measure of protection to the Virgin brand.

The critical issue for Virgin, then, will be to manage the business as its consumers (and Branson) age and as it mushrooms into an ever-broader range of ventures. Can Virgin maintain its strategic position across all of its product categories and hold onto its energetic personality over time? A clear strategic position, and being able to implement it, will be the key to meeting that challenge.

IBM

Strategic positioning (or the lack thereof) has been an important element of IBM's fortunes over the years. In the 1950s, it changed from being a punch card processing business to being a computer manufacturer. In the 1960s, IBM evolved from a purveyor of hardware into a firm that delivered systems solutions reliably and competently. The adage that no one ever got fired for buying IBM reflected the incredible equity supporting that position. An antitrust settlement requiring the company to separate its service from its hardware systems undercut a central part of the IBM strategic position, however, and led to a difficult period. In the middle to late 1980s, IBM lost its way. Its systems consulting business had atrophied, clones had undercut its PC position, and Microsoft (among others) had grasped the leadership role in software. IBM lacked a visible strategic position, and it was in crisis as a result.

When Lou Gerstner took over as CEO in the spring of 1993, one of his first initiatives was to create a strategic position.[3] A series of focus groups among executives in management of information systems (MIS) revealed that IBM was perceived as smart, innovative, a technological leader, and a producer of high-quality equipment. Nevertheless, these same executives would not buy IBM products. They were very emotional in claiming that IBM had betrayed their trust and support, disappointing the whole computer field by becoming too arrogant and turning away from customers. Further research revealed that MIS executives were looking for systems solutions, for firms that could integrate computer technology and apply it to their business problems with a systems perspective and scope (as opposed to a component orientation).

Gerstner took several steps to change the IBM culture, beginning with a programme to have top managers (including himself) talk to customers on a regular basis. He stopped internal consideration of breaking up the company, making clear that the IBM brand and the synergy of the organisation would be a strategic point of advantage. Gerstner also identified the most promising initiatives in products and operations and made sure they were funded. All of these actions established a new strategic position that maintained IBM's image as the *global technology leader* while removing the appearance of being aloof and uncaring. An advertising campaign developed by Ogilvy & Mather symbolically drove home this message. One ad showed two Czech nuns walking down a road, saying (in English subtitles) things like 'I can't wait to get my hands on OS/2.' The tagline, 'solutions for a small planet' expressed the message of global leadership in a soft, understated way and it returned IBM to its roots as a customer- and solutions-oriented firm. This strategic position was credited with helping to bring IBM back from the brink of destruction.

Only a few years later, though, IBM faced a relevance problem. The Internet had progressed from buzz to reality, and IBM was seen as less connected to this new world than Cisco, Sun, and others, in part because of its product legacy and size. In response, an augmented and refocused strategic position around the e-business concept was developed to signal IBM's relevance to the Internet age and to represent its strategically important service business oriented toward creating systems solutions. From the introduction of the e-business label in late 1996, IBM ultimately spent over $5 billion communicating the concept. A host of products and programs (including a series of 'e' subbrands, such as e-servers) provided substance and credibility for the new position.

In 2003 Sam Palmisano became IBM's CEO and created a new business strategy and accompanying position based on the 'on-demand' e-business concept. On-demand means that unused computer capacity could be accessed by those with a need for it through a managed network grid. Again, the IBM organisation was mobilised from top to bottom in order to deliver on this new promise, with a host of on-demand products and services.

Products have had a large role in the strategic position of IBM over time. In the mid-1960s (when computers meant UNIVAC, not IBM), the company forged its dominance with the 360, a hugely successful mainframe computer that set the standard for years with a flow of upgrades and refinements. The 360 was the message and substance behind the strategic position of computer leadership. Three small consumer products also played instrumental roles in shaping the IBM strategic position, even though each had only a minor portion of the company's sales. The first, in the early 1980s, was the original PC, which legitimised the personal computer world and IBM's place in it. This breakthrough reinforced the company's leader as a dominant leader in the field that could also be nimble and innovative. The second was the PCjr, a strategically sound idea whose execution cost IBM most of the lustre earned by the PC. The intent was to create a home computer related to the PC many customers used at work, but the product had an inadequate keyboard, no hard drive, and could not be hooked up to a printer. Even worse, the introductory ad campaign (with a humorous Charlie Chaplin character) became the focal point of ridicule. The PCjr thus revived the bureaucratic, out-of-touch perceptions of the IBM brand while dialling down the relevant, can-do elements. The third product, the IBM ThinkPad, featured a striking design, innovative features (including the red TrackPoint), light weight, and solid performance. As it became a high-end leader in a very visible space, tracking studies showed customers' attitude toward IBM going up significantly, the company's only significant upward movement in a five-year time period.

Ryanair – An Unparalleled Strategic Position[4]

Since it pushed back from the brink of financial collapse in 1991, the Ryanair story has been about the relentless drive for, and communication of, its position as a low cost airline. Founded by the well-known Irish entrepreneur, Tony Ryan, and his family, Ryanair began its life as a local airline in 1985. It began to fly to London (Luton) and other UK cities, committing itself to a high-quality service for customers and to a transparent pricing policy. The incumbents, Aer Lingus and British Airways responded with price cuts and a price war ensued. The result was Ryanair posting an accumulated loss of £20 million in 1990.[5] A strategic position which was competitive, sustainable and capable of guiding the business as well as resonating with customers was required. That solution was found in the low cost carrier model pioneered by Southwest Airlines.

Upon his appointment as CEO in 1991, Michael O'Leary set about achieving and communicating the low-cost position both within and beyond the airline and using it to drive growth and profitability. The initial elements of the strategic position were cut price fares, the use of secondary airport destinations and point-to-point travel. Low fares allowed the company to build its customer base, attracting a casual traveller and encouraging them to fly more often than they normally would. Flying to secondary airports gave Ryanair the twin advantages of quicker turnaround times (secondary airports are not as busy) and lower airport charges (many smaller airports even paid Ryanair to fly there). For the casual traveller the need to land at a major city airport was not a keen requirement and in some cases worked in their favour. The commitment to point-to-point travel meant that Ryanair did not have to suffer any of the costs of supporting onward travel. In 1995 Ryanair carried more than 2.25 million passengers.

The deregulation of the European airline market in 1996 and the flotation of Ryanair in 1997 meant that the company had the opportunity and the means to expand from its Ireland-UK routes to other European destinations. It duly did this, opening routes into Scandinavia and continental Europe. In 2001 it opened its first continental European hub at Brussels Charleroi. The purpose of these hubs is to extend Ryanair's destination range while maintaining its point-to-point flight strategy. By 2006 Ryanair had 16 bases around Europe.

As passenger numbers grew Ryanair put the next piece of the low costs strategic position in place. Most airline costs are fixed and much of those costs relate to the aircraft used and their maintenance. In order to gain maximum benefit from staff expertise and reduce the costs of holding parts and training, Ryanair needed to adopt a single aircraft type in its fleet. Earlier in its life it had committed itself to the Boeing 737, in 1998 it placed an order for 45 new Boeing 737-800s, following this up with another order for 155 737-800s in 2001, both to meet expected demand but also to take advantage of discounts from Boeing as the airline business suffered in the post 9/11 travel environment. In 2003 another 100 of the same aircraft were ordered. These aircraft have higher passenger capacity and lower fuel consumption than their older counterparts. The average age of the Ryanair fleet is under three years; this reduces the costs of maintenance.

In addition to these major moves, Ryanair has made continuous cost reduction its goal. For example, the company has recently announced charges for bags that go into the baggage hold at the same time as increasing the weight of bags allowed in the cabin. The objective being to reduce the amount of baggage passengers bring, reducing the weight on aircraft and the need for ground crews. Window shades have been removed, as have seat pockets and reclining seats. Passengers have long been encouraged to take their rubbish with them from the plane when they disembark. One of its early big moves to cut costs was with internet bookings, adopted with the launch of Ryanair.com in January 2000. Ninety-eight per cent of all Ryanair bookings are now made via the website, cutting out the costs of travel agents' commission. Ryanair. com is the largest travel website in Europe and the fifth most recognised brand on Google.[6] This high volume of visitors to the website also provides the company with opportunities to generate ancillary revenues through car rentals and hotel bookings and other advertising on the website. In addition the company has plans to launch onboard gaming to boost revenues. Reinforcing the Ryanair low cost charter internally pilots are required to pay for their own training, staff pay for their own uniforms and are not allowed to recharge their mobile phones while at work.

By the end of 2005 Ryanair carried more than 31 million passengers and by 2012 will have aircraft capacity for 70 million. This growth will come as low fares continue to expand the market for air travel and as routes in Spain, Portugal, central and Eastern Europe are opened up.

The Ryanair story tells of how absolute commitment to the achievement of a particular strategic position can lead to extraordinary commercial and financial success. It also demonstrates the need to adapt that strategic position as opportunities arise (the emergence of Internet booking) as well as the need to be creative (such as the removal of seat pockets highlights) and opportunistic (such as the purchasing of aircraft at a time of depressed aircraft prices).

STRATEGIC POSITION OPTIONS

There are as many strategic positioning avenues as there are products, markets, and business strategies. Successful positions can be based on the competitive strategy options discussed in the preceding three chapters:

- *The quality player with a defined product space.* For example, the Victronox Swiss Army Knife is the best pocket knife on the market. Harrods Department Store in London is one of the greatest retailers in the world. Accenture hopes to be perceived as the best management consulting firm with an expanding scope of activities. To be successful with this strategic position, a firm must both deliver on the promise of being the best and manage the category definition that dictates the perceived set of competitors.

- *The value option.* Skoda, Ryanair, Aldi and Argos are all positioned primarily as value players. Success in a value position generally requires a cost advantage, and again, it is important to carefully manage the perceived competitive set. Argos, for example, is only a value player when compared against traditional department stores, and Aldi similarly provides value among a well-defined set of competitors. When Aer Lingus adopted a value approach, reducing its fares and its costs base, it was competing on two fronts, with discount airlines on fares and flag carrier/alliance airlines on service and routes.

- *The innovator.* SAP, Apple, Nokia, and Zara all present themselves as innovators. Creating this perception among customers is easiest when it is based on product or service innovations, as SAP and Apple have shown. Perceived innovation can also be driven, however, by indicators of leadership and energy. Zara, the Spanish fashion retailer, has built a reputation for being innovative through its strong presence in the high street as well as through its product. P&G has its own innovator-in-chief. And Virgin enhanced its innovative image with publicity stunts (often by Richard Branson, its CEO) that created enormous energy.

- *A narrow product focus.* The essence of Rolex, Land Rover, and Ferrari cars is their narrow product offering. As such, they are imbued with credibility that they know their product well. The challenge is to be disciplined about not expanding the product scope in a way that would dilute this credibility.

- *A target segment focus.* A media business with focus is The Economist Group, which provides analysis on international business, political and financial matters. It does this through a number of media including The Economist newspaper, The Economist Intelligence Unit and international conferences. Hamley's of London, one of the world's largest toy stores, has built its reputation on providing a unique experience for children of all ages. This is achieved through offering a vast range of children's toys and games over seven floors and creating an in-store buzz with demonstrations of new products. Positioning with respect to a target segment can help ensure that the organisation keeps its eye on the ball by keeping the product experience responsive and relevant to that segment.

- *Being global.* HSBC is a global financial institution. Louis Vuitton is a global fashion brand. IKEA is a global retail company. Being global provides functional benefits in that you can access the services of HSBC or buy Louis Vuitton products anywhere. It also provides the prestige and assurance of knowing that the firm has the business capabilities to compete successfully in other countries. Awareness that IKEA is strong in Europe, for example, helps the firm in the US, where customers might otherwise see it as a modest player.

There are, of course, a host of additional dimensions on which to base a strategic position as suggested by Figure 12.2. Some, but not all, are based on a strategic option. The following have proven their ability to drive success:

- product category
- product attributes and functional benefits
- breadth of product line
- organisational intangibles
- emotional self-expressive benefits
- experience
- being contemporary
- brand personality
- competitor position

Strategic Positions	Firms
The best	Accenture, Harrods
Value	Skoda, Aldi
Innovator	Nokia, SAP
Product focus	Rolex, Land Rover
Target segment	Hamleys, Mothercare
Product categories	Red Bull, Remy Martin
Product attributes	Saab, Duracell
Product line scope	Tesco, Amazon
Organisational intangibles	HP, Sorbonne
Emotional benefits	MTV, BBC Radio Five Live
Self-expressive benefits	Puma, Mercedes
Experience	Harvey Nichols, Guardian Unlimited
Contemporary	U2, Zara
Personality	Patek Philippe, Volcom
Competitors	Visa, Virgin

Figure 12.2   Strategic positions

As they are discussed and illustrated, it will become clear that many of these dimensions are interrelated. A purely one-dimensional strategy position is rare.

Product Category

The choice of a product category with which a business will associate itself can have enormous strategic as well as tactical implications. Schweppes positioned its tonic in Europe as an adult soft drink and the popularity of new-age adult drinks has carried it to a dominant position. In the US, however, Schweppes (perhaps wanting to avoid the Coke/Pepsi juggernaut) positioned its entry as a mixed drink, which relegated it to being a minor player when the market changed. The cereal bar market has achieved high growth by creating a category, based on healthy ingredients and distinct from chocolate bars. Danone's Frusion (known as Dannon in the US) expanded its market by positioning as an alternative to yoghurt rather than being in a category with milk drinks.

Maintaining Relevance

As suggested in Chapter 5, the relevance concept can help with the difficult task of managing an evolving category with emerging and receding subcategories. Relevance is, in essence, being perceived as associated with the product category in which the customer is interested. In the Brand Asset Valuator, the product of Young & Rubicam's mammoth study of global brands, relevance was one of four key dimensions identified (along with differentiation, esteem, and knowledge). Although differentiation got top billing in the study's results, relevance may be as powerful in dynamic markets. After all, if a business loses relevance, differentiation may not matter.

The ability of a firm to maintain relevance varies along a spectrum, as shown in Figure 12.3. At one extreme are trend neglectors – firms that miss or misinterpret trends, or are so focused on a particular business model that they ignore them. Such firms are often characterised as having inadequate strategic analysis capability,

Figure 12.3   Staying relevant

organisational inflexibility and/or a weak brand portfolio strategy; they eventually wake up in surprise to find that their products are no longer relevant. At the other end of the spectrum are trend drivers, the firms who actually propel the trends that define the category. In the middle are trend responders who track closely the trends and the evolution of categories, making sure that their products stay current.

Virgin Atlantic Airlines, IBM and Ryanair all have been trend drivers. Virgin has created new subcategories by introducing and owning new services such as massage services in first class. IBM was able to define a category with its e-business and on demand e-business services, supported by enormous brand-building resources. Ryanair defined a new age of low cost air travel in the European airline market.

Trend responders – those firms that can recognise trends, evaluate them accurately, and then implement a response – can sustain success in dynamic markets. Zara has built its business model upon being able to rapidly respond to customer demands and staying abreast of fashion trends. Although it has been conservative in terms of product introduction, Coca Cola has identified a large segment of young men who are committed to healthy lifestyles but do not regularly buy diet drinks. To meet the needs of this group it has introduced Coke Zero, a calorie-free product aimed at this group. Hyundai successfully entered the US and European market as a brand of low-cost quality car. Once established, the Hyundai brand evolved to offer affordable luxury models. Adapting quickly to the digital age, Fuji Film became a leader with its Super CCD high-quality image sensor for digital cameras (the fourth generation of which was introduced in 2003) and products such as digital photo printers.

Being a successful trend responder, however, is not easy. As suggested in Chapter 5, it can be difficult to identify and evaluate trends well enough to separate them from mere fads. It is also difficult to respond to emerging subcategories, especially if they start small and if the existing business and brand are established. Consider, for example, the difficulty that McDonald's and other fast food companies have had in responding to the healthy eating trend. They were simply not good at product development and delivery in that arena because it is not in their DNA; they lacked the people and culture to be successful. Further, their brands have become a liability as the firms attempt to change perceptions established over decades.

Product Attributes/Functional Benefits

When a business is blessed with a strong, sustainable product attribute or functional benefit that is valued by the market, that element should be a prominent part of the strategic position. Volvo has historically been associated with safety and reliability. This position is based on the long list of innovations that it introduced to the car market. For example Volvo cars were the first to feature safety cages, ABS (anti-lock brakes) and driver airbags. As safety features become less of a differentiator across makes, Volvo has found the need to introduce more emotional benefits to its strategic position, with models such as the C70 to the fore of this effort.

In some product classes, different brands will target different 'benefit segments' and be positioned accordingly. For example, Volvo has stressed durability, showing commercials of 'crash tests' and telling how long its cars last. Range Rover has emphasised its distinctive styling and design. BMW, in contrast, talks of performance, fun in driving and engineering innovations, with the tag line 'the ultimate driving machine'. Mercedes stresses comfort and luxury. Each of these car makers has selected a different attribute/benefit on which to base its strategic position.

Attribute/benefit positioning is powerful because it often provides a reason to buy and thus resonates with customers. Finding an attribute that is important to a major segment that is not already occupied by a competitor, however, is often a challenge. Neau is a brand of water sold in Holland that offers buyers a unique benefit. It is the same price as other bottled waters and the bottle is similar to its competitors. The differentiator is that the bottle does not contain water but a leaflet that explains the brand's purpose is to raise consciousness amongst Dutch consumers that while they enjoy access to a high-quality water supply, many people in the world do not. The second is to raise funds to provide fresh water in a number of developing countries.

Breadth of Product Line

A broad product offering signals substance, acceptance, leadership, and often the convenience of one-stop shopping. For example, the strategic position that drove Amazon's operations and marketing was never about selling books, even at the beginning. (It was no accident that the company was not called books.com.) Rather, the firm positioned itself as delivering a superior shopping/buying experience based on the 'Earth's Biggest Selection' – an array of choices so wide that customers would have no reason to look anywhere else. This position allows Amazon to enter a variety of product markets although it also puts pressure on the company to deliver in each venue.

Breadth also works well as a dimension for other firms, such as Renault, Tesco, and Bosch. As noted above, however, product and/or market focus is the key to competitive strength for most brands. Especially in the online world, businesses must resist enormous pressures to add functions and segments that appear to offer marginal revenue at almost no cost.

Why? On the one hand, product expansion exploits assets such as brand equity and distribution, creates synergies for the customer and the firm, and can develop associations of acceptance and leadership. On the other, a poorly handled expansion can degrade the brand asset, create inefficiencies, and divert needed resources. Sometimes the worst damage happens when the firm goes halfway – stepping away from a focused strategy, but not achieving worthwhile breadth.

Organisational Intangibles

Companies love to make product claims. They often engage in shouting matches attempting to convince customers that their offering is superior in some key dimension: Ronseal does exactly what it says on the tin and so is easier to use. Solpadeine provides more effective pain relief. Cadbury's chocolate has a glass-and-a-half of full-cream milk in every half pound. Shredded Wheat has no added ingredients. A server has more capacity. A plane has more range.

There are several problems with such specmanship. First, a position based upon some attribute is vulnerable to an innovation that gives your competitor greater effectiveness makes it easier to use, healthier or greater range. In the words of Regis McKenna, the Silicon Valley marketing guru 'you can always get outspeced.'

Second, when firms start a specification shouting match, they all eventually lose credibility. After a while, nobody believes that any pain reliever is more effective or faster acting than another. There have been so many conflicting claims that all of them are discounted.

Third, people do not always make decisions based upon a particular specification anyway. They may feel that small differences in some attribute are not important, or simply lack the motivation or ability to process information at such a detailed level.

Fourth, the addition of features to new product models may not be a pathway to success in the market place. Product managers, particularly in FMCG markets, often add features to products and their packaging without removing other features first. The result can be a product or service with a range of legacy features, each contributing to the cost of producing the product and so affects its bottom line. Another perspective on this issue is 'feature fatigue', which arises particularly in technology markets.[7] This term has been coined to address the common experience of consumers dissatisfaction at owning technology that they cannot operate. This is a more complicated problem than it may initially seem. Consumers like to buy multifeature products but very often they cannot use the features and the brand gets the blame. The task for the marketer is to balance the number of features needed to get the sale against the number likely to cause consumer dissatisfaction.

In contrast to attribute positioning, intangible factors can differentiate a business more effectively and in a more enduring fashion. Organisational attributes, such as being global (BP), innovative (Nokia), quality driven (Siemens), customer driven (Zara), or concerned about the environment (DHL), are usually longer lasting and more resistant to competitive claims than product-attribute associations. Not only are they harder to copy (because they are based on the people, culture, values, and programmes of the entire organisation) but it is difficult for a competitor to demonstrate that it has overcome a perceived intangible gap. It is easier to show that a competitor's printer is faster, for example, than to show that its organisation is more innovative.

A laboratory study of cameras demonstrated the power of an intangible attribute. Customers were shown two camera brands, one of which was positioned as being more technically sophisticated, and the other as easier to use. Detailed specifications of each brand, which were also provided, clearly showed that the easier-to-use brand in fact had superior technology as well. When subjects were shown both brands together, the easy-to-use brand was rated superior on technology by 94 % of the subjects. However, two days later (when the specifications were not fresh in their minds) only 36 % of respondents felt that it had the best technology. Using technology as an abstract attribute dominated the actual specifications.

Emotional and Self-expressive Benefits

Another way to move beyond attribute/functional claims is to create a position based on emotional or self-expressive benefits. *Emotional benefits* relate to the ability of the offering to make the customer feel something during the purchase or use experience. The strongest identities often include emotional benefits. Thus, a buyer or user can feel:

- safe in a Volvo
- exhilarated in a BMW
- energised while drinking Redbull
- important when at Harrods
- healthy when drinking Evian
- warm when making or drinking Barry's or PG Tips tea
- strong and rugged when driving a Range Rover

Cadbury's Flake is an example of a brand that extended its association from just another chocolate bar to a reward. Carlsberg has used the 'If Carlsberg made…' campaign to position its product both as of superior quality and also as a sociable and entertaining brand. Thus, the position of a product class (with all its associations of calories, sugar, and alcohol) is replaced with the emotional benefits of a reward for a job well done or source of entertainment, which is linked to positive feelings and people.

Emotional benefits are all about the 'I feel…' statement: 'I feel energised', 'I feel warm', 'I feel elegant'. To see if an emotional benefit can play a role in differentiating a brand, try the 'I feel' question with customers. If the hard-core loyalists consistently come up with a particular emotional benefit, then it should be considered as part of the strategic position.

Self-expressive benefits reflect the ability of the purchase and use of an offering to provide a vehicle by which a person can express him or herself. To illustrate, a person might express a self-concept of being:

- adventurous or daring by owning a Burton snowboard
- cool by buying fashions from Diesel
- sophisticated by wearing Prada
- successful, in control, and a leader by driving a Mercedes
- frugal and unpretentious by shopping at Lidl
- competent by using i-tunes
- a nurturing mother by preparing Shredded Wheat cereal in the morning

Self-expressive benefits are all about the 'I am…' statement: 'I am successful', 'I am young', 'I am a great athlete'. To see if a self-expressive benefit can play a role in differentiating a brand, try the 'I am' question with loyal customers and see if any consistent self-expressive benefits emerge.

xperience

⌐he experience of using the brand could include emotional or self-expressive benefits without any functional advantage, but when an experience combines both it is usually broader and more rewarding. The experience at Harvey Nichols includes a host of factors (such as the merchandise, the ambiance and the service) that combine to provide a pleasant, satisfying time. The experience of using Puma combines functional, emotional, and self-expressive benefits, to provide a depth of connection and passion that competitor brands lack.

The *Guardian* newspaper in the UK is one of the most respected newspapers in the world. It also offers reader access to its content via a range of websites under the brand of Guardian Unlimited. Football Unlimited offers football fans access to the current and archived pieces of its journalists. In addition, it provides minute-by-minute match commentary on important games. It also invites reader to draw or photoshop famous footballers and submit them to the Football Unlimited Gallery. The best ones are then made available for all to see. Finally, subscribers (free) receive a daily e-newsletter that takes a humorous and informative look at the day's football news. The brand experience for Football Unlimited offers fans is exceptional and long term. This is reflected in its user profile, which is higher social class, salary and education profile than the average internet users.[8]

Being Contemporary

Most established businesses face the problem of remaining or becoming contemporary. A business with a long heritage is given credit for being reliable, safe, a friend, and even innovative if that is part of its tradition. However, as noted earlier, it also can be perceived as 'your father's (or even grandfather's) brand'. The challenge is to have energy, vitality, and relevance in today's marketplace – to be part of the contemporary scene.

In 1985 *Rolling Stone* magazine named the Dublin rock band, U2, the band of the 1980s. More than twenty years later U2 won five Grammy awards for its album *How to Dismantle an Atomic Bomb*. U2 present a master class in maintaining their status as a contemporary act. Having built their reputation with early albums from *Boy* to *Rattle and Hum* and the concert tours that support them (developing a particular competence in stadium gigs), U2 built a loyal global following. The key to maintaining their contemporary status has been their commitment to pushing the boundaries of rock and their own abilities as artists particularly in albums like *Unforgettable Fire*, *Achtung Baby* and *Pop*. On each occasion capturing the zeitgeist of the moment and drawing in new fans. However, the vital element has been that while pushing the boundaries they were always able to draw on what they had achieved in the past, artistically falling back to the U2 sound (in albums like *All That You Can't Leave Behind*) and commercially to their loyal fan base.

Brand Personality

As with human beings, a business with a personality tends to be more memorable and better liked than one that is bland, nothing more than the sum of its attributes. And like people, brands can have a variety of personalities, such as being professional and competent (Volvo and the *Financial Times*), upscale and sophisticated (Jaguar and Mont Blanc), trustworthy and genuine (BBC and Marks & Spencer), exciting and daring (Aston Martin and Diesel), or active and tough (Adidas and Victronox). Certainly, Virgin is a brand whose strategic position includes a strong personality.

Harley-Davidson has a strong personality reflecting a macho, America-loving, freedom-seeking person who is willing to break out of confining social norms. The experience of riding a Harley (or even the association that comes from wearing Harley-Davidson clothing) helps some people to express a part of their personality, which results in intense loyalty. More than 1 million of these people belong to one of the local chapters of the Harley Owners Group (HOG) around the world. Regular events and tours are held around Europe. One such event is European Bike week, which more than 100 000 Harley riders attend. Harley is much more than a motorcycle; it is an experience, an attitude, a lifestyle, a vehicle to express 'who I am'.

Joie de Vivre is a San Francisco firm whose boutique hotels are each inspired by a theme that reflects a personality. The 'Rolling Stone' Phoenix hotel attracts rock-and-roll and other entertainment personalities with its irreverent sense of cool and funky, adventurous decor. The 'New Yorker' Rex hotel is clever and sophisticated, with a literary sensibility. The '1920s luxury liner' Commodore Hotel, with its Titanic Café, looks and feels like a party straight out of The Great Gatsby. The 'movie palace' Hotel Bijou has a miniature movie theatre in the lobby, accompanied by dramatic Hollywood portraits.

Competitor Position

Letting the competitor be the anchor of the strategic position can be effective, especially when the competitor already has an established position. Visa, for example, has continually and successfully fought for market share by offering both functional and self-expressive benefits that are superior to those offered by MasterCard. The strategic position, however, is against American Express, a less formidable competitor whose upscale associations Visa would like to share. One way this positioning is implemented is by noting prestigious Visa-sponsored venues that do not accept American Express.

The classic competitor position is of Avis in the US, which was having trouble differentiating itself from two other major rental car agencies (Hertz and National) and several lesser players such as Budget. With Hertz capitalising on being the leading firm, Avis brilliantly stepped forward with the slogan 'we're Number 2, we try harder.' By proclaiming itself the logical alternative to Hertz, Avis deftly positioned National and others as also-rans. Further, it provided a point of differentiation along a dimension (effort, plus the spirit of an underdog) that resonated with customers.

Multiple Strategic Positions

Arbitrarily insisting that a strategic position should apply to all products or market segments can be self-defeating. Rather, consideration should be given to adapting the position to each context. A shared strategic position that is augmented with additional dimensions in each market will ensure that a consistent message is received, without the unnecessary limitations of a 'one-size-fits-all' philosophy. For example, Honda is associated with youth and racing in Japan, in the US it has a family orientation while in Europe it is associated with quality and engineering. Similarly, Heineken is projected more as a premium brand in East Asia than in Europe. Liquid Wit is an Internet firm that provides marketing and communication companies with names, taglines, ad copy and guerrilla marketing within a short time frame. By tapping freelance talent, its offering is positioned as contemporary (real time, in the know, and continuously relevant), substantial (a solid organisation that will be around) and eccentric (inventive, extraordinary, a wide range of interests). In addition, the position is augmented differently for potential buyers of the service and the members who do the work. To clients, LiquidWit means fresh ideas and leverage (using existing organisational processes as opposed to outsourcing). To members, it offers the stimulation of being challenged by different problems and the rewarding feeling of being paid based on your results rather than your resume.

Capturing the Essence of the Strategic Position

The strategic position, as in the case of Virgin Atlantic Airways, often requires three to six dimensions to be expressed. There are times, however, when a single conceptual phrase can represent the essence of the strategic position and the organisation. For example, consider the following essence statements:

- *Nokia* – connecting people
- *Diesel* – for successful living
- *Intel* – leap ahead
- *HSBC* – the world's local bank
- *Henkel* – a brand like a friend
- *London Business School* – transforming futures

An essence statement needs to communicate the strategic position both inside and outside the organisation. Thus, it is not necessarily a tagline, which is designed to communicate to customers. It can be understated ('it simply works better') or aspirational ('the passionate pursuit of perfection'). In either case, a successful statement should capture the very soul of the organisation, inspire those implementing the strategy, resonate with customers and differentiate the company from its competitors.

DEVELOPING AND SELECTING A STRATEGIC POSITION

How should a business select the position(s) that will drive its strategy, both internally and externally, and create compelling and sustainable competitive advantages? As suggested in Figure 12.1, the process parallels the dimensions that should guide strategic decisions (set forth in Chapter 7). The strategic position should resonate with customers, differentiate the firm from its competitors, and reflect and be supported by the overall business strategy. It therefore follows that a position needs to be supported by analyses of the organisation's customers and competitors, as well as its own strengths, initiatives, and strategies.

- *Resonate with the target market.* Ultimately the market dictates success, and thus the strategic position needs to create a point of difference that resonates with customers. Associations that create emotional or self-expressive benefits can add value beyond the usual, practical reasons to buy a product. Certainly the act of opening a Asprey package is more intense than opening a Debenham's package, and the wearer of an Asprey bracelet will usually feel more special than if a similar bracelet had been purchased at a department store.

- *Differentiate from competitors.* Differentiation is often the key to winning. As noted earlier, the Brand Asset Valuator data from Young & Rubicam showed differentiation to be the single most important predictor of brand strength. The same research provided evidence to support the notion that up-and coming brands lead with differentiation, and fading brands lose differentiation first.

- *Reflect the culture, strategy, and capabilities of the business.* Don't try to be something you are not. Creating a position that is different than what the brand delivers is not only wasteful, but strategically damaging – it will undermine the basic equity of the brand – by making customers skeptical about future claims.

Proof Points and Strategic Imperatives

A business needs to deliver on its promise. This goal involves proof points and often strategic imperatives as well. *Proof points* are programmes, initiatives, and assets already in place that provide substance to the strategic position, helping to communicate what it means. Skinkers is the leading player in the desktop alerts market. A proof point is its comprehensive product range, including promotions and e-CRM products. An additional proof point is the number of high profile clients who use its products including Sky News, BBC and Manchester United. Marks and Spencer has a customer service position supported by the following proof points:[9]

- a strong reputation for exceptional customer service
- the 'Our Service Style' training programme, which every staff member is required to attend
- a well-known and credible return policy
- one in six customer assistants being coaches for other staff mean improvement is ongoing on the shopfloor

- the quality of the staff, the Marks & Spencer recruitment process and a very low staff turnover by industry standards
- a rigorous monitoring of customer service via customer surveys and mystery shopping

A gap between what the brand now delivers, even given the proof points, and the promise implied by the strategic position should lead to strategic imperatives. A *strategic imperative* is an investment in an asset or program that is essential if the promise to customers is to be delivered. What organisational assets and competencies are implied by the strategic position? What investments are needed in order to establish any of those assets and competencies that do not already exist? If a bank aspires to deliver a relationship with customers, for instance, two strategic imperatives might be needed. First, a CRM system might need to be installed so that each customer contact person has access to all of a given customer's accounts. Second, a programme to improve the interpersonal skills of these employees (including both training and measurement) might be needed.

KEY LEARNINGS

- A strategic position specifies how the business is to be perceived relative to its competitors and market by customers, employees, and partners. It should differentiate the company from its competitors, and resonate with customers. It should also drive strategic initiatives and the culture and values of the organisation, as well as communication programmes.
- Virgin Atlantic Airways is positioned with respect to extraordinary service quality, value for money, being the underdog, and a desire to flaunt the rules.
- IBM's strategic position evolved over the years as its market changed. A particularly defining moment was in the mid-1990s, when Gerstner arrived with the e-business position.
- Ryanair has expanded its strategic position over time from being a regional European airline to become one of the largest and most respected airlines in Europe.
- Among the strategic positions described in the preceding two chapters are being the quality player, brand equity, the focus business, the value option, the innovator, customer intimacy and the global player.
- Other options include positioning with respect to product category, product attributes, breadth of offering, organisational intangibles, emotional/self-expressive benefits, experience, being contemporary and being distinct from competitors.
- In coping with dynamic environments, trend drivers create new categories, trend responders adapt to emerging subcategories and trend neglectors ignore them.

- A strategic position needs to reflect the culture and strategy of the business, to differentiate it from its competitors, and to resonate with the target market. Proof points and strategic initiatives are needed to make sure that the brand delivers on the aspirational promise.

FOR DISCUSSION

1. How is Virgin Atlantic Airlines positioned? Are the dimensions, particularly the high quality and high service, inconsistent with its personality? If so, how is that handled? How has the positioning been brought to life? What are the proof points? Why don't more brands emulate Virgin's brand-building programs?

2. Trace the positions of Hyundai cars through the years. How has the firm evolved? How would you advise Hyundai to implement its desired new luxury position? What are the keys to success? Why was the logic behind it?

3. Ryanair has adopted an aggressive positioning versus major stakeholders such as regulators, airport authorities and governments. Identify each position. In each case, is the positioning a liability with respect to its growth ambitions?

4. Pick out three brands from a particular industry. How are they positioned? Which is the best in your view? Does that brand's positioning provide any emotional or self-expressive benefits? How would you evaluate each brand's positioning strategy? Hypothesise proof points and strategic imperatives for each brand.

5. Consider how U2 have approached the task of remaining contemporary. What are the lessons of this for newer brands like Innocent or Google? What are the problems with implementing a strategy like this? How would you deal with these problems?

6. Consider the Joie de Vivre hotel concept. Think of themes stimulated by magazines or movies, and discuss how you would design a hotel around each concept. For each theme, choose five words that reflect that theme.

NOTES

1. For more information, see David A. Aaker (1996) *Building Strong Brands*, The Free Press, New York and David A. Aaker and Erich Joachimsthaler (1999) *Brand Leadership*, The Free Press, New York.

2. Pantea Denoyelle and Jean-Claude Larreche, Virgin Atlantic Airways, Case publication INSEAD, 595-023-1.

3. Louis V. Gerstner, Jr. (2002) *Who Says Elephants Can't Dance?* Harper Business, New York.

4. Ryanair as a consumer growth company: inside the 21st century European travel phenomenon. Davy Stockbrokers, Dublin, 28 March 2006. Analysts report downloadable at http://www.ryanair.com/site/about/invest/docs/analyst/davy_2006-03-29.pdf.

5. Http://www.ryanair.com.

6. Ryanair as a consumer growth company: inside the 21st century European travel phenomenon. Davy Stockbrokers, Dublin, 28 March 2006. Analysts report downloadable at http://www.ryanair.com/site/about/invest/docs/analyst/davy_2006-03-29.pdf.

7. Roland T. Rust, Deobra Viana Thompson and Rebecca W. Hamilton (2006) Defeating feature fatigue. *Harvard Business Review*, February. pp. 98–107.

8. Forrester UK Internet User Monitor No. 2005; HBX March 2006 from Guardian Unlimited.co.uk.

9. Marks and Spencer Annual Review and Summary Financial Statement, 2006.

CASE CHALLENGES FOR PART III

CASE STUDY I: DEVELOPING A STRATEGIC POSITION

Neau

Bottled water consumers in the Netherlands have a unique and highly original alternative to consider when they want to quench their thirst. Launched in 2003, this new brand is called Neau (pronounced 'no') and is priced at the same level as the market leaders (€1.80 for 33cl). It also looks like other brands of water with a clear blue plastic PET bottle. But the bottle contains not water, but a leaflet. This leaflet reminds Dutch consumers that the quality of tap water in Holland is so good that there is no reason for them to pay a massive premium to buy bottled water. Instead they can be continuously refreshed by buying Neau and filling and refilling the bottles with tap water. All of the profits from the sale of Neau go to water projects in developing countries through cooperation with Dutch NGOs such as Unicef Nederland and Plan Nederland, which is part of the internal children's charity, Plan International.

For Menno Liauw, founder of Stichting Neau (the Neau Foundation) and a Dutch advertising executive, the proposition goes much wider than a means of providing financial support for worthy projects. 'When you drink a bottle of Neau ... you indirectly provide a refugee camp in Sudan with seventeen litres of clean drinking water. Every draught for you is ten draughts for them, drinking here is drinking there. . . We sell conscientiousness and social responsibility.'[1]

Such consciousness is of increasing importance. A 2003 report from the European Union, *Water for Life*[2] noted that more than 1.1 billion people in the developing world have no regular access to clean drinking water and over 2.4 billion lack basic sanitation facilities. In addition, more than 6000 children die every day from conditions associated with this lack of access to water and sanitation and half of all the hospital beds in the world are occupied by patients with preventable water borne diseases. At the same time the consumption of water is doubling every twenty years, more than twice the rate of population growth. A person in the developing world typically consumes 20 litres of water per day, while those in the developed world use ten times that much!

The roll-out of the Neau brand involved a range of partnerships, with companies such as Ikea Nederland supplying its employees with a Neau bottles. Kuyichi, the fashion design house, with a strong commitment to social responsibility and investment distributed Neau at shows. The company also sold its product during concerts and events such as World Harbour Days in Rotterdam, and the Navy Days (Vlootdagen) of the Royal Dutch Marine. The product was also distributed through Plaza 21C Store which specialises in environmentally friendly products.[3] Other partners included PriceWaterhouse Coopers (PWC) and innovative design house, Droog Design.

Globally the market for bottled water is estimated in volume terms at 154 billion litres, in value terms at about €65 billion and is growing at 7% to 10% per annum. The explosive growth in bottled water consumption over recent years can be simply explained: it is not expensive, it can be easily carried or put in a bag, it has few restrictions on usage situation and it is healthy and noncarbonated. More than all of this the awareness of the need for proper hydration and the sheer ubiquity of use by people in all walks of life has made the consumption of bottled water cool.

While there are two main types of bottled water, noncarbonated (including purified, filtered and spring) and carbonated (natural and manufactured) and many varieties within these categories, differentiation based on attributes is difficult to sustain. One water is much the same as another. Consequently, as US consumers have become more confident in their choices of water the distribution strengths of global soft drinks, firms such as Coke and Pepsi have come to the fore. Their Dasani and Aquafina brands, respectively, both filtered water products, now lead the American market.

While the American market for bottled water only gained real scale in the 1970s when Perrier entered the market, European bottled water has a much longer history. Europeans have always had a different relationship with bottled water, not least due to poor quality of tap water in many countries even as recently as the 1970s. The result has been the emergence of strong national brands such as San Pellegrino of Italy, Perrier of France, Ramlosa of Sweden and Gerolsteiner of Germany. A second historical consequence is that the average consumption of mineral water in Europe is higher than that of the US. For example, in 2004 the per capita consumption of mineral water in Italy and Spain was 183.6 and 136.7 litres per capita respectively, while in the US it was 90.5 litres.[4]

The Dutch bottled water market is somewhat different from other markets. The most obvious difference is the relatively low per capita consumption of bottled water, at about 20 litres. The primary reason for this is the exceptional quality of Dutch tap water. Rigorous national water standards apply more than 60 different quality tests. However, like other markets, consumption of bottled water is growing in the Netherlands. This growth is being driven, as in other markets, by young people who are more aware of the need for proper hydration and feel that this is easier to achieve with bottled water. The higher status of bottled water is also attractive to younger consumers. Like other markets the trend is away from carbonated drinks and towards still and flavoured waters. The headline market growth figure in the category as a whole is about 3% per annum but this low figure reflects sluggishness in sales of carbonated waters.

The bottled water market in Holland is dominated by two brands, Spa and Bar le Duc. Spa is owned by Spadel Nederland and is the largest bottled water brand on the market with about 65% of off-trade volume in 2005. The Spa brand name is ubiquitous with bottled water – so much so that Dutch consumers will often refer to a Spa when they mean any bottled water product. The brand is recognised in two colours, red for carbonated and blue for still. Bar le Duc commanded about 20% of the off-trade volume in 2005. Other smaller brands include Aqua Viva and Aquell.[5] In the European market as a whole, global brands of bottled water have fallen from 57% of the market in 1997 to 40% in 2004.[6] But, as in other regards, the Dutch market is different and private label commands less than 4% of total volume in the market, although private label growth was strong in other areas of the soft drinks market. The major international brands of bottled water such as Evian, San Pellegrino and Perrier, while occupying their place at the premium end of the market, do so from a position of limited distribution in restaurants and foods shops.

In general the level of promotional activity in the bottled water market is low and competitors generally appear more interested in developing other interests in soft drinks and less concerned with growing the nonflavoured bottled water market. In 2005 the flavoured water market in the Netherlands grew by 9% to a volume of 14 million litres. The leading brands in this segment are Vrumona's Crystal Clear and Spadel's Spa Clear. Vrumona was the first to enter this market with Crystal Clear, which was very clearly positioned for younger women. The brand is available in nine flavours and is strongly supported with advertising and sales promotions. Spadel has launched new products under the Spa Clear brand and it appears that this segment will be a strongly contested one in the future.

The next stage of Neau's growth is its entry to the water cooler market. In the Netherlands about 8% of coolers take advantage of the quality of tap water and operate on a mains water basis, rather than the more widely employed bottled water alternative. In collaboration with a leading mains water cooler company, Water Care Nederland, a Neau water cooler is now available. The proposition for buyers is that each Neau cooler comes with 25 Neau bottles and that the staff of the firm receive a regular e-newsletter about the investments made with the profits from Neau.[7]

Questions

1. Using the characteristics identified in figure 12.1, can you summarise the strategic position of Neau?
2. How vulnerable is Neau's strategic position to the major market trends in the bottled water market in the Netherlands and Europe?
3. Neau has positioned itself in direct opposition to leading brands such as Spa and Bar le Duc in the Dutch market. Should these brands respond? If so, how, bearing in mind the negative publicity that might result from damaging a brand with such positive values?
4. What are the lessons arising from the Neau case for other not-for-profit marketers? What general lessons can be drawn?

References

1. Neau – no water, Erwin Wijman, *Brandchannel.com*, 3 October 2005. http://www.brandchannel.com/features_profile.asp?pr_id=252
2. *Water for Life* (2003), Office for Official Publications of the European Communities, Luxembourg.
3. Neau – no water, Erwin Wijman, *Brandchannel.com*, 3 October 2005. http://www.brandchannel.com/features_profile.asp?pr_id=252
4. Beverage Marketing Corporation, cited in John G. Rodwan, Jr. (2005 Bottled water 2004: US and international statistics and developments. *Bottled Water Reporter*, April/May.
5. Bottled water in the Netherlands, *Euromonitor International*, June, 2006.
6. The big brands go begging in Europe' BusinessWeek online, 23 March 2005.
7. Neau – no water. Erwin Wijman, *Brandchannel.com*, 3 October 2005. http://www.businessweek.com/magazine/content/05_12/b3925071_mz054.htm

CASE STUDY II: COMPETING AGAINST INDUSTRY GIANTS

Innocent

Innocent Drinks was established in 1999 by three college friends who chose a jazz festival in London's Parsons Green to test their new product. They set up their stall at the festival with £500 worth of fresh fruit to be blended into a smoothie containing no sugar, water or concentrates and two rubbish bins marked with yes and no asking customers if they should give up their jobs to make the smoothies. If tasters thought they should, they put their empty cups in yes and if not, no. At the end of the festival the yes bin was overflowing with cartons and the next day they gave up their jobs.[1] Innocent Drinks had been created. Since then, their total market share has increased to 61 % of the smoothie market in 2006.[2] The number of employees in the company has expanded from three in 1999 to 93 in 2006 and turnover in 2000 was £1.8 million increasing to £37 million in 2006. They are the largest fruit buyer in Europe and the UK's leading smoothie manufacturer.

Innocent Drinks was established in recognition of a reduction in the popularity of traditional sugar based soft drinks and the emerging healthier living trend. Innocent tapped into the emerging culture of health conscious, cash-rich, time-short consumers who were willing to pay a premium for products that are natural, convenient and healthy. Consumers wanted healthy options not just in their supermarkets but also in their convenience stores where they could have easy access with minimal effort. Innocent was able to address this real customer demand by supplying their product to local convenience stores. But Innocent Drinks is not a passing fad with the smoothie market just beginning to emerge and growing at a phenomenal rate. Innocent is growing at an average of 60 % in each year they have been in business and succeeded were many have failed by making fruit fun and being healthy easy. Innocent has managed to maintain its market position by listening to customers, monitoring and understanding customer trends and innovating its product line to take advantage of these opportunities. For example, as the trend of healthy eating extended to parents' concerns over what their children are eating, Innocent launched a range for children.

The company takes pride in their products being natural, pure fruit juice and nothing else, with the selling proposition 'No sugar. No water. No concentrates.' But the UK fruit beverage market is already abundant with strong competitors like The Feel Good Drinks Co. and PJ Smoothies, all promising pure, fresh, natural, healthy ingredients, so what was it that provided Innocent with its strategic position?

Innocent's phenomenal success is based on the strength of their brand and their marketing strategy. This involved developing a strong, clear brand proposition of 'makes sense, feels good' and a unique positioning strategy so customers know what to expect when they buy an Innocent product. It also involved maintaining consistency across their communications, brand image and all aspects of the brand from the language to the product, the packaging design, labelling, the website, their cow delivery vans and their delivery systems, the banana phone and even their offices known as 'Fruit Towers' and how they reward staff. This enabled them to make a dramatic impact on the fruit beverage market and the saturated beverage market where brands have to compete with global giants like Coke.

While the company has experienced dramatic growth in sales it has managed to avoid the dangers associated with a fast growing business by careful strategic planning. Developing the brand as an asset and building its image and reputation to a leadership position has allowed Innocent to enter the market with a premium pricing strategy that customers are willing to pay. With little money spent on advertising initially this meant that price premium revenues were pumped straight back into the company. It has enabled them to achieve a leadership position in smoothie industry with higher market share and volume growth as demand for the product increases. Their position as a brand leader in the smoothie market has also enabled them to achieve economies of scale that allows them to achieve lower costs.

At the centre of Innocent Drinks' success is the use of the words 'simple', 'honest' and 'fresh', which make a powerful statement about the unique nature of their products, the brand and the company. Even the name itself is simple, honest and easy to remember, leaving no doubt in the customers mind about the product. Innocent focused on differentiating their brand as an asset by developing a fun, sense-of-humour brand personality that epitomised feeling good.

While their competitors also used fun language in their own products to help sell their brand Innocent took their fun brand personality a step further. For example, on the ingredients list on the side of an Innocent drink hidden among the real product ingredients they often included 'a few small pebbles' between the blueberries and strawberries then at the end of the list they would include 'we lied about the pebbles'. Innocent represents feel-good consumerism. The packaging they use is simple, plain coloured, straight to the point, with fun, witty, alternative labelling on a clear plastic bottle not only telling customers to recycle the bottle but to go camping or bounce on a trampoline. It is an extremely clever representation of the brand and an effective brand differentiator when all the other brands on the shelf use brightly coloured opaque bottles. Buying the Innocent brand means that you are buying into the ideal of a healthier, happier, fun lifestyle. The simple, friendly, fun approach also extends to other areas of the business. The language and design that they use on their website also adopts a simple but powerful approach, for example, a 'Bored?' section for visitors. The website also has a unique feel to it: one of light-heartedness and fun where they poke fun at themselves and at customers. For example, 'we wanted people to think of Innocent as their one healthy habit; like going to the gym, but with the communal shower after.'[3] On the company fact sheet, along with basic information about company, they include Richard's shoe size and Adam's waist size (two of the original founders) to lighten the tone and show customers that they do not really take themselves seriously. The company has also published its own book called *Stay Healthy. Be Lazy,* which is consistent with the overall image and personality of the company with an honest, simple, straightforward tone. The company uses unique 'cow vans' complete with fur, horns, eyelashes, udders, tails and names to promote the brand's sense of humour and raise brand awareness.

Innocent have also developed a socially responsible brand image by working to do things that the founders believe are right. They donate 10% of their profits to the Innocent Foundation that gives away drinks to the homeless, donates to the Third World and recycles and plants trees. If the company was to be called Innocent the founders believed that they had a responsibility to be innocent and they were promoting many of the current topical issues like kids health, ethical trading and environmental issues long before other companies had even started. Staff are also treated exceptionally well, they are given money on the birth of a child, scholarships to achieve dreams and a free snow-boarding trip each year. The environment that the staff work in is conducive to entrepreneurship and innovation. Innocent recognise that energetic brands have a human face that captures the public's interest.

Innocent began selling products in 1999 with three recipes, which increased to 24 in 2006 and product lines have expanded to include smoothies containing blended fresh fruit, thickies containing live probiotic yoghurt and honey, really lovely juice containing pure fresh orange juice, juicy waters containing juice and spring water, super smoothies which are naturally functional smoothies designed for a specific purpose like fighting off colds, smoothies for children and the one litre take-home carton. Product innovations are continuous and are based on listening to customers and what they feel that they are good at. Some new products have been rejected on the grounds that they are deviating from the strategic position of the company. For example, Innocent have decided against exploiting the current trend for adding vitamins, health and medicinal ingredients to drinks as this is not something that they are experts at, instead they prefer to focus on the enjoyment, fun and taste of their products. Recipe innovations that are created in their Fruit Towers London office are tested on people in the surrounding offices, the product ingredients are sourced from all around the world and regular sampling is conducted to ensure that the best ingredients with the best flavour are used in their smoothies.

The main problem Innocent have encountered while producing their product has been the short shelf life of the product, as all of the ingredients were fresh and no preservatives or additives were added. Careful production and high-technology packaging was developed to give their drinks the longest possible shelf life but without interfering with the fresh, natural ingredients of the product. The company has continued to research ways that their product life cycle can be extended. In 2004, with the introduction of their one litre take-home carton, the life of the product increased to four days once opened as opposed to the previous two days.

Innocent have pursued a premium pricing strategy, which targets health-conscious consumers who are willing to pay a premium price for the health benefits that the product contains. The price of an Innocent drink varies from the recommended retail price of £1.75–£1.99 for smoothies and thickies, £1.49–£1.69 for really lovely juices, £1.49–£1.69 for Juicy Waters, £3.29 for one litre cartons and £2.99 for four kids' drinks.[5]

Until 2003, Innocent had not spent any money on advertising, with their marketing strategy based around low-cost, high-impact marketing based on word of mouth. These communication techniques were very successful and they built brand awareness of 35 % in three years on a budget of less than £100,000.[6] The company is proud that they were able to save money and still communicate with customers using unconventional channels. For example, in the summer of 2003 Innocent's summer marketing campaign featured a double-decker bus covered in astro turf grass offering customers free smoothies and free rides around London. Word of mouth was key to their marketing campaign and the theory behind this is that if they made a good product people would tell their friends and they felt that advertising might bring the perception of corporate dishonesty to a brand that is based on an image of honesty, simplicity, wholesomeness and innocence. In fact, Innocent has always strived to distance its brand from the corporate image that success brings and its alternative, simple, 'fruity', witty, brand image is an effective marketing strategy in a world that has lost faith in the traditional corporate world.

After six years of getting the product and distribution right they started using advertising to promote the brand. They were aware that any advertising that they did use needed to be consistent with their brand image and a true reflection of what the company really was. In March 2005 Innocent began advertising on television and to keep in line with the quirky, witty personality of the Innocent brand, they shot the ad themselves, which featured a talking carton in a sea of fresh fruit, over a weekend in a local park.

As a company they also see the relationship benefits that can be created as part of a marketing campaign. For example, they have developed marketing activities that enable them to talk directly to their customers such as the annual music festival called 'Fruitstock'. This is a free music festival that Innocent hosts to say 'thank you' to its customers for using their brand. This festival offers good commercial value for the company, improves its customers' perceptions of the brand and allows it to raise money for charity.

Its first venture into the market was very modest with a local shop around the corner from where the founders worked agreeing to stock some of their drinks. Innocent supplied them with 20 bottles, all of which were sold out at the end of the first day. Over the first weekend that Innocent was on sale in 50 shops it was an immediate success, with 45 shops wanting more.[7] Initially, most of the sales came from delicatessens and sandwich shops, but Coffee Republic, which at the time was also a young growing business agreed to stock their product in eight or nine shops. Since then, Innocent developed its distribution network to include supermarkets as well as smaller local convenience stores. In 2006 it supplied smoothies to over 6000 retailers, selling over one million smoothies per week.

Future challenges for the company include how to continue using the brand to drive growth without stepping over the mark and undoing all that the brand has achieved. The company has opened other market fronts by adding product lines that deviate from the original product and many more product lines could be tested to see if they fit the company's brand image. For example, could the brand be extended to include baby food or alcoholic drinks? The fear is that by launching new product extensions it will undermine the brand and dilute it rather than strengthen it. It is also now in a position where, as demand increases, it is faced with the decision to either restrict the distribution of the brand and move it upmarket or continue and get as many distribution outlets and sales as possible. But the question is what implications will this have on the strength of the brand, its image and its pricing? While the brand image and personality are so easily understood and enjoyed in the UK, Innocent faces cultural and language challenges as they begin to expand internationally. With the aim of becoming 'Europe's favourite little juice company', how can they overcome these challenges of growth? While Innocent continues to research packaging technology that will enable it to achieve a longer shelf life the short shelf-life of the product also poses problems for Innocent as it looks to expand further into Europe. As distribution of the products increase what steps can Innocent take to ensure that the natural quality of the product, which made it so successful in the UK, will not hinder its expansion into Europe?

FOR DISCUSSION

1. How was the Innocent strategic position conceived? How strong is its position?

2. How did the position that Innocent achieved drive sales growth for the company?

3. How should Innocent maintain the relevance of its position in a fast-moving, developing market?

4. As Innocent expands into Europe how can it overcome the challenges associated with the growth of their position, brand name and its personality? How will it overcome production problems associated with a shelf life in international markets?

NOTES

1. "Forming a company- Innocent Drinks" bCentral
   http://bcentral.co.uk/startingup/formingacompany/innocent-drinks.mspx
2. "Juicy Fruit" The Sunday Times, 9 April 2006.
3. www.innocent.co.uk
4. "Juicy Fruit" The Sunday Times, 9 April 2006.
5. www.innocent.co.uk
6. "Innocent by Name" Times Online, 16 July 2003.
   http://business.timesonline.co.uk/article/0,,12090-746240,00.html
7. "Innocent Drinks" www.startups.co.uk
   http://www.startups.co.uk/Innocent_Drinks.Yfou1uVoyivadQ.html

PART FOUR

GROWTH STRATEGIES

Growth Strategies: Penetration, Product-Market Expansion, Vertical Integration and the Big Idea

Marketing should focus on market creation, not market sharing.
—*Regis McKenna*

Results are gained by exploiting opportunities, not by solving problems.
—*Peter Drucker*

Only the paranoid survive.
—*Andrew Grove*, former CEO, Intel

*M*any firms have focused on improving performance by downsizing, restructuring, redeploying assets, and reducing costs. Most have, or will soon, come to the point of diminishing returns; there is a limit to how much you can improve profits with efficiency programmes. Only so many people and offices can be eliminated. Further, downsizing can eventually be debilitating to the organisation. Muscle needed to create and support growth opportunities is lost along with the fat. Employees and partners will lose motivation when they see that productivity innovations will cost them roles and jobs.

There is thus an increasing realisation that the road to improved performance must involve a renewed emphasis on growth. Growth not only provides the potential for enhanced profitability but it also introduces vitality to an organisation by providing challenges and rewards. It is simply more fun and stimulating to create growth than to improve productivity by downsizing. A renewed focus on growth does not mean that operational efficiency is ignored, only that it is not dominant.

257

Both are needed for a successful long-term strategy. Achieving profitable growth involves some fundamentals of sound strategic management, such as the following:

- Excel at the base business. Growth options may be tempting but they can also distract from the core business, which has growth potential and ultimately funds growth in other growth directions.
- Withdraw resources from areas that lack future growth prospects or do not fit strategically with the firm. Resources to fund growth cannot be squandered on futile attempts to turn around problem business areas.
- Develop skills in strategic analysis, especially the ability to detect emerging trends and subcategories.
- Develop options for future offerings. Growth options can be created internally by understanding and applying creative thinking methods. They also can be sourced externally through a network of partners that can supply products (or assets and competencies) that will fuel or enable growth.
- Develop and leverage core assets and competencies. Growth arenas will require these, and success probabilities go up when they are already in place.

Figure 13.1 shows a way to structure alternative growth strategies based, in part, on the product-market matrix introduced in Chapter 2. The first set of growth

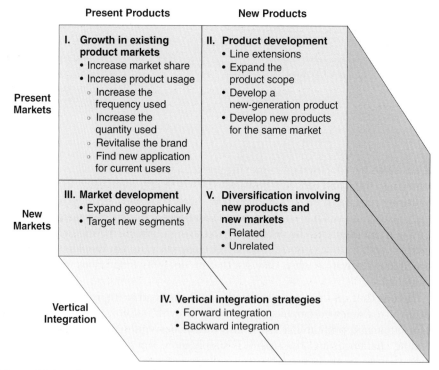

Figure 13.1   Alternative growth strategies

strategies involves existing product markets. The next two concern product development and market development. The fourth concerns vertical integration strategies, and the fifth, diversification strategies, which will be covered in Chapter 13. The distinctions between some of these categories may be blurred, but the structure is still helpful in generating strategic options.

GROWTH IN EXISTING PRODUCT MARKETS

Existing product markets are often attractive growth avenues. An established firm has a base on which to build and momentum that can be exploited. Furthermore, the firm may have experience, knowledge, and resources (including human resources) already in place. Growth can be achieved in existing product markets by increasing share through capturing sales held by competitors. Alternatively, product usage among existing customers can be increased.

Increasing Market Share

Perhaps the most obvious way to grow is to improve market share. A programme based on tactical actions (such as advertising, promotion, or price reductions) can be expensive and unprofitable, however, resulting in transitory share gains from attracting price-sensitive customers. Firms can generate a more permanent share gain by delivering solid value and thereby creating customer satisfaction and loyalty. Developing the assets and competences that lead to this result, though, often involves more heavy lifting than designing a price promotion. Another expensive and risky approach is to pursue increased market share by focusing on competitors and their customers. The worst-case scenario of this strategy was played out in the long-distance telephone battles, where people were rewarded for being disloyal. In contrast, increasing the loyalty of existing customers is not only much easier but also more rewarding. When existing customers are made to feel like winners, new customers – and a market share gain – will usually follow.

Increasing Product Usage

Attempts to increase market share will very likely affect competitors directly and therefore precipitate competitor responses. The alternative of attempting to increase usage among current customers is usually less threatening to competitors. When developing programmes to increase usage it is useful to begin by asking some fundamental questions about the user and the consumption system in which the product is embedded. Why isn't the product or service used more? What are the barriers to increased use? Who are the light users, and can they be influenced to use more? What about the heavy users?

Heavy users are usually the most fruitful target. It is often the case when heavy users shoulder greater spending on a particular product, such as coffee. It is helpful to look at the extra-heavy user subsegment – special treatment might solidify and expand usage by a substantial amount. Consider the special services offered to British Airways Executive Club gold members, including lounge access even when not flying BA, complimentary upgrades for the members and a guest and reservation assurance guaranteeing access to BA flights. Many firms own premium boxes at elite sporting and cultural venues such as Wembley, Croke Park and Santiago Bernabéu and invite valued customers to attend events. Perhaps the best known example of this might be the legendary treatment provided to high rollers by Las Vegas casinos.

Light users should not be ignored because there may be a way to unlock their potential. Who are the light users and why don't they use more? Nestlé noted that people in their early twenties were light coffee users. Exploiting a sweet tooth in this segment, the company successfully introduced the new Nescafé Cappuccino product. Launched in 2002 in many markets worldwide, this new product has attracted young consumers. Denby Pottery's premium image in the tableware market, while competitive, also meant that the product was not used regularly and so the replacement cycle was retarding sales. Additionally, buyers bought different brands for everyday use. To address this, Denby repositioned the product as being for everyday use. Advertisements and the website showed Denby with the slogan 'love food, love Denby' and with the tableware being used with everyday foods such as chips.

CREATIVE THINKING METHODS

Not all growth strategies are obvious. In fact, the obvious ones are likely to be marginal in terms of likely success and impact, so it is useful to look for breakthrough ideas. Methods and concepts of creative thinking, as described in books by Edward de Bono and others, can help in this process. Among the guidelines suggested most often are the following:

- Pursue creative thinking in groups, as multiple perspectives and backgrounds can stimulate useful alternatives.

- Begin with warm-up exercises that break down inhibitions. To make whimsy acceptable, for example, ask individuals to identify what animal expresses their personality and to imitate the sound made by that animal. To stretch minds, ask someone to start a story based on two random words (for example, blue and sail) then ask the group to create a position for a brand based on that story.[1]

- Focus on a particular task, such as how to exploit an asset (a brand name, for example), or a competence (such as the ability to design colourful plastic items).

- Develop options without judging them. Discipline in avoiding evaluation while generating alternatives is a key to creative thinking.

- Engage in lateral thinking to change the perspective of the problem. Challenge an obvious assumption ('What if we had two telephones in a booth?') or simply pick a random word or object (such as 'beer', or 'the Eiffel Tower') to stimulate a new line of thought.

- Evaluate the options based on potential impact without regard to how feasible they are.

- Engage in a second stage of creative thinking aimed at improving the success chances of an attractive option – possibly one with high potential impact that seems too expensive or too difficult to implement.
- Evaluate the final choices not just rationally ('What do the facts say?') but emotionally ('What does your gut say?').
- Create an action plan to go forward.

Greater usage can be precipitated in two ways, by increasing either the frequency of use or the quantity used. In either case, there are several approaches that can be effective as Figure 13.2 suggests.

Provide Reminder Communications

For some use contexts, awareness, or recall of a brand, is the driving force. People who know about a brand and its use may not think to use it on particular occasions without reminders. Reminder communication may be necessary. Thedoghouse.co.uk offers customers the opportunity to be reminded of important, dates, birthdays and anniversaries as well the opportunity to buy gifts for the occasion. Other companies try to use communications to encourage use of products that are easily overlooked. For example, the Fresh Food Company is a UK-based organic food firm which provides information on produce which is in season and a cookbook that supports the use of the organic produce.

Routine functions such as dental checkups or car maintenance are easily forgotten and reminders can make a difference. Some car dealers provide small maintenance items (such as the replacement of bulbs) for free and regular club activities in order to provide a strong link to their customers who will be accessing their maintenance and repair business.

Position for Regular or Frequent Use

Provide a reason for more frequent use. On websites, what works is to have information that is frequently updated. People go to BBC.co.uk, Guardian Unlimited or

Strategy	Examples
Provide reminder communications	Send e-mail about upcoming birthday
Position for frequent use	Checking stocks on Yahoo!
Position for regular use	Flossing after meals
Make use easier	Microwaveable containers
Provide incentives	Frequent-flyer miles
Reduce undesirable consequences	Gentle shampoo for frequent use
Revitalise the brand	New VW Beetle
Find new applications	Jell-O salads

Figure 13.2 Increasing usage in existing product markets

elpais.es to see the latest headlines or catch up on the on their favourite football team, as often as every few minutes when important things are happening. Other incentives might include a new cartoon each day (the *Daily Telegraph* drives traffic to its website each day by making its cartoons Alex and Matt available) or a best-practices bulletin board at a brand consulting site. The image of a product can change from that of occasional to frequent usage by a repositioning campaign. For example, Kellogs Special K has used the Special K Challenge to increase the frequency of usage of its product. Similarly, Danone has invited consumers to use its Activia yoghurt daily for two weeks to reduce digestive discomfort. The use of programmes such as the MANGO Girls Book Club UK, CD clubs, Beer of the Month Club, DVD clubs, and flower-of-the-month or fruit of-the-month delivery can turn infrequent purchasers into once-a-monthers.

Make the Use Easier

Asking why customers do not use a product or service more often can lead to approaches that make the product easier to use. For example, disposable plates and cups or paper-towel dispenser encourages use by reducing the usage effort. Packages that can be placed directly in a microwave make usage more convenient. An online reservation service can help those who must select a hotel or similar service. Many ready-to-cook foods, pizzas, salads, speciality breads, dips, pasta, soups, sauces and prepared fruits serve as examples of product modifications that increased consumption by making usage more convenient.

Provide Incentives

Incentives can be provided to increase consumption frequency. Promotions such as double mileage trips offered by airlines like British Airways, with frequent-flyer plans, can increase usage. American Express Blue, offers users a 1% cashback on purchases to encourage usage frequency and value. A challenge is to structure the incentive so that usage is increased without creating a vehicle for debilitating price competition. Price incentives, such as 'two for the price of one', can be effective but they also may stimulate price retaliation.

Reduce Undesirable Consequences of Frequent Use

Sometimes there are good reasons why a customer is inhibited from using a product more frequently. If such reasons can be addressed, usage may increase. For example, some people might believe that frequent hair washing may not be healthy. A product, such as Johnson's baby hair shampoo, that is designed to be gentle enough for daily use, might alleviate this worry and thereby stimulate increased usage. Demand for snack products has fallen as consumers become concerned about their calorie, sodium or fat intake. In response some manufacturers, have introduced healthier product extensions, such as Tayto Honest, whereas others have changed the ingredients and manufacturing of their existing product (for example, Walkers crisps have reduced the amount of fat and salt in their products without changing their taste). The brand that becomes associated with a product change will be in the best position to capitalise on the increased market.

Revitalise the Brand

Especially for a leading brand, it is easy to become stale over time. Customers may perceive the brand to be of excellent quality but something their parents (or worse, grandparents) would buy. The challenge is to revitalise the brand, to introduce some energy, vitality, and buzz into it. In Chapter 15, approaches to revitalisation involving new products, new markets and new applications are discussed. However, revitalisation can occur often by simply acting young again within the same product-market-application space. Whiskey brands are seeking to use revitalised marketing to attract new users to the product category.[2] The expectation is that as current 28–40 year olds shift their consumption patterns from quantity to quality, that whiskey can fill the gap as a premium and prestige product choice. The major spirits firms have introduced new products to meet this opportunity. Diageo's J&B −6 °C is a pale-coloured Scotch intended for those currently drinking white spirits. Johnnie Walker Green Label serves the blended malt market. Brands within the whiskey market have also embraced tools such as sponsorship, visitor centres and events in order to enhance the relevance of their brands to emerging segments of customers.

The best firms continuously inject excitement and news into their operations with specific programmes. Disneyland, for example, adds and updates rides so often that it is worth going twice a year just to see what is new. Ryanair has had a continuous flow of announcements on how it is reducing and even eliminating fares in order to remind customers of their strategic intent and to leave them wondering what they will do next.

New Applications for Existing Product Users

The detection and exploitation of a new functional use for a brand can drive business growth. A classic story is of Viagra, which was originally developed as a drug to deal with blood pressure and angina. Initial trials suggested that its maximum efficacy was in dealing with erectile dysfunction, rather than its intended use, and so a blockbuster drug was born, with sales in its first two years in excess of US$1 billion. Another classic story from the US is Arm and Hammer baking soda, which saw annual sales grow tenfold by persuading people to use its product as a refrigerator deodoriser. An initial 14-month advertising campaign boosted the use of Arm and Hammer as a deodoriser from 1 % to 57 %. The brand subsequently was extended into other deodoriser products, dentifrices, and laundry detergent.

Another tactic is to look at the applications of competing products. But new uses can perhaps best be identified by conducting needs analysis to determine exactly how customers use a brand. Britvic has a long history as a brand leader and innovator in the mixer and juice sold in pubs. In response to demand from consumers for healthy drinks and from publicans for premium juice brands, Britvic has launched a range of premium 100 % juices: Britvic Squeezed Orange juice and Britvic Pressed Apple Juice. In the confectionery market one counter trend to health concerns has been for products which afford consumers the opportunity for indulgence products. In response Nestlé has launched Aero Chocolate Truffle and Mars offers its Galaxy range.

Sometimes a large payoff will result for a firm that can provide applications not currently in general use. Thus, surveys of current applications may be inadequate.

Biotech firms, such as Amersham, sponsor forums and conferences for scientists to encourage them to develop new applications of their products in scientific research. For a product, such as stick-on labels, which can be used in many ways, it might be worthwhile to conduct formal brainstorming sessions or other creative exercises.

PRODUCT DEVELOPMENT FOR THE EXISTING MARKET

As reflected in Figure 13.1, product development can occur in a variety of ways, and it is helpful to distinguish among them. They include the addition of product features, the development of new-generation products, and the development of new products for an existing market.

Line Extensions

One type of product development is the addition of features to a firm's current product. The right feature can dramatically change the competitive dynamics. Head and Shoulders has been an aggressive policy of line extension. For instance, General Mills' Yoplait overtook long-time category leader Dannon with Go-Gurt, the yoghurt in a tube that kids slurp up. This 'lose the spoon' yoghurt redefined the category for this important segment. To maintain balance, Yoplait followed this success with the adult flavors of Yoplait Expressé. A car maker could add a transmission or sun roof option that would improve its penetration of an existing market. Adding product features involves almost total commonality of marketing, operations, and management. Because additional features represent such visible growth opportunities and are accomplished relatively easily, they can be very enticing. They still absorb resources, however, and should be resisted if the prospective ROI is unsatisfactory.

Product modifications can also occur when high-tech or industrial firms are asked by a customer to produce a special-purpose version of a product. Such development work can lead to substantial sales and even to new products but the attraction of a visible customer need can be overly enticing. If this type of activity is permitted to preempt more ambitious development programs, the long-term health of an organisation can suffer.

Developing New-generation Products

Growth can also be obtained in an existing market by creating new-generation products. Google is under threat from a new generation of search engines that go beyond keyword search. Nextaris.com takes search to the next level by combining search with social networking. As users search the Web they can save results in online folders which can then be kept confidential or shared with online friends.[3]

In the late 1980s Yamaha revitalised a declining piano market by developing the Disklavier, whose electronic control system allowed a performance to be recorded and stored in memory, thus creating a modern version of the old player piano. The technology could be used by a student, a professional player, or a composer, in addition to those who wanted the feeling of having a great pianist play in their home.

While the outsider has nothing to lose and much to gain from pursuing an innovation that will disrupt the marketplace, the established market participant faces the 'incumbent's curse,' two forces that inhibit innovation. First, even if the new technology is successful, often the best result is that a significant investment will be required just to maintain the same level of sales and profits. And the new technology could present problems that add time and expense and reduce customer acceptance – hardly an attractive incentive. Second, the existing market participants need to focus on improving costs, quality and service for the existing offering, which leaves little time and effort to explore a totally new technology. Although new technologies, such as personal video recorders (PVRs) can disrupt an established business, they can also create profitable growth opportunities. Existing market participants should be aware of their biases against detecting and exploiting such opportunities. If the biases are visible, the chances that they will inhibit the organisation from participating in a new technology will be reduced.

Expand the Product Scope

Existing customers might be served further by broadening the use context. Thus, instead of being in the orange juice business, a firm might choose to be in the breakfast business. Instead of selling only footballs, it might consider making goals and nets.

GE's Jack Welch has said that dominant companies in slow growing businesses in particular should redefine their markets, looking for a broader scope that will have more opportunities. Coca-Cola considers its largest competitor to be water. The manager and originator of Microsoft Office, Jeffrey Raikes, was inspired by Welch's concept. As a result, he decided to develop products not just for office workers but for anyone who uses information, including pilots, nurses, factory workers, and truck drivers.[4] Toward that end, Microsoft has researched customer needs and tested innovations in prototypical workplaces of the future.

Slywotsky and Wise make a similar suggestion in their book *How to Grow When Markets Don't*.[5] They recommend identifying and serving the customer needs that emanate from the use of existing products. Boots Group plc is the dominant pharmacy chain in the UK. In recent years they have diversified their business from a traditional pharmacy to one offering a wider range of goods and services including one-hour photo-processing, opticians, and with partners, health checks and wines. O2's acquisition of a broadband provider, Be, was completed in order to allow the company compete in the converging communications market in which customers will be using a single provider to watch TV and video, listen to music and make telephone calls.

New Products for Existing Markets

A classic growth pattern is to exploit a marketing or distribution strength by adding compatible products that share customers with, but are different from, existing products. Synergy is usually obtained at least in part by the commonality in distribution, marketing and brand-name recognition and identity. Newbridge Silverware has a long history as a maker of cutlery, competition in that market and a broad demise in the use of cutlery led them to expand their commitment to quality and brand equity in silverware to expand into giftware and jewellery. The UK high street retailer Monsoon used its design-led retail concept to develop the Accessorise chain with its range of high fashion accessories.

Leveraging brand equity into other product categories is a route to product extension that will be explored in Chapter 14. Examples of this would include Nivea's Toddies wipes, Evian Skincare, Green & Black's organic ice cream, Kellog's nutrigrain bars, Gillete's Venus shaving range for women, Mars Galaxy instant chocolate drinks and Elastoplast Spray Plaster. Each has strong name identification and associations that can drive success in the new category. Managers must make sure that the extension fits the brand, that it provides helpful associations, and that it does not damage or dilute associations of the brand. One of the issues facing Kit-Kat, at one stage the market leading confectionery brand in Europe, is that it has overused product extensions.

A rationale for product additions is to achieve synergies. Sometimes, however, synergies are simply illusory. A packaged food firm had little in common with a fast-food restaurant chain that it acquired, even though both involved food. More often, synergy exists but its benefit is modest and does not overcome the costs and problems associated with the new area.

There is significant risk to any new product venture, especially with respect to customer acceptance. In 2002 Nestlé and Coca-Cola came together to produce Choglit, a diary-based drink intend to appeal to the youth market and the broader concern about the health implications of soft drinks. Dasani was withdrawn from the UK market in 2004 after it was revealed that it was regular tap water rather than spring water and following a scare on the bromate content of the product. The brand owner, Coca-Cola, had never claimed that Dasani was a spring water but the expectation of the category was that it would be. Even the use of an established brand cannot guarantee success. Masterfoods failed with its bisc& range which featured biscuits covered with Twix, Mars, Bounty and M&Ms. Although operating in the high-growth sweet biscuit market and featuring leading brand names, the brand was withdrawn after two years on the market.

Product-line expansion will be based on many factors, of course, but will often involve consideration of the following questions:

- *Will customers benefit from a systems capability or service convenience made possible by a broad product line?* The inclusion of a software line and printers with a line of computers provides the potential of offering a more complete system. However, customers may want not only systems design but also systems support.

- *Do potential manufacturing, marketing, or distribution cost efficiencies exist from an expanded product line?* To the extent that there are shared costs, the experience and scale effects on costs will be enhanced. The question is whether, even with this cost advantage, the proposed product line expansion will have a satisfactory ROI.

- *Can assets or competencies be applied to a product-line expansion?* The most prominent asset is often the brand name itself. In the next chapter, brand extensions will be treated in more detail. Do not automatically assume, though, that assets and competences can work in new contexts.

- *Does a firm have the needed competencies and resources in R&D, manufacturing, and marketing to add the various products proposed?* Sometimes an apparently simple line extension, such as adding wood stains to a line of paints, can involve a totally new manufacturing effort, raw materials technology, or marketing effort and thus may not fit the capabilities of the firm.

MARKET DEVELOPMENT USING EXISTING PRODUCTS

A logical avenue of growth is to develop new markets by duplicating the business operation, perhaps with minor adaptive changes. With market expansion, the same expertise and technology and sometimes even the same plant and operations facility can be used. Thus, there is potential for synergy and resulting reductions in investment and operating costs. Of course, market development is based on the premise that the business is operating successfully. There is no point in exporting failure or mediocrity.

Expanding Geographically

Geographic expansion may involve changing from a regional operation to a national operation, moving into another region, or expanding to another country. HSBC, Tesco, Marks & Spencer, Carrefour and BMW have successfully exported their operations to other countries. Many companies are looking to countries such as China, India and Russia to fuel growth in the coming decades. They realise that success will involve significant investment in logistics, distribution infrastructures, and organisation building and adaptation.

Moving from local to regional to national to international is another option. Often, however, this expansion is best implemented by connecting, through an alliance or merger, to a partner that already has the capability to market more broadly. Remaining geographically focused may also be a profitable pathway. As the major branded firms such as Nestlé and Unilever refocus on major global brands, local brands have come into closer focus. Although they would require massive investment to achieve global status, such brands can often be very profitable in the domestic market. An Irish firm, Jacobs Fruitfield, led by Michael Carey, have taken advantage of this and bought up many local foods brands such as Bewley's Coffee, Chef sauces, Mikado biscuits and Fruitfield jams. With revitalised marketing these iconic Irish brands offer profitability and growth potential in the local market.

Expanding into New Market Segments

A firm can also grow by reaching into new market segments. There are a variety of ways to define target segments and therefore growth directions:

- *Usage.* The nonuser can be an attractive target. An audio electronics firm could target those who don't own an audio system.

- *Distribution channel.* A firm can reach new segments by opening up a second or third channel of distribution. Many fashion retail brands offer the product thought single brand stores, other retailers and through online stores. A direct marketer such as Oriflame could introduce its products into department stores under another brand name.
- *Age.* Johnson & Johnson's baby shampoo was languishing until the company looked toward adults who wash their hair frequently.
- *Attribute preference.* An instrumentation firm might extend its line to include more precise equipment to serve a segment that requires greater accuracy.
- *Application-defined market.* An airline offered a door-to-door, same day package delivery service in conjunction with a shipping service. A customer places an order on a website, a courier picks it up and delivers it to the aircraft, and another courier then delivers it to the recipient.

A key to detecting new markets is to consider a wide variety of segmentation variables. Sometimes looking at markets in a different way will uncover a useful segment. It is especially helpful to identify segments that are not being served well, such as the women's calculator market or the fashion needs of older people. In general, segments should be sought for which the brand can provide value. Entering a new market without providing any incremental customer value is very risky.

Evaluating Market Expansion Alternatives

Although synergy can potentially be high, several other considerations are involved in a market expansion:

- *Is the market attractive?* Will customers value the product or service? Does it really offer meaningful and distinctive value? How formidable and committed are competitors? Can their assets and competencies be neutralised by the right strategy? Are market and environmental trends supportive?
- *Do the resources and will exist to make the necessary commitment in the face of uncertainties?* Does the move make strategic sense? Compaq exited the printer business despite having a superior product because the prospects of catching Hewlett Packard and the other leaders were too formidable. The commitment was lacking.
- *Can the business be adapted to the new market?* To the extent that conditions differ, is there a convincing plan to adapt the business? It is often said that France is the European country most resistant to American culture. However, one of America's most iconic brands, McDonald's, known in France as McDo, has been in France since 1979, has more than 1000 restaurants around the country and is their most profitable market in Europe. To achieve this McDonald's has adapted its menu to meet French tastes, including offering French yoghurts, French coffee and French soft drinks.

The company has also promoted its commitment to French suppliers by advertising how many cows, chickens, lettuces and tomatoes it buys in France each year.[6]

- *Can the assets and competencies that are at the heart of business success be transferred into the new business environment?* Wal-Mart experienced problems with its entry to Europe with problems in the German market. Its entry was via the acquisition first of Wertkauf and later of Interspar, which should have provided a smooth path. However, the reluctance of suppliers to participate in its centralised supply system, the challenge of introducing American managers to German business and later regulatory problems with its low prices all caused problems for the retail giant. Its entry to the UK market via the acquisition of Asda was smoothed as a result of this experience as Wal-Mart gave local management a greater role and focused instead on offering them the benefits of their expertise in IT and included them in their global buying operations to reduce prices for Asda customers.[7]

The experience of FedEx when it first attempted to duplicate its concept in Europe illustrates the last two issues.[8] Setting up a hub-and-spoke system in Europe was inhibited by regulatory problems. Attempts to short-circuit regulations by acquiring firms with related abilities resulted in something of a hodgepodge – FedEx ended up owning a barge company, for example. The firm also lacked a first-mover advantage in Europe because DHL and others had employed the FedEx concept years earlier. A reliance on the English language and a decision to impose a pickup deadline of five o'clock in Spain (where people work until eight) caused additional implementation problems.

VERTICAL INTEGRATION STRATEGIES

Vertical integration represents another potential growth direction. Forward integration occurs when a firm moves downstream with respect to product flow, such as a manufacturer buying a retail chain. Backward integration is moving upstream such as when a manufacturer invests in a raw material source. A good way to understand when vertical integration should be considered and how it should be evaluated is to look at the possible benefits and costs of a vertical integration strategy. Vertical integration potentially provides:

- access to supply or demand
- control of the quality of the product or service
- entry into an attractive business area

But introduces:

- the risks of managing a very different business
- a reduction in strategy flexibility

Access to Supply or Demand

Access to Supply

In some contexts, a key success factor is access to a supply of raw material, a part, or another input factor; backward integration can reduce the availability risk. Thus a packaging firm might buy timberland or develop a paper recycling capability, as Smurfit Kappa has done, in order to guarantee supply. Owning the source in this case also allows paper and packaging firms to ensure that the forests are managed in a renewable way. Nokia was able to gain a market share advantage over Ericsson when a chip plant in Mexico, which supplied them both, burned down. Nokia took an urgent approach to sourcing new supply and working with the supplier, Philips, to ensure that its production was not disrupted. Ericsson on the other hand took time in responding – and its access to a crucial resource, and sales, suffered as a result.[9]

Access to Demand

Similarly, forward integration could be motivated by a concern about product outlets. Thus, an insurance firm could buy regional insurance agents to provide sales outlets. BP is the second largest fuels' retailer in Europe, and number one or two in most national markets. This access to the European market provides BP with an opportunity to sell both its fuel and lubricant products.

Control of the Product System

It may become necessary to integrate vertically in order to gain sufficient control over a product or service to maintain the integrity of a differentiation strategy. For example, a vital component may need to be made with precision, and outside contractors may be unable to provide it or unwilling to make an investment in the specialised assets required. Vertical integration may be the only way to ensure that the desired quality is achieved.

Samsung has made a dramatic transformation since the mid-1990s. Once a manufacturer of low-priced consumer electronic equipment with adequate quality distributed through value retailers, the Korean firm now sells its high-priced, top-quality wares through premium channels. One reason behind this turnaround was Samsung's emergence as a product leader in mobile phones and flat-screen television sets and computer monitors. The company attributes its ability to make these product advances – and get the resulting buzz – to its backward integration into microprocessors and memory chips. By inventing, manufacturing, and owning its advances, Samsung can get (and stay) ahead of competition that must rely on an outside supplier.

Sony has lived with the memory of its superior Beta format being overrun by the consortium of VHS firms. The final nail was hammered in when the movie studios stopped producing films in the Beta format. Sony has since become a one-stop shop for entertainment with two entertainment groups, Sony BMG Music Entertainment and Sony Pictures Entertainment, which incorporates Columbia Tristar Pictures, MGM, United Artists and other businesses. Sony has substantial control over supplier decisions and in the future it can guarantee a supply of software for its hardware products.

Entry into a Profitable Business Area

Many manufacturers have struggled because of margin pressures. Those that have prospered have often vertically integrated downward to the customer, because that is where the money is. From cars to telecommunications to computers, the size of the installed base is much larger than the new unit sales. In corporate computing, for example, the average company designates only about one-fifth of its annual personal-computer budget on buying boxes – the rest goes to technical support. Four different downstream business models can be considered:

Comprehensive Services

Suites of services are packaged along with the product. Sony has established Sony centres to guarantee the widest choice of Sony products and after sales service. BMW and other premium car firms have seen much of their growth and profits come from services that augment their products. In many cases, the product is the tail that wags the dog.

Distributor/Retailer

When a distributor or retailer is used they will command a substantial margin. By going direct to customers as Oriflame and Dell do with a direct model and Vodafone and O'Briens Sandwiches do with their retail sites, the potential for a profitable business may exist.

Embedded Services

With digital technology advances, services that once were external to the product can be built in. Microsoft plans to have a feature in its next operating system software that will warn users that a disk drive is about to fail and give notice of the need to back-up files.[10] Stryker makes surgical equipment that can be controlled through voice recognition. Each of these augmentations extends the product's value.

Integrated Solutions

Nokia illustrates how a firm can combine products and services into a seamless offering that addresses a customer need. When it recognised that telephone carriers (its customers) were struggling with the conversion from analogue to digital and a massive growth in demand, Nokia broke into a leadership position by creating an array of cellular products, including handsets, transmission equipment, and switches. In addition to deploying these products with a range of services, the company helped the carriers plan and manage their networks.

Two sets of questions will help guide any downstream option. First, can it be successfully implemented by your organisation? Can the needed assets and competencies be developed? Second, is the opportunity attractive in terms of profitability?

Will the demand support the business? Will the competitive landscape allow health margins?

Risks of Managing a Different Business

Vertical integration involves adding an operation whose required organisational assets and competences may differ markedly from those of the firm's other business areas. Dell, for example, would require a very different type of organisation if it attempted to manufacture disk drives or microprocessors, than the one it has developed for selling finished computers. Similar would be the case of Domino's Pizza if it wanted to provide services similar to Pizza Hut. The difference between managing packaged goods like Pepsi-Cola and restaurants such as KFC and Pizza Hut helped PepsiCo decide to get out of the restaurant business. Another influence on the decision was the problem with being a competitor to large customers (some pizza chains in the US were reluctant to offer Pepsi in their locations, given that PepsiCo owned a rival in Pizza Hut). Running an integrated organisation introduces added complexities.

Reduction in Strategic Flexibility

The increased commitment to a business and its market reflected by vertical integration reduces strategic flexibility. If that market is healthy, then integration may enhance products. On the other hand, if the market turns down, integration may cause a larger drop in profits. Integration also raises exit barriers. If the business becomes weak, the additional investment and commitment created by integration will inhibit consideration of an exit alternative. Furthermore, if one operation becomes dependent on the other, an exit strategy may be inhibited.

Alternatives to Integration

Several alternatives to integration exist, such as long-term contracts, exclusive dealing agreements, asset ownership, joint ventures, strategic alliances, technology licenses and franchising. For example, a winery can have a long-term contract with vineyards that protects both. Exclusive dealing agreements that link a manufacturer and a retail chain or distributor can provide the needed information transfer, strategy coordination, and transaction and distribution efficiency. Automobile firms that own the special tooling used by their suppliers provide a technological and financial link that helps insure reliable supply. Most of these alternatives involve difficulties, especially as circumstances and power relationships change over time, but they also provide many of the advantages of integration with fewer disadvantages. They should usually be considered before commitments to integration are pursued. Although net profit as a percent of sales does increase with vertical integration, the return on investment (ROI) may not because of the increase in investment. One study of 1650 businesses suggested that the most profitable businesses are at the extremes of the vertical integration spectrum.[11] A V-shaped relationship between vertical integration and profitability was found. Thus, manufacturers should be wary of taking a middle course.

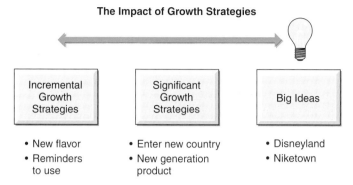

The Impact of Growth Strategies

Incremental Growth Strategies	Significant Growth Strategies	Big Ideas
• New flavor • Reminders to use	• Enter new country • New generation product	• Disneyland • Niketown

Figure 13.3   The impact of growth strategies

The business that puts together systems and farms out component production will tend to minimise investment, seek out low prices, and have maximum flexibility. The heavily integrated firm will maximise the benefits of vertical integration.

THE BIG IDEA

The foregoing has introduced five paths to growth. Each path comprises a spectrum of strategies that range from the incremental to really big ideas, as Figure 13.3 suggests. Although incremental growth strategies can and should be the foundation for growth, some significant growth initiatives and big ideas ought to be on the table as well. If no big ideas are ever considered, there is virtually no chance to create breakthrough strategy – so expand your horizon and look for the Disneyland and Niketown type of ideas.

Creativity and innovation comes from a diversity of ideas and idea sources. Get multiple sources and perspectives involved, then test the best ideas. Since it is hard to predict what will be a significant growth initiative or a big idea, don't be afraid to take five lesser ideas and see which one surprises you.

Strategy as Revolution

Gary Hamel has put forward the thesis that the real payoff results from development of revolutionary strategies that break out of industry norms or operations. Dell Computer, for example, sold computers by mail when that was just a hypothetical idea. Ryanair, one of Europe's most controversial companies, provided services at exceptionally low fares and challenged what Ryanair calls the 'establishment' within the airline industry, similar to its American counterpart, Southwest Airlines. IKEA furniture pioneered in modern designing of self-assembly and the use of more sustainable approaches to mass consumer culture.

Revolutionary strategies, when successful, can lead to strategic advantage and avoid the difficult task of improving on the same strategies used by competitors. How can revolutionary strategies be developed, especially within an organisation committed to the accepted ways of operation? The answer involves some creative thinking. Use the guidelines suggested on p. 260. During external and internal analysis look for revolutionary ideas. Hamel suggests some additional guidelines:[12]

- List the fundamental beliefs that incumbents in your industry share. What new opportunities would exist if one or more of these were relaxed? What if hotels operated similarly to rental-car agencies, selling rooms on a 24-hour basis instead of using a rigid check-in system?
- Look at the functional benefits received by the customer and consider different ways of supplying those benefits.
- Consider how assets or competencies could be exploited in different settings or in different ways.
- Look at the discontinuities in the industry and let them lead to unconventional strategy options.
- Consider offering a scaled-down version of the product or service, such as bed-and-breakfast inns or microbreweries. Or, think about an expanded version, from local to global, perhaps.
- Push the boundaries of universality. For example, make disposable cameras that children can use.
- Add excitement or fun to the product or service, thereby redefining the offering. For example, a supermarket added a children's crèche, a football team added a jazz band and gourmet picnic food, and Asda's added fashion to food retailing.
- The most fruitful growth area is often to increase product usage within the existing product market by increasing the frequency or quantity used, by finding new applications or revitalising the brand.

Searching for Blue Oceans

Similarly to Hamel, W. Chan Kim and Renée Maulborgne have identified that above average growth can not be achieved without looking beyond existing strategy norms and rules. For them, most firms seek growth in 'red oceans' where strategy is characterised by confrontation with competitors, the exploitation of existing demand and trading off value for costs. However, the best quality growth exists in 'blue oceans' or new market spaces in which competition is nonexistent.[13] Think of the first entrants into each new market for a sense of how this might look.

In order to identify blue-ocean opportunities Kim and Maulborgne suggest the need first to identify the dimensions upon which competitors in the industry invest and compete. For example, in a particular section of the retail industry the investment might be seen as being in stores with competition being around price and range. Having done this blue ocean opportunities can be identified through asking four questions:

- Which of the dimensions on which the industry competes could be *reduced well below* the industry's standard?
- Which dimensions should be *raised well above* the industry's standard?
- Which factors should be *created* that the industry has never offered?
- Which of the dimensions that the industry takes for granted should be *eliminated*?[14]

KEY LEARNINGS

- The most fruitful growth area is often to increase product usage within the existing product market, where assets and competences are in place and only need to be leveraged. Growth within a product market can involve adding product features, new-generation products, expansion of the product scope, or new products.

- Developing new products, a second route to growth, can involve line extensions, expanded product scope, or new generation products.

- A third growth route, market development, involves expanding the market either geographically or by targeting new market segments.

- A key consideration of any growth strategy is how to achieve synergy by leveraging current assets and competences.

- Vertical integration, another growth direction, can provide access to supply or demand, control of the quality of the product or service, and entry into an attractive business area. It also, however, introduces the risks of managing a very different business and reducing strategy flexibility.

- Outsourcing rather than vertical integration makes it easier to change strategic direction in response to threats and pressures for the market.

- Growth can be achieved with incremental growth strategies, significant growth initiatives, or big ideas.

- All businesses should strive to uncover and implement big ideas, and discontinuous growth opportunities because they are usually the source of breakthrough strategies.

FOR DISCUSSION

1. Pick an industry and a product or service. Engage in a creative thinking process (as outlined in the insert in the chapter) to generate an improved offering. Do the same to create an entirely new offering that uses one or more of the assets and competencies of the firm.

2. Pick a firm and business and use the ideas proposed by Gary Hamel or W. Chan Kim and Renée Maulborgne to come up with a big idea.

3. How would you increase the usage of products if you were the manager of:
   a. Head and Shoulders anti-dandruff shampoo
   b. Nokia mobile phone handsets
   c. Zara

4. The Body Shop was recently acquired by L'Oréal and Green & Blacks Organic Chocolate was acquired by Cadbury. How might their new owners

drive growth of these brands? In each case, what assets or competencies are being leveraged? Were these wise acquisitions?

5. Dell is planning to expand its service business, as it has higher margins and is a growth area. What must Dell do to be successful in this arena? What suggestions would you make as to the business model that will allow easyJet to compete with HP and IBM?

NOTES

1. Suggestions with respect to this second bullet, as well as the seventh bullet following, come from Alexander Biel an active and successful creative thinking innovator and facilitator.

2. Ian Buxton (2006) Blending heritage with innovation. *Marketing*, 4 May, p. 17.

3. Olga Kharif (2005) New generation of search sites threaten Google. *Business Week*, 8 March.

4. Jay Greene (2002) Beyond the office. *Business Week*, 16 September, pp. 54–6.

5. Adrian Slywotsky and Richard Wise (2003) *How to Grow When Markets Don't*, Warner Business Books, New York.

6. Burger and fries à la française. *The Economist*, 15 April 2004.

7. Wendy Zellner, Katherine Schmidt, Moon Ihlwan, Heidi Dawley (2001) How well does Wal-Mart Travel. *Business Week*, 3 September.

8. Daniel Pearl (1991) Federal express finds its pioneering formula falls flat overseas. *Wall Street Journal*, 15 April, pp. A1–A6.

9. Yosef Sheffi (2005) *The Resilient Enterprise*, MIT Press, Cambridge MA.

10. Computer, heal thyself. *Business Week*, 5 December 2005.

11. Robert D. Buzzell (1983) Is vertical integration profitable? *Harvard Business Review*, January–February, pp. 92–102.

12. Gary Hamel (1996) Strategy as revolution. *Harvard Business Review*, July–August, pp. 69–81.

13. W. Chan Kim and Renée Maulborgne (2004) Blue ocean strategy. *Harvard Business Review*, October, pp: 76–84.

14. W. Chan Kim and Renée Maulborgne (2005) *Blue Ocean Strategy*, Harvard Business School Press.

CHAPTER FOURTEEN

Diversification

'Tis the part of a wiseman to keep himself today for tomorrow, and not venture all his eggs in one basket.
—*Miguel de Cervantes*

Put all your eggs in one basket and – WATCH THAT BASKET.
—*Mark Twain*

Diversification is a popular story in the business world. A pharmaceutical firm buys a chemical company, a bank enters the insurance business, a consumer electronics company goes into medical devices, a newspaper publisher buys an online listings business. Such diversification moves represent both the opportunity for growth and revitalisation and the substantial risk of operating an unfamiliar business in a new context.

Diversification is the strategy of entering product markets different from those in which a firm is currently engaged. Two growth strategies discussed in Chapter 13 – product expansion and market expansion – usually involve entry into new product markets, thus representing diversification. However, diversification can also involve both new products and new markets. A diversification strategy can be implemented by either an acquisition (or merger) or a new business venture. It is helpful to categorise diversification as related and unrelated. In a related diversification, the new business area has meaningful commonalities with the core business. Meaningful commonalities provide the potential to generate economies of scale or synergies based on an exchange of assets or competencies. The resulting combined business should be able to achieve improved ROI because of increased revenues, decreased costs, or reduced investment. As noted in Chapter 8, meaningful commonalities can involve sharing of:

- customers and sometimes customer applications (potentially creating a systems solution)
- a sales force or channel of distribution
- a brand name and its image

- facilities used for manufacturing, offices, or warehousing
- R&D efforts
- staff and operating systems
- marketing and marketing research

The product expansion growth strategy normally involves the same market and distribution system, so it would qualify as a related diversification. The market expansion growth strategy is usually also a related diversification because it applies the same production technology and often involves a similar market and distribution system. Vertical integration is usually an unrelated diversification, however, because it typically lacks an area of commonality.

An important issue to consider in any diversification decision is whether, in fact, there is a real and meaningful area of commonality that will affect the ultimate ROI. An unrelated diversification (a diversification lacking meaningful commonalities) may still be justifiable, but a different rationale would be needed. Thus, the concept of related diversification is more than an issue of definition. In the following section we consider the rationale and risks of related diversification and then those of unrelated diversification.

RELATED DIVERSIFICATION

Exporting or Exchanging Assets and Competencies

Related diversification provides the potential to attain synergies by sharing assets or competencies across businesses (see Figure 14.1). When related diversification is accomplished by internal expansion, the goal is to export assets or competencies. When acquisition of or merger with another business is the vehicle, the goal is to combine two sets of complementary assets and competencies, with each party contributing what the other lacks. In either case, a business exploring related diversification should consider three steps.

The first step is to inventory assets and competencies in order to identify real strengths that are exportable to another business area. Recall the discussion in Chapter 4 on identifying assets and competencies. Among exportable assets and competencies are brand names, marketing skills, sales and distribution capacity, manufacturing skills, and research-and-development capabilities.

The second step toward related diversification is to find a business area where the assets and competencies can be applied to generate an advantage. A line of greeting cards sold through pharmacies might be able to use the distribution assets and competencies of an over-the-counter drug marketer. Although Reuters is best known to the world as an international news provider, in fact more than 90% of its revenue is

Figure 14.1   Leveraging assets and competencies

derived from its financial services business. Reuters provides financial services organisations with information and specialised tools for decision making. The news brand builds an exceptional profile for Reuters and supports its position in the financial services industry.

One fruitful exercise is to examine each asset for excess capacity. Are some assets underutilised? An accounting firm that considered this question took advantage of excess office space to offer legal services. A supermarket chain with obsolete sites went into the discount off-licence business. A bakery began making sandwiches. The advent of multiscreen cinemas exploited the excess capacity of the staff. If a diversification can use excess capacity, a substantial, sustainable cost advantage could result.

Finally, implementation problems need to be addressed. Assets and competencies may require adaptations when applied to a different business. Further, new capabilities may have to be found or developed. When acquisitions are involved, two organisations with different systems, people, and cultures will have to be merged. Many efforts at achieving synergy falter because of implementation difficulties.

Brand Name

One common exportable resource is a strong, established brand name – a name with visibility, associations, perceived quality, and loyalty among a customer group. The challenge is to take this brand asset and use it to enter new product-markets. The name can make the task of establishing a new product more feasible and efficient because it makes developing awareness, trust and interest easier. Many firms have built large, diverse businesses around a strong brand, including Sony, Nestle, IBM, UBS, Siemens, Philips, Samsung, Cadbury and Danone.

Disney, founded in 1920 as a cartoon company with Mickey Mouse (then known as Steamboat Willie) as its initial asset, might be the most successful firm ever at leveraging its brand. In the 1950s, the company built Disneyland and launched a TV show linked to the theme park, dramatically changing the brand by making it much richer and deeper than before. Particularly after extending Disneyland to Florida, Paris, Japan and Hong Kong and establishing its own retail stores, resorts, and a cruise ship, Disney can deliver an experience that goes far beyond watching cartoons. As a result of this brand power, the Disney Channel is arguably one of the strongest TV channels available, an incredible achievement if you consider what others have put into that space.

It is instructive to see why Disney has done so well with an aggressive brand extension strategy. First, from the beginning the company has known what it stands for – magical family entertainment, executed with consistent excellence. Everything Disney does reinforces that brand identity; when it went into films for mature audiences, it did so under the name Touchstone rather than Disney. Second, Disney has relentless, uncompromising drive for operational excellence that started with Walt Disney's fanatical concern for detail in the earliest cartoons and theme parks. The parks are run so well that Disney holds schools for other firms seeking to learn how to maintain energy and consistency. The cruise ship was delayed, despite ballooning costs, until everything was judged perfect. Third, the organisation actively manages a host of subbrands that have their own identities, including Mickey Mouse, Donald Duck, a mountain (the Matterhorn), a song (*It's a Small World*), film characters like

Mary Poppins or the Lion King, and on and on. Fourth, Disney understands synergy across products. The Lion King is not only a film but supports video/DVD sales, the Disney store, an exhaustive set of promotions, and a musical.

It should be noted, however, that in the brand extensions the roads were always uneven. When Disneyland first opened its theme park in 1992 in Paris, attendance was disappointingly low. Five hundred thousand guests were expected on opening day but only a fraction of this number turned out, and the numbers fell further after the first three months. The park failed to plan for certain cultural issues – such as initially not offering wine in its restaurants and trying to offer more French food on its menus to visitors who were more interested in distinctly American cuisine. High entrance fees were also blamed for the lack of visitors. Furthermore, the theme park faced protests by commentators who thought a Disney park in France would harm French culture with its American influence; some went as far as to call the project a 'cultural Chernobyl'.

More recently Disneyland Paris was again under pressure, although its problems seemed to be less cultural and more marketing related. The Disneyland Paris theme park is generally full of guests and was the most popular tourist attraction in France in 2003. However, the opening of a second theme park, Walt Disney Studios, in 2002 coincided with a post-9/11 drop in visitors to France. In addition, one of the company's main sources of revenue, hotels, was affected by the opening of competing hotels. The key driver of (particularly repeat) attendance at theme parks is the opening of new rides and attractions. In 2004 there had been no new rides at Disneyland Paris for some time. In late 2005 the company announced plans to more aggressively manage the yield from its hotel business as well as its intentions to launch major new attractions in 2006, 2007 and 2008.[1]

The brand-extension decision is largely based on three questions. Each must be answered in the affirmative for the extension to be viable.[2]

- *Does the brand fit the new product context?* If the customer is uncomfortable and senses a lack of fit, acceptance will not come easily. The brand may not be seen as having the needed credibility or expertise, or it may have the wrong associations for the context. In general, a brand that has strong ties to a product class and attributes (for example, Airbus, Shell or Renault) will have a more difficult time stretching than a brand that is associated with intangibles such as fashion, value, German engineering, or active lifestyles. Certainly, all of the Disney extensions fit because they were supporting or part of the 'magical family entertainment' brand identity. The Disney store, for example, fits because it is full of Disney characters, videos and spirit.

- *Does the brand add value to the offering in the new product class?* A customer should be able to express why the brand would be preferred in its new context. Despite the fact that cruise ships are difficult to tell apart, nearly anyone could verbalise rather clearly how a Disney Cruise ship would be different from others – it would have Disney characters aboard, contain more kids and families and provide magical family entertainment. If the brand name does not add value in the eyes of the customer, the extension will be vulnerable to competition. For example, easyJet is one of the best known consumer brands in Europe today. It has recently extended its brand to a range of men's grooming products, easy4men. It is less obvious how the brand proposition of the easyGroup might add value in this category. Sometimes a brand's value for extension can be reduced through overuse. At one point Pierre Cardin was used on over 800 products. A concept test can help determine what value is added by the brand. Prospective customers can be given only the brand name, then they can be asked whether they would be attracted to the product and why. If they cannot articulate a specific reason why the offering would be attractive to them, it is unlikely that the brand name will add significant value.

- Will the extension enhance the brand name and image? The ideal is to have an extension that will provide visibility, energy, and associations that support the brand. Monsoon's sister stores Accessorise supports its position as a concept fashion retailer. Disney's extension into theme parks in Europe and Asia, retail stores and cruises all reinforced the brand. The extension of the original easyJet brand to online shopping (easyValue.com), job search (easyJobs.com), mobile phones (easyMobile.com) and online personal finance (easyMoney.com) and its ongoing move into other areas all provide an energy and momentum to the brand and help to attract new groups of customers to the brand and other offerings.

If an extension will damage the brand, another branding option needs to be found. The fashion brand Prada wished to have a presence in the larger, but more price conscious segment of the fashion market. To use the Prada brand to do this could potentially have undermined the parent brand. It thus entered this market with the Miu Miu brand.

Subbrands and Endorsed Brands

Two unfortunate realities can interfere with brand extensions. First, a new brand may not be feasible because the space is too cluttered and the organisation does not have the size or resources to build a new brand in that context. Second, the existing brand may have the wrong associations or risk being damaged by the extension, perhaps because the latter's perceived quality or personality is incompatible with the brand.

In these cases the answer may lie in the use of subbrands or endorsed brands. Sony has used subbrands effectively to enter a range of new markets such as gaming (Playstation), computers (Vaio), entertainment robots (AIBO), television (Brava). A subbrand lets the offering separate itself somewhat from the parent brand, and it offers the parent brand some degree of insulation. For example, in 2006 Sony announced that the AIBO entertainment robots would be discontinued. This exit is achieved without casting any doubt on its commitment to or achievement in the other areas of consumer entertainment in which it is active.

An endorsed brand offers even more separation. For example, Tesco recognised the growth potential of two segments of the UK retail market. The first was the 'top-up' retail market, when consumers need a newspaper, milk or a chocolate bar. In response they launched the Tesco Express format, local stores, often located in petrol stations, to meet the demand. They also saw the potential for a wider retail format and launched a further endorsed brand, Tesco Extra selling a wide range of goods such as homewares and electrical goods. These two are added to the existing endorsed brand of Tesco Express and the standard Tesco superstore. These endorsements indicate that Tesco as an organisation stands behind each and that customers can be confident that the stores would deliver on the core brand promise. Leveraging a brand by using it to endorse other brands, often provides a trust umbrella.

Marketing Skills

A firm will often either possess or lack strong marketing skills for a particular market. Thus, a frequent motive for diversification is to export or import marketing skills. Procter & Gamble's (P&G's) acquisition of Gillette in 2005 was substantially about deploying and acquiring marketing skills. At a very basic level P&G had great skills in marketing to women. Its brands include Olay, Camay and Max Factor. On the other hand Gillette, with its range of innovative razors and shaving products, had been regularly cited as the firm which understood the men's personal care market better than anyone else. Adding the two groups together widens the product mix in a logical way and provides avenues for market learning on both sides.

Applying marketing skills is not always as easy as it appears. Prada sought to take advantage of its exceptional marketing skills in the creation of high fashion accessories, particularly in handbags, with the acquisition of a variety of other labels including Fendi, Helmut Lang and Jil Sander. The latter two were both sold in 2006 having failed to make a profit for Prada.

Capacity in Sales or Distribution

A firm with a strong distribution capability may add products or services that could exploit that capability. Thus, Tesco's store network and later its strength as an online store helped provide a boost to its financial services business. Post Offices have strengths in distribution and security that provide them with an asset that can be exploited. In the UK the Post Office uses these strengths to offer foreign exchange, insurance and investments. Similarly, in Ireland the national postal service, An Post, offers money transmission and banking services.

E-commerce firms usually have operations that can add capacity just by adding a button to access another product group. The result can be additional sales and margins to offset the fixed costs of the operation.

Manufacturing Skills

Manufacturing or processing ability can be the basis for entry into a new business area. Cadbury's expertise in the manufacture of flake and in extrusion allowed them to create TimeOut. The ability to make small products has been a key for Sony as it has moved from product to product in consumer electronics.

Research and development

Expertise in a certain technology can lead to a new business based on that technology. Nokia is often cited as a packaging firm that became a mobile phone manufacturer.

While this is true it masks the full story of its historical involvement in cable manufacture, then electronics and telephone exchange equipment. What is common amongst these areas and the driving force of its excellence is a commitment to research-and-development-driven innovation. The challenge is to be open to channel research and development toward new business areas. Too often there is a tendency to focus exclusively on evolving the existing business. Dyson has been very successful at using research and development to develop new business, developing from the ball barrow to the dual cyclone vacuum cleaner, to the two-drum washing machine.

Achieving Economies of Scale

Related diversification can sometimes provide economies of scale. Two smaller consumer products firms, for example, may not each be able to afford an effective sales force, new product development or testing programmes, or warehousing and logistics systems. However, the combination of these firms may be able to operate at an efficient level. Similarly, two firms, when combined, may be able to justify an expensive piece of automated production equipment. Sometimes a critical mass is needed in order to be effective. For example, a specialised electronics firm may need a research-and-development effort, but research-and-development productivity may be low if it is not feasible to have several researchers who can interact and a range of lab equipment to work on. A significant aspect of the P&G/Gillette merger was related to achieving economies of scale in communications and distribution. P&G is one of the largest advertisers in the world, spending more than €4 billion, while Gillette spends more than €1.25 billion. Together these budgets should allow the combined entity to secure better terms from communications agencies. More importantly, consumer goods firms face the challenge of doing business with giant retail chains such as Wal-Mart and Tesco who put continuous downward pressure on supplier prices. A larger supplier of strong brands should be better placed to resist margin pressures and to work with retailers as new consumer markets in India and China develop.

THE MIRAGE OF SYNERGY

Synergy, as suggested in Chapter 8, is an important source of competitive advantage. However, synergy is often more mirage than reality. Synergy is often assumed when, in fact, it does not exist, cannot be realised because of implementation problems, or is vastly overextended.

Potential Synergy Does Not Exist

Strategists often manipulate semantics to delude themselves that a synergistic justification exists. In the pharmaceutical industry, mergers have been justified on the basis that global marketing and research-and-development muscle are required to drive drug development and success. Such a motive underlay the €24 billion merger of Glaxo Wellcome and SmithKline Beecham in 2000, but the benefits in term of new blockbuster drugs were slow to emerge.

Potential Synergy Exists, but Implementation Barriers Make it Unattainable or Difficult

This happens when a diversification move integrates two organisations that have fundamental differences. Morrisons is one of the UK's most successful retailers, concentrated mainly on the north of England it has a long history of sales and profit growth. In 2004 it moved to acquire the Safeway supermarket chain. The logic was unquestionable. Safeway's southern England concentration would compliment the northern bias of Morrison's. However, a number of problems quickly came to the fore. Morrison's maintained tight control over its stores, while Safeway had traditionally allowed its store managers more autonomy. Safeway had a much larger range of products than Morrison's. There were also difficulties in integrating the two companies' IT and finance systems, which added to costs and reduced the level of control senior management had over the business. Finally there was a sense that Morrison's simply did not appreciate that the southern English customer was different from those of the north. The result was Morrison's posting its first ever loss in 2006.

Synergy is about resources more than products. One firm making industrial thermostats decided to leverage its technology by capitalising on a growth market for household thermostats. Three years later, the effort was written off as an expensive failure because of the company's lack of expertise in design, packaging, mass production, and distribution to marketers and contractors.[3] The ultimate integration challenge is when a group of entities are combined to provide an integrated customer solution. Lou Gerstner indicated that integrating the country, product and service silos at IBM was his most significant legacy.[4] He also noted, though, that it took five years to accomplish the progress that was made. Citing the failures of many firms to create true financial supermarkets, multiservice telecommunication companies, and fully integrated entertainment companies, he opined that integrating decentralised operations is a struggle at which few have been successful.

Potential Synergy is Overvalued

One risk of buying a business in another area, even a related one, is that the potential synergy may seem more enticing than it really is. BMW bought the Rover car company in 1994 for about €1.1 billion, with the objectives of gaining access to the Land Rover brand as an entry point to the growing four-wheel drive market, and to use BMW's upmarket engineering and marketing skills to push the Rover brand up the prestige ranks. BMW began by allowing exiting management to continue to manage the business. It became apparent quite quickly both that this would not work and also that Rover was in a far worse condition than BMW had thought. These miscalculations meant that the integration of the two business and the resulting synergies were never realisable. When BMW disposed of Rover in 2000 (it kept the profitable Land Rover and Mini brands) the total losses were in excess of €1 billion and they had to write off additional investments in the region of €3 billion.

The acquisition of The Learning Company – a popular children's software publisher with titles like *Reader Rabbit*, *Learn to Speak*, and *Oregon Trail* – seemed like a logical move by Mattel, the powerful toy company with Barbie among its properties. Yet less than a year-and-a-half after paying $3.5 billion for it, Mattel basically gave The Learning Company away to get out from under mounting losses.

One study of 75 people from 40 companies that were experienced at acquisition led to several conclusions. First, few companies do a rigorous risk analysis looking at the least and most favorable outcome. With optimistic vibes abounding, it is particularly wise to look at the downside: What can go wrong? Second, it is useful to set a price over which you will not pay. Avoid getting so exuberant about the synergistic potential that you ultimately pay more than you will ever be able to recoup.[5]

THE ELUSIVE SEARCH FOR SYNERGY

The concept of a total communications firm that comprises advertising, direct marketing, marketing research, public relations, design, sales promotions, and now Internet communications has been a dream of many organisations for two decades. The concept has been that synergy will be created by providing clients with more consistent, coordinated communication efforts and by cross-selling services. Thus, Young & Rubicam had the 'whole egg' and Ogilvy & Mather talked about 'Ogilvy orchestrations'. Despite the compelling logic and considerable efforts, such synergy has been elusive. Because each communication discipline involved different people, paradigms, cultures, standards, and processes, the disparate groups had difficulty not only working together but even doing simple things like sharing strategies and visuals. A related problem was a reluctance to refer clients to sister units who were suspected to deliver inferior results, which created client-relationship ownership issues. Young & Rubicam has been perhaps the most successful, in large part because it merged its direct marketing, public relations, Internet communications and advertising firms into one organisation, with shared locations and client-relations leadership. Each major account has a director and dedicated space. With these four units together already, it became easier to include a design firm such as Landor in client engagements. DDB Needham has had success with virtual client teams drawn from its family of communication companies. These cross-discipline teams create their own culture and processes that allow them to provide the coordinated communication that clients need. The lesson here is that synergy does not just happen, despite logic and motivation. It can require real innovation in implementation – not just trying harder.

UNRELATED DIVERSIFICATION

Unrelated diversification lacks enough commonality in brands, marketing, distribution, channels, manufacturing, or R&D thrust to provide the opportunity for synergy through the exchange or sharing of assets or competencies. The objectives are therefore mainly financial, to generate profit streams that are either larger, less uncertain, or more stable than they would otherwise be. Figure 14.2 summarises the motivations for both unrelated and related diversification.

Related Diversification	Unrelated Diversification

• Exchange or share assets or competencies, thereby exploiting a
  ○ Brand name
  ○ Marketing skills
  ○ Sales and distribution capacity
  ○ Manufacturing skills
  ○ R&D and new product capability
• Economies of scale
	• Manage and allocate cash flow
	• Obtain high ROI
	• Obtain a bargain price
	• Refocus a firm
	• Reduce risk by operating in multiple product markets
	• Tax benefits
	• Obtain liquid assets
	• Vertical integration
	• Defend against a takeover
	• Provide executive interest

Figure 14.2   Motivations for unrelated and related diversification

Managing and Allocating Cash Flow

Unrelated diversification can balance the cash flows of business units. A firm with businesses that merit investment might buy or merge with a cash cow (a business with a substantial cash flow) to provide a source of financial resources. Conversely, a firm with a cash cow may enter new markets seeking growth opportunities. Tobacco firms, for example, have used their enormous cash flows to buy firms such as Kraft Foods.

Entering Business Areas with High ROI Prospects

One basic motivation for diversifying is to improve ROI by moving into business areas with high growth prospects. The French giant Danone has global strength in three areas: biscuits, dairy products and water. The latter two categories are particularly high growth and have attracted attention from a variety of firms seeking to access those growth markets. Skype was a particularly attractive acquisition target for a number of firms, including its eventual buyer eBay, because of its leadership role and growth potential (it adds about 150 000 new users a day) in the VOIP market.

Many disastrous mergers or acquisitions have been motivated by the enticement of ROI prospects. In some cases, the catastrophe was caused in part by an inability to manage the resulting organisation, as well as a mistaken promise of synergy. Other times, however, it was caused by an overestimation of the ROI prospects by a firm unfamiliar with the industry. Avon, for example, lost a fortune buying Tiffany & Co. and perfumer Giorgio Beverly Hills, in part because it overpaid for those businesses.

Obtaining a Bargain Price for a Business

There are certainly bargains for the astute buyer. Bargains are most likely when there has been a crash. In the property business, one truism is that the second (or third) buyer – after the first has gone bankrupt – will be successful. This can happen in other sectors. After the dot-com crash, many viable firms were available for reasonable prices for those who could identify the businesses with real assets. On average, instead of getting bargains, acquiring firms fail to realise value because they misread market prospects and threats, fail to capture hoped-for synergy, mismanage the integration of firms (often because cutting costs takes precedence over delivering customer satisfaction) and are unable to combine cultures and operate the acquired business. Numerous studies have explored the stock-return payoff when an acquisition is made. One review of some 41 such studies concludes that the acquired stock was purchased at a premium of around 22%.[6] Another study of acquisitions over time showed that around 60% of them resulted in the total market-adjusted return of the acquiring company going down upon the announcement and, in most cases, staying down for the next year.[7] The business model for too many firms is to acquire a business with a low price–earnings multiplier, which will create 'earnings growth' when combined with the acquiring company. The result is apparent financial success as long the bargains persist, acquisitions continue, and investors remained convinced that the earnings growth is real. The problem is that eventually the absence of a real strategy and operational excellence will show through, and the house of cards will collapse.

The Potential to Refocus a Firm

An acquisition can provide the basis for a refocus of the acquired firm, the acquiring firm or both. Not incidentally, the thrust of change may result in investors' perceiving a firm to be in more attractive industries, thus causing its stock price to rise.

The key is to identify firms that are undervalued with respect to their potential after a refocus. One approach suggested by Booz Allen acquisition specialists is to group a firm's businesses into four categories:[8]

- *Core businesses.* A core business might represent 25% to 60% of sales. Strategically, the core business should be strong and have some sustainable competitive advantages on which to build.
- *Successful diversifications.* These would be the firm's stars with strong positions in attractive markets.
- *Unsuccessful diversifications.* An undervalued firm typically has a substantial proportion of sales in unsuccessful diversifications, which is a major drag on performance.
- *Nonoperating investments.* These could be stock investments or physical assets carried below market value. Unsuccessful diversifications and their effect on performance may generate associations and perceived risks that cause a firm to be undervalued. The core business, successful diversifications, and nonoperating investments may be worth much more than the current firm as a whole. Liquidating or divesting the unsuccessful diversifications would be one way to realise that value. Another possibility would be to spin off the core business, which by itself may be valued relatively highly, and thereby use the successful diversifications as a base to generate a new core business. If the original core business is in an industry not highly regarded by the stock market, the revised core could be valued higher.

Reducing Risk

The reduction of risk can be another motivation for unrelated diversification. This risk might arise from an overreliance on a single product line, or from the entry of competitors to an adjacent area of the market. Microsoft's move into mobile telephony and computer games was intended to reduce the risk that the high and growing software content of these product areas might allow rivals, such as Sony and Nokia, to develop software skills that would eventually rival those of Microsoft itself. In 2005, Novartis, the Swiss pharmaceutical giant, acquired one of Europe's largest generic drug manufacturers, Hexal, as well as a large share in one of America's largest generic manufacturers Eon Laboratories. The logic of the acquisitions was to provide Novartis with access to the strong growth of the generics market and to provide it with a counter balance against the blockbuster drug cycle.

Stockholder Risk versus Management Risk

Diversification may reduce the market risk facing a firm and thus protect the firm's employees, customers, and managers. Managers, in particular, face the loss of job and reputation from a business downturn over which they may have no control and thus they may be motivated to diversify. However, risk reduction obtained from unrelated diversification is of no value to stockholders, who are free to diversify by holding a portfolio of stocks. Based on the premise that stockholders are the only relevant stakeholders of a business, it can be argued that the reduction of risk is not a legitimate objective.

Even stockholders cannot diversify from systematic risk, that portion of variation of the stock return correlated with general economic conditions. Thus, a diversification that would reduce a firm's systematic risk would be of value to stockholders. For example, an upscale chain of restaurants might acquire a set of fast food outlets, which would do well when the economy is down.

Tax Implications

Tax considerations can stimulate mergers or acquisitions of unrelated firms. Firms can accumulate large tax-loss carryovers, which they can exploit. Thus, a firm with a large series of losses from its automatic teller machines purchased a profitable sweater manufacturer, which could utilise the losses to reduce taxes. Mergers have also been motivated by firms that have underutilised tax incentives to make capital investments.

Obtaining Liquid Assets

A firm can become an attractive acquisition candidate because of substantial liquid assets that can be readily deployed or because of a low debt-to-equity ratio that provides the potential to support debt financing. Banks and insurance companies can be attractive acquisition targets because they provide access to money.

Vertical Integration Motivations

A vertical integration is usually an unrelated diversification. In Chapter 13, some of the motivations for vertical integration were discussed, such as gaining access to supply or demand, controlling quality, and gaining entry into attractive business areas.

Defending Against a Takeover

The threat of an unfriendly takeover can lead to an acquisition. One firm bought a small banana company to generate an antitrust obstacle to a takeover by United Fruit. Martin Marietta responded to a takeover move by Bendix by attempting to buy Bendix with the help of a third firm, United Technologies. The complex and expensive manoeuvring ended with a fourth company, Allied Corporation, buying Bendix, while Martin Marietta remained independent.

Providing Executive Interest

For the executives making the decision, diversification can be stimulating. It can also lead to the prestige of a larger organisation. A study in which 14 merger experts were queried as to the motivations involved found that enhancement of personal power as measured by the sales volume controlled by a chief executive may be a moderately important motivation in merger decisions.[9] Another related conclusion was that the merger decisions were ultimately made by one person, the CEO.

Risks of Unrelated Diversification

The very concept of unrelated diversification suggests risk and difficulty because, by definition, there is no possibility of synergy. Many knowledgeable people have made blanket statements warning against unrelated diversification. Peter Drucker claims that all successful diversification requires a common core or unity represented by common markets, technology, or production processes.[10] He states that without such unity, diversification never works; financial ties alone are insufficient. Among the major risks:

- attention may be diverted from the core business
- managing the new business may be difficult
- the new business may be overvalued

Unrelated diversification, if unsuccessful, may actually damage the original core business by diverting attention and resources from it. When Paolo Scaroni took over as CEO of Enel, the Italian energy giant, he had 30 managers, each representing different businesses reporting to him. The wide spread and a lack of depth meant that the company had limited ability to achieve excellence in any one area and the share price suffered accordingly. To tackle this, Scaroni reduced the business to two divisions, Gas & Electricity and Telecoms & Power Generation with the expectation that this would be further reduced over time.

The potential for difficulties in managing a diversification is magnified when an unrelated business is acquired. The new business may require assets, competencies and an organisational culture that differ from those of the core business. Furthermore, a skilled, valued management team in the acquired company might leave and be difficult to replace. One of the problems with Morrison's takeover of Safeway was that many professional staff members, particularly in the finance area, left Safeway prior to the takeover as part of a redundancy package.

A new business area might be incorrectly evaluated. For example, environmental threats may be overlooked or misjudged. If an acquisition is involved, its strategic liabilities, weaknesses, and problems may be undiscovered or miscalculated.

Performance of Diversified Firms

A case can be made for a focused strategy – keep your eye on the ball, stick to your knitting, and so forth. Although of little value to a shareholder, however, diversification can provide a firm with strategic flexibility and a cushion against bad events (the operative cliché in this case being not to put all of your eggs in one basket). One research study by a McKinsey group suggests a middle ground, noting that moderate diversification may, on average, be better than either extreme.[11]

In the study, a total of 412 of the S&P 500 companies were classified as focused (deriving at least 67% of revenues from one business), moderately diversified (with at least 67% of revenues from two segments), or diversified (with less than 67% of revenues from two segments). Total return to shareholders between 1990 and 2000 for the moderately diversified firms was 13% more than for their industry peers, as compared to 8% for the focused companies and 4% for the diversified firms.

Why might moderately diversified firms perform better? More diversified firms tend to suffer from spreading their resources and culture too broadly, resulting in a reduced ability to gain efficiencies and market leadership. More focused firms, conversely, may find it difficult to manage market dynamics because of what is termed 'strategic stubbornness' in Chapter 8. In an example of moderate diversification, O2 one of the UK and Ireland's leading mobile phone operators, diversified into secure digital radio networks, with its O2 Airwave division. The technology behind this service allows for encryption, making it impossible for anyone to listen in to the communications of emergency service workers. The multi-functional handsets provide digital radio and data as well as phone services. This technology played a vital role in supporting the recovery efforts following the 7/7 incident in London.[12]

ENTRY STRATEGIES

When the decision is made to enter a new product market, the entry strategy becomes critical.[13] Figure 14.3 summarises eight alternative strategies with their advantages and disadvantages. The most common entry routes are internal development and acquisition.

Developing a new business internally means that a concept, strategy, and team can be created without the limitations, liabilities, or acquisition costs represented by acquiring an existing business. An internal venture is a variant in which a separate entity within the existing firm is established, so that the new business will not be constrained by existing organisational culture, systems and structure.

Entry Strategy	Major Advantages	Major Disadvantages
Internal Development	• Uses existing resources • Avoids acquisition cost especially if unfamiliar with product/market	• Time lag • Uncertain prospects
Internal Venture	• Uses existing resources • May keep talented entrepreneurs	• Mixed success record • Can create internal stresses
Acquisition	• Saves calendar time • Overcomes entry barriers	• Costly—usually buy redundant assets • Problem of integrating two organisations
Joint Venture or Alliance	• Technological/marketing unions can exploit small/large firm synergies • Distributes risk	• Potential for conflict in operations between firms • Value of one firm may be reduced over time
Licensing from Others	• Rapid access to technology • Reduced financial risk	• Will lack proprietary technology and technological skills • Will be dependent on licensor
Educational Acquisition	• Provides window and initial staff	• Risk of departure of entrepreneurs
Venture Capital and Nurturing	• Can provide window on new technology or market	• Unlikely alone to be a major stimulus of firm growth
Licensing to Others	• Rapid access to a market • Low cost/risk	• Will lack knowledge/control of market • Will be dependent on licensee

Figure 14.3   Entry strategies

Source: Adapted from Edward B. Roberts and Charles A. Berry (1985). Entering new businesses: selecting strategies for success. *Sloan Management Review*, Spring, pp. 3–17. Copyright © 1985 by Massachusetts Institute of Technology. All rights reserved. Distributed by Tribune Media Services.

The acquisition route saves calendar time. An acquisition can mean that a firm becomes an established player in a matter of weeks instead of years. Perhaps more important, it means that substantial entry barriers such as distribution or brand name recognition are overcome. A variant is an educational acquisition in which a small firm that is not established as a major force is acquired in order to obtain a window into a technology or market, as well as knowledge, experience, and a base from which to grow. The other options shown in Figure 14.3 represent reduced risk and commitment, as well as a reduced chance that the route will lead to an established business supported by SCAs. A joint venture will share the risk with others and provide one or more missing and needed assets and competencies. For example, a small firm that possesses a new technology could enter into a joint venture with a larger firm that has financial resources and access to distribution. Licensing a technology from others provides a fast way to overcome one entry barrier but makes it difficult to gain control of that same technology in the future. Both entry options are important in international business contexts and are discussed in detail in Chapter 11. An alternative to a joint venture is an alliance in which the parties share assets to attack a market. For example, Sony's cooperative technology-sharing arrangements with a host of small high-tech firms serve to keep Sony on the cutting edge of technology and also provides the small firms with access to Sony's production, engineering, and marketing assets.

The lowest involvement options are licensing others to use and market a technology or entering into a business as a venture capital investor. Astrazeneca and Glaxosmithkline are among firms that have made minority investments in young and growing high-tech enterprises in order to secure some relationship to a new technology. Both licensing and becoming a venture capital investor offer the potential to increase involvement over time, if the business does well, and to control any risk.

Selecting the Right Entry Strategy

Roberts and Berry suggest that the selection of the right entry strategy depends on the level of a firm's familiarity with the product market to be entered.[14] They define familiarity along two dimensions: (1) market and (2) technology or service embodied in the product. With respect to market factors, three levels of familiarity are defined:

- *Base.* Existing products are sold within this market.
- *New/familiar.* The company is familiar with the market because of extensive research, experienced staff, or links with the market as a customer.
- *New/unfamiliar.* Knowledge of and experience with the market are lacking.

An analogous set of three levels of familiarity with the technologies or services embodied in the product is set forth:

- *Base.* The technology or service is embodied within existing products.
- *New/familiar.* The company is familiar with the technology because of work in related technologies, an established research-and-development effort in the technology, or extensive focused research in the technology.
- *New/unfamiliar.* Knowledge of and experience with the technology are lacking.

The basic suggestion is that as the level of familiarity on these two dimensions declines, the commitment level should be reduced. Figure 14.4 shows the baseline entry strategy recommendations that follow from a familiarity assessment. Of course, there will be contexts in which a high-commitment approach in the new/unfamiliar cell will make sense. However, Roberts and Berry suggest, on the basis of experience and theory, that substantial risk is associated with such an approach and the option of gaining familiarity should be seriously considered.

Technologies or Services Embodied in the Product

Market Factors		Base	New/ Familiar	New/ Unfamiliar
	New/ Unfamiliar	Joint ventures	Venture capital or educational acquisitions	Venture capital or educational acquisitions
	New/ Familiar	Internal market developments or acquisitions (or joint ventures)	Internal ventures or acquisitions or licensing	Venture capital or educational acquisitions
	Base	Internal base developments (or acquisitions)	Internal product developments or acquisitions or licensing	Joint ventures

Figure 14.4   Optimal entry strategies

Source: Adapted from Edward B. Roberts and Charles A. Berry (1985). Entering new businesses: selecting strategies for success. *Sloan Management Review*, Spring, pp. 3–17. Copyright © 1985 by Massachusetts Institute of Technology. All rights reserved. Distributed by Tribune Media Services.

KEY LEARNINGS

- Related diversification involves the potential to attain synergies by exporting or exchanging assets or competences.
- The brand is one asset that often can be leveraged. Disney and easyJet are examples of brands that have provided the basis for a broad array of businesses.
- A brand should fit a proposed new product market and add value. And, importantly, the new product market context should enhance and reinforce the brand (and certainly should not damage it).
- Synergy can be illusory, being perceived when in fact it does not exist, or when implementation barriers make it unachievable, or it is overvalued.
- There are 11 motivations for unrelated diversification, including to manage cash flow, to obtain attractive businesses, to refocus a firm, and to reduce risk.
- Figure 14.3 illustrates eight approaches to market entry based on how new the technology or market is to the organisation.

FOR DISCUSSION

1. What is the difference between related and unrelated diversification? Are the following related or unrelated? Why?

   a. Dell selling TV sets

   b. Barclay's Bank owning theme parks

   c. Crest purchasing a chain of dental surgeries

   d. Caterpillar manufacturing cars

   e. Domino's Pizza owning exercise clubs

2. Pick a branded offering, such as Ryanair. Come up with 20 products or services that are alternative extension options. Include some that would be a stretch. Evaluate each of the extension options using the three criteria listed in the chapter.

3. Consider the following mergers and acquisition. In which cases would synergy be logically possible? What would inhibit this synergy? Consider operations, culture, and brand equities.

   a. Mittal Steel's acquisition of Arcelor

   b. Telefonica's acquisition of O2

   c. Grupo Ferrovial's acquisition of BAA

4. Consider the alliance of Starbucks and Barnes & Noble, in which Starbucks cafés were opened inside the bookstores. Evaluate this alliance from both sides. When Barnes & Noble opened stores in areas where Starbucks had no presence, the cafés were branded Barnes & Noble but sold Starbucks coffee. Would you accept this arrangement if you were Starbucks? (Eventually, it was applied to nearly all of the cafés.) Again, comment from both sides.

NOTES

1. Trouble in le Royaume Magique. *The Economist*, 5 August 2004; Euro Disney SCA. Consolidated Financial Results, Fiscal Year 2005, Analysts Conference Call, 16 November 2005. http://www.eurodisney.com./en/pdf/fy05_presentation.pdf.

2. David A. Aaker (1991) *Managing Brand Equity*, The Free Press, New York, Chapter 9 and David A. Aaker and Erich Joachimsthaler (2000) *Brand Leadership*, The Free Press, New York, Chapter 5.

3. David J. Collis and Cynthia A. Montgomery (1998) Creating corporate advantage. *Harvard Business Review*, May–June, pp. 71–83.

4. Louis V. Gerstner, Jr. (2002) *Who Says Elephants Can't Dance*, Harper Business, New York, pp. 251–2.

5. Robert G. Eccles, Kersten L. Lanes, and Thomas C. Wilson (1999) Are you paying too much for that acquisition? *Harvard Business Review*, July–August, pp. 136–43.

6. Deepak K. Datta, George E. Pinches, and V. K. Narayanan (1992) Factors influencing wealth creation from mergers and acquisitions: a meta-analysis. *Strategic Management Journal* 13, pp. 67–84.

7. Robert G. Eccles, Kersten L. Lanes, and Thomas C. Wilson (1999) Are you paying too much for that acquisition? *Harvard Business Review*, July–August, pp. 126–42.

8. Michael G. Allen, Alexander R. Oliver and Edward H. Schwallie (1981) The key to successful acquisitions. *Journal of Business Strategy*, Fall, pp. 14–24.

9. Wayne I. Boucher (1980) The Process of Conglomerate Merger. Prepared for the Bureau of Competition, Federal Trade Commission, June 1980.

10. Peter Drucker (1981) The five rules of successful acquisition. *Wall Street Journal*, 15 October, p. 16.

11. Neil W. C. Harper and S. Patrick Viguerie (2002) Are you too focused? *McKinsey Quarterly*, 2, pp. 28–37.

12. Bobbie Johnson and Michael Cross (2005) Technology to the rescue. *Guardian*, 14 July.

13. Edward B. Roberts and Charles A. Berry (1985) Entering new businesses: selecting strategies for success. *Sloan Management Review*, Spring pp. 3–17.

14. Ibid.

CHAPTER FIFTEEN

Strategies in Declining and Hostile Markets

Anyone can hold the helm when the sea is calm.
—*Publilius Syrus*

Where there is no wind, row.
—*Portuguese proverb*

There is nothing so useless as doing efficiently that which should not be done at all.
—*Peter Drucker*

Strategic planning is often associated with a search for healthy, growing markets and the development of strategies to penetrate those markets. However, as the discussion in Chapter 5 makes clear, there are a variety of risks in high-growth contexts, including the possibility that a market can be crowded with competitors, each trying to find a niche. On the other hand, declining markets as well as mature markets can represent real opportunities for a business following the right strategy, in part because they are not as attractive to competitors. Thus, declining markets are not always to be avoided.

A declining market involves a fall in demand, often caused by an external event such as the creation of a competing technology, a change in customer needs or tastes, or a shift in government policy. Of course, a participant in a declining market will attempt to obtain sustainable competitive advantages (SCAs) and compete successfully. In a market characterised by zero or negative growth, however, the options of milking and even exiting should be considered, as suggested by the portfolio models. Thus, it is important to understand these options as well. In this chapter several strategic alternatives especially relevant to declining markets are considered:

- Create a growth context by revitalising the industry so that it becomes a growth industry or by focusing on a growth submarket.

- Be the profitable survivor in the industry by dominating the market, thus encouraging others to exit.
- Milk or harvest. Withdraw resources so that they can be invested elsewhere.
- Exit or liquidate. Salvage existing assets.

Hostile markets are those with overcapacity, low margins, intense competition and management in turmoil. Hostility has two primary causes. The first is a decline in demand. The second and most important cause of hostility is competitive expansion. Though there are many reasons for startup failures in the high-tech industry the retaliation of much larger firms plays an important role. Thus, even a growing market can be hostile.

Hostile markets are all too common. Even in markets that have traditionally been characterised by monopoly, such as telecoms and other utilities, more and more intense competition has been creeping in. It is thus important to understand the dynamics of hostile markets and why some competitors do better than others in such environments. In the final section of this chapter, the life cycle of a hostile market will be described and the strategies of above-average performers will be discussed.

CREATING GROWTH IN DECLINING INDUSTRIES

It is usually assumed that existing participants have already fully exploited the market potential of a stagnant or declining industry. If that assumption is untrue, a dramatic opportunity exists for a business to participate in revitalising the industry and achieve a commanding position in the new growth context. As suggested by Figure 15.1, there are at least seven routes to revitalising a stagnant market.

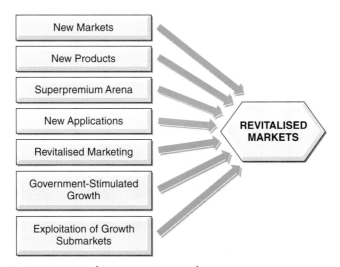

Figure 15.1   Routes to revitalising a stagnant market

New Markets

An obvious way to generate growth is to move into neglected or ignored market segments that have the potential for new growth. Consumer electronics companies could focus on women or the elderly, both of which are underserved markets. Some industries have seen international expansion fuel growth. Carmakers like Volkswagen, for example, have found growth in new markets in East Asia, although the level of competition is rising rapidly in these markets as competitors also see the opportunities.

New Products

Sometimes a dormant industry can be revitalised by a product that makes existing products obsolete and accelerates the replacement cycle. The market for TVs is one that has been continuously revitalised by innovation. The industry has seen a succession of innovations designed to increase the number of TV's which each home owns and to drive replacement cycles, these have included colour TV, portable TV, the remote control, and flat panel display TV. In each case the new product has created sales vitality in what is a mature market. A new product variant can also add interest in mature markets, such as the introduction of functional yogurt or mobile phones with picture and video cameras.

The Superpremium Arena

In many hostile market environments, from ice cream to water to cars to banking, there is a superpremium category that has healthy margins and product vitality. In the ice-cream market the super premium brands such as Ben & Jerry's and Häagen Dazs have built significant market share despite being priced at a hefty premium to the rest of the market. The crowded 4 × 4 market has seen the emergence of superpremium brands such as the Range Rover Sport and the Porsche Cayenne. In the vodka market, super premium brands such as Grey Goose, Vox and Stoli Elit command 50–100 % price premiums over competitors.

New Applications

A new application for a product can stimulate industry growth. In Chapter 13, the graphic example of baking soda and its use as a deodoriser was given. When the US paper towel brand Bounty wished to enter the fast growing, private-label dominated UK market it used new applications as its vehicle. The unique quality of Bounty was its strength when wet. Bounty used a series of commercials with the endline 'have you tried it wet yet' to emphasise the potential for Bounty to be used differently to other paper towels. The advertising led to paper towels being used for a wider variety of tasks, with more sheets being used each day and growth in the number of sheets used per task.[1] The small refrigerator opened up new sources of sales in offices and student dormitories. A prime way to find promising applications is to learn how existing customers are using the product or service.

Revitalised Marketing

A product class may be revived by a fresh marketing approach, such as changing the distribution channel by using new types of stores or direct selling, selling the product to firms to use as giveaway promotion items, changing the pricing structure, or perhaps changing the advertising. The Vespa scooter, an Italian design classic, has always had a loyal following in the US. Prior to its relaunch in 2000 there were two dozen shops dedicated to restoring old Vespa scooters. However, in order to drive sales in the American market Vespa has strongly revitalised its marketing. Firstly working with local government officials to educate them in 'Vespanomics' or the particularly strong environmental logic behind encouraging people to travel by scooter. Secondly, they have adopted a direct to consumer communications approach using a blog, Vespaway, to establish a dialogue with users, potential users and admirers.[2]

Government-Stimulated Growth

There is an old adage, 'if all else fails, change the rules of the game.' Strategically, the idea is to change the environment so that industry sales will be enhanced. A governmental body can provide incentives for change, such as tax incentives for installing insulation, building nursing homes or investing in public infrastructure such as roads and bridges. Or a government might dictate a new hygiene standard for hospitals, bars or the restaurant industry thus stimulating the growth of new disinfection products.

Exploitation of Growth Submarkets

Some firms have been successful in declining or mature industries because they have been able to focus on growth subareas, pockets of demand that are healthy and perhaps even growing nicely. The low calorie and sodium sections are growing in the mature snack market. Cars, buses and motorcycles with low carbon emissions are a new growth segment in the automobile industry.

Sometimes a growth submarket has the same visibility and risk as another growth market, but it is neglected because its parent industry is unattractive. As a result, it is likely to receive less competitive attention.

BE THE PROFITABLE SURVIVOR

The conventional advice is to avoid investing in declining markets and to milk or exit businesses that are trapped in a declining situation.[3] However, an aggressive alternative is to invest in order to obtain or strengthen a leadership position. A strong survivor may be profitable, in part because there may be little competition and in part because the investment might be relatively low. The cornerstone of this strategy is to encourage competitors to exit. Toward that end a firm can:

- Be visible about its commitment to be the surviving leader in the industry.
- Raise the costs of competing by price reductions or increased promotion.

- Introduce new products and cover new segments, thereby making it more difficult for a competitor to find a profitable niche.
- Reduce competitors' exit barriers by assuming their long-term contracts, supplying spare parts and servicing their products in the field, or supplying them with products. For example, a bakery could supply private label products to a retailer, thus enabling the retailer to exit from doing its own baking and encouraging others to consider doing the same.
- Create a national, dominant brand in a declining industry that is fragmented.
- Purchase a competitor's market share and/or its production capacity. This is the ultimate removal of a competitor's exit barriers and ensures that a tired competitor won't be taken over by a more vigorous organisation. In the past few years, Finsbury Food Group Plc, one of the UK's leading manufacturers of premium added-value cakes and speciality breads has acquired a number of its competitors allowing it to widen its own product range and benefit from economies of scale.

MILK OR HARVEST

A milk or harvest strategy aims to generate cash flow by reducing investment and operating expenses, even if that causes a reduction in sales and market share. The underlying assumptions are that the firm has better uses for the funds, that the in-volved business is not crucial to the firm either financially or synergistically, and that milking is feasible because sales will decline in an orderly way.

A milking strategy can be precipitated by a new entrant that turns a market hostile. Chase & Sanborn was once a leading coffee in the US; the 'Chase & Sanborn Hour', starring Edgar Bergen, was one of the most popular radio shows of its time. After the Second World War, though, Chase & Sanborn decided to retreat to a milking strategy rather than fight an expensive market retention battle against the rising popularity of instant coffee and the appearance of the heavily advertised Maxwell House brand.

There are variants of milking strategies. A *slow milking* strategy would sharply reduce long-term investment but continue to support operating areas such as market-ing and service. A *fast milking* strategy would be disciplined about minimising the expenditures toward the brand and maximising the short-term cash flow, accepting the risk of a fast exit.

Conditions Favouring a Milking Strategy

Several conditions support a milking strategy rather than a hold or exit strategy:

- The decline rate is pronounced and unlikely to change but not excessively steep and pockets of enduring demand ensure that the decline rate will not suddenly become precipitous.
- The price structure is stable at a level that is profitable for efficient firms.
- The business position is weak but there is enough customer loyalty, perhaps in a limited part of the market, to generate sales and profits in a milking mode. The risk of losing relative position with a milking strategy is low.

- The business is not central to the current strategic direction of the firm.
- A milking strategy can be successfully managed.

Implementation Problems

Implementation of a milking strategy can be difficult. One of the most serious problems is that if employees and customers suspect that a milking strategy is being employed, the resulting lack of trust may upset the whole strategy. As the line between a milking strategy and abandonment is sometimes very thin, customers may lose confidence in the firm's product and employee morale may suffer. Competitors may attack more vigorously.

All these possibilities can create a sharper-than-anticipated decline. To minimise such effects it is helpful to keep a milking strategy as inconspicuous as possible. Another serious problem is the difficulty of placing and motivating a manager in a milking situation. Most business managers do not have the orientation, background, or skills to engage in a successful milking strategy. Adjusting performance measures and rewards appropriately can be difficult for both the organisation and the managers involved. It might seem reasonable to use a manager who specialises in milking strategies, but that is often not feasible simply because such specialisation is rare. Most firms rotate managers through different types of situations, and career paths simply are not geared to creating milking specialists.

When the Premises Are Wrong

One advantage of milking rather than divesting is that a milking strategy can often be reversed if it turns out to be based on incorrect premises regarding market prospects, competitor moves, cost projections, or other relevant factors. A resurgence in product classes that were seemingly dead or in terminal decline gives pause. The bicycle, for example, has shown signs of growth, as people have become more health and environmentally conscious. The mechanical watch, invented in the nineteenth century, was almost killed by the appearance of electronic watches in the 1970s. However, the combination of nostalgia and a desire for prestige has provided a major comeback for the luxury mechanical watch.

Forecasting and Managing the Flow of Funds from Milking

The flow of funds from a milking strategy needs to be both forecasted and managed properly. In markets with slow changing technology such an approach is practical. The lessons of a variety of market such as telecoms and digital imaging is how radical innovation can often make forecasting and managing flow of funds from milking difficult.

The Hold Strategy

A variant of the milking strategy is the hold strategy, in which growth-motivated investment is avoided, but an adequate level of investment is employed to maintain product quality, production facilities, and customer loyalty. A hold strategy is appropriate when an industry is declining in an orderly way, pockets of enduring demand exist, price pressures are not extreme, a firm has exploitable assets or competencies, and a business contributes by its presence to other business units in the firm. A hold strategy would be preferable to an invest strategy when an industry lacks growth opportunities and a strategy of increasing share would risk triggering competitive retaliation. The hold strategy can be a long-term strategy to manage a cash cow or an interim strategy employed until the uncertainties of an industry are resolved. A problem with the hold strategy is that if conditions change, reluctance or slowness to reinvest may result in lost market share.

DIVESTMENT OR LIQUIDATION

As Figure 15.2 suggests, when a business environment and business position are both unfavourable then the final alternative, divestment or liquidation, is precipitated. Among the conditions that would suggest an exit decision rather than a milking decision are the following:

- The decline rate is rapid and accelerating, and no pockets of enduring demand are accessible to the business.
- The price pressures are expected to be extreme, caused by determined competitors with high exit barriers and by a lack of brand loyalty and product differentiation. Thus, a milking strategy is unlikely to be profitable for anyone.
- The business position is weak; one or more dominant competitors have achieved irreversible advantage. The business is now losing money, and future prospects are dim.
- The firm's strategic direction has changed, and the role of the business has become superfluous or even unwanted.
- Exit barriers can be overcome.

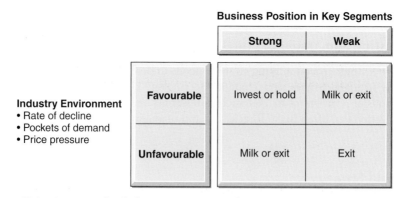

Figure 15.2   Strategies for declining or stagnant industries

A set of exit barriers can inhibit an exit decision. In particular:

- Specialised assets such as plant and equipment may have little value to others.
- Long-term contracts with suppliers and with labor groups may be expensive to break.
- The business may have commitments to provide spare parts and service backup to retailers and customers. For example, although Sony decided to stop production of its Clie PDA product in 2005 they have maintained the support website with drivers, software and a troubleshoot facility. Anything other than this might have damaged the reputation of the overall Sony brand.
- Firms' financial and management resources are being absorbed when they could be employed more effectively elsewhere.
- An exit decision may affect the reputation and operation of other company businesses.
- Government restrictions can effectively prohibit an exit decision. Rail service, for example, cannot simply be terminated.

Managerial pride may also be a factor. Professional managers often view themselves as problem solvers and are reluctant to admit defeat. Several anecdotes describe firms that have had to send a series of executives to close down a subsidiary, because each executive convinced himself or herself after arriving that a turnaround was possible, only subsequently to fail at the effort. Furthermore, there may be an emotional attachment to a business that has been in the 'family' for many years or that was even the original business on which the rest of the firm was based. It is difficult to turn your back on such a valued friend.

Many firms avoid divestiture decisions until they become obvious or are forced on the firms by external forces. The better-managed – and, according to one study, more profitable – organisations will actively manage these decisions by systematically evaluating the strategic fit and future prospects of each business, then regularly making divestiture decisions or placing business units on a probationary status.[4] Jack Welch, during his first four years as GE's CEO, divested 117 business units accounting for 20% of the corporation's assets. Such divestitures can generate cash at a fair (as opposed to a forced sale) price, liberate management talent, help reposition the firm to match its strategic vision and add vitality. The divested businesses will often benefit as well, as they will likely move to environments that will be more supportive in terms of not only assets and competencies but also the commitment to succeed.

SELECTING THE RIGHT STRATEGY FOR THE DECLINING ENVIRONMENT

The spectrum of investment alternatives ranges from invest to hold to milk to exit. In order to determine the optimal alternative in a declining environment, a firm needs

SOME STRATEGIC UNCERTAINTIES
Market Prospects
1. Is the rate of decline orderly and predictable?
2. Are there pockets of enduring demand?
3. What are the reasons for the decline—is it temporary?

Competitive Intensity
4. Are there dominant competitors with unique skills or competencies?
5. Are there many competitors unwilling to exit or contract gracefully?
6. Are customers brand loyal? Is there product differentiation?
7. Are there price pressures?

Performance/Strengths
8. Is the business profitable? What are its future prospects?
9. What is the market-share position and trend?
10. Does the business have some SCAs with respect to key segments?
11. Can the business manage costs in the face of declining sales?

Interrelationships with Other Businesses
12. Is there synergy with other businesses?
13. Is the business compatible with the firm's current strategic thrust?
14. Can the firm support the cash needs of the business?

Implementation Barriers
15. What are the exit barriers?
16. Can the organisation manage all the investment options?

Figure 15.3   The investment decision in a declining industry

to consider strategic uncertainties in the five areas summarised in Figure 15.3 and discussed next.

Market Prospects

A basic consideration is the rate and pattern of decline. A precipitous decline should be distinguished from a slow, steady decline. One determining factor is the existence of pockets of enduring demand, segments that are capable of supporting a core demand level. The vacuum-tube industry had replacement demand even after vacuum-tubes had all but disappeared from new products. In the leather industry, leather upholstery is still a healthy market.

Another factor affecting the decline rate, particularly in dynamic industries, is product obsolescence. When one-time use syringes were introduced, the sale of glass syringes dramatically declined.

A related issue is the predictability of the pattern. If the pattern is based on demographics, such as the size of the teen population, then it may be predictable. In contrast, fashion and technology can change quickly and therefore predictions based on them are riskier. A slow decline may accelerate, or a declining market may suddenly be revived. One area where decline is predictable is in the disposable nappy market. The declining birth rate in most Western European countries is a significant barrier to growth but its impact is entirely predictable.

Competitive Intensity

Another consideration is the level of competitive intensity determined by the industry structure. Are there dominant competitors that have substantial shares and a set of unique assets and competencies that form formidable sustainable competitive advantages? Is there a relatively large set of competitors that is not disposed either to exit or to contract gracefully? If the answer to either of these questions is yes, the profit prospects for others may be dismal. Another perspective comes from customers. A key to making a profit in a declining industry is price stability. Are customers relatively price insensitive, as are sports fans buying the shirts of their favourite clubs? Is there a relatively high level of product differentiation and brand loyalty? Or has the product become a commodity? Are costs involved in switching from one brand to another?

Performance/Strengths

A business position appraisal should focus on business strengths and capabilities, as well as on current performance. Sources of strength in a declining environment are usually quite different from those in other contexts. The strengths must reflect the reality that there are fewer products to make and fewer customers to serve. Thus, such sources of strength as economies of scale, vertical integration, and technological leadership may not be needed or may even be liabilities. Helpful strengths in a declining industry are:

- Strong established relationships with profitable customers, especially those in pockets of enduring demand.
- A strong brand name. At this stage it will be difficult for competitors to alter their images significantly. Thus, the nature of an established image can be most important.
- The ability to operate profitably with underutilised assets.
- The ability to reduce costs as business shrinks; flexibility in applying assets and resources.
- A large market share if economies of scale are present.

An analysis of current profitability is important to the assessment of future position, but care is needed, especially if an exit decision is involved. Book assets, for example, may be overstated, because their market value may be small or even negative if they have associated obligations. Some overhead items that would have to be shifted to other businesses under an exit alternative might be properly omitted from some analyses.

Interrelationships with Other Businesses

Interrelationships among businesses should be considered in a firm's investment decision. A business may support other businesses within the firm by providing part of a system, by supporting a distribution channel, or by using excess plant capacity or a byproduct of another production process. If the firm is vertically integrated, a decision to leave a particular business may affect the other components.

Visibly closing down a business may generate a credibility problem for the parent corporation, especially if a large write-off is involved. Closing down could affect access to financial markets and influence the opinion of dealers, suppliers, and customers about the firm's other operations. When Kodak announced plans to close its 35 mm Kodachrome film processing plant in Switzerland, buyers of the product were concerned that it was a signal that Kodak was exiting the market. When PSA Peugeot Citroen decided to close its plant in the UK the workers union launched an advertising campaign urging people not to buy Peugeot cars.

Implementation Barriers

Finally, the possible implementation problems associated with each option must be considered. Exit barriers affect the exit option. The milk option presents difficult management problems in that both the managers and customers involved will have to accept a disinvest context. The hold option is also a delicate issue, because a passive investment strategy can inadvertently lead to a loss of position.

HOSTILE MARKETS

Declining markets can create hostile markets – markets usually associated with overcapacity, low margins, intense competition and management in turmoil. However, hostile markets can also occur in growth contexts if there is overcapacity caused by too many competitors. It is not an exaggeration to say that most industries are either hostile or in danger of becoming hostile. It is thus useful to take a close look at hostility. Fortunately, a major study is available to provide insights. Windemere Associates, a management consulting firm, has systematically studied more than forty hostile industries. Its findings are reported in two articles by Don Potter.[5] These reports suggest that hostility can be precipitated by competitors who are attracted to – and who tend to minimise the risks of – growth contexts in which margins and profits are high. Therefore, high prices and profits should be a cause for concern as well as celebration, and it might be worthwhile in the long run to forgo them or to build other barriers to discourage competitors from entering the market.

A Hostile Industry – Six Phases

The Windemere study identified six phases of hostile markets (shown in Figure 15.4) that could span decades. Although they don't always occur in the order set forth, most do occur. An understanding of this six-phase life cycle can help firms prevent or manage hostile environments.

Phase 1—Margin pressure
Phase 2—Share shifts
Phase 3—Product proliferation
Phase 4—Self-defeating cost reduction
Phase 5—Consolidation and shakeout
Phase 6—Rescue

Figure 15.4   Six phases of hostility

Phase 1 – Margin Pressure

Predatory pricing to gain share, stimulated in part by overcapacity, leads to margin erosion; the prime beneficiaries are large customers. As a result, competitors attempt to create or find protected niches. However, others eventually will encroach on attractive niches. Note that efforts to isolate Japanese companies in the low end of copiers, cars, motorcycles, and semiconductors failed, as they eventually moved their product lines up, attacking the high-margin niche markets.

Phase 2 – Share Shifts

Each year, 1% to 5% of the share in a hostile market will shift from one group of companies to another. One cause is the leader's trap, when a leading company, often the biggest and best firm, will not match discounting in its market, believing that a superior product and customer loyalty will support a large price premium. This strategy rarely works. The leader's prices eventually fall but only after market share (which is difficult to regain) is lost and customers have become convinced that the leader's prices before the adjustment were excessive. The experience of PC brands that clung to high prices long after competitors such as Dell had established lower price points is illustrative. Another cause of share shift is a flight to quality, when a company, such as DHL, simply delivers more reliability or has more accessible distribution. A third cause is acquisitions, which occur when competitors become desperate to achieve economies of scale.

Phase 3 – Product Proliferation

Competitors compete for market share by attempting to generate value for the customer through product proliferation. The product might be upgraded by bundling additional features or functions, such as a suite hotel room, colour-tinted cement or not form concentrate orange juice. A snack company might add new lines, such as low-sodium crackers or biscuits without trans fats. An insurance company might offer new insurance items with service variants. Product proliferation rarely results in winners, but raises the ante for all. Further, other firms such as Accor's budget hotel Etap offer versions of the product that delete features and services.

Phase 4 – Self-defeating Cost Reduction

A pressure to maintain margins leads to self-defeating cost reductions. A company intent on limiting investments may fail to match product and quality improvements of competitors, which can be costly in terms of share. Heinz is under pressure in Europe and the US as its operating profits fall and it faces strong competitive pressure from branded and own-label players in its major product markets. The major criticisms levelled at Heinz are a failure to invest sufficiently in its brands, a timid approach to new product introduction and a tendency to see cost cutting rather than innovation as the path to growth.[6] Even more serious is the failure to keep pace with rising industry quality standards. As General Motors and many others have learned, it is hard to recover from a damaged reputation. Attempting to squeeze margins out of the distribution channel or sales force may provide illusory short-term savings at the expense of market position.

Phase 5 – Consolidation and Shakeout

Consolidation, generally geared to reducing overhead, occurs in three waves. The first is internal and involves reducing the workforce, closing facilities, and pruning businesses. The second involves mergers and acquisitions, with stronger firms buying weaker ones, in part to reduce overhead. The third is global in scope, with combinations of international players being formed, such as the successful cross-shareholding based alliance between Renault and Nissan.

Phase 6 – Rescue

Industries can emerge from hostility, some in as few as five years, but most after a decade or longer. One route is consolidation, when three or four key players control more than 80% of the market and all players have given up trying to win share through price competition. Procter & Gamble and Kimberly-Clark have achieved such a consolidation in the disposable nappy market. However, it can take 15 to 20 years (as it did in appliances) for consolidation to play out. Industries may emerge from hostility more quickly if demand grows enough to soak up overcapacity. The necessary growth in demand may be fuelled by expanded customer markets or shifts in the value of international currencies that stimulate export demand.

Strategies That Win in Hostile Markets

The Windemere study identifies two types of firms that have achieved above-average sales growth and profitability within the hostile industries. The first type, termed Gold competitors, holds the number one or two position and includes such firms as FedEx, American Airlines and Canon Copiers. The second, termed Silver competitors, includes firms such as Airborne Express, Alaska Airlines, Pitney Bowes copiers, Tamko roofing and Freightline trucks. Silver competitors are smaller and occupy number three slots, or lower, in sales. An examination of how these two types of firms have succeeded in hostile conditions is illuminating. Their recipe for success has five basic ingredients.

Focus on Large Customers

Volume, which is crucial because it drives the cost structure, comes from a relatively small subset of customers. Gold competitors are the prime suppliers to the industry's largest customers, although they serve others as well. Their weapons are a strong brand identity with end users and close relationships with the large-volume distribution channels. They adapt well to channel shifts. Owens Corning Fiberglass, for example, added a strong retail marketing programme to its wholesale distribution when retail channels became important. In industries without channels of distribution, Gold companies will attempt to create a large customer out of medium-sized firms. FedEx for example, created a parts bank programme that maintained an inventory of parts for firms in order to expedite shipment.

Because Silver companies rarely possess the infrastructure to serve the largest customers as effectively as their Gold competitors, they focus instead on developing strong relationships with medium-sized customers. Freightline focuses on selling its trucks to small fleet owners, for example. These second-tier customers tend to empha-sise good service and reasonable prices to their own end-user customers.

Silvers can thus service their customers without sacrificing margins. To attract these customers, Silvers often adopt industry specialties. Ball, for example, has become the major supplier of wide mouth jars to the food industry.

Differentiate on Reliability

The top firms tend to differentiate on intangibles such as reliability and a relationship of trust and confidence rather than on product features and attributes, which are easier to copy. The focus is on providing the end user with a product or service that works consistently and the channel member with efficient and reliable delivery. Gold companies use widespread physical presence and advertising to create a large share of mind and a strong brand identity with end users. With channel customers, Golds reduce costs by investing in information technology.

Silvers offer service levels that are higher and more consistent than those of their rivals. Pitney Bowes guarantees a four-hour response time on a copier service call, for example. Silvers tend to have strong channels and often offer exclusivity of territories to protect them.

Cover Broad Spectrum of Price Points

Golds will offer a broad array of products covering the high, medium, and low ends of the market. They avoid leaving niches available to others and end up with a product mix that mirrors the market. Silvers will usually participate in the high-end market but will not feel constrained by a niche segment. Rather, they will introduce products that are responsive to their largest customers.

Turn Price into a Commodity

In the early stages of hostility, price differences can be as large as 10% to 15%. How-ever, price differentials eventually converge to within 5% and become less important. Golds, such as FedEx in air express and IBM in personal computers, drop their price umbrella so that smaller competitors can grow and price at the market. They basically match the price of peers, thereby removing price from the customers' buying crite-ria. Their superior performance is rewarded by customer loyalty. Silvers gain share initially by discounting, but eventually their discount level is reduced and their focus shifts to delivering superior performance for key customers.

Have an Effective Cost Structure

The most successful companies in hostile markets have an effective cost structure. Golds such as Gallo in table wine and John Deere in farm equipment achieve high productivity not only by exploiting economies of scale but also by investing in automa-tion and information systems to reduce costs. Silvers target the high end of the market where returns are better and focus intently on key customers. They are also customer focused in their R&D, and they stretch their marketing budgets by concentrating on existing customers and avoiding advertising directed at gaining new customers.

In summary, the companies that outperform others in hostile industries tend to focus attention on large customers, differentiate on reliability, cover a wide spectrum of price points, turn price into a commodity, and have effective cost structures. However, the Golds compete very differently from the Silvers. Golds enjoy significant economies of scale, have a broad presence in share of shelf and share of mind, and offer efficiencies to channel partners. Silver firms are smaller, offer above-standard service, compete at higher price points, protect the margins of their channel partners, and focus on low unit cost with key customers.

KEY LEARNINGS

- One strategic option in a declining or stagnant industry is to create a growth context, revitalising the industry by seeking new markets, technologies, applications-marketing tactics, government-stimulated demand, and growth submarkets.

- Another option is to be the profitable survivor by strengthening a leadership position and encouraging others to exit, perhaps by buying their assets.

- A milking or harvest strategy (generating cash flow by reducing investment and operation expenses) works when the involved business is not crucial to the firm financially or synergistically. For milking to be feasible, though, sales must decline in an orderly way.

- The exit decision can be optimal, even though it is psychologically and professionally painful and usually must face organisational barriers. A proactive divestiture policy will be better than waiting until the situation deteriorates to the point that the decision is obvious.

- The investment decision in declining markets should rely on an analysis of market prospects, competitive intensity, business strengths, interrelationships with other businesses in the firm, and implementation barriers.

- Hostile markets, caused by too many competitors as well as declining demand, typically go through phases: margin pressures, share shifts, product proliferation, self-defeating cost reductions, consolidation, and rescue.

- Two strategies to gain above-average returns in hostile markets are represented by Golds (number one or two firms with economies of scale and substantial presence) and Silvers (number three or lower firms that focus on a smaller segment, usually at the high end of the market).

FOR DISCUSSION

1. Identify examples of brands that have created growth in stagnant or declining industries. What revitalisation routes were taken?

2. Identify profitable survivors in declining markets. Why can some firms maintain profits over time? Why did others leave the marketplace?

3. Identify brands that are employing a milking strategy. What are the risks?

4. Consider a divestment strategy. Why is it hard to divest a business? Jack Welch divested hundreds of businesses during his tenure. What are some of the motivations that led to these divestitures?

5. Summarise the hostile market theory. What are the key assumptions? Evaluate the theory. How would you test it?

NOTES

1. Sam Dias and Fiona Keyte (2004) How advertising caused a seismic change in the UK's use of paper towels. *IPA Effectiveness Awards.* Institute of Practitioners in Advertising, London, 2004. © copyright and database rights owned by WARC.

2. www.vespa.com.

3. Some excellent research has been done on strategy development in declining industries, on which the balance of this chapter draws. It has been reported in Michael E. Porter (1980) *Competitive Strategy*, The Free Press, New York, Chapter 8; Kathryn Rudie Harrigan (1980) *Strategies for Declining Businesses*, Lexington Books, Lexington MA. Kathryn Rudie Harrigan and Michael E. Porter (1983) End-game strategies for declining industries. *Harvard Business Review*, July–August, pp. 111–20.

4. Lee Dranikoff, Tim Koller and Antoon Schneider (2002) Divestiture: strategy's missing link. *Harvard Business Review*, May, pp. 75–83.

5. Donald V. Potter (1991) Success under fire: policies to prosper in hostile times. *California Management Review*, Winter pp. 24–38. Donald V. Potter (1994) Rare Mettle: Gold and Silver strategies to succeed in hostile markets. *California Management Review*, Fall, Vol. 37 Issue 1, pp. 65–82.

6. Claire Murphy (2006) The trouble with Heinz. *Marketing*, 14 June 2006, p. 26–8.

CASE CHALLENGES FOR PART IV

CASE STUDY I: GROWTH THROUGH BRAND ASSETS

Dove

Unilever launched the Dove brand in 1957 with a patented, mild cleansing bar of soap positioned as a beauty bar that contained one-fourth moisturising cream to moisturise skin. Dove is now the world's number one cleansing brand competing against Olay, Nivea and Neutrogena and is Unilever's third biggest brand behind Knorr and Lipton.[1]

The Dove brand portfolio consisted of a wide range of personal care products including beauty bars, body wash, face care and deodorant. But amidst this success Dove faced a strategic problem: although soap was only about half of their sales, customers viewed Dove as a soap brand. In the face of strong competition Dove needed to shift its brand asset to a beauty brand in order to accelerate sales of existing products and provide it with the scope to drive further brand extensions. But how could Dove be a distinctive voice in the industry? How could they change their core message without losing their loyal customers and damaging the brand's credibility? How could they differentiate themselves when there were already hundreds of brands in the beauty market?

Most beauty brands promote an idea of beauty as flawless, physical perfection. Dove recognised that there was a disparity between what the beauty industry was saying to women and women's attitudes and therefore made the decision to explore this gap for opportunities. In 2004 Dove published a global study on women and beauty titled 'The real truth about beauty: a global report.' This study of over 3 000 women in ten countries examined the effects of perceptions of beauty on women and young girls' lives. The results of the study showed how advertising was affecting young women's self-esteem, identified the pressure women feel the beauty industry places them under, as well as the need for a broader definition of what female beauty is. Dove management felt that an alignment between their brand promise and these important concerns could provide their brand with the type of dynamic it needed for its future development.

The first expression of Dove's new Real Women manifesto was the UK launch of Dove Body Firming Lotion in 2004. This was presented with an advertising campaign with the theme 'Let's celebrate curves.' The idea behind the campaign was that women did not like the usual promises of the unnaturally thin, toned, youthful woman and found them patronising. The message was that beauty comes in all shapes, sizes and forms and used poster ads featuring a group of women, who were not models, wearing only their underwear. Dove's target market was women in their 30s who were conscious of wanting a firmer and more toned body.

The campaign was a marketing risk in a society in which the pursuit of physical perfection was so strongly embedded. Companies have played with the idea of using 'real women' in ads for some time but had never really succeeded. Most recent was the Marks & Spencer 'I'm normal' campaign, which provoked a backlash.[2] But Dove had a background in the use of real women in its advertising as they had historically used non-actor women in marketing communications talking about how the brand

312

helped them. More subtle though, was the matching of the real women theme with the rise of reality entertainment. The use of ordinary people in celebrity roles elevates the ordinary woman, using Dove, as a symbol of beauty.

This new strategy incorporated some basic objectives. Dove hoped to raise awareness of issues of low self-esteem amongst women and girls, and advertise to women the need to change the way they view beauty and themselves in order to raise their self-esteem and reinforce their attractiveness despite the conditioning of conventional media.

The campaign had a moral purpose, but the real beauty ads still needed to sell to women the idea that they needed these products to become more beautiful. Their proposition to women was to question the images that were depicted by the beauty industry by showing that beauty comes in all shapes and that women, by seeking their own idea of beauty they can bring themselves closer to beauty, rather than closer to the media-ideal of physical perfection. Essentially, they proposed to them that with Dove Firming Lotion, women can show off their curves. This strategy was not without risk.

The execution of the campaign consisted of broadcast, print and outdoor supported by a strong public relations campaign, which was essential for provoking the debate that surrounded the campaign and was an integral part of its success. It focused on Germany, Italy, Spain, the UK, the Netherlands and France with marketing expenditure in the region of €20 million.[3]

The success of the campaign was breathtaking and genuinely groundbreaking, generating unprecedented amounts of PR coverage for the company and its brand, and promoting awareness around the world about the need to re-examine how women's beauty is defined in media. It has helped position the Dove brand as one that challenges the current beauty ideal and replaces it with a more refreshing alternative. By associating the brand with normal women they positioned the brand closer to the heart of these women. It also succeeded in revitalising and changing perceptions of the Dove brand from an old-fashioned soap brand to a more energetic, beauty-focused brand capturing the imagination and loyalty of women.

The campaign was enormously successful for Dove's sales and market share. The campaign enabled Dove to double sales of their firming lotion within a month of the campaign starting. Sales exceeded forecast by 110% in Western Europe and in the UK sales rose from 280 000 bottles in 2003 to 2.3 million bottles in the first half of 2004.[4] It also increased its volume share by 80% and its value share by 13.5% across its six biggest European markets.[5]

Encouraged by their success in Europe, a global campaign was developed to extend the concept to other markets and the resulting Campaign for Real Beauty was launched in September 2004. The intention of this campaign was to extend the concept beyond that of just a marketing strategy and to develop it into a global action plan or women's rebellion against the prevailing ideals of beauty. Dove wanted to continue to raise awareness of the issues surrounding beauty and stereotypes, but also create a forum which could facilitate and encourage public participation in the debate surrounding the concept and definition of beauty.

Dove developed a website, www.campaignforrealbeauty.com, which was integral for campaign success and in 2005 the website was active in 16 European markets.

On their website they have included details of their campaign, their products, real women's stories and images to pose beauty questions on which visitors can vote between possible responses. They have also included a copy of the Dove Global Study and details of the Dove Self-Esteem Fund, a charitable trust with the objective of supporting women's growth as individuals and to oppose the impossibly perfect media ideals that they are surrounded by. The website has also provided a forum and discussion room for customers to debate the issues that surround the campaign. This element of public debate has been essential for creating awareness of the brand and the campaign.

FOR DISCUSSION

1. Why was Dove's action so successful? Why did the use of 'Real Women' work for them when it had failed for others? How sustainable is this brand association for Dove?

2. How should Dove's competitors respond to their action? Would it be easy for them to imitate the Campaign for Real Beauty? If not, are there alternative themes which appeal to women which they could use to counter Dove?

3. How useful is the repositioning of Dove for brand extensions? What other product areas might they consider extending into?

4. Why did Dove launch of the Campaign for Real Beauty website? What are the short term benefits of this website? What are the long-term benefits?

NOTES

1. "Dove" Brand Profile, WARC, http://www.warc.com/ © 2006 Copyright and database rights owned by WARC

2. Alicia Clegg "Dove gets real" Brancchannel.com, 18 April 2005, http://www.brandchannel.com/features_effect.asp?pf_id=259.

3. "Dove- Celebrating Curves" Euro-Eiffes 2005, http://www.warc.com/ © 2006 Copyright and database rights owned by WARC

4. Inge Selawny "How real curves can grow your brand" (OgilvyOne Worldwide-Copenhagen), Viewpoint Online Magazine, Viewpoint 9, April 2005. http://www.ogilvy.com/viewpoint/view_ko.php?id=42707&iMagaId=9

5. "Dove- Celebrating Curves" Euro-Eiffes 2005, http://www.warc.com/ © 2006 Copyright and database rights owned by WARC

6. Inge Selawny "How real curves can grow your brand" (OgilvyOne Worldwide-Copenhagen), Viewpoint Online Magazine, Viewpoint 9, April 2005. http://www.ogilvy.com/viewpoint/view_ko.php?id=42707&iMagaId=9

CASE STUDY II: CREATING BRAND ASSETS TO SUPPORT A GROWTH STRATEGY

Cadbury's acquisition of Green & Black's

Green & Black's was founded in 1991 when Craig Sams, founder of Whole Earth, an organic food company, and his wife, Josephine Fairley, made the world's first organic chocolate, a high-quality, bittersweet dark chocolate bar, containing 70% cocoa solids. Green & Black's Maya Gold chocolate is a blend of dark chocolate with a twist of orange, cinnamon, nutmeg and vanilla. It is also the UK's first product to be awarded the Fair Trade mark.

The company uses direct trade with Mayan farmers in Belize, paying them a premium for their organic cocoa and an additional Fairtrade price. Today, Green & Black's is the fastest-growing confectionary brand in the UK,[1] is the UK's number one organic chocolate player[2] and sales are growing at extraordinary rates. One part of the reason for the explosive growth in the brand is the emergence of an indulgence based chocolate buyer whose consumption is typically of higher quality product in a lower volume. For these consumers the high sugar content of mainstream brands was not what they wanted.

The company produces a range of chocolate bars, as well as ice cream, biscuits, hot chocolate and cooking products, which are sold through retailers such as Tesco and Sainsbury's. All of their products are organic and premium-priced. While Green & Black's has been successful in exploiting emerging trends of premium, organic market niches, this alone does not fully account for Green and Black's success of more than quadrupling sales between 2001 and 2004. While Green & Black's business policies have strong ethical considerations, their marketing strategy has also emphasised their premium product quality image and great taste, with good distribution. Their decision to pursue such a strategy lies in their recognition that their ethical dimension may not be sufficient to develop a long-term market position and that they needed to develop a wider customer base by appealing to other segments based on taste and product quality and then emphasise the added ethical benefits of the product.

In 2005 Green & Black's was acquired by Cadbury Schweppes for an undisclosed fee believed to be in the region of £20 million.[3] So why did Green & Black's sell their organic low-sugar chocolate to one of the world's leading confectionary companies with seemingly different products and corporate values?

The acquisition was seen as necessary for several reasons. Green & Black's needed to forge a link with one of the big three confectioners, Mars, Cadbury or Nestle, in order to reach its full potential. Green & Black's also needed an investor who could insulate them against short-term losses. Green & Black's can learn a lot from Cadbury's manufacturing and quality control technologies.

Cadbury also offers Green & Black's the advantage of its experience of pursuing international expansion as well as providing the financial support and distribution channels to make it happen. This is particularly important in the US, where organic chocolate bars are achieving 200% growth year on year. The US market is characterised by long supply lines which are difficult for a small company like Green & Black's to handle without help from a larger manufacturer. While Cadbury only exports a small percentage of its turnover to the US it has just set up a subsidiary in Connecticut and is in the process of hiring a team there.

Currently Green & Black's sells primarily in supermarkets but supermarkets only have 60 % of the confectionery market, with most sweets sold as an impulse purchase in newsagents. Green & Black's can take advantage of Cadbury's salesforce to begin distributing and selling through smaller shops and convenience stores.

Green & Black's hope the acquisition by Cadbury will enable them to bring their ethical message and commitment to fair trade to a wider international consumer audience and to other confectionery manufacturers.

For Cadbury, the acquisition of Green & Black's offers them several benefits. Financially the company is very successful and very attractive, and under Cadbury's ownership its international expansion would further increase its financial attractiveness as sales and turnover increase. Green & Black's operations and annual turnover hardly compare to Cadbury, with Cadbury's sales about 20 times that of Green & Black's. But Cadbury has recognised that Green & Black's are the biggest organic chocolate brand in the UK and the fastest-growing UK confectionery brand with a year-on-year growth in the region of 70 %. In the UK they had a first mover advantage which helped them achieve a strong market position. Its revenues rose 49 % in 2005 compared to the overall rise in the UK confectionery market of just 2 %.

The acquisition of the well-established Green & Black's brand is also a powerful asset in Cadbury's brand portfolio as it provides an entry point to both the premium and organic chocolate markets. Green & Black's have positioned their products as not only organic and fairly traded but also as a premium product due to their high cocoa content. Both of these sectors are growing faster than the overall chocolate confectionery market. Green & Black's occupies a prime position in the premium chocolate market sector which grew by 21 % between 1999 and 2005. Cadbury has underperformed in this market with some classic brands like Roses and Milk Tray suffering in price and brand image terms.

Cadbury's objective is to achieve higher growth in their UK confectionary market, which has been slow due to lack of innovation in the market as a whole. Therefore, they are planning to refocus their innovation efforts to shift their brands upmarket. For example, they plan to extend their mainstream chocolate brands like Roses and Flake into the premium market. The acquisition of Green & Black's also allows Cadbury to counter the growth of Switzerland's Lindt, their main competitor in the premium and luxury chocolate market.

Cadbury had not developed any of their own organic products and have tapped into the growing appetite of consumers for organic chocolate through their purchase of Green & Black's. This is at a time when health-conscious consumers are buying more products that are low in sugars and fats. It enables Cadbury to consolidate its position in the UK chocolate market and gain a share in the rapidly growing organic chocolate sector by acquiring a brand that already enjoys significantly wider distribution than many other organic products.

Finally, Cadbury's acquisition of Green & Black's allows them to add an ethical dimension to their business. Many consumers believe that multinational companies do not have high enough ethical standards. Therefore, larger, established confectionary companies like Cadbury, keen to establish credentials in the booming ethical market, are taking over smaller companies known for their ethical principles and counter-culture approach, which have tapped into the emerging, ethical, organic consumer trend like Green & Black's have managed to do. Cadbury can learn a lot from Green & Black's about organics, fair trade and corporate social responsibility.

Questions

1. If you were Craig Sams or Josephine Fairley would you have sold your business to Cadbury? Why?
2. What synergies exist in this acquisition? How realisable are they? What are the likely barriers to achieving synergies in this acquisition?
3. Does ownership by Cadbury undermine the Green & Black's brand message? Why?
4. Should Cadbury consider branding the Green and Black's product with its own brand name? What are the options for doing this? What are the advantages and disadvantages of each option?

NOTES

1. "Cadbury gobbles up organic rival" BBC News, 13 May 2005. http://news.bbc.co.uk/1/hi/business/4543583.stm
2. "Going organic: Cadbury acquires Green & Blacks" Euromonitor International, 20 May 2005.
3. ibid
4. Andrew Purns "How a £1.50 chocolate bar saved a Mayan community from destruction" *Observer Food Monthly*, 28 May 2006.
5. Stuart Jeffries "I Should Cocoa" The Guardian, 16 May 2005. http://www.guardian.co.uk/g2/story/0,,1484605,00.html
6. Jenny Wiggins "Premium chocolate market for Cadbury", Financial Times, 22 February 2006.
7. Jenny Wiggins "Premium chocolate market for Cadbury", Financial Times, 22 February 2006.

PART FIVE

IMPLEMENTATION ISSUES

CHAPTER SIXTEEN

Organisational Issues

All progress is initiated by challenging current conceptions and executed by supplanting existing institutions.
—George Bernard Shaw

Structure follows strategy.
—Alfred Chandler, Jr.

Those that implement the plans must make the plans.
—Patrick Hagerty, Texas Instruments

W hen Mercedes Benz and Chrysler merged in 1998 the logic seemed impeccable. Mercedes was a luxury carmaker seeking a foothold in the volume car market. Chrysler was a profitable volume carmaker who could go further with fresh investment. The new DaimlerChrysler seemed a merger made in a $36 billion heaven. However, Daimler management had failed to appreciate the challenges involved in implementing the merger strategy and realising its goals. Although Chrysler was profitable it had achieved this through early entry into the 1990s growth market of light trucks. Their follow up products were not as successful due to pricing and quality problems and a tougher and more competitive business environment. In addition many Chrysler managers left post merger, leaving the business without many of those who had led to success in the first place.[1] Finally, Daimler management waited for two years before they inserted their own management as they feared that the Mercedes brand would be adversely affected by too close an association with Chrysler and also that the German and American management cultures might not mix well.[2] After a German CEO was appointed to Chrysler a round of cost cutting, an emphasis on quality and new products led the firm to profitability in 2004 and 2005. However, by that time Mercedes was facing troubles of its own, primarily quality problems in its volume C and E class saloons. Although there was optimism that a new CEO could turn the situation around. In mid 2006 the value of the DaimlerChrysler was about half what it was at its most euphoric peak following the merger in 1999.[3]

The DaimlerChrsyler merger clearly illustrates the importance of strategy implementation. Strategy implementation is essential for success so the assessment of any strategy should include a careful analysis of organisational risks and a judgement about the nature of any required organisational changes and their associated costs and feasibility. Toward that end, this chapter first develops a conceptual framework that will help in analysing an organisation.

A CONCEPTUAL FRAMEWORK

The conceptual framework shown in Figure 16.1 can be used to identify and position organisational components and their interactions. The heart of the framework is a set of four key constructs that describe the organisation: structure, systems, people, and culture. The figure includes strategy, which must successfully interact with the four organisational components, and organisational performance. It also includes external analysis and internal analysis, which provide a link to Figure 2.1 and the strategy development process. Recall that a strategy involves the product-market investment decision, the value proposition, the selection of functional area strategies, and the identification of bases for sustainable competitive advantage.

Consideration of organisational components can help a business identify actual and potential implementation problems, as well as determine how its organisation would adapt to a new strategy. The first section of this chapter discusses each central component and its link to strategy. The need for achieving a fit or congruence among these four organisational components and strategy is then considered. Finally, ways by which an organisation can become more innovative and responsive to change are suggested.

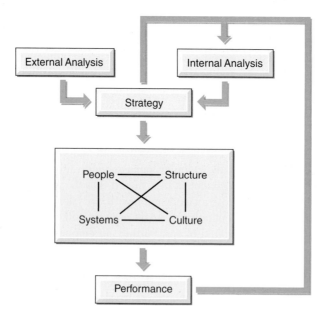

Figure 16.1   A framework for analysing organisations

STRUCTURE

Organisational structure defines lines of authority and communication and specifies the mechanism by which organisational tasks and programmes are accomplished.

Decentralisation versus Centralisation

Nearly every organisation, from the Virgin Group to Unilever, Siemens, Henkel and Nestlé prides itself on being decentralised. And with good reasons. Autonomous groups running distinct businesses have enormous inherent advantages. The managers are close to the market and can therefore understand customer needs. They are also intimate with the product technology and thus can chart the direction of product offerings. Being empowered to act quickly in an environment means no delays in making and implementing strategic decisions, a difference that is vital in dynamic markets. As distinct business units can be held accountable for investments and results, business performance will also be known in a timelier and less ambiguous manner. The most impressive feature of decentralisation, however, is that it fosters incredible energy and vitality. Managers are empowered and motivated to innovate, to gain competitive advantage by providing superior value propositions to the customers.

Nevertheless, there are challenges as well. One challenge facing a decentralised organisation is creating cross-business synergy. Potential synergy is often unrealised because having a host of silos can involve duplication, inefficiencies, and lost opportunities to create value for customers. In addition, it may be hard for a business to support a world-class marketing, IT, or sales function unless it finds a way to combine resources with other units. The failure to achieve synergies can be debilitating when competition for customers is intense and margins are under pressure.

A second challenge is to respond strategically at the firm level to market dynamics. What is strategically optimal for a business unit may not be the best for the firm as a whole. Brand portfolio strategy, for example, is easily undermined if a brand is shared across business units, with each using the brand to its local advantage. Conversely, a major technology process change that could result in advantage for several business units might not be justified when evaluated at the business level.

One way to address these problems is with centralised control, the polar opposite of decentralisation. In this model, a centralised team makes all the strategic and tactical decisions and has a strong functional capability to implement them (or at least manage their implementation). Such a group will create business strategy from a firmwide perspective, and it can make sure that synergy opportunities are detected and exploited. To succeed, the central team needs to have credible knowledge of the products and the markets, the necessary resources, and the authority add stature to get things done. It will work best when the business scope is limited or there is a seasoned, knowledgeable CEO who has earned respect throughout the organisation.

A central management team can influence decentralised business units even without controlling them by utilising the approaches described in Chapter 11 – namely, playing the role of a service provider, consultant, or facilitator. In the service provider role, the central team will manage a variety of support functions, such as sponsorship, marketing research, IT, advertising and performance tracking. Business units would buy services from the central team. In the consultative role, the central team will develop insights and recommend strategies. As a facilitator of strategy development, the central team would be less aggressive in suggesting strategies but would support and facilitate them, using the resources and processes of the organisation.

Whatever management style used by the central team – controlling, service provider, consultative, or facilitative – needs to match the organisational heritage and culture. If it is too disparate, it may be rejected like an incompatible transplanted organ in a human body. Sometimes a change agent is needed, though, and some organisational stress may be healthy. Whatever style is used, the central team will be most effective when it has resources, market knowledge, product knowledge, and respect. If it lacks any of these, it will be marginalised.

Matrix Organisation

A matrix organisation allows a person to have two or more reporting links. Several business units could share a sales force by having the salespeople report to a business unit as well as to the sales manager. A research-and-development group could have a research team that reports both to the business unit and to the research-and-development manager. As a result, the salespeople and the research team in these examples are each supported by a critical mass of employees and infrastructure that allows them to excel while still being a part of the business unit. A person might also be attached to a task force (assigned, for instance, to explore a new market opportunity). That person would report to both the task force manager and his or her business unit. The concept of dual reporting requires coordination and communication that can be stressful and costly but it also provides the flexibility needed to deal with a fast-moving market.

The Virtual Corporation

The virtual corporation is a team of people and organisations specifically designed for a particular client or job. The organisations brought together may be suppliers, customers, and competitors. The people can be drawn from a variety of sources and might include contract workers who are hired only for the project at hand. The virtual corporation can sometimes be formed or modified in a matter of days, which means it is the ultimate response in a fast-moving environment.

Communication firms, for example, are now forming teams tailored to the needs of particular clients. Some members of the team will come from subsidiary firms specialising in corporate design, packaging, direct marketing, and promotions. Others may come from firms that specialise in brochures and the media. The core of the team is likely to be located in a single building, but some team members will be connected via computer workstations that share visual images and in-process advertising. Thus, clients do not have to wait for an agency with the optimal set of characteristics to evolve; it can be formed almost overnight. WPP, the world's largest communication firm, has formed an ongoing virtual firm around health-care marketing services that has become a dominant force in its market, with the virtual firm's CEO as the only employee.[4]

One of the legacies of the Dot.Com era has been the idea that the Internet could facilitate the virtual structuring of organisations around a series of outsourcing deals. Many firms in consumer goods sector found this idea attractive and engaged in outsourcing deals with low cost manufacturers, with them focusing on marketing and brand development.

The story has not gone in the straight line that this early logic suggested. For the perfect virtual corporation business model to work economies of scale dictate that production must be ordered well in advance and that last minute changes to quantities or features are minimised. In the clothing/fashion industry this doesn't work as tastes change rapidly and unexpected success for particular lines require increased production at short notice is common. In response some corporations have adapted the virtual model and developed deeper relationships with partners in geographically closer countries. Production is still low cost, albeit a little more expensive but the flexibility offered outweighs the costs involved.

Alliance Networks

In the global environment, markets and competitors can change significantly and it is important to be able to respond quickly. There may not be time to develop needed assets and competencies, and responses that require large commitments to new technologies or distribution channels may be risky, especially for a firm with little relevant background. One way to be able to go online immediately with necessary business changes is to form a network of alliances and joint ventures with suppliers, customers, distributors, and even competitors. With such a network, needed assets can be made available instantly, the firm can focus on what it does best, the risk of failure is shared, and many more opportunities can be funded. The use of strategic alliances, their motivations, and how to make them work are discussed in detail in Chapter 11. These alliances play an especially important role in global strategy development.

SYSTEMS

Several management systems are strategically relevant. Among them are the budgeting/accounting, information, measurement and reward, and planning systems.

Accounting and Budgeting System

Accounting and budgeting are key elements in any management system. The risk that these systems cannot be adapted to the needs of a new strategy can be very real. An accounting and budgeting system that is well conceived and contains valuable historical data may not fit the reorganised structure required by the new strategy. Or a system that worked well for an electronic instruments firm may not work when applied to a new service business. Another concern is the system's influence on investment decisions, especially when a new strategy is proposed that does not fit a familiar pattern.

Information System

The information system and the technology, databases, models, and expert systems on which it is based can fundamentally affect strategy. The link between manufacturers and retailers, for example, is increasingly being forged by information technology.

EASY STEPS TO DESTROYING REAL VALUE

By Henry Mintzberg[5]

1. Manage the bottom line (as if companies make money by managing money).
2. Make a plan for every action. (No spontaneity please, definitely no learning.)
3. Move managers around to be certain they never get to know anything but management well, and let the boss kick himself upstairs so that he can manage a portfolio instead of a real business.
4. When in trouble, rationalise, fire, and divest; when out of trouble, expand, acquire, and still fire (it keeps employees on their toes); above all, never create or invent anything (it takes too long).

New systems control inventory and handle ordering, pricing, and promotions. The ability to control the information generated by retail scanners can be key to strategies of manufacturers and retailers. The creation, organisation, and use of knowledge banks can be a significant strategic asset. Thus, understanding the current capability and future direction of an organisation's information system is a key dimension of strategy development.

Measurement and Reward System

Measurement can drive behaviour and thus directly affect strategy implementation. The key to strategy is often the ability to introduce appropriate performance measures that are linked to the reward structure. One concern is to motivate employees to cooperate, communicate, and create synergy. Rewards that are based too closely on a business unit's performance can work against this motivational goal. As a result, many companies deliberately base a portion of their bonuses or evaluations on the results of a larger unit. Prophet, a brand strategy consulting firm with seven offices, encourages cross-office support by making its bonuses conditional on firmwide performance. Another business may focus on divisional performance because synergy across divisions is not realistic. Another prerequisite is to create measures reflecting a long-term perspective in order to balance short-term financial results. Thus, measures such as customer satisfaction, customer loyalty, quality indicators, new products brought to market, or training programme productivity may be useful to gauge the progress of strategic initiatives.

Planning System

An annual strategic planning process is almost always useful because it forces managers to take time out to consider strategic uncertainties. Without that impetus, routine tasks will generally absorb management's available time. Workshops and retreats are often crucial elements in dedicating quality time to planning. Creative, out-of-the-box thinking (perhaps aided by formal creative-thinking exercises) is a vital part of any planning system. Too often, strategic planning is nothing but an extrapolation of past strategies, with a financial spreadsheet as the dominant tool. There are two problems with this approach. First, it will not lead to the breakthrough strategies that can reinvent a business when needed. Second, it will not provide the consideration of strategic options that provides the basis for adapting to new events or trends. When Eisenhower said, 'Plans are nothing, planning is everything' in part he meant that the process of examining a variety of strategic options makes the manager more capable of adapting or changing when necessary. Planning should not be separated from the values, culture, and energy of the organisation. According to Mintzberg, successful planning is often based on a committing, rather than a calculating style of management: 'Managers with a committing style engage people in a journey. They lead in such a way that everyone on the journey helps shape its course. As a result, enthusiasm inevitably builds along the way.' Mintzberg paraphrases the sociologist Philip Selznick when he says that 'strategies only take on value as committed people infuse them with energy.' The output of strategic planning should have soul as well as logic.[6]

PEOPLE

A strategy is generally based on an organisational competency that, in turn, is based on people. Thus, strategies require certain types of people. For each strategy, it is important to know how many people, with what experience, depth, and skills, are needed for:

- functional areas, such as marketing, manufacturing, assembly, and finance
- product or market areas
- new product programmes
- management of particular types of people
- management of a particular type of operation
- management of growth and change

Make, Buy, or Convert

If a strategy requires capabilities not already available in the business, it will be necessary to obtain them. The make approach, developing a broad managerial or technical base by hiring and grooming workers, ensures that people will fit the organisation, but it can take years.

STRATEGY AND PEOPLE DEVELOPMENT AT GE

Jack Welch, the legendary former GE CEO, created a system and culture to develop both strategy and people throughout his 20-year tenure. Five elements were involved:[7]

- Each January, the top 5000 GE executives gathered in Boca Raton to share best practices and set major business priorities. Webcasts of the event were available to the whole organisation.
- Each quarter, top executives met in two-day retreats facilitated by Welch and focused on initiatives related to the agenda set in Boca Raton. This was a key place for future leaders to emerge, earn respect, and demonstrate growth.
- Twice a year, Welch and others focused on personnel needs for each business, such as how to handle each unit's top 20% and bottom 10% of employees.
- Similar biannual sessions (one in the spring and one in the fall) looked at each business over a three-year horizon.
- The entire effort was supported by the GE social architecture of informality, candour, substantive dialogue, boundaryless behaviour, emphasis on follow through, and making judgments on qualitative business dimensions.

The convert approach, converting the existing workforce to the new strategy, takes less time. AT&T is an example of a firm that attempted to change its orientation from that of service to marketing, largely by retraining existing staff. A host of strategies, particularly those precipitated by acquisitions, have failed because of the faulty assumption that an old staff could adapt to a new context. A car components buying team, for example, could not be easily adapted to the needs of a plane manufacturer. The buy approach, bringing in experienced people from the outside, is the immediate solution when a dramatic change in strategy needs to be implemented quickly, but it involves the risk of bringing in people who are accustomed to different systems and cultures.

Motivation

In addition to the type and quality of people, the motivation level can affect strategy implementation. There are, of course, a variety of ways to motivate people, including the fear of losing a job, financial incentives, self-fulfillment goals, and the development of goals for the organisation or groups within the organisation, such as teams or quality circles. Motivation is usually enhanced if employees are empowered to accomplish their goals even when a departure from the routine response is required. People who are inhibited from using their initiative will eventually lose interest and become cynical. Motivation also is enhanced when employees are linked to the corporate culture and objectives. Companies can accomplish these links in a number of ways, most simply by providing titles, such as 'host' (Disney), 'crew member' (McDonald's). Henkel have used a company song ('we together') and a short film ('in motion') to connect staff and other stakeholders to its core message of 'A brand like a friend' and the impact that implementing the Henkel brand can have on the lives of customers.[8] Embracing the concept of brand communities, as Saab has long done, not only deepens relationships between customers and provides an opportunity for employees to engage directly with the firm's culture through its customers.

CULTURE

As suggested by Figure 16.2, an organisational culture involves three elements:

- A set of shared values or dominant beliefs that define an organisation's priorities.
- A set of norms of behaviour.
- Symbols and symbolic activities used to develop and nurture those shared values and norms.

Shared Values

Shared values or dominant beliefs underlie a culture by specifying what is important. In a strong culture, the values will be widely accepted, and virtually everyone will be able to identify them and describe their rationale. Shared values can have a variety of foci. They can involve, for example:

- A key asset or competency that is the essence of a firm's competitive advantage: we will be the most creative advertising agency.
- An operational focus: SAS focused on on-time performance.
- An organisational output: We will deliver zero defects or 100% customer satisfaction.
- An emphasis on a functional area: Black & Decker transformed itself from a firm with a manufacturing focus to one with a market-driven approach.
- A management style: This is an informal, flat organisation that fosters communication and encourages unconventional thinking.
- A belief in the importance of people as individuals.

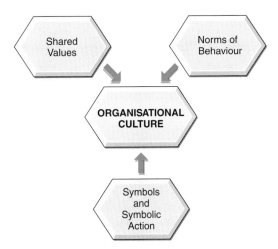

Figure 16.2   Organisational culture

- A general objective, such as a belief in being the best or comparable to the best: Patek Philippe sets out to produce the world's finest timepiece; Carlsberg is probably the best beer in the world; Samsung endeavours to create superior products and services.

Norms

To make a real difference, the culture must be strong enough to develop norms of behaviour – informal rules that influence decisions and actions throughout an organisation by suggesting what is appropriate and what is not. Charles O'Reilly of Stanford University talks of culture as a social control system with norms as behaviour guides.[9]

The fact is that strong norms can generate much more effective control over what is actually done or not done in an organisation than a very specific set of objectives, measures, and sanctions. People can always get around rules. The concept of norms is that people will not attempt to avoid them because they will be accompanied by a commitment to shared values.

O'Reilly suggests that norms can vary on two dimensions: the intensity or amount of approval/disapproval attached to an expectation and the degree of consensus or consistency with which a norm is shared.[10] It is only when both intensity and consensus exist that strong cultures emerge.

Norms encourage behaviour consistent with shared values. Thus, in a quality service culture, an extraordinary effort by an employee, such as renting a helicopter to fix a communication component (a FedEx legend) would not seem out of line and risky; instead it would be something that most in that culture would do under similar circumstances. Furthermore, sloppy work affecting quality would be informally policed by fellow workers, without reliance on a formal system. One production firm uses no quality-control inspectors or janitors. Each production-line person is responsible for the quality of his or her output and for keeping the work area clean. Such a policy would not work without support from a strong culture.

Symbols and Symbolic Action

Corporate cultures are largely developed and maintained by the use of consistent, visible symbols and symbolic action. In fact, the more obvious methods of affecting behaviour, such as changing systems or structure, are often much less effective than seemingly trivial symbolic actions. A host of symbols and symbolic actions are available. A few of the more useful are discussed next.

The Founder and Original Mission

A corporation's unique roots, including the personal style and experience of its founder, can provide extremely potent symbols. The innovation culture of Dyson and its commitment to innovative marketing is due almost entirely to its founder James Dyson. Akio Morita, the co-founder of Sony, instilled a commitment to branding and internationalisation into the company's DNA. The concept of furniture developed by

Ingvar Kamprad, the founder of Ikea, the better value business model of Ben Dunne Snr. of Dunnes Stores, the vision of Zara's Amancio Ortega to use manufacturing as a competitive advantage, continue to influence the cultures of their firms today.

Modern Role Models

Modern heroes and role models help communicate, personalise, and legitimise values and norms. The boundless ambition of Ryanair's Michael O'Leary has encouraged other entrepreneurs and managers to expand the limits of their ambition. The commitment of Anita Roddick, founder of The Body Shop, to using business to make the world a better place has inspired a range of entrepreneurs in the profit and not-for-profit sector.

Activities

A manager's use of time can be a symbolic action affecting the culture. An airline executive who spends two weeks a month obtaining a firsthand look at customer service sends a strong signal to the organisation. Patterns of consistent reinforcement can represent another important symbolic activity. For example, a firm that regularly recognises cost-saving accomplishments in a meaningful way with the visible support of top management can, over time, affect the culture.

Questions Asked

An executive of a major bank reportedly shifted concern from revenue to profit by continually asking about profit implications. When a type of question is continually asked by top executives and made a central part of meeting agendas and report formats, it will eventually influence the shared values of an organisation.

Rituals

Rituals of work life, from hiring to eating lunch to retirement dinners, help define a culture. One of the early success stories in Silicon Valley was a firm with a culture that was based in part on a requirement that a person commit before knowing his or her salary. A high growth Irish firm found it difficult to build internal relationships as so many of its employees travelled internationally developing new business and servicing existing account. To overcome this they developed a ritual of meeting each Friday afternoon at 5.30 p.m. in a Dublin city centre pub.

OBTAINING STRATEGIC CONGRUENCE

Figure 16.3 lists a set of questions that provide a basis for analysing an organisation and its relationship to a proposed strategy. As discussed earlier, a strategy must match the structure, systems, people, and culture of the organisation. In addition, each organisational component needs to fit with the others. If an inconsistency exists, it is likely that implementation of the strategy will be affected. The concept of organisational congruence suggests that interactions between organisational components should be considered, such as:

- *Do the systems fit the structure?* Does the compensation system emphasise teamwork rather than individual performance when teamwork and cooperation are required?

- *Do the people fit the structure?* Can they operate within the organisational groups and integrate mechanisms to complete the task? For example, creative or entrepreneurial managers may be uncomfortable in a highly structured organisation.

- *Does the structure fit the culture?* Does the structure complement the values or norms of the organisation? For example, a top management group accustomed to controlling dedicated resources may be less effective in a matrix organisation, in which persuasion and coordination are more important.

Corporate Culture and Strategy

Organisational culture provides the key to strategy implementation because it is such a powerful force for providing focus, motivation, and norms. Many strategies con-

---

STRUCTURE
- What is the organisation's structure? How decentralised is it?
- What are the lines of authority and communication?
- What are the roles of task forces, committees, or similar mechanisms?

SYSTEMS
- How are budgets set?
- What is the nature of the planning system?
- What are the key measures used to evaluate performance?
- How does the accounting system work?
- How do product and information flow?

PEOPLE
- What are the skills, knowledge, and experience of the firm's employees?
- What is their depth and quality?
- What are the employees' expectations?
- What are their attitudes toward the firm and their jobs?

CULTURE
- Are there shared values that are visible and accepted?
- What are these shared values and how are they communicated?
- What are the norms of behaviour?
- What are the significant symbols and symbolic activities?
- What is the dominant management style?
- How is conflict resolved?

STRATEGY
- Where would the new strategy fit into the organisation?
- Would the new strategy fit into the strategic plan and be adequately funded?
- Would the systems and culture support the new strategy?
- What organisational changes would be required for the new strategy to succeed?
- What impact would these changes have? Are they feasible?

Figure 16.3   Obtaining information about organisational components

REPRESENTING CULTURE AND STRATEGY WITH STORIES, NOT BULLETS

Research has shown that stories are more likely than lists to be read and remembered. Nevertheless, most business strategists rely on bullet points to communicate both culture and strategy. 3M is one firm that has based its culture on classic stories – how initial failures of abrasive products led to product breakthroughs; how masking tape was invented; how a scientist conceived of Post-it Notes when his bookmarks fell out of a hymnal, and how the Post-it-Notes team, instead of giving up in the face of low initial sales, got people hooked on the product by flooding a city with samples. These stories communicate how innovation occurs at 3M and how its entrepreneurial culture operates.

At 3M, business strategy is also communicated via stories rather than the conventional bullets, which tend to be generic (the goal of increased market share applies to any business), skip over critical assumptions about how the business works (will increased market share fund new products, or result from new products?) and leave causal relationship, unspecified (if A is done, B becomes effective). A strategic story will involves several phases – setting the stage by describing the current situation, introducing the dramatic conflict in the form of challenges and critical issues, and reaching resolution with convincing stories about how the company can overcome obstacles and win. Presenting a narrative motivates the audience, adds richness and detail, and provides a glimpse into the logic of the strategist.[11]

centrate on an organisational asset or competency, such as the product quality level, service system, or customer support, or on a functional area, such as manufacturing or sales. A culture can provide support if it is congruent with the new structures, systems, and people required by a new strategy. If it is not congruent, however, the culture's motivations and norms could cripple the strategy.

THE E-ORGANISATION

E-organisations use the Internet to transform their business by fundamentally changing the way they interact and conduct business with suppliers, partners, and customers. These firms, such as Cisco, have developed very new organisational forms. In particular:

- Structure. Rather than hierarchical structures, flat, flexible, decentralised team- and alliance-based organisations are needed to allow fast and focused responses to strategic opportunities and problems around the world. Alliance partners have become an integral part of the firm at Dell and Cisco. Business units and teams are more likely to be organised around customers.

- Systems. At firms like Dell, suppliers, partners, and customers are integrated into virtually all systems. The latest information systems are required in order to improve customer service and increase personalisation. Intranets become a key instrument in communicating experiences and managing initiatives.

- People. Leadership is now the province of the many rather than the few. An army of people is empowered to achieve change and support others in responding to emerging opportunities and threats. British Telecom, for example, created a team of evangelistic visionaries and mavericks who could quickly find markets for the firm's cutting-edge research.

- Culture. The culture tends to emphasise the customer, change, and innovation. Customer focus is a driving force at Cisco and IBM, for example, where customer-obsessed CEOs lead the way. Change, even fundamental business model change, is supported by the culture. Innovation is the norm for e-organisations and acceptance of failure is often a visible value.[12]

A new strategy's fit with an organisation's culture is of greater concern than the strategy's fit with the other organisational components because culture is so difficult to change. For example, an oil company CEO developed elaborate diversification plans that failed because they were incompatible with the firm's oil business culture. BT, however, has managed to successfully complete a radical transformation from a highly bureaucratic organisation to a highly innovative company, essentially, by implementing an ongoing programme of structural and cultural reform. Not everyone embraced the changes at BT with open arms. Radical change often gives rise to uncertainty and unease, meaning that opposition is almost inevitable. When major change is occurring it is imperative to have everyone pulling in the same direction as much as possible. It goes without saying that any organisation's leaders have a crucial role to play in trying to sustain harmony during transitional periods. Harmony is a by-product of trust, but trust will only develop through fair treatment. BT clearly comprehends this because its leaders have nurtured an environment in which employees' needs and concerns are recognised.[13]

When a new strategy is proposed, it is important to understand the relationship of that strategy to the shared values and norms of the organisation. Is it compatible? Will the culture have to be modified? If so, what impact will that have on the organisation? Often the worst case develops when a strong positive culture is sacrificed to accommodate a new strategy, and the result is an absence of any positive culture.

Hit-Industry Topology

The need for congruence between strategy and organisational components can be illustrated by the three very different types of firms that compete in hit industries.[14] A hit industry is one in which the goal is to obtain, produce, and exploit a product that will have a relatively short life cycle. Examples of such industries include movies, music, fashion, publishing, video games, computer software, venture capital (especially in high-tech areas), and oil. Industries with short life cycles are interesting because many of their organisational problems are more intense and graphic. The model in Figure 16.4 divides a hit industry into three functions, which are shown as being performed by different organisations, although often two or more will coexist within the same organisation. An oil industry analogy provides the conceptual framework.

The first organisational type is termed drillers. They are the wildcatters who find oil fields and drill wells, the coaches of young football players, the talent scouts and artists of the record industry the producers and writers in the movie industry and the editors and authors in the publishing industry. A key success factor is to locate or create the new wells, properties or projects. An ultimate goal in the record business, for example, would be to get a lock on performing talent and keep the artists so happy that they would not consider leaving the company. Key people tend to be creative, high-energy, decisive risk takers. They thrive in a flat organisation with little structure and high bottom-line incentives. The second organisational type is termed pumpers. They are the well operators and refiners of the oil business, the DVD pressers, the movie directors, and the printers in publishing. The key success factors in a pumping organisation are operations, production engineering, and an ability to exploit the experience curve. The key people are disciplined, cost and production-oriented, in production and control jobs, and risk avoiders. A centralised organisation with tight controls provides an appropriate context.

The third type specialises in distribution. The distributors are the pipeline operators and retailers in the oil industry and the distributors and retailers in the film, DVD, and publishing industries. The key success factors in a distribution business usually include marketing, promotion, physical distribution, and access to or even control over distribution channels. The key people are in marketing and distribution. A decentralised structure with loose controls and some bottom-line incentives is often effective.

The hit-industry topology shows how the lack of fit between organisational components can develop. Typically, an organisation starts as a drilling company. After establishing some products and experiencing rapid growth, the company finds that it desperately needs to control production costs, develop a secure, effective distribution channel and professionalise the marketing effort. As a result, pumping and

Strategy	Drillers	Pumpers	Distributors
Structure	• Flat, loose • Amorphous	• Centralised • Tight control	• Decentralised • Loose control
Bottom-line Performance Incentives	• High	• None	• Low
People	• Product development	• Production control	• Marketing and distribution
Culture	• Stay loose • Move fast • Take risks	• Disciplined • Cost oriented • Avoid risks	• Promotion-oriented • Control risks
Key Success Factors	• Finding and keeping key people • Idea source • Get products to market quickly	• Exploit the experience curve • Operations • Production • Engineering	• Distribution channels • Inventory • Promotion • Positioning • Pricing

Figure 16.4   A model of hit industries

distribution people are brought in. The organisation then takes the form of either a pumper or a distributor, depending on which function is most critical or which type of person becomes the CEO. In any case, the system, structure, and culture of the organisation change and the drillers who started the business become uncomfortable and leave, perhaps to start a competing business. When the existing wells dry up or are damaged by competition, no one in the organisation is available to create new ones.

It is a challenge in any business to keep access to drillers. One approach is to keep the drillers satisfied by financial incentives and organisational mechanisms, such as *ad hoc* groups with extraordinary freedom and autonomy. However, these special incentives may create inequities and disincentives for others. If entrepreneurial engineers are becoming millionaires, while those charged with maintaining existing products are on a fixed salary, tensions are bound to mount. Furthermore, the entrepreneurial groups may need access to the facilities and expertise of the pumpers and distributors, and providing that access may compromise their separateness. Another way to approach a fit problem is to restrict a business to one function and allow other organisations to perform the other functions. Venture capital firms restrict themselves to being drillers and do not become involved in the other functions. Publishers are largely distribution companies; their production is farmed out and the drillers are actually the authors, who are not part of the organisation. A business without in-house drillers may have limited access to new ventures, however, because other firms may successfully contract with the best independent drillers. The price for the proven drillers may also become so high that profits are limited.

Problems can also arise when pumpers and distributors share an organisation. If one of the two clearly dominates the problem is minimised. If each is equally significant, however, there could easily be a fit problem.

ORGANISING FOR INNOVATION

Although the achievement of high congruence among an organisation's components and strategy leads to organisational effectiveness in the short to medium term, it can also inhibit desirable and even necessary change. An organisation can become so integrated and the culture so strong that only compatible changes are tolerated. For example, when faced with a technological threat, firms often respond with even greater reliance on the obsolete familiar technology. The challenge is to create an organisation that can successfully operate a congruent strategy and still have the ability to detect the need for fundamental change. If a significant change in strategy is needed, a major organisational change undoubtedly will be required as well. Also, even in the context of a congruent strategy, there needs to be a capacity for ongoing innovation – the ability to create new or improved products or processes and enter new markets. Several approaches, including decentralisation, task forces, skunk works, kaizen, and reengineering, are being used successfully to promote change and foster innovation.

Decentralisation – Keeping Business Units Small

Michael Tushman and Charles O'Reilly have identified three firms that are good at both evolving and improving operations and generating revolutionary change: HP

(Hewlett-Packard), Johnson & Johnson, and ABB (Asea Brown Boveri).[15] Each of these firms emphasises autonomous groups. Johnson & Johnson has 165 separate operating companies, ABB has over 5000 profit centres with an average staff of 50 each, and HP has over 50 divisions and a policy of splitting any division that gets larger than a thousand or so people. Small units are closer to customers and trends, can be agile and fast moving, and create motivated employees who feel an ownership of the operation. The result is a vital, innovative organisation relatively unencumbered by a central bureaucracy.

Task Forces

Sometimes a firm will find that it must make a substantial change in operations because of a significant challenge, such as a deterioration in competitive position, or opportunity, such as a technological breakthrough. A cross-functional task force can look at the issues in depth and form a response that provides a meaningful change in direction. Japanese companies infuse task forces with a sense of urgency to create significant change agents. The sense of urgency will usually involve a competitor oriented goal, such as 'beat Cat' in the case of Komatsu; specific objectives, such as reduction of costs by 20%; a tight timetable; and a process, such as total quality control or 'just-in-time'. The result is extreme pressure to work hard and perform and to break out of the mould and find creative new approaches.

Skunk Works

Major new business ventures may require separate entrepreneurial units because the slow decision-making process, the resource allocation biases against risky new businesses and the overhead burden of the core organisation are too great a handicap. Small, autonomous groups of people representing all the important functions join together to create a product or a business and nurse it through the early stages of life, often in an off-site garage operation called a skunk works. Used by 3M, Intel, Google, and many others, such a group is usually autonomous enough that it can bypass the usual decision process and resist pressures to conform to existing formal and informal constraints. A key to entrepreneurial units is to have a business champion committed to the concept. Texas Instruments reviewed 50 new product introductions and found that every failure lacked a voluntary product champion.[16]

Kaizen

Kaizen, which means ongoing improvement involving everyone from top management on down, has been the basis of an increase in productivity for many Japanese firms.[17] Particularly Japanese, it does not easily fit into the European context because it focuses on process rather than on results and because it depends on many small improvements rather than on a quick fix based on a dramatic new product or technology. The bottom line is never the motivation. Rather, the goal is continuous improvement throughout the organisation.

Reengineering

Reengineering, the antithesis of kaizen, is the search for and implementation of radical change in business operations to achieve breakthrough results.[18] The basic idea is to start with a clean sheet of paper and ask 'If we were to start a new company, how would we operate?' Rather than attempting to refine and improve, the effort is to create a revolution from within. The key to reengineering is to break down the old functional units and approach the problem from an interdisciplinary view using cross-functional teams. The starting point is usually considering how customers would like to deal with the firm, rather than how the firm would like to deal with customers.

For example, a phone company discovered that customers wanted a single phone number to call about any problem, rather than separate numbers for the repair, billing, and marketing departments. As a result it started a customer care centre staffed by people who could field and deal with any inquiry. The goal was to have the people and systems in place so that 70 % of all calls could be handled without being passed on to another department. This approach was indeed a radical departure, which ended up not only improving service, but also reducing costs.

Reengineering, both risky and expensive, is most appropriate when there is a strong threat from a changing environment or competitor and marginal improvements in the old operation simply will not get the job done. Without a major change in operations, the business will be in jeopardy.

Seeking Radical, Breakthrough Innovation

A truly paradigm-shifting, breakthrough innovation – as opposed to one that sustains the present course – can result in an enormous strategic payoff. Robert Stringer, a strategic consultant, suggests a variety of 'breakthrough' strategies that successful companies can use (in addition to skunk works and decentralisation) to reinvent themselves and their markets.[19]

- Make breakthrough innovations a strategic and culture priority, as General Mills has done in the cereal market.
- Hire more creative and innovative people. Philips has established a Simplicity Advisory Board with external members from the worlds of design, medicine and academia to advise them on how they might continue with their drive towards simplicity in product design.[20]
- Create 'idea markets' where the best ideas in the organisation compete for funding.
- Become an ambidextrous organisation, meaning that the ability to commercialise radical innovation exists in the conventional organisation (this solution is efficient, but difficult to implement).
- Use acquisitions, joint ventures, and alliances to bring in innovation. Airbus and Volvo are case studies on how to do this.
- Participate in a corporate venture-capital fund or internal corporate venturing, whereby new businesses are managed apart from a company's

existing business in order to provide entrepreneurs the level of autonomy that they value.

A RECAP OF STRATEGIC MARKET MANAGEMENT

Figure 16.5 provides a capstone summary of the issues raised in both strategic analysis and strategy development/refinement. It suggests a discussion agenda to help an organisation ensure that the external and internal analysis has the necessary depth,

---

CUSTOMER ANALYSIS
- Who are the major segments?
- What are their motivations and unmet needs?

COMPETITOR ANALYSIS
- Who are the existing and potential competitors? What strategic groups can be identified?
- What are their sales, share, and profits? What are the growth trends?
- What are their strengths, weaknesses, and strategies?

MARKET ANALYSIS
- How attractive is the market or industry and its submarkets? What are the forces reducing profitability in the market, entry and exit barriers, growth projections, cost structures, and profitability prospects?
- What are the alternative distribution channels and their relative strengths?
- What industry trends are significant to strategy?
- What are the current and future key success factors?

ENVIRONMENTAL ANALYSIS
- What environmental threats, opportunities, and trends exist?
- What are the major strategic uncertainties and information-need areas?
- What scenarios can be conceived?

INTERNAL ANALYSIS
- What are our costs, strategy, performance, points of differentiation, strengths, weaknesses, strategic problems, and culture?
- What is our existing business portfolio? What has been our level of investment in our various product markets?

STRATEGY DEVELOPMENT
- What strategic options should be considered—quality, value, focus, innovation, global, product attributes, product design, product-line breadth, corporate social responsibility, brand familiarity, and customer intimacy.
- What assets and competences will provide the basis for an SCA? How can they be developed and maintained? How can they be leveraged?
- What value proposition will be the core of the offering?
- What are the alternative functional strategies?
- What strategies best fit our strengths, our objectives and our organisation?
- What alternative growth directions should be considered? How should they be pursued? What investment level is most appropriate for each product-market—withdrawal, milking, maintaining, or growing?

Figure 16.5   Strategy development: a discussion agenda

breadth and forward thinking and that the strategy creation and refinement process yields winning, sustainable strategies.

KEY LEARNINGS

- Four key organisational components are structure, systems, people, and culture. All must be in sync with each other and with the business strategy.
- The fit between components is illustrated by the hit-industry topology, which contrasts the functions of drillers (who develop products), pumpers (who focus on production), and distributors (who specialise in marketing and distribution).
- Organisational structure defines the lines of authority and communication and can vary in the degree of centralisation and formality of communication channels.
- Management systems – including budgeting and accounting, information, measurement and reward, and planning – can all influence strategy implementation.
- People profiles and their motivation provide the bases of competencies needed to support SCAs.
- Because organisational culture – which involves shared values, norms of behaviour, symbols, and symbolic activities – is difficult to change, the fit between culture and strategy is particularly important.
- A final challenge is to create an organisation that can change rapidly through use of decentralisation, task forces, skunk works, kaizen, and reengineering.

FOR DISCUSSION

1. Strategy execution did not go according to plan in the DaimlerChrysler example at the beginning of this chapter. How could these problems have been avoided?

2. What are the advantages of decentralisation? Some people argue that more centralisation in needed to develop and implement strategy in these dynamic times. Express your opinion, and illustrate it with examples. When would you recommend that the central team use a facilitative role, rather than impose its advice?

3. Evaluate Mintzberg's easy steps to destroying value. Which is the most common step?

4. GE's Jack Welch believes that people are the most important ingredient to success. What are the implications of that belief?

5. Assume that you are CEO of a company, which sells entertaining, electronic-based learning devices for customers ranging from infants to secondary school students. Describe the culture you would like to develop and maintain. How would you do that?

6. Consider Tesco, the strategy for which is summarised in the case on p. 134. What are implications for the culture, structure, systems and people arising from the nature of the industry and the company?

7. Pick a bank or other service firm. Evaluate the organisational routes to innovation.

NOTES

1. Schrempp's last stand. *The Economist*, 1 March 2001.

2. The new European order. *The Economist*, 2 September 2004.

3. In tandem (at last). *The Economist*, 30 March 2006.

4. Michael E. Raynor and Joseph L. Bower (2001) Lead from the center. *Harvard Business Review*, May, p. 97.

5. Henry Mintzberg (1996) 'Musings on management. *Harvard Business Review*, July–August, pp. 61–7. Reprinted by permission of *Harvard Business Review*. Copyright © 1996 by the Harvard Business School Publishing Corporation. All rights reserved.

6. Henry Mintzberg (1994) The fall and rise of strategic planning. *Harvard Business Review*, January–February, pp. 107–14. Quotes are from p. 109. Reprinted by permission of *Harvard Business Review*. Copyright © 1996 by the Harvard Business School Publishing Corporation. All rights reserved.

7. GE's ten-step talent plan. *Fortune*, 17 April 2000, p. 232.

8. www.henkel.com.

9. Charles O'Reilly (1989) Corporations, culture, and commitment: motivation and aocial control in organisations. *California Management Review*, Summer, pp. 9–25.

10. Charles O'Reilly, op cit. p. 13.

11. Gordon Shaw, Robert Brown and Philip Bromiley (1998) Strategic stories: how 3M is rewriting business planning. *Harvard Business Review*, May–June 1998, pp. 41–50.

12. This material draws on Gary L. Neilson, Bruce A. Pasternack and Albert J. Viscio (2000) Up the e-organisation! *Strategy and Business*. First Quarter, pp. 52–61.

13. BT rings the changes: Managing the transition from public to private. *Strategic Direction*, 21 May 2005, 5, pp. 27–30.

14. The hit-industry topology was developed in discussions with Dr Norman Smothers.

15. Michael L. Tushman and Charles A. O'Reilly (1997) *Winning through Innovation: A Practical Guide to Leading Organisational Change and Renewal*, Harvard Business School Press, Boston MA.

16. Thomas J. Peters and Robert H. Waterman (1982) *In Search of Excellence: Lessons from America's Best-Run Companies*, Harper & Row, New York, p. 203.

17. Masaaki Imai (1984) *Kaizen*, McGraw-Hill, New York.

18. Thomas A. Stewart (1993) Re-engineering: the got new managing tool. *Fortune*, 23 August, pp. 41–8.

19. Robert Stringer (2000) How to manage radical innovation. *California Management Review*, Summer, pp. 70–88.

20. www.philips.com/global/.

CASE STUDY I: THE CHALLENGES OF STRATEGY IMPLEMENTATION

Vodafone

In 2006 Vodafone had over 170 million customers around the world and, either directly or through partnerships, operations in 30 countries across five continents. It was the largest telecommunications network company in the world in terms of turnover and had a market value of approximately $134 billion. Vodafone's previous CEO, Sir Christopher Gent, transformed the group into a global giant and the number one or number two mobile service provider in more than 12 international markets. Gent's strategy for Vodafone consisted of two main pillars, the first that Vodafone would strive to be the world's global mobile operator and would use this global reach to drive economies of scale. Second, that the company would deploy a mobile-only approach to allow it to focus on the fast growing wireless segment. In 2006 this strategy, which had driven the success referred to above, was failing and both pillars of Vodafone's strategy were coming under fire with questions as to whether the strategy that the company was pursuing should be maintained.

In 2003 when Sir Christopher Gent handed over to his successor as CEO, Arun Sarin, the Vodafone business was generating record levels of cash and customer numbers. While Christopher Gent acquired a large portfolio of mobile operators around the world, including the controversial acquisitions of US company Airtouch, German telecoms giant Mannesman and a 45% share in US telecommunications company Verizon Wireless, it was the job of the new CEO to manage the integration of this global collection and fit them together to achieve economies of scale for the company and justify that Vodafone's 'bigger is better' strategy.

However, a year after Gent's departure, due to specific problems at Vodafone, investor sentiment had changed and the shares had fallen by 20%. The questions of investors revolved around a couple of issues. Vodafone's mantra of building a global footprint had seemed questionable given the poor performance of Vodafone Japan. The Japanese mobile market is the largest market in the world in revenues terms but Vodafone had suffered at the hands of Japanese rival mobile operator KDDI, who were winning more customers due to advanced Japanese handset technology and 3G technology. Vodafone's bulkier handsets proved inferior in comparison to the competition's product offering. This was a result of Vodafone's failure to invest sufficiently in 3G technology and handsets. Profits in Japan plummeted in 2004 and eventually in 2006 it sold its Japanese business to Softbank Corporation. Issues also arose around the role of acquisitions in the strategy of Vodafone. In 2004 Vodafone failed in their attempts to bid for US based AT&T Wireless. This produced poor sentiments among Vodafone's investors as many were under the impression that the new management's focus would be on Vodafone operations rather than acquisition deals. They felt that Vodafone had concentrated on expansion by focusing on the difficult US and Japanese market but had done this at the expense of execution.

This poor sentiment continued and from 2004 Vodafone's share price underperformed the market in comparison to the shares of the smaller mobile operator O2. In

May 2006 Vodafone announced the largest corporate loss in European history of £22 billion as a result of writedowns on its previous acquisitions. This led to continued doubts over whether its strategy of using acquisitions to enhance its geographical expansion was appropriate and also to the belief that Vodafone has failed to live up to the promises of their strategy of 'bigger is better'.

This strategy is based on the ability of Vodafone to provide economies of scale to their business processes but this is undermined by their use of technology in different regions, namely a GSM technology in all of its markets except that of the US and Japan. This presents a restriction on what Vodafone can do with the brand in the US as they use a different incompatible wireless technology called CDMA. Scale gave them cost advantages but it meant that their emphasis was on expansion rather than efficiency. Instead, shareholders felt that Vodafone should concentrate on growth in emerging markets like Africa and Eastern Europe, while moving away from ventures that it did not have a controlling stake in, like Verizon Wireless. At the beginning of 2006, Vodafone was under pressure from shareholders to sell off their 45% stake in Verizon Wireless and replace it with something that enabled it to have control over the equipment, name and branding in order to perform well in the US market, which still holds potential growth. However, to sell out their share in Verizon would mean that Vodafone would lose out on its global number one position and the negotiating power that this allows them with suppliers.

The second pillar of Vodafone's strategy, its mobile-only approach, also came under attack as what was an advantage a few years ago is in danger of becoming a burden. Globally telecom operators had begun to integrate their fixed and mobile services allowing them to offer customers special deals if they bought combined services. Some even went so far as to offer quadruple services of fixed, mobile, broadband and television services. Vodafone's one-dimensional, one-technology strategy left it isolated and open to attack from competitors who could offer customers a better deal and greater value for money. It was particularly under threat from wireless operations and cheap Internet technologies like Skype, which threatened to spread from fixed to mobile services.

While the two pillars of strategy remain in place for the time being, the sale of their Japanese business appeared to mark a shift in their global strategy. In addition, in June 2006 Vodafone announced plans for a new range of services called Mobile Plus, which offered customers a less expensive rate when they use their mobile in the vicinity of their home, instead of going down the wireless and fixed-line route. Arun Sarin insisted that the company was monitoring technologies and already offered corporate customers fixed and mobile deals. Emphasis has been placed on simplifying the business by taking a few key actions in order to ensure that Vodafone can gain the benefits of its global scale. He has unified Vodafone's sprawling divisions and implemented standard technology at all of Vodafone's national affiliates under his 'One Vodafone' project. This has allowed Vodafone to achieve a measure of the economies of scale that they desire as it allows them to cut costs when developing a new service which can be introduced in several markets simultaneously. Mr Sarin has also restructured Vodafone's management by changing the lines of reporting to gain more direct control and enable more effective execution of business.

FOR DISCUSSION

1. Sarin seems to lack support for his decision to maintain Vodafone's `bigger is better' strategy. How important is stakeholder buy-in for a CEO's strategy? How can a CEO gain more support for his strategy?

2. Evaluate the changes Vodafone made to its strategy in response to stakeholder pressure. Are they enough to satisfy external stakeholders?

3. Evaluate the problems faced by Sarin (or any CEO) in inheriting a strategy designed by another. What are the challenges in building on a strategy which has been successful in the past but which may not be in the future?

4. Identify the problems Vodafone had with its American and Japanese business units? Why did these occur?

5. How would you change the reward system to reflect the change in strategy at Vodafone? In the past success appears to have been measured by growth, how should it be measured in the future? How would you implement any changes?

3M, 333
7up, 130
99 lives, 101
accounting systems, 325
active partnerships, 49–50
activities, 331
actual market size, 80–81
administrative distance, 211
Airbus, 10
Airness, 111
Aldi, 184–85
all hat, no cattle model, 217
alliances
    diversification, 291
    networks, 325
    organisational issues, 325, 333
    strategic, 218–23
    synergies, 148
alternative strategies, 141–254
    global strategies, 206–24
    identification, 17–18, 28–31
    misconceptions, 159
    opportunism, 149–51, 154–56, 160
    positioning strategies, 225–46
    selection, 31–33
    strategic options, 162–205
    stubbornness, 151–54, 160
    sustainable competitive advantages, 141–47,
        160
    synergies, 147–49, 160
    vision, 149–51, 156–60
analysis. *See* external analysis; internal analysis
anarchy model, 217
Anglo-Irish Bank, 45
application
    scope, 78
    segmentation, 45
application-defined markets, 268
ASDA, 136–38
assets
    alliances, 221
    business strategies, 9, 31
    competitor analysis, 62–63, 67–69
    exporting/exchanging, 278–79
    growth strategies, 258, 267, 269, 278–79,
        312–17
    leveraging, 199
    market analysis, 89
    sustainable competitive advantages, 142–43

synergies, 148–49
    vision, 150
attractiveness, 76, 123–26
attributes
    positioning strategies, 237–38
    preference, 268
    strategic options, 165
average costing, 118

backward integration, 62
Ballygowan, 132
bargaining power, 84, 86
BCG consulting group, 124–26
being alive, 101
benchmarking, 119–20
benefit segmentation, 44
Big, Hairy, Audacious Goals (BHAGs), 26–28,
        33–34
big ideas, 273–75
blue ocean opportunities, 274
BMW, 52, 71–73, 168, 284
The Body Shop, 9
Boeing, 10
brand. *See also* positioning strategies
    aggregation, 5
    associations, 24, 116, 176–77, 179, 208
    awareness, 174–75
    bureaucracy model, 217
    customisation, 211–13
    declining markets, 305
    equity, 172–81
        building and maintaining, 178–80
        challenges, 180
        financial benefits, 178
        growth strategies, 266
        positioning strategies, 234, 244
        sources, 174–77, 180
    expansion, 78
    experience, 240
    extension, 279–82, 312–14
    images, 70–71, 214, 253–54
    loyalty
        customer analysis, 44–45
        internal analysis, 24, 115–16
        programmes, 201–2
        strategic options, 177
    management, 215–18
    personality, 240–41
    portfolios, 179

brand (*Continued*)
  relevance, 79–80
  revitalisation, 263
  standardisation, 209, 211–13, 223
breakthrough innovations, 338–39
BRIC economies, 56
British Airways, 259–60
budgeting systems, 325
business
  portfolio analysis, 123–26
  scope, 6
  units, 4–5
  vision, 26–28, 33–34
business strategies, 3–16
  assets, 9, 31
  brand aggregation, 5
  business units, 4–5
  competencies, 9, 31
  core purpose, 27
  customer value propositions, 7–9, 163–64, 181
  definitions, 4–10
  dynamics, 6
  feasibility, 164
  functional strategies/programmes, 9–10, 31
  positioning strategies, 227
  product-market investment strategy, 5–7
  relevance, 164
  resource allocation, 5
  scope, 6
  SMM characteristics and trends, 11–14
  strategic options, 10–11, 31, 162–64
  sustainability, 164
buy approach, 328
buy-in, 150
buyer hot buttons, 47–48
buyer sophistication/knowledge, 83
buzz marketing, 175

C&C (Ireland) Ltd, 131–33
Cadbury's, 315–17
capabilities-based competition, 149
capital costs, 178
Capri-Sun, 131
cash cows, 125
cash flow
  alternative strategies, 32
  brand equity, 178
  diversification, 286
  internal analysis, 127–29
Castrol Motor Oil, 192–93
centralisation, 323–24, 336–37
change management
  business strategies, 15
  market analysis, 80

Chase & Sanborn, 300
Chrysler, 321, 340
Cisco, 333–34
Clarks, 49
Coca-Cola, 5, 130–31
cocooning, 101
cocreating personalised experiences, 50
collaboration. *See* alliances
common enemies, 27
commonalities. *See* synergies
communication
  global strategies, 215–16
  growth strategies, 261
  horizontal/vertical, 14
  positioning strategies, 227
community creation, 201
competencies
  alliances, 221
  business strategies, 9, 31
  competitor analysis, 62–63, 67–69
  exporting/exchanging, 278–79
  growth strategies, 258, 267, 269, 278–79
  market analysis, 89
  sustainable competitive advantages, 142–43
  synergies, 148–49
  vision, 150
competition
  capabilities-based, 149
  sustainable competitive advantages, 142–43
competitive
  intensity, 305
  overcrowding, 90–91
  strength grid, 71–73, 74
competitor analysis, 18, 19–20, 56–75, 339
  assets and competencies, 62–63, 67–69
  competitive strength grid, 71–73, 74
  cost structure, 20, 66
  current and past strategies, 20, 65
  customer choices, 59, 74
  customer-based approaches, 57–59
  evaluation, 57
  exit barriers, 60, 66
  identification, 57–62
  image and positioning strategy, 20, 64
  information gathering, 73–74
  objectives and commitment, 20, 64–65
  organisational culture, 20, 65
  performance, 20, 64
  potential competitors, 62–63
  product-use associations, 59
  projecting strategic groups, 61–62
  strengths and weaknesses, 20, 66–73, 74
  strategic groups, 59–62
  understanding competitors, 63–67
comprehensive services, 271

congruence, strategic, 331–36
consistency, 179
consolidation, 308
constraints
  internal analysis, 25, 111, 120–21
  market analysis, 92–93
consultative model, 217–18
convenience shoppers, 46
convert approach, 328
core assets/competencies
  growth strategies, 258, 267, 269
  synergies, 148–49
core values/purpose, 26–27
corporate culture. *See* organisational culture
corporate social responsibility (CSR)
  brand assets, 312–13
  positioning strategies, 251–52
  strategic options, 166–67, 181
cost advantages, 117–18, 188–92
cost structures
  competitor analysis, 20, 66
  hostile markets, 309
  market analysis, 21, 77, 86–87
creative thinking
  customer analysis, 53
  external analysis, 40
  growth strategies, 260–61
CRM. *See* customer relationship management
cross-subsidisation, 209
CSR. *See* corporate social responsibility
culture. *See also* organisational culture
  brand image, 253–54
  global strategies, 211, 214, 216–17
  trends, 100–102
current ratio, 127
current strategies, 119
customer analysis, 18, 19, 41–55, 339
  active partnerships, 49–50
  applications, 45
  benefits, 44
  buyer hot buttons, 47–48
  characteristics, 43
  choices, 59, 74
  communities, 50
  competitor analysis, 57–59, 70, 71
  creative thinking, 53
  demographics, 43
  disinterest, 83
  diversity, 50
  focus strategies, 45–46
  ideal experience, 53
  motivations, 42, 46–50, 54, 67–68, 214
  multiple segments, 45–46
  priorities, 49
  problem research, 51–52

  product-related segmentation, 43
  qualitative research, 48–49, 51
  segmentation, 42–46
  trends, 78–79
  unmet needs, 42, 50–53, 54
customer relationship management (CRM)
  global strategies, 220
  market analysis, 78
  problems, 202–3
  strategic options, 199–203
customer satisfaction
  internal analysis, 24, 115–16
  strategic options, 167–68, 171–72
customer service, 201
customer value propositions
  business strategies, 7–9, 163–64, 181
  innovation, 197
customisation, 201, 211–13

DaimlerChrysler, 321–22, 340
debt-to-equity ratio, 128
decentralisation, 323–24, 336–37
decision making
  business strategies, 12–13, 14
  external analysis, 37–38, 53
  internal analysis, 121–23
declining markets, 296–306
  detecting, 83
  divestiture, 302–3, 310
  government-stimulated growth, 299
  hold strategy, 301–2
  milking strategy, 300–302, 310
  new applications, 298
  new markets, 298
  new products, 298
  profitable survivors, 299–300, 310
  revitalised marketing, 299
  superpremium arena, 298
  uncertainties, 304–6
Deep RiverRock, 132
defensive strategies, 63
Dell, 333–34
demand access, 270
demographics
  customer analysis, 43
  environmental analysis, 23, 102–3
  market analysis, 82
depreciation, 129
depth of analysis, 41
deregulation, 61–63, 232
determinants of strategic options, 18, 25–26, 119–21
Diageo, 5
direct
  competitors, 58–59
  sales, 60–61, 271

Direct Line, 157
Disney, 279–81
disruptive technologies, 96–97
distribution
    growth strategies, 268, 271, 282
    market analysis, 21–22, 77, 87, 93
    organisational issues, 335–36
diversification, 277–95, 315–17
    assets and competencies, 278–79
    brand name extension, 279–82
    capacity, 282
    cash flow, 286
    economies of scale, 283
    entry strategies, 290–93
    executive interest, 289
    liquid assets, 288
    marketing skills, 282
    performance, 290
    pricing, 286–87
    refocusing acquired firms, 287
    related, 278–83
    research and development, 282–83
    return on investment, 286
    risk, 288, 289–90
    synergies, 283–85
    takeovers, 289
    tax implications, 288
    unrelated, 285–90
    vertical integration, 289
divestiture, 126, 302–3, 310
dogs, 125
Dove, 312–14
down-aging, 101
downsizing, 257
downstream business models, 271–72
drift, strategic, 155–56, 160
drillers, 334–36
dynamic niche markets, 130–33
dynamic vision, 156–59

e-organisations, 333–34
early market leaders, 197–99
easyGroup, 185–86
economics
    environmental analysis, 96, 99–100
    internal analysis, 129
economies of scale, 186–87, 189–90
    declining markets, 305
    diversification, 283
    global strategies, 208, 213–14, 220, 223
educational acquisitions, 291, 293
embedded services, 271
emerging submarkets, 20–21, 76–80
emerging technologies. *See* new technologies
Emissions Trading Scheme (ETS), 99

emotional benefits, 239
empirical research, 13–14
endorsed brands, 281–82
enthusiastic shoppers, 46
entrepreneurial thrust, 13
entry barriers, 60
entry strategies
    diversification, 290–93
    vertical integration, 271–72
environmental analysis, 18, 22–23, 95–109, 339
    cultural trends, 100–102
    demographics, 102–3
    economics, 96, 99–100
    environmental impacts, 99
    governmental regulations, 96, 98–99
    technology, 96–98
    uncertainties, 23
environmental impacts, 99
essence statements, 242
ethics
    corporate social responsibility, 166–67, 181,
        251–52, 312–13
    Fair Trade products, 315–17
    privacy, 202, 203
ethnography, 51
ETS. *See* Emissions Trading Scheme
Evian, 132
executive interest, 289
existing customers, 84–85
exit barriers
    competitor analysis, 60, 66
    divestiture, 303, 310
experience curve, 186–87, 190–91
external analysis, 18–23, 37–110
    competitor analysis, 18, 19–20, 56–75, 339
    creative thinking, 40
    customer analysis, 18, 19, 41–55, 339
    decision making, 37–38, 53
    environmental analysis, 18, 22–23, 95–109,
        339
    frequency/timing, 41
    global strategies, 207
    impact analysis, 95, 103–6
    market analysis, 18, 20–22, 76–94, 339
    market definition, 40–41
    objectives, 37–39
    scenario analysis, 95, 106–9
    uncertainties, 39–40, 53, 95, 103–9
external market orientation, 12

facilitator model, 218
fads, 88–89
Fair Trade products, 315–17
Fanta, 130–31
fantasy adventure, 101

fast milking strategy, 300
faulty assumptions of the future, 152
feasibility, 164
financial performance
    brand equity, 178
    internal analysis, 112–19, 126
    strategic options, 169–70
financial resources
    competitor analysis, 69–70
    internal analysis, 25, 120–21
Finches, 131
first-mover advantage, 197–99
five-factor model of profitability, 83–86, 123
flexibility
    alternative strategies, 32
    growth strategies, 272
    vision, 158–59
focus
    positioning strategies, 194–95, 233, 237
    resources, 193–94
    segmentation, 45–46
    strategic options, 192–95, 203
follower strategies, 199
Ford, 49, 186–87
formal joint ventures, 219, 222
forward integration, 62
founders, 330–31
frugal shoppers, 46
functional
    benefits, 236–37
    strategies/programmes, 9–10, 31
future strategies, 150

General Electric, 147, 327–28
generic customer need, 29
geographic expansion, 267
ghost potential, 80–81
global strategies, 206–24
    alliances, 218–23
    brand associations, 208
    brand management, 215–18
    business strategies, 13
    communication, 215–16
    cross-subsidisation, 209
    customisation, 211–13
    delivering brilliance, 218
    dysfunctional management styles, 216–17
    indicators, 209–10
    leadership strategies, 213–15
    low-cost labour/materials, 208, 220, 223
    market selection, 210–11, 220, 223
    national investment incentives, 208–9
    planning structure, 216–18
    positioning strategies, 234
    scale economies, 208, 213–14, 220, 223

    standardisation, 209, 211–13, 223
    trade barriers, 207, 209–10, 220
Gold competitors, 308–10
Golden Wonder, 3–4
government-stimulated growth, 299
governmental regulations, 96, 98–99
Green & Black's, 315–17
Green Shield Stamps, 135
growth strategies, 257–317
    big ideas, 273–75
    business strategies, 30
    case studies, 312–17
    competitor analysis, 20, 64
    declining markets, 296–306, 310
    disappointing, 91–92
    diversification, 277–95, 315–17
    driving forces, 81–82
    existing product markets, 259–64, 275
    forecasting, 82–83
    high-growth markets, 89–93, 296
    hostile markets, 297, 306–10
    market analysis, 21, 77, 81–83, 89–93
    market development, 267–69, 275
    penetration, 259–64, 275
    product development, 264–67, 275
    related diversification, 278–83
    sources, 83
    synergies, 266, 275, 283–85
    unrelated diversification, 285–90
    vertical integration, 269–73, 275, 289
growth-share matrix, 124–26

harvest strategy, 300–302, 310
heavy users, 259–62
Hewlett Packard, 5
high-growth markets, 89–93, 296
hit-industry topology, 334–36, 340
hold strategy, 301–2
horizontal communication, 14
hostile markets, 297, 306–10
hostile takeovers, 289
human resources, 24, 118–19

IBM, 100, 147, 218–19, 230–31, 244
ideal experience, 53
image. *See* brand
impact analysis, 95, 103–6
implementation. *See also* organisational issues
    alternative strategies, 32–33
    barriers, 151–52, 284, 306
    business strategies, 13
incentives, 102, 135, 262
indirect competitors, 58–59
inflation, 129
informal agreements, 219

information
  gathering, 73–74
  systems, 12, 325–26
  technology, 101–2
information-need areas, 11, 40
Innocent Drinks, 250–54
innovation
  competitor analysis, 69, 70
  customer value propositions, 197
  first-mover advantage, 197–99
  organisational issues, 330–31, 336–39
  positioning strategies, 227, 233
  strategic options, 195–99, 203
intangibles, 237–38
integrated solutions, 271–72
interim strategies, 17
internal analysis, 18, 23–26, 111–29, 339
  benchmarking, 119–20
  brand loyalty, 24, 115–16
  brand/firm associations, 24, 116
  business portfolio analysis, 123–26
  capabilities, 120
  cash flow, 127–29
  constraints, 25, 111, 120–21
  customer satisfaction, 24, 115–16
  decision making, 121–23
  determinants of strategic options, 18, 25–26,
    119–21
  financial resources, 25, 120–21
  human resources, 24, 118–19
  market share, 122–23
  new product activity, 24, 118
  organisational capabilities, 25
  performance, 18, 24, 112–19, 126
  product portfolio analysis, 24
  product/service quality, 24, 116
  profitability, 113–15
  relative cost, 24, 117–18
  sales, 112–13
  shareholder value analysis, 113–15, 126
  strategic problems, 25, 120
  strategy reviews, 25
  strengths and weaknesses, 25, 111, 121
internal transformation, 27
Internet Protocol Television (IPTV), 21–22
interrelationships, 305–6
investment
  decisions, 38
  global strategies, 208–9, 220
  internal analysis, 114, 125–26
  strategies, 30–31
IPTV. *See* Internet Protocol Television

joint ventures, 219, 222, 291, 293

Kaizen, 337
key success factors (KSFs)
  market analysis, 22, 76–77, 86–87, 89, 91
  organisational issues, 335
  sustainable competitive advantages, 144
knowledge management, 12
KSFs. *See* key success factors

language barriers, 214
large customers, 308–9
lead users, 52
leadership strategies, 213–15
Lexus, 167–69
licensing, 291, 293
lifetime customer value (LTCV), 202
light users, 259–62
line extensions, 264
liquid assets, 288
liquidation. *See* divestiture
long-range view, 14
L'Oréal, 9, 45
low-cost
  cultures, 191–92
  labour/materials, 208, 220, 223
loyalty programmes, 201–2
LTCV. *See* lifetime customer value
Lucozade, 131–32
Lynx, 172–74

make approach, 327
manufacturing, 69, 70
margin pressure, 307
market analysis, 18, 20–22, 76–94, 339. *See also*
    declining markets; growth strategies
  attractiveness, 76
  brand relevance, 79–80
  cost structures, 21, 77, 86–87
  development, 267–69, 275
  distribution, 21–22, 77, 87, 93
  emerging submarkets, 20–21, 76–80
  expansion, 62
  growth, 21, 77, 81–83, 89–93
  high-growth markets, 89–93
  hostile markets, 297, 306–10
  key success factors, 22, 76–77, 86–87, 89, 91
  market definition, 29, 40–41
  market trends, 22, 77, 87–89
  profitability, 21, 77, 83–86
  prospects, 304
  size, 21, 77, 80–81
market share
  global strategies, 214
  growth strategies, 259
  internal analysis, 122–23

market-attractiveness–business position matrix, 123–26
marketing
   competitor analysis, 70–71
   diversification, 282
Marks & Spencer, 7
matrix organisations, 324
maturity, 83
meaningful commonalities. *See* synergies
measurement systems, 326
Mercedes Benz, 321, 340
metrics, 202
milking strategy, 300–302, 310
mobility barriers. *See* entry barriers; exit barriers
modern role models, 331
motivation, 328
multidomestic strategies, 206
multinational strategies, 206
multiple segments, 45–46
multiple strategic positioning, 241–42

narrow scope specifications, 41
national investment incentives, 208–9
Neau, 247–49
negative customer experiences, 169
Nestlé, 5
net working capital, 127
NetJets Europe, 50
new
   applications, 298
   markets, 298
   products, 24, 118, 264–65, 298
   technologies, 79, 91, 97–98
newbie shoppers, 46
niche markets, 78, 130–33, 220
no-frills products/service, 184–86, 188
Nokia, 195
nonoperating investments, 287
norms, 330

O'Brien's Sandwich Bars, 192
Ocean Spray, 131
online analysis, 12–13
operations efficiencies, 185, 188–89
opportunism, 149–51, 154–56, 160
optimal strategies, 17
options. *See* strategic options
organisational issues, 321–44
   alliance networks, 325
   capabilities, 25
   case study, 342–44
   (de)centralisation, 323–24, 336–37
   conceptual frameworks, 322, 334–36

   culture, 329–34, 340
      competitor analysis, 20, 65
      positioning strategies, 225, 227, 243
   e-organisations, 333–34
   hit-industry topology, 334–36, 340
   innovation, 330–31, 336–39
   intangibles, 237–38
   management systems, 325–27, 332, 333, 340
   matrix organisations, 324
   people, 327–28, 332, 333–34, 340
   strategic congruence, 331–36
   structure, 323–25, 332, 333, 340
   synergies, 9
   virtual corporations, 324–25
   vision, 32
original missions, 330–31
outsourcing, 114, 149
overcapacity, 83
overserved customers, 97

paradigm shifts, 152–53
past strategies, 119
penetration, 259–64
Pepsi, 130–31
perceived
   quality, 169–70, 176
   value, 163–64, 181, 191
performance
   analysis, 18, 24
   competitor analysis, 20, 64
   declining markets, 305
   diversification, 290
   financial, 112–19, 126, 169–70, 178
personalised experiences, 50
personality, 228–30, 240–41
planning
   structure, 216–18
   systems, 326–27
pleasure revenge, 101
points of differentiation (PODs), 144
points of parity (POPs), 144
Porter's five-factor model of profitability, 83–86, 123
positioning strategies, 31, 225–46
   brand equity, 179
   brand experience, 240
   brand personality, 240–41
   case studies, 247–54
   competitor analysis, 20, 64
   competitors, 241, 243
   developing, 242–44, 247–49
   emotional benefits, 239
   essence statements, 242
   focus, 194–95, 233, 237
   functional benefits, 236–37

positioning strategies (*Continued*)
  multiple, 241–42
  organisational intangibles, 237–38
  product attributes, 236–37
  product category, 235
  proof points, 243–44
  relevance, 226, 235–36, 240
  selecting, 242–44
  self-expressive benefits, 239
  strategic imperatives, 243–44
potential
  competitors, 62–63
  customers, 84–85, 97
  market size, 80–81
  markets, 210–11, 220, 223
preempted positions, 214
price instability, 92
price sensitivity, 44
pricing strategies. *See also* value
  brand equity, 178–79
  diversification, 286–87
  hostile markets, 309
  positioning strategies, 252–53
primary value activities, 68–69
privacy, 202, 203
proactive strategies, 12
problem children, 125
problem research, 51–52
product
  attributes, 165, 236–37
  category, 235
  class repositioning, 78
  control, 271
  definition, 29
  design, 165–66
  development, 264–67
  differentiation, 83
  expansion, 62, 278
  line breadth, 166
  portfolio analysis, 24
  proliferation, 307
  quality, 24, 116
  scope, 265, 275
  segmentation, 43
  usage, 259–62, 267, 275
  use associations, 59
product-market investment strategies, 5–7, 29–31, 143
profitability
  competitor analysis, 20, 64
  growth strategies, 257
  internal analysis, 113–15
  market analysis, 21, 77, 83–86
profitable survivors, 299–300, 310
promotions, 102, 135, 262

proof points, 243–44
pumpers, 336

qualitative research, 48–49, 51
quality
  positioning strategies, 228, 233
  strategic options, 167–72, 176
quality of life, 101
questions asked, 331
quick ratio, 128

R & D. *See* research and development
real value, 326
Red Herring, 108
reengineering, 338
refocusing acquired firms, 287
related diversification, 278–83
relative cost, 24, 117–18
relevance
  brand equity, 178
  business strategies, 164
  positioning strategies, 226, 235–36, 240
reliability, 309
reluctant shoppers, 46
reminder communications, 261
repositioning, 78
rescue phase, 308
research and development (R & D), 282–83
resources
  allocation, 5, 14
  constraints, 92–93
  focus, 193–94
  vision, 150
retaliatory strategies, 63
return on assets (ROA), 113
return on investment (ROI), 286
revitalised marketing, 299
revolutionary strategies, 273–74
reward systems, 326
Ricola, 50
risks
  diversification, 288, 289–90
  high-growth markets, 89–93
rituals, 331
ROA. *See* return on assets
ROI. *See* return on investment
role models, 27, 331
Ryanair, 232–33, 244

Sainsbury's, 136–38
sales
  goals, 27
  internal analysis, 122–23
  patterns, 82
Salomon, 40

Samsung, 270
San Pellegrino, 132
saturation, 83
scale economies, 186–87, 189–90
   declining markets, 305
   diversification, 283
   global strategies, 208, 213–14, 220, 223
SCAs. *See* sustainable competitive advantages
scenario analysis, 31–32, 95, 106–9
scope
   application, 78
   business strategies, 6
   external analysis, 41
   growth strategies, 265
   product, 265, 275
secondary value activities, 69
segmentation
   customer analysis, 42–46
   external analysis, 41
   growth strategies, 267–68
selective investment, 125
self-defeating cost reductions, 307
self-expressive benefits, 239
Senokot, 26
service provider model, 217
service quality, 24, 116
shakeout, 308
share shifts, 307
shared values, 329–30
shareholder value analysis, 113–15, 126
Sheraton, 171–72
Shouldice Hospital, 192
shouting matches, 237–38
signals of high quality, 171–72
Silver competitors, 308–10
skunk works, 337
slow milking strategy, 300
small indulgences, 101
small is beautiful, 81
smart cards, 102
social responsibility. *See* corporate social
      responsibility
Sony, 147, 196–97, 270–71
specification positioning, 237–38
sponsorship, 175
Sprite, 130
standardisation, 209, 211–13, 223
stars, 125
strategic. *See also* assets; competencies;
      positioning strategies; uncertainties
   congruence, 331–36
   drift, 155–56, 160
   groups, 59–62
   imperatives, 243–44
   intent, 157–58, 160

problems, 25, 120
shoppers, 46
strategic analysis. *See* external analysis; internal
      analysis
strategic options, 10–11, 14, 31, 339
   brand equity, 172–81
   business strategies, 162–64
   corporate social responsibility, 166–67, 181
   cost advantages, 188–92
   customer relationship management, 199–203
   determinants, 18, 25–26, 119–21
   external analysis, 38
   financial performance, 169–70
   focus, 192–95, 203
   innovation, 195–99, 203
   product attributes, 165
   product design, 165–66
   product line breadth, 166
   quality, 167–72
   signals of high quality, 171–72
   sustainable competitive advantages, 146–47
   total quality management, 170–71
   value, 184–92, 203
strategy reviews, 25, 33
strategy selection, 28–33
stubbornness, 151–54, 160
subbrands, 281–82
submarkets. *See also* market analysis
   competitor analysis, 73
   emerging, 20–21
   growth strategies, 299
substitute products, 83, 84, 85
superior competitive entry, 91
superpremium arena, 298
supply access, 270
sustainability, 164
sustainable competitive advantages (SCAs),
      339
   alternative strategies, 32, 141–47, 160
   assets, 142–43
   business strategies, 9
   competencies, 142–43
   competition, 142–43
   competitor analysis, 67–68, 71
   declining markets, 296
   environmental analysis, 101–2
   examples, 144–46
   focus, 194
   global strategies, 206–7
   internal analysis, 115
   key success factors, 144
   market analysis, 87
   product-market selection, 143
   strategic options, 146–47
   value propositions, 143

sustaining technologies, 96–97
symbolic actions, 330
synergies
  alternative strategies, 32, 147–49, 160
  diversification, 277–78, 283–85
  growth strategies, 266, 275
  implementation barriers, 284
  nonexistent, 283
  overvalued, 284–85

takeovers, 289
target segment focus, 234
task forces, 337
tax implications, 288
Tesco, 134–36, 138
threats, 19
time horizons, 13
Tod's, 7–9
total debt-to-equity ratio, 128
total quality management (TQM), 170–71
trade barriers, 207, 209–10, 220
tradeoffs, 41
trends
  drivers, 236, 244
  market analysis, 22, 77, 87–89
  neglectors, 235–36, 244
  responders, 236, 244
tribing, 100
Tropicana, 131

uncertainties
  competitor analysis, 73
  declining markets, 304–6
  environmental analysis, 23
  external analysis, 39–40, 53, 95, 103–9
  growth strategies, 268
  immediacy, 104, 105
  impact analysis, 95, 103–6
  management, 105–6
  probabilities, 108
  scenario analysis, 95, 106–9
underdogs, 228

Unilever, 5
uninformed dictator model, 216–17
unmet needs, 42, 50–53, 54
unrelated diversification, 285–90
user gap, 80, 93
user-developed products, 52

value
  added, 87
  alliances, 220–21
  brand equity, 178–79, 181
  brand names, 280–81
  chains, 68–69
  experience curve, 186–87, 190–91
  low-cost cultures, 191–92
  no-frills products/service, 184–86, 188
  operations efficiencies, 185, 188–89
  organisational issues, 326
  perceived, 163–64, 181, 191
  positioning strategies, 228, 233
  propositions, 7–9, 31–32, 143, 197
  scale economies, 186–87, 189–90
  strategic options, 184–92, 203
venture capital, 291, 293
vertical communication, 14
vertical integration, 30
  business strategies, 5
  growth strategies, 269–73, 275, 289
Virgin Atlantic Airlines, 227–30, 244–45
virtual corporations, 324–25
vision, 149–51, 156–60
Vodafone, 122–23, 342–44
volume, 308–9
Volvic, 132
Volvo, 43, 72–73

Wal-Mart, 136–37
Walkers, 3–4
Webnography, 51
Windemere Associates study, 306–8

Xerox, 29